SAINT BONAVENTURE

AND

THE ENTRANCE OF GOD INTO THEOLOGY

AFTERWORD: SAINT THOMAS AND THE ENTRANCE OF GOD INTO PHILOSOPHY

BY EMMANUEL FALQUE
TRANSLATED FROM THE FRENCH BY BRIAN LAPSA
REVISED BY WILLIAM C. HACKETT

SAINT BONAVENTURE AND THE ENTRANCE OF GOD INTO THEOLOGY

THE *BREVILOQUIUM* AS A *SUMMA THEOLOGICA*

BY

EMMANUEL FALQUE

WITH A NEW PREFACE TO THE ENGLISH EDITION BY THE AUTHOR

*TRANSLATED FROM THE FRENCH BY BRIAN LAPSA AND
SARAH HORTON
REVISED BY WILLIAM C. HACKETT*

© 2018 Franciscan Institute Publications,
St. Bonaventure University

Cover Art: Michelangelo, Sistine Chapel (open source)
Cover Design: Jill M. Smith

ISBN 978-1-57659-425-4
E-ISBN 978-1-57659-426-1

Library of Congress Cataloging-in-Publication Data

Library of Congress Control Number: 2018952720

Printed and bound in the United States of America.
Franciscan Institute Publications makes every effort
to use environmentally responsible suppliers and materials in the publishing of its
books. This book is printed on acid free, recycled paper that is FSC (Forest Stewardship
Council) certified. It is printed with soy-based ink.

FROM THE SAME AUTHOR
Works that have already appeared in English

Crossing the Rubicon : The Borderlands of Philosophy and Theology (*Passer le rubicon. Philosophie et théologie : essai sur les frontièrs*, 2013), trans. Reuben Shank, 2016.

The Wedding Feast of the Lamb : Eros, the Body, and the Eucharist (*Les Noces de l'Agneau* : Essai philosophique sur le corps et l'eucharistie, 2011), trans. George Hughes, 2016.

God, the Flesh, and the Other : From Irenaeus to Duns Scotus (*Dieu, la chair et l'autre : de Irenée à Duns Scot*, 2008), trans. William Christian Hackett, 2014.

The Metamorphosis of Finitude : An Essay on Birth and Resurrection (*Métamorphose de la finitude* : *Essai philosophique sur la naissance et la résurrection*, 2004), trans. George Hughes, 2012.

The Loving Struggle, Phenomenological and Theological debates (Le combat amoureux, Disputes phénoménologiques et théologiques, 2014), trans. Bradley B. Onishi and Lucas Mc Craken, 2018.

The Guide to Gethsemane, Anxiety, Suffering, Death (Le passeur de Gethsémani, Angoisse, souffrance et mort, Lecture existentielle et phénoménologique, 1999), trans. Georges Hughes, 2018.

The Guide of Gethsemane : Anxiety, Suffering, Death (Le passeur de Gethsémani, 1999), trans. George Hughes, 2018.

The Loving Struggle : Phenomenological and theological debates (Le combat amoureux, 2014), trans. B. Onishi and L. MCCraken, 2018.

WORKS EXISTING ONLY IN FRENCH

Parcours d'embûches: S'expliquer, 2016.

Ça n'a rien à voir, Lire Freud en philosophe, 2018.

Le livre de l'expérience, D'Anselme de Cantorbéry à Bernard de Clairvaux, 2017.

SEE ALSO

Une analytique du passage: Rencontres et confrontations avec Emmanuel Falque, ed. Claude Brunier-Coulin, 2016.

Penser Dieu autrement. L'oeuvre d'Emmanuel Falque, Alain Saudan, 2013.

Author's Note to the American Edition

This book is not just the translation of a work that originally appeared in French, *Saint Bonaventure et l'entrée de Dieu en théologie*. Properly original, the new version of this essay intends both to nourish debate and differentiate points of view. In its new articulation, the book justifies work that has been carried out since. It justifies the sense of Franciscan rootedness that has never been denied and at the same time opens to the discovery of another reading of the Dominican Thomas Aquinas. The preface specially composed for this American edition, the opening debate with famous medievalist Etienne Gilson, and above all the afterword entitled "Saint Thomas Aquinas and the entrance of God into Philosophy" make it a radically new book. None of this would have been possible without the hard work of the translators (Brian Lapsa and Sarah Horton), reviser (William C. Hackett) and the enthusiastic welcome of the Franciscan Institute for the publication of this book. Let them be here, each one, warmly and fraternally thanked.

Saint Bonaventure University, NY
On the Feast of Saint Bonaventure
15 July 2017

NOTE ON THE REVISION

My revision of Brian Lapsa's translation of *Saint Bonaventure et l'entrée de Dieu en Théologie* only requires a few comments. In keeping with a convention I found necessary in translating *Dieu, la chair et l'autre*, citations are almost always direct translations of the author's own use of French editions, or of his translations of the originals. Following a process begun by Lapsa, where necessary, originals were consulted, and English renderings modified. (And sometimes the decision is discussed in a translator's note.) Usually, the author's own distinctive use, and (more often than not) rich modification, of the French editions demanded a direct rendering of the French into English. To replace such a profoundly hermeneutical engagement with citations of standard English translations would completely bypass these essential philosophical moments crucial to the author's style and method. The reader will quickly see what I mean. However, I left in place Lapsa's general references to available English editions in case the reader would like to take the author's hermeneutical engagement into their own intellectual foyer, layering that over Falque's, Lapsa's and/or my own. The same strategy was undertaken in regards to Sarah Horton's translations of the Preface, the "Opening" and the Afterword. This latter text in particular, "Saint Thomas Aquinas and the Entrance of God into Theology," is crucially important to a full understanding of the present work in the context of Emmanuel Falque's thought, regarding both its entire breadth and historical development.

A quick comment on some difficult decisions. I found both Lapsa and Horton to have sound intuitions. This gave me confidence in the work of revision, which played itself out in the final decisions I made. I refer to three here: One could translate (and I settled on it) *originarité* as "originarity"—not a word in the OED. According to *Le Trésor de la langue française*, in philosophical and theological contexts, *originaire* can bear the same sense as *original(e)*, "original"—present from the beginning as source. The fact is that the word is common in French philosophy. Originarity [*originarité*] means, generally: the quality (-ity) of that which belongs to the origin. The French translation of Bonaventure's *Breviloquium* used by Falque translates *sentire* as *sentir*: pretty straightforward. The standard English translation of the key passages involved usually translates *sentire* as "to conceive." One will find both to be good translations but between the French and English only a heavy amount of theological labor could build a bridge. The connection between French *sentir*, Latin *sentire*, English "to sense," "to feel" and "to conceive," as well as to Falque's use of co-/auto-affectivity in the text on this Franciscan theologian is a theologically dense constellation worth keeping in mind. This is highlighted in a translator's note in chapter four. And in this constellation there is also the play between *sentir* and *res(s) entir* that I will allow the reader the pleasure of discovering in due course (there is an explanatory note at the end of § 8).

Finally, the most consequential: one has to deal aggressively with Falque's own use of a modern neologistic enterprise called on in chapters one and three, involving first the words "principiel –elle" (adj.) and "principiellement" (adv.), located within the philosophically fruitful constellation governed by the two great lights of *principe* (n.) and *principal* (n.)—in relation to the Latin *principaliter*, *principalis*, *principium*, *princeps*, etc. The word *principiel, -elle* is found, representatively, in Barthes (1953: *Essais critiques*, p. 21) and Jankélévitch (1957: *Le Je-ne-sais-quoi et le Presque-rien*, p. 238). It means (according to *Le Trésor*, on which I rely again), "relative to the principle as first cause of something." But *principiellement* is a hapax legomenon of Sartre's, from *Être et Néant* (1943: p. 479). It means "in principle": a "consistent attitude to the Other" would only be possible, for Sartre, if we could approach it as revealed as both subject and object, as "transcendance-transcendante" and as "transcendance-transcendée": this is in principle ("in theory," "at root") impossible ("ce qui est *principiellement* impossible"). Falque decides to translate the Latin *principaliter* (first found at the beginning of the *Breviloquium*, I 1, 1) by *principiellement* instead of the usual *principalement* (as his French edition of Bonaventure has it): theology treats of God, the Three in One *principaliter*, "*principiellement*" (not *principalement*). Falque gives his reasons for this in a footnote to §1(b) below. The short of it is that he wants to emphasize the connection between the allusion to the opening words of the Gospel of John and the Book of Genesis with which Bonaventure starts ("in principio," which can mean both "in the beginning" and "in the principle") and his (immediately following) description of the content of theology (as the English translation of Bonaventure has it: "theology deals principally with the First Principle— God, three and one.").[1] Suffice to say that a lot in Falque's interpretation is manifest through this distinction. And it has only a little to do with

---

[1] St. Bonaventure, *Breviloquium*, ed. Dominic Monti, OFM *Works of St. Bonaventure* vol. IX. NY: Franciscan Institute, 2005, p. 27.

Sartre's neologism: he borrows the word but uses it for his own ends. Whereas French only has one adverb (*principalement*) for both *principal* and *principe*, Falque wants to introduce *principiellement* in order to raise their distinction onto the adverbial plane as well. "In principle" for *principiellement* is not sufficient. For this English text, Lapsa proposed a neologism: "princ*e*pally," to distinguish it from the common English word "principally." Falque also introduces a later hapax related to this context, *principialité*. I decided to render it, simply, "principiality" given there is an uncommon English term "principial," meaning (according to the OED) "standing at the beginning; initial," which is only a little less uncommon in philosophical-theological contexts as "constituting a source or origin; primary; original; basic; fundamental" (in *The Perennial Philosophy*, for example, the younger Huxley distinguished between "the mental activities of the ego" and "the principial consciousness of the Self;" 1946, p. 178). This allows the play between "beginning" and "principle" of the Latin *principium* that Falque wanted to capture with *principialité*. I decided not to render it with "princ*e*pality" since the distance, in Falque's French, between *princepiellement* and *principialité* (not *princepialité*) seems to eschew the wisdom of it. Besides, if he wanted to distinguish his term (in part) from *principalité* (or, granted, *principauté*) by introducing an "i," it works best, vis-à-vis the English "principality," to do the same.

WCH

TABLE OF CONTENTS

PART THREE
THE MANIFESTATION AND NAMING OF GOD

In honor of Théodore Farnham Léonard, S.J.
(1929-1999)

ACKNOWLEDGMENTS

My special thanks go to my wife, my children, and all my friends and loved ones, who have supported me step by step throughout this project; to Théodore Farnham Léonard and Marc Ozilou for following the progress and development of this work over the years—the former with respect to its form, and the latter with respect to its content; to Jean-Luc Marion, for so rightly directing me toward Bonaventure, and for the constancy of his confidence and friendship; to Jean Jolivet for his extremely valuable advice on publication and to Alain de Libera, in gratitude from one of his very first students; to Jérôme de Gramont, for graciously and thoroughly reading drafts of the present work; and finally, to the members of my doctoral committee, who so warmly supported not only this project, initially defended as a thesis at the Université Paris IV-Sorbonne, but also its author: Jean-Luc Marion (my supervisor), Jean-François Courtine, Jean Jolivet, Olivier Boulnois, and Philippe Capelle.

Author's Preface to the American Edition

"We must start from the beginning" – *Incohandum est ab exordio*. This formula of St. Bonaventure, placed as an epigraph to the present work, certainly first states the necessity of ascending to an identified origin, of not confounding causality and paternity, or of discovering a source for the entirety of the created. The fact remains that what has philosophical (the beginning) and theological (the origin) sense first possesses a methodological signification. *St. Bonaventure and the Entrance of God into Theology* was indeed, in my own journey, that by which it was necessary to "begin." It is thus not nothing for an author, as likewise for the future of the books he has written, to make a return to his own works. Certain works, when one returns to them and they are one's own, indeed make visible the path travelled, the turns taken, and the decisions yet to come. Such is the case for the book that you are going to read. One never knows, in reality, where thought leads. One follows it rather than preceding it, and to believe that everything was foreseen in advance, and that the attempts succeeded each other as if a single logic sufficed to preside over everything, is to have never experienced a work, be it literary, artistic, or philosophical.

Some authors certainly stick to a single idea and do nothing but exploit it. And that is already a great deal. One cannot but admire the constancy with which the beginning is sometimes given identically at the end, albeit deployed mainly in premises that had not then been suspected. Others, if not rarer then at least more difficult to pin down, do not cease to change, or rather to use detours by which they let themselves be transformed. Did not the painter Picasso have periods (blue, rose, cubism, surrealism) that make his genius rather than marking an inconstancy in the project undertaken? Or again, does one not find an immense distance between the first and last Platonic dialogues, even though everything already seemed to be in position there, in embryo, at the heart of the first thoughts? "Beginning by a beginning" aimed at as the moment *ab initio* of the introductory works is not the same as turning *in fine* toward the works that were drawn from them. The prelude bears in embryo the symphony that is yet to be played but also announces certain themes to develop elsewhere.

A certain number of works have thus appeared since, in medieval philosophy of course (*God, the Flesh, and the Other: From Irenaeus to Duns Scotus*) but also in phenomenology (*The Loving Struggle*), in philosophy of religion (*The Guide of Gethsemane; The Metamorphosis of Finitude; The Wedding Feast of the Lamb*), and even in the guise of a methodological breakthrough (*Crossing the Rubicon; Parcours d'embûches*). One enters by the porch (St. Bonaventure) only by measuring it against the edifice (philosophy of religion, phenomenology, etc.). Or rather, this entrance gives a sense to the whole and makes visible its unity, for the initial intuition was never denied in spite of certain turns taken in thought. I was and remain of Bonaventurian inspiration, even though a certain Thomistic inflection has since taught me another manner of relating oneself to God or to the creature. From the "Trinitarian monadology" or from the "interpretation of the *Canticle of Creation*" (St. Bonaventure) to the "subsistent relation" or to the "five ways for ascending to God" (Thomas Aquinas), there is not such a distance as one could sometimes think. St. Bonaventure and St. Thomas Aquinas give us two ways of saying God and for thinking him that are, if not "complementary" (Gilson), at least original but not in competition. Their contemporaneity in the 13th century is not an obstacle to their comparison but rather marks the *kairos* by which a renewal is born, teaching us today also what it is to philosophize differently.

The choice of St. Bonaventure the Franciscan, and of the *Breviloquium* as a veritable "summa of theology" in the manner of Thomas Aquinas, is not here a mere chance born of the university, nor is it only the response to a passage that is required for obtaining a diploma. I have since pronounced this avowal in the work concerning my own journey (*Parcours d'embûches*) in response to a colloquium held in Paris on my work where I was interrogated (*Une analytique du passage*). There is, and there was, in my past youth, at a semi-adolescent age when everything was being decided (seventeen years old), a spiritual experience in Assisi at St. Francis's bedside, which has made it so that Franciscanism will never for me be only an object of study, but also something lived and even practiced. The "ontology of poverty" with which the present work deals does not amount only to "giving the gift" in a phenomenology that is certainly engaged, but to inscribing in God himself, and in our own thought, the Trinitarian possibility of a givenness that makes it so that God is experienced rather than conceptualized and that he is felt and sensed rather than merely thought. One will therefore read this book as a "confession," in the manner of St. Augustine in another place and another time. The itinerary certainly will not cease to be transformed, but the point of departure is the same one by which we should start: St. Bonaventure and the Franciscan root that will always be with me.

I also certainly admit that I have changed. Or rather, turns were taken that, far from forgetting my past, give it a certain value along a winding and turbulent road. This work bears the mark of my beginnings and of my rootedness in a "phenomenology of givenness" that had not yet been questioned. And yet, everything was already in place in embryo, or awaiting deployment. For the recognition that *Denys the Areopagite is in no instance Bonaventure,* and that, therefore, the "saturated phenomenon" or the "phenomenology of the extraordinary" (J.-L. Marion) is to be distinguished from the "limited phenomenon" and from the "phenomenology of the ordinary" (my perspective), is probably one of the central theses of the book that you are going to read. Neither philosophy nor theology are referred exclusively to the apophatism of language or of God himself. There is also a form of cataphatism or of God's hypercognizibility that makes it so that the Word, in his kenosis, made himself known to us (*pro nobis*) to the point of becoming hyper-known by us (*a nobis*). Christianity is not about "distance" only but also about "proximity" – an aim that Franciscanism, like the *Spiritual Exercises* of St. Ignatius of Loyola, in reality do not cease to deploy. The incarnated summons the limit, and it is by inhabiting our created Being (être) that we abide as that very thing that God wanted us to be and that we remain. Certainly the "overcoming into the ineffable" states God's glory and transcendence (Denys), but with the counterpoint of a "divine condescension" that inhabits our immanence and stands in the "flesh" of a transformed and waiting humanity (Bonaventure). We will not see in this two opposed ways but rather two different and complementary manners of envisioning phenomenology on the one hand (the saturated/ the limited) and theology on the other (glory/kenosis).

The "confrontation with Étienne Gilson" inserted as an opening to this book, and even more the "St. Thomas Aquinas and the Entrance of God into Philosophy" added as an afterword, show the present work in its full relief, making visible both the possible turn and the rootedness in the beginning. For, as with any stage of a work, this book is inscribed in a history, in that Bonaventure is not for me a forgotten point of departure but rather an undeniable foundation. Moreover, the "phenomenological practice of medieval philosophy," amply justified in the introduction to the work that followed (*God, the Flesh, and the Other*) has definitively conceptualized, from the point of view of the method, the exercise that here was practiced for the first time. Far from remaining confined to their mere "historicity," the texts of the Fathers and the medievals also refer to an "experience" that we must today find again phenomenologically. It is by meeting each other, and by mutually enriching each other, that medieval historians and phenomenologists will come, if not to understand each other, at least to recognize that the texts need both to be scientifically established and analyzed (medievalists) and to be actualized and rooted in the experience that they attempt to describe and to show (phenomenology).

We will therefore read here, to follow the title, *St. Bonaventure and the Entrance of God into Theology.* The interrogation is born, as we will see, from Martin Heidegger and from his call for a God before whom one can also "fall to one's knees, play instruments, pray, sing, and dance" (sic.). But there is also a *St. Bonaventure and the Ontology of the Sensible* – for the originality of the Franciscan concerns not only givenness and the Trinity but also creation and corporeality. This sequel, never written and yet announced, has found in the sixth chapter of *God, the Flesh, and the Other* ["The Conversion of the Flesh (Bonaventure)"], if not its summary, at least its outlines. I will therefore refer the reader to it, as he can there read the prolongation that is demanded: the "language of the flesh" on the one hand (Bonaventure the Brother Minor or the Franciscan) and the "flesh of language" on the other (Thomas Aquinas the Preacher Brother or the Dominican). Moreover, one will find, as an afterword to the present work, and as a "loving struggle" this time, what I have since called *St. Thomas Aquinas and the Entrance of God into Philosophy* (and no longer into theology), because man's "limit" (philosophy) is also that by which God comes to reveal himself (theology).

Letting "God enter into theology" (Bonaventure, *the present work*), bringing forth from this a possible "ontology of the sensible" (*God, the Flesh, and the Other*, ch. 6), and ensuring that God does not enter "into theology alone" but also "into philosophy" (Thomas Aquinas, *afterword*), structures the entirety of an approach made less of oppositions than of transformations, less of exclusions than of confrontations. Neither so-called "natural" theology nor the term "Being" (être) attributed to God are necessarily to be condemned today, provided that they can also be phenomenologically reread and justified. An entire section of contemporary phenomenology has plunged into the aforementioned "overcoming of metaphysics" and the "critique of ontotheology." Probably the overcoming has now been overcome – and our later works have constantly shown this. *"Crossing the Rubicon"* is not a leaping from one bank to the other but a crossing the river and letting oneself be transformed by the crossing and by what one has met. The "other discourse" (of charity, of prayer, of liturgy, or of the Incarnation) that contemporary phenomenology has so much called for perhaps no longer goes without saying, or at least deserves to be questioned. Through privileging the "rupture" over the "overlapping," the "leap" over the "tiling," one forgets what is *common* to man and God, thereby falling into an angelism that can certainly draw us toward the heights but can also make us fall from our grandeur: "man is neither an angel nor a beast," Pascal reminds us, "and unfortunately he who wishes to act the angel acts the beast" (*Pensées*, L.678/B.358).

Boston, September 5, 2016
(Translated by Sarah Horton)

OPENING:
CONFRONTATION WITH ÉTIENNE GILSON[1]

It is an outrageous gamble, even an act of temerity, to dare compare, as an opening to the translation of the present work, Étienne Gilson's masterwork on Saint Bonaventure [*The Philosophy of St. Bonaventure* (1924)] and the work presented here [*St. Bonaventure and the Entrance of God into Theology* (2000)]. We will, however, dare the duel, at least because the two books confront each other across a distance of nearly three-quarters of a century [1924 / 2000], from the same French publisher [Vrin], and in the same collection [Études de philosophie médiévale], itself founded by Étienne Gilson. One will, in addition, be all the more assured of the possible confrontation in that my later work of medieval philosophy [*God, the Flesh, and the Other: From Irenaeus to Duns Scotus*] establishes, this time definitively, the method employed – the "phenomenological practice of medieval philosophy" (Introduction) – and finishes what here is still only announced: an ontology of the sensible designated as a "conversion of the flesh" (ch. 6).[2] Furthermore, my "St. Thomas Aquinas and the Entrance of God into Philosophy," which is presented as an afterword to the present translation and is, to my eyes, one of my most important texts ["Theological Limits and Phenomenological Finitude"], shows to what extent in my "confrontation with Étienne Gilson" one finds a community of thought and entirely differentiated paths. Bonaventure and Thomas Aquinas remain the two great common masters through whom all medievalists must pass, albeit

---

[1] One will find here, as an opening to the American translation of *Saint Bonaventure and the Entrance of God into Theology*, a revised version of a text initially published in Études franciscaines, volume 2, January-March 2009, pp. 7-20: "Autour de saint Bonaventure: un essai de confrontation avec Etienne Gilson."

[2] See *God, the Flesh and the Other: From Ireneus to Duns Scotus*, trans. William Christian Hackett, Evanston, Illinois, Nothwestern University Press, 2015, chapter 6, pp. 167-201: "The Conversion of the Flesh" (Bonaventure). For what concerns the specificity of Franciscan thought in general, I refer to my dialogue with L. Solignac, "Penser en franciscain," in *Etudes franciscaines*, October-December 2014 (n° 7), pp. 297-325; as well as to the preface of the new French edition of St. Bonaventure's *Short Treatise* in a single volume, "*Breviloquium*," Paris, Editions franciscaines, 2016.

according to divergent perspectives that the work which follows and the afterword that is added to it suffice to show.[3]

We are thus "like dwarves sitting on the shoulders of giants," as Bernard of Chartres aptly emphasized.[4] We might as well, therefore, endeavor to lean on them, if not to see farther than they do, at least to see otherwise than they do. What applies here to my relation to the tradition in general applies all the more to this narrow bond that binds me to that French grandmaster of medieval philosophy who was Étienne Gilson and to the lineage that he engendered. *His* "Bonaventure" and *mine* certainly bear no resemblance to each other, and yet they both open a "career path" [1924 for Gilson and 2000 for me] the future of which shows how much these beginnings counted. "Disagreements (*différends*)" create "differences (*différences*)," but it is by measuring them that the originality of each thinker and the possibility of positioning oneself emerge. Although the work you are going to read is in no way directed against the celebrated French medievalist, nor is it even addressed to him as if one has to decide between us, one will nevertheless see born here a new method regarding medieval philosophy, more phenomenological than metaphysical, descriptive rather than explanatory, with moving boundaries rather than remaining confined to disciplinary delimitations. What is essential is not to be in opposition but to trace one's own way by which one accesses the received heritage differently. Recognizing one's debt is not paying a bill from which one would like to exempt oneself but is entering into the "recognition"[5] of one who knows all the better what he owes for having also traveled the path by which he liberated himself from it.

We must indeed admit it. The eras are different, and that is why the aims are also. At the time of writing his *St. Bonaventure,* in 1924, Étienne Gilson had in reality but a single goal: breaking with a narrow rationalism that confined medieval philosophy to an abstract and strict Thomism. The Seraphic Doctor served, then, as it were, as a counterpoint to the Angelic Doctor but was always visualized through him – Thomas Aquinas or the

---

[3] On this point, see my response to Solignac in *Parcours d'embûches: S'expliquer*, Paris, Editions franciscaines, 2016, § 28, pp. 236-246: "Fidélité bonaventurienne et thomasienne." This work serves as a response to the international colloquium that was organized in France on my work (July 5-7 2014) and published under the title *Une analytique du passage: Rencontres et confrontations avec Emmanuel Falque*, Cl. Brunier-Coulin (ed.) Paris, Editions franciscaines, 2016 (720 pages).

[4] Bernard of Chartres, cited by John of Salisbury, *Metalogicus* (1159), trans. J. B. Hall, Turnhout, Belgium, Brepols Publishers, 2013, 3.4, p. 257. "Dicebat Bernard Carnotensis nos esse quasi nanos, gigantium humeris incidentes."

[5] [The French *reconnaissance* can mean both "recognition" and "gratitude," and both senses of the word apply here. – Trans.]

sense of the word "nature" (*natura*) serving, for example, as a prism for a reading of St. Bonaventure, who hardly ever uses it, always preferring to it, in my view, the word "creature" (*creatura*): "with St. Bonaventure," as the work's ending emphasizes, "[the mystical element of the doctrine] for the first time achieved full expression. [...] This undoubtedly is its gravest fault in the eyes of many of our contemporaries. Philosophy must treat of nature; mysticism can treat only of grace, and is, therefore, the business of none but the theologian. But we should be clear, to begin with, as to the meaning of the word 'nature.'"[6] The major problem of the "status of philosophy" is therefore the essential object of Gilson's work, as it would be, moreover, up through the debate about Christian philosophy. St. Bonaventure, and the book that is devoted to him, would thus serve Étienne Gilson as a fulcrum for criticizing and rejecting all attempts at a "separated philosophy": "While the Aristotelians saw the evil effect upon Christian truth of a definite metaphysical error and accepted battle upon the ground of pure philosophy, the Augustinians chose to remain upon the field of Christian wisdom and block the advance of Averroism by denying the very principle of a separated philosophy."[7] Whether the figure of St. Bonaventure is that *of a philosopher or of a theologian*, whether the ambition of a *critique of natural philosophy* is or is not appropriate to him, and whether the question of *the existence of God* is really the one to be posed (to him): such are the three lines that will here serve as a spearhead for this *a posteriori* confrontation with the work of Étienne Gilson. Thus the Seraphic Doctor will appear, at least today, as *a philosopher and a theologian "of the body and the world*," questioned mystically and phenomenologically rather than being explained metaphysically and in a still-scholastic manner.

1. ST. BONAVENTURE, PHILOSOPHER OR THEOLOGIAN?

The opposition here established between a Bonaventurian Augustinianism and a Thomistic Aristotelianism certainly remains too radical. One can even add that the sequence of Bonaventurian studies has had no other task but the nuancing of this statement, up to positing the hypothesis of an "Augustinizing Aristotelian" Bonaventure (Van Steenbergen), a thesis, moreover, taken up and discussed by a certain

---

[6] E. Gilson, *The Philosophy of St. Bonaventure* (1924), trans. Dom Illtyd Trethowan and Frank J. Sheed, Paterson, New Jersey, St. Anthony Guild Press, 1965, p. 445-446 [henceforth SBPH].

[7] Gilson, SBPH, 25. [Translation modifed. – Trans.]

Joseph Ratzinger in his *The Theology of History in St. Bonaventure*.[8] It remains, however, that what Étienne Gilson would later name "Christian philosophy" is not, or is no longer entirely, the "separated philosophy" justly "rejected" in his work on *St. Bonaventure*. The idea of "revelation as an indispensable auxiliary to reason" [definition of "Christian philosophy" in *The Spirit of Medieval Philosophy*[9]] simultaneously includes the indispensable subalternation of philosophy to theology, inherited from St. Bonaventure (against Latin Averroism's temptation to separation), and the autonomy of reason, directly linked this time to Thomas Aquinas (against Augustinian illuminism). There does not exist, as is often believed, a Gilson of mysticism on the one hand [Bonaventure (1924), Augustine (1929), Bernard of Clairvaux (1934)] and a Gilson of philosophy on the other [Thomism (1921), Christianity and philosophy (1936), Introduction to Christian philosophy (1960), etc.]. "Christian philosophy" remains *mystical* in its attachment to Bonaventure and claims to be entirely *philosophical* in its descent from Thomas Aquinas. The work on St. Bonaventure thus largely exceeds the question of Bonaventure alone. Étienne Gilson knows this and emphasizes it precisely in the introduction to his *St. Bonaventure:* "It was not a question of this or that philosophic doctrine, but the very notion of philosophy that was at issue: and the battle then joined was so important that its result was to be decisive for the future of modern thought."[10]

But there is more, and better, in the reinterpretation for today of Gilson's *St. Bonaventure,* according to a remark that this time leads directly to my own Bonaventurian work presented here [*St. Bonaventure and the Entrance of God into Theology*]. In 1974, at a distance of exactly half a century from the publication of *St. Bonaventure and Philosophy* (1924) and a few years before his death (1978), Étienne Gilson admitted, at a colloquium celebrating the seventh centenary of St. Bonaventure's death, that "this attempt to define St. Bonaventure as a *philosopher* is no less grave a deformation of his thought [...].Genuine *supernatural theology*, in the spirit of St. Bonaventure, is the sort found in the *Brief Discourse (Breviloquium)* and in the *Collationes in Hexaemeron*. It is in these writings, which in their form are rather free, that the distinctiveness

---

[8] J. Ratzinger, *The Theology of History in St. Bonaventure* (1959), trans. Zachary Hayes, Chicago, Franciscan Herald Press, 1971, § 15, p. 120-134: "The Modern Controversy Concerning Bonaventure's Anti-Aristotelianism."

[9] Gilson, *The Spirit of Medieval Philosophy* (1932), trans. A. H. C. Downes, New York, Charles Scribner's Sons, 1936, p. 37.

[10] SBPH, 25.

of Bonaventure's teaching becomes apparent."[11] One could not have been clearer, in a turn that was at the very least surprising but was already the sign of a change of era. The true fidelity to Bonaventure (in 1974) was not to attempt always, and by a *tour de force,* to define him above all as a philosopher (as in 1924); and his principal aim was not only and negatively the "critique of natural philosophy" (ch. 2 of *St. Bonaventure and Philosophy* [1924]), but also and positively the "exposition of supernatural theology," but in terms that I, for my part, think could be philosophical. The present work attempts therefore, as it were, to take Étienne Gilson literally and to push him to his limits, be it in order better to take leave of him. If there is an "entrance of God into theology" it is because the Trinitarian and Christian God "does not" enter "directly into philosophy," or rather (as I have written) because "he first enters into it as if not entering into it, or at the very least not as we would want to force him to enter into it."[12] If the question of "the entrance of God" certainly and explicitly refers to the Heideggerian debate on the onto-theological constitution of metaphysics (the supposedly necessary "entrance of God into philosophy when he enters into theology"), it is no less an extension of Gilson's interrogation of the necessity of centering, or not, all studies of St. Bonaventure on philosophy alone: "that to which the historians many times have indeed applied the critical term 'illusion of separated philosophy,'" as I will demonstrate by already distancing myself somewhat from Étienne Gilson, "has wrongly turned them from the properly *positive* aim of the Seraphic Doctor: the truth of an 'anchored theology' (in Scripture)."[13]

One will, therefore, have understood this: our work extends and at the same time takes leave of that of Étienne Gilson. The matter is the same (St. Bonaventure), the ambition also (not separating philosophy from theology), but the manner remains different (no longer isolating the philosophical, but rooting it in the theological). To the debate about "separated philosophy" (Gilson) is therefore here opposed the debate about "anchored theology" (Falque) – otherwise named in the act of what I have since called "Crossing the Rubicon."[14] But in both cases, as in all cases, it will *first* be a question of "doing philosophy" and of speaking "as a philosopher," provided that the difference between philosophy and theology consists, in my view, less in a *distance in contents* (one can

---

[11] Gilson, *S. Bonaventura, 1274-1974*, Collegio S. Bonaventura, Grottaferrata, Roma, 1974, Vol. I, pp. 2-5. [My translation. – Trans.]

[12] See introduction, below.

[13] See introduction, below.

[14] *Crossing the Rubicon: The Borderlands of Philosophy and Theology*, trans. Ruben Shank, New York, Fordham University Press, 2016.

treat theological themes philosophically [the Trinity as gift, resurrection as birth, the Eucharist as body, etc.]) than in a *difference in points of departure* (the point of view of man and the point of view of God) and *in accomplishment* (the possible and the actual).[15]

2. A CRITIQUE OF NATURAL PHILOSOPHY?

The chapter devoted to the "critique of natural philosophy" by St. Bonaventure remains famous, and it remains one of the most commented-on chapters of Étienne Gilson's work (ch. 2). In the era of the book's publication, in a context that we have difficulty imagining today, it was first a question, according to a critic in 1924 (G. Théry), of "restoring to St. Bonaventure his true features and making him, from a merely endearing figure, into a historical one."[16] St. Bonaventure did not only have to "be a philosopher" and enter into the "snare of Thomism," as it was ordinarily put in that era, but it was also necessary to show and respect his theological and mystical dimension. Saying, with Étienne Gilson, that St. Bonaventure's philosophy was not "a hesitant Thomism that [...] never came to completion" and that it was no longer fitting to "perpetually judge it from the point of view of a philosophy which is not his" (introduction to *St. Bonaventure and Philosophy*)[17] was therefore conferring on the Seraphic Doctor an autonomy and a rightful place that he had never before received. In its own time, therefore, the attempt was audacious and freed, as it were, Franciscan thought from its Thomastic vise. St. Bonaventure and St. Thomas Aquinas organize their doctrines "from different starting points," as the work's famous finale emphasizes, and "never envisage the same problems in the same aspect."[18]

A question is posed, nevertheless, and it is one that I myself have even already addressed to the famous Bonaventurian in the present work, at least in order to radicalize its aim [ch. II]. In view of the firstly "theological and mystical" intention of the Franciscan Doctor, can we, and must we, still and always take the aforementioned "critique of natural philosophy" as the point of departure for a study on St. Bonaventure? Accepting this beginning is on the one hand negatively defining the Seraphic Doctor (in critique) and on the other hand making natural theology a question, even his question (in its very formulation). Certainly we must be grateful to

---

[15] Ibid., chapter 5, pp. 121-136: "Tiling and Conversion."

[16] G. Théry, *Revue des Sciences philosophiques et théologiques* (RSPT), Recension, 1924, p. 551. [My translation. – Trans.]

[17] Gilson, SBPH, 8.

[18] Gilson, SBPH, 449.

Étienne Gilson for having brought out the importance of the debate on the status of (natural) philosophy in the conflict that opposed Bonaventure and Thomas Aquinas within the *Collationes in Hexaemeron* (1270-1274). But this refusal of the Dominican position by the Franciscan relies, in reality, on a thought that is proper to him. The theological questions of the "content of Scripture" (Gilson, p. 83),[19] of the "infused light" (p. 85), or of Christ's Incarnation (p. 85) arise precisely in order to call into question "natural philosophy" or the hypothesis of a "knowledge of things that men can acquire by means of reason alone" (p. 81). The fact remains that in 1924 it was still necessary to fear being accused of being a theologian when one was a philosopher, and certain critics (J. Bittremieux) even reproached him for having too much favored theology in his *St. Bonaventure*: "At first glance, Monsieur Gilson can sometimes seem to deviate somewhat from his subject and to enter too often into the domain of theology."[20] In short, the boundaries having been established on the basis of a given concept of "natural philosophy" that was in no way Bonaventurian, Étienne Gilson himself projected unawares the Thomistic light onto the Bonaventurian aim, because the debate then consisted, for the French medievalist, in showing how Bonaventure was *not* Thomas Aquinas, but always *starting from* Thomas Aquinas. The aforementioned "philosophy" (natural or not) remained the common basis of debate, without any calling into question of the boundaries or any possible evaluation of the "counterblow" of theology on philosophy, to the point of transforming philosophy itself.[21]

My own approach is thus distinct from Étienne Gilson's project (necessary, of course, in his era) in that it does not keep theology at a distance and never speaks of it as of a content supposedly separated from philosophy, in a distinction still nearly nonexistent at the end of the 12th century and the beginning of the 13th. The treatment, for example, that the medievalist reserves for the Trinity is in this sense, in my view, one of the most exemplary. Certainly we must emphasize with the exegete that the pure philosopher ignores the true reality of God since "he thinks he is reasoning about a mere unity whereas in fact he is reasoning about a trinity" (p. 97).[22] But what does such a trinity of persons signify, properly speaking, in Bonaventure, without directly treating of the distinction of the appropriations of the Father, of the Son, and of the Holy Spirit? There

---

[19] [Translation modified. – Trans.]

[20] J. Bittremieux, *Revue théologique de Louvain*, 1924 (Recension), p. 585. [My translation. – Trans.]

[21] This hypothesis of the "*choc en retour*" (*backlash* or *counterblow*) of theology on philosophy is found in *Crossing the Rubicon*, op. cit., p. 149-150: "The Counterblow."

[22] [Translation modified. – Trans.]

Gilson says nothing, at the risk, of course, of passing for a theologian – or of having crossed, unawares, the "Rubicon."

I will therefore endeavor, in my own project and according to my own perspective, to take Bonaventure and the Trinity at their word. I will refuse, in this sense, to speak "of" God with regard to Bonaventure, as Étienne Gilson never ceases to do. The Seraphic Doctor, as soon as he has the leisure to do so, indeed cites by name the Father, the Son, or the Holy Spirit, rather than the essence of a concept of God. Moreover, the very term "principle" (*principium*) at the beginning of the *Breviloquium* (Brev. I, 1) does not state the metaphysical principiality of an idea, as is sometimes wrongly believed, but the theological primacy of a person, the Father in his fontality: "the name of principle (*ratio principii*) pertains to God principally for what concerns the person of the Father" (I Sent. d. 29, a. 1, q. 1 ; concl.). The "true metaphysician," as a famous passage of the *Hexaemeron* indicates (I, 13), does not consider God under the name "of principle, means, and final end" (which is simply the work of the "metaphysician"), but under the name "of exemplar of all things," as "Father, Son, and Holy Spirit" (the work of the "true metaphysician"). One does not, therefore, speak "of" God and even "of" the Trinity in Bonaventure, at the risk again of making him a concept, but one thinks only "from" or "on the basis of" the Trinity, that is to say by the influence (*influentia*) of the differentiated action of the persons in man.

We must therefore recognize this, and even make it the principal track of this work after Étienne Gilson's belated admission concerning St. Bonaventure (1974): the definition of Bonaventure as a "philosopher" gravely deforms his thought. Is this to say, however, that there is no study of Bonaventurian thought save a theological one? Certainly not. For if the corpus is theological, its examination can and must also be philosophical. Treating, for example (just as I have attempted to do in the present work) of the diffusion of the Father in terms of givenness (the power of giving himself unto giving the gift) shows that certain of philosophy's contemporary inquiries (the question of givenness) find in theology their strongest and most exemplary modes of thought. But what is true of the "gift" (debate with J.-L. Marion) can also be extended, and has already been extended in my own work, to the no less essential phenomenological and Bonaventurian questions of the "Incarnation" (debate with M. Merleau-Ponty), of "perichoresis" as a form of *khôra* (debate with J. Derrida), or of "creation" as facticity (debate with J.-Y. Lacoste).[23] One will therefore not limit this early Bonaventurian work

---

[23] See *Le combat amoureux: Disputes phénoménologiques et théologiques* [*Loving Struggle* (translation forthcoming)], Paris, Herman, 2014 : ch. 1 (Derrida), ch. 2 (Merleau-Ponty), ch. 4 (Marion), ch. 7 (Lacoste).

only to the era when it was written (2000), but one will see in it the seeds of what would later and newly be engendered, from the point of view of method [*Crossing the Rubicon*] as also of content [*God, the Flesh and the Other*] and of debate [*Loving Struggle*]. I have said this from the preface to the present work onward. St. Bonaventure remains *for me* "the" source, as does Denys the Areopagite for Jean-Luc Marion in his youthful works (*The Idol and the Distance*), but in an entirely distinct way. The ways thus give themselves as entirely different, but also as complementary – like two possible manners of conceiving of appearing, the sense of Christianity, and the relation to the tradition: the "saturated phenomenon" on the one hand (J.-L. Marion) and the "limited phenomenon" on the other (my own perspective).[24]

3. GOD'S EXISTENCE IN QUESTION(S)?

The feedback mechanism from Thomistic philosophy onto Bonaventurian philosophy, even as he nevertheless wants to defend himself against it (the case of natural philosophy), is thus repeated according to the same process for what concerns "the evidence for God's existence" (Gilson, ch. 3). Certainly, it fell exclusively to Étienne Gilson to show the distance in matter between St. Bonaventure and St. Thomas Aquinas. "[O]ur experience of God's existence is the very condition of the inference by which we claim to establish that God exists," the medievalist justly emphasizes (p. 114). Proving God, or rather accessing God according to "ways" is therefore not for Bonaventure an exercise of reason for finding God at the end (*in fine*) but a mode for discovering that he is already there at the beginning (*ab initio*).

But here again a question is posed, and it is one that I have not failed to raise here in "my" *St. Bonaventure*. If God is not to be proved, is this only because he is "unprovable," that is to say beyond our concepts in his Trinity – in the Dionysian manner, for example? The response is

---

[24] The distinction between the saturated phenomenon and the limited phenomenon is fully established in the afterword to the present work: "St. Thomas Aquinas and the Entrance of God into Philosophy: Theological Limit and Phenomenological Finitude": "Deficiency as Limit." One will find the explanation of this in terms of philosophy in *Le combat amoureux*, op. cit. ch. 6: "Phénoménologie de l'extraordinaire" (J-L. Marion), by way of philosophy of religion in *The Metamorphosis of Finitude*, § 5, pp. 19-20: "Christian Specificity and the Ordinariness of the Flesh," and put into methodological perspective in *Crossing the Rubicon*, § 19 (3), pp. 145-147: "The Limited Phenomenon." For a view of the totality, if not of the controversy then at least of the new position, I refer to *Parcours d'embuches: S'expliquer* (response to *Une analytique du passage*), op. cit. ch. 3, pp. 85-105: "La finitude en question."

just as clear as it is trenchant, and it implicitly, here and already, takes its distance from what a certainly "Gilsonian" but also "Marionian" interpretation of St. Bonaventure would be. God is not to be proved not because he exceeds the order of proofs (Denys, the Syrian monk) but because he is everywhere and always already proved (Bonaventure, the Franciscan): "yet God is always and everywhere (*semper et ubique*), and absolutely always and everywhere (*et totus semper et ubique*)," as we read in the *Commentary on the Sentences* (I *Sent.* d. 8, p. I, a. 1, q. 2, concl.). "For this reason, one cannot think that he is not. This is the reason that Anselm gives in his book against the fool." Étienne Gilson certainly also exploits, justly, this reference to Anselm to say and to see that, for St. Bonaventure as for the Abbot of Bec, "the divine being, *considered in itself*, is absolutely evident" (p. 115, emphasis added).[25] But we must, in my view, once more radicalize this approach (as I do below) and show that the fidelity to Anselm is in fact a false fidelity. It is not "the divine being *considered in itself*" that is according to Bonaventure absolutely evident (Gilson), but his Trinitarian manifestation *for us* (Falque). It is not at all a question here of "proofs" or of "ways" for saying God, but only of "theophanies" of a personal and identified God.

If Bonaventure is thus faithful to St. Anselm's *Proslogion* with regard to God's absolute evidence via his grandeur, he nevertheless remains entirely unfaithful to him with regard to the manner of showing God. "Grandeur" (*majus*) no longer designates only *God* in his concept, but the Father's power of diffusion in an explicit and, to say the least, differentiated Trinity: "this diffusion is so extreme that He who produces gives all that he can," as the *Hexaemeron* remarkably indicates (Hex. 11, 11). And the destinary of this givenness is no longer man exceeded by so much grandeur, but the Son himself in whom we are contained (Col 1:16-17), and who is alone able to receive it: "it is possible to think of something greater than any creature, and the creature can think of something greater than itself. But in the Son, production is *as* in the Father (*sicut in Patre*). Consequently, if nothing can be thought that is greater than the Father (*si ergo Patre nihil maius cogitari potest*), the same is true of the Son (*ergo nec Filio*)."[26]

One will, therefore, have understood. What is truly at stake in the so-called "proofs" or "absence of proofs" of the existence of God in

---

[25] [Translation modified. – Trans.]

[26] For an interpretation of the so-called "ontological" argument of St. Anselm, I refer to my contribution "L'argument théophanique" in Abbaye Bec Helloin (éd.), *Saint Anselme. Un penseur et un saint pour notre temps. Actes du colloque à l'occasion du IXème centenaire de l'anniversaire de sa mort* (12 septembre 2009), Bec-Helloin, Les Ateliers du Bec, 2009, pp. 63-118.

Bonaventure is not his possible risk of ontologism, but the Trinitarian reinterpretation of the aforementioned ontological argument, such that it becomes, this time, entirely theological (equality of the Father and the Son that accounts for the Father's power of givenness and the Son's capacity for reception). Is this to say that it is here only a question of theology? We cannot and dare not believe this. For thinking the Father in the present work as "absolute givenness" unto "giving the gift of himself" (ontology of poverty [§ 10]) and making the Son the "Trinitarian manifesto of the grandeur of God's expression [§ 11]) is not enclosing oneself in the sole sphere of the theological but opening, and opening oneself, *by* theology itself to the philosophical thought of "givenness" (by the Father), of "manifestation" (by the Son), and of "Being to oneself (être à soi) as Being to God (être à Dieu)" (by the Spirit) – contemporary categories of philosophy to renew as well on the basis of the corpus of theology.[27]

Certainly Étienne Gilson can with reason display "ways" for going to God in Bonaventure, and this by relying on the *Commentary on the Sentences* (p. 110-115). But the term *"viae"* does not appear in Bonaventure, except to set forth "mystical degrees" for elevating ourselves towards the divine (*Itinerarium*), and not "proofs" or "arguments" for justifying its existence (Thomas Aquinas). Moreover, when he is free from all preliminary obligations (in the *Breviloquium* or the *Short Treatise* that I, for my part, have analyzed), the Seraphic Doctor is purely and simply silent on the question of proofs of God's existence, which is *precisely* a proof, if there is one, that God is truly known by us when he gives himself to us, in an entirely Franciscan "divine hypercognizibility" that we should oppose, it seems to me, to the Dionysian schema of the unknowability of God [§ 5].

For, and we must insist on this, making Bonaventure too immediately the disciple of Denys is once again reading Bonaventure through Thomas Aquinas. To say that Bonaventurian analogy is not an "analogy of Being" (Thomas Aquinas) but an "analogy of faith" (Barth) does not suffice. What marks the gap is not the possibility of bringing the world back to God, since the Seraphic Doctor also carries this out by his interpretation of the *Canticle of Creation,* but the suppression of, or rather the Son's journey through, in his Incarnation, the space that separates man and God. Certainly a mystical theologian, Bonaventure does not leave God in the "distance" of his ineffability. On the contrary, and as a good Franciscan, he places the divine in a hyper-proximity of man to God that our own grandeur for its part struggles to conceive, dazzled as it is

[27] See below, ch. 6.

not only by God's height or his splendor (the God Most High), but by so much smallness or humility (the God Most Low): "the depth of God made man, that is, the humility," as Bonaventure remarkably emphasizes in the *Hexaemeron*, "is so great that reason fails."[28]

4. A THEOLOGY OF THE BODY AND THE WORLD

We must ultimately compare Étienne Gilson's *St. Bonaventure* to *God, the Flesh, and the Other* [ch. 6: "The Conversion of the Flesh (Bonaventure)"] to measure the gap that yet separates me from the celebrated medievalist – if not concerning matter, at least concerning manner. We will be grateful, certainly, to the professor at the École Pratique des Hautes Etudes (Paris) for having exhibited Bonaventure's themes of the "*book of the world*" [ch. 7: "Universal Analogy"] and also of the "*stigmata*" [ch. 1.2: "The Franciscan"]. It remains that the "book" is still and always written in metaphysical terms for the medievalist ("analogy"), whereas in my view it could not be formulated otherwise than in mystical or hermeneutical terms ("interpretation" of the world). Moreover, the stigmata of Brother Francis, certainly defined philosophically as an essential root of the Franciscan experience (the marks of the nails on the body), are however waiting, again in my view, for their mystical implication in order to say what their possible philosophical and theological translation is (the theme of the "conversion of the senses," which is surprisingly absent, or nearly so, from Gilson's work).[29]

Let us beware, however. Saying, as I have emphasized, that "God is always and everywhere, and absolutely always and everywhere" and that "for this reason, one cannot think that he is not" (I *Sent*. d. 8, p. I, a. 1, q. 2, concl.), does not suffice for reading and discovering God's presence in the world on the basis only of the redefinition of divine exemplarism, and this in the manner of a number of post-Gilsonian Bonaventurians (Bissen, Mouiren, Berubé, Bougerol, etc.). The perspective here is not first metaphysical, without denying its validity (analogy). It is first hermeneutical (interpretation) – in which the "use of metaphor"

---

[28] Bonaventure, *Collations on the Six Days* (*Collationes in Hexaemeron*), trans. José de Vinck, Paterson, New Jersey, St. Anthony's Guild, 1970, VIII, 5, p. 124. [Translation modified to follow more closely the wording of Falque's quotation from the French. – Trans.]

[29] See *God, the Flesh, and the Other* [GFO], op. cit. (Northwestern University Press, 2015), ch. 6, pp. 167-201: "The Conversion of the Flesh (Bonaventure)" [Language of Flesh and Flesh of Language / From Symbol to the Spiritual Senses / The Limit Experience of the Stigmata].

probably indicates one of St. Bonaventure's greatest originalities, which Paul Ricœur perhaps should have, or could have, developed. "Universal analogy" (*sic*.) certainly sees that "the visible universe is a book of which particular beings (êtres) are the words" (*The Philosophy of St. Bonaventure*, p. 195). But the act of reading is always oriented, metaphysically in Gilson, towards the object or the text that is to be read ["by nature every creature is the image and likeness of the Creator" and "the image or the vestige is a substantial property of every creature" (p. 195)[30]], rather than towards the hermeneutical attitude of the reading subject. The detour, or rather the return, towards the *Collations on the Six Days* (XIII, 12) rather than towards the *Commentary of the Sentences* (II Sent. d. 16) would, however, have conferred an entirely other sense on the analysis, in a probably more finished stage of Bonaventurian thought: "when man had fallen, since he had lost knowledge," as the Seraphic Doctor emphasizes in a famous text of the *Hexaemeron*, "there was no longer any one to lead creatures back to God. Hence this book (*iste liber*), that is, the world (*scilicet mundus*) became as dead and deleted. This is why another book (*alius liber*) was necessary, by which man would be enlightened for interpreting the metaphors of things (*ut acciperet metaphoras rerum*). This book is that of Scripture (*autem liber est Scripturae*)."[31]

Without again taking up here an exegesis that I have, moreover, already performed,[32] let me indicate only that everything here is a matter of "reading" or of "reception" (*accipere*) of the book of the world by the believing subject, rather than of the "substantial property of every creature" (Gilson, p. 195), concerning which it did, however, fall to the medievalist to show the gap between it and the "vestige" in St. Augustine. As Adam no longer knew how to "read" the presence of God in the world (*liber mundi*) because his own sight was obscured by sin, God gave him this gift of the book of Scripture (*liber Scripturae*) as a bridge to the book of the world that was "*as* dead and deleted." What is objectively to be read (the world or Scripture) matters less, in my view, than the personal acuity of the believing and reading subject (in clarity or in obscurity). The vast, but just, panegyric of a "universal analogy" of all creatures to God [Gilson] here gives way, therefore, to a "hermeneutic of facticial life" because for St. Bonaventure, living in the Middle Ages turns out to be first, and mystically, being in the world (être au monde) and in God (à Dieu), and not solely resembling him in an immediately given

---

[30] [Translation modified. – Trans.]

[31] Bonaventure, *Collations on the Six Days*, XIII, 12, pp. 190-191. [Translation modified to follow more closely the wording of Falque's quotation from the French. – Trans.]

[32] GFO, pp. 182-184: "Reading the Book."

metaphysical structure (a supposedly "non-Thomistic" sense of the human composite [p. 315]).

We will, in this sense, certainly be grateful to the medievalist for emphasizing to what extent the initial intuition of Brother Francis came justly to be conceptualized by the Seraphic Doctor: "What St. Francis had simply felt and lived, St. Bonaventure was to *think*" (p. 60). The fact remains that the carnal experience of Brother Francis (ch. I: life and its milieu [the "quasi-auditory" hearing of Saint Damian's crucifix, the nudity at Assisi, being marked with the stigmata on Mount Alverna, etc.]) could have further enriched the totality of the conceptualization (ch. 12.1: "The Illumination of the Intellect [The Senses and the Imagination]). That "St. Bonaventure binds the soul more closely to the matter than St. Augustine had done" (information of corporeal matter after the information of spiritual matter) incontestably states the philosophical originality of the Franciscan Doctor (p. 321), but not his properly theological and spiritual aim, in that the philosophical attempt necessarily had, however, to lead there. The exterior senses, as we have therefore also shown [*God, the Flesh, and the Other* (ch. 6)], lead toward the interior senses to constitute in reality a veritable "divine sensorium." We will not, therefore, be satisfied to describe the philosophical mode of sensation (analogy and conformity), but we will radicalize it unto giving it sense in a theological experience of the "divine touch," because also it humanizes us at the same time as it deifies us: "When man possesses the spiritual senses (*sensus spirituales*)," as St. Bonaventure explains with originality in the *Breviloquium*, "he *sees* (*videtur*) the supreme beauty of Christ under the aspect of his Splendor (*Splendoris*), he *hears* (*auditur*) the sovereign harmony under the aspect of the Word (*Verbi*), he *tastes* (*gustatur*) the sovereign sweetness under the aspect of Wisdom (*Sapientiae*) [...], he *smells* (*odoratur*) the sovereign scent under the aspect of the Word inspired in the heart (*Verbi inspirati in corde*), and he *embraces* (*astringitur*) the sovereign sweetness under the aspect of the incarnate Word (*Verbi incarnati*)...."[33] "Seeing" God in Christ or in one's brother, "tasting" him in his wisdom or in the Eucharist, "hearing" him in his harmony or in his Word, "touching" him in his Incarnation or in prayer, and "feeling" him in the aspiration of the heart or by the scent of incense are thus so many manners of placing one's senses, and therefore "the entire human being" (*totum hominem*), in the service of God's apparition to the senses.

---

[33] Bonaventure, *Breviloquium* V (The Grace of the Holy Spirit), Paris, Éditions franciscaines, 1967, VI, 6, pp. 73-75. Cited and commented on in GFO, pp. 187-189: "A Divine Sensorium." [Translation following Hackett, *GFO*. Emphasis added by Falque. – Trans.]

The stigmata, in this sense, and far from any valorization of suffering, are not content to state a certain mode of the "substantial unity of the body and the soul" [Gilson, ch. 11: "The Human Soul"]. They signify, on the contrary or rather to a greater extent, the mode of expression of a corporeality that is able to represent God even in our own flesh converted to him: "This itinerary (*itinerarium*) to be followed is nothing but the ardent love of the crucified (*ardentissimum amorem Crucifixi*), [...]," as the prologue of the *Itinerarium* famously indicates. "This love so impregnates the soul of St. Francis that it finishes by showing through his *flesh* (*in carne patuit*), when he carried about in his *body* (*in corpore suo deportavit*) the sacred stigmata of the Passion."[34] The "touching" disciple is here "touched," and in this quasi-phenomenological chiasmus, the possible mode of an intercorporeality from man to God is expressed.[35]

CONCLUSION: AN EXIT FROM THE ALTERNATIVE

One will, therefore, have understood. This plea for Bonaventure, and the demand for a still more theological reading of the Seraphic Doctor, be it in order to bring out his firstly philosophical consistency, is not contrary to the masterwork of Étienne Gilson – far from it. The intention is different – more metaphysical and neo-Scholastic on the one hand (1924), more mystical and phenomenological on the other (2000) – but the content remains the same: an originality proper to St. Bonaventure, independent from or beyond his vis-à-vis with St. Thomas Aquinas. Moreover, my last attempt [*God, the Flesh, and the Other*] relies precisely, and explicitly, on the celebrated medievalist to found its position, to radicalize its aim, and perhaps also to accomplish what he himself only dared to outline: "Experience reveals," as the exegete indeed confides in a crucial text on "Les recherches historico-critiques et l'avenir de la scolastique" ["Historical-Critical Research and the Future of Scholasticism"] (reprinted in Études médiévales, Vrin, 1983), "that the more we re-integrate historical studies with their *theological* syntheses, the more the *philosophies* of the Middle Ages appear original."[36] Medieval studies, at least in France, have since spent several decades endeavoring to dispense with such a position. It was necessary to show a Middle Ages that was purely philosophical against those who had made it

---

[34] Bonaventure, *Itinerarium mentis in Deum*, Prologue, 2-3 (V, 295), Paris, Vrin, 1960, p. 21 [translation modified]. Cited and commented on in GFO, pp. 197-199: "The Stigmata of Brother Francis."

[35] GFO, pp. 195-197: "The Disciple Touching and Touched."

[36] Cited and commented on in GFO, Introduction, pp. 15-17.

theological, sometimes under dogmatic influences (think in particular of Pope Leo XIII's encyclical *Aeterni Patris* referring on the one hand to Bonaventure and Thomas Aquinas and invoking on the other hand his wish for a possible "Christian philosophy").[37] These times, in my view, have passed, or at the very least have been consummated. It is no longer the moment of the quarrel between philosophy and theology, at least in that the former no longer belongs to the philosophers alone (in its extension as in its vulgarization) and that the latter is no longer the jurisdiction of theologians alone (the philosophers, and in particular the phenomenologists, are countless who today do theological work by practicing philosophy first and explicitly [M. Henry, J.-L. Marion, J.-L. Chrétien, J.-Y. Lacoste, etc.]).

Must we then confine ourselves, in medieval philosophy also, to Bonaventure alone, for fear of losing our turf, and therefore never leave an alternative that we must, however, overcome [Bonaventure / Thomas Aquinas]? The question is posed here, for myself included, several centuries after Étienne Gilson. We know that it would be necessary in reality to wait for the 50's, or at the very least for the publication of *L'Être et l'essence [Being and Essence]* (1948), for the reference to Thomism to be no longer only historical in the medievalist's view (as in *The Philosophy of St. Thomas Aquinas* [1921]), but also philosophical, even dogmatic. Christian philosophy will thus later become an "art of being Thomists" (*The Philosopher and Theology*, p. 172) once Thomas Aquinas becomes *the* reference beside, and even beyond, all previous references (Augustine, Bernard of Clairvaux, Bonaventure, etc.).

Without entering into the reasons for such a turn, perhaps it is thus the destiny of any Bonaventurian to discover later that he is at the same time a Thomist – hence the afterword to the present work ["St. Thomas Aquinas and the Entrance of God into Philosophy"], which, far from constituting a simple addition, also brings forth another manner of seeing, or also of thinking. For my part, the insistence, in other essays as well (*The Guide to Gethsemane, The Metamorphosis of Finitude,* or *The Wedding Feast of the Lamb*), on "finitude" as modern man's horizon to be assumed and converted in Christianity leads more toward a philosophy of the limit (Thomas Aquinas) than to a philosophy of pure givenness (Bonaventure).[38] Where the path was first divine and then human or

---

[37] On this point, see the clear and precise introduction of Th-D. Humbrecht, in Gilson, *Introduction à la philosophie chrétienne,* Vrin (Reprise), 2007, p. 7-26 (in particular p. 19 for the reference to Leo XIII).

[38] See *The Guide of Gethsemane: Anxiety, Suffering and Death,* trans. George Hughes, New York, Fordham University Press (forthcoming); *The Metamorphosis of Finitude: An Essay on Birth and Resurrection,* trans. Hughes, New York, Fordham University Press,

taken into God (the "creative Trinity" in St. Bonaventure), it is now discovered as human first, be it in order then to be assumed by God and converted by him (man *in via*, in distinction to man *in patria* in Thomas Aquinas). The perspectives, here anew, do not oppose each other but "complete each other" (Gilson, p. 449),[39] or rather "succeed each other" (Falque):[40] "God cannot be seen in his essence by a mere human being (*ab homine puro*)," as article 11 of question 12 of the first part of the *Summa Theologica* remarkably emphasizes, "except he be separated from *this mortal life*. [...]. [O]ur soul, *as long as we live in this life,* has its being (être) in corporeal matter, hence naturally it knows only what has a form in matter [...]. Hence it is impossible for the soul of man *in this life* to see the essence of God."[41] The limit here, in the Angelic Doctor (and no longer the Seraphic Doctor) this time, is what gives the form that is the condition of the fullness of desire. We will thus remain philosophers *first,* be it in order then to work as philosophers in theology. "Crossing the Rubicon," radicalizing and transforming the initial position of Étienne Gilson (still mistrustful of the theological drift), and possibly returning next and also towards Thomas Aquinas (towards a philosophy of the limit rather than of revelation) – such is, therefore, what we have been taught by this necessary and *a posteriori* conversation between two works that face each other, less to defy each other than to orient themselves otherwise: *St. Bonaventure and Philosophy* on the one hand (1924) and *St. Bonaventure and the Entrance of God into Theology* on the other (2000).[42]

(Translated by Sarah Horton)

2012; *The Wedding Feast of the Lamb: Eros, Body and Eucharist,* trans. Hughes, New York, Fordham University Press, 2016. As for a possible and new reinterpretation for today of Thomas Aquinas, see my contribution as an afterword to the present work: "St. Thomas Aquinas and the Entrance of God into Philosophy: Theological Limit and Phenomenological Finitude."

[39] [Translation modified. – Trans.]

[40] *Crossing the Rubicon,* chapter 5, pp. 121-136: "Tiling and Conversion" [Duns Scotus, Thomas Aquinas, Bonaventure].

[41] *S. th.* Ia, q. 12, a. 11: "Whether anyone in this life can see the essence of God?" trans. The Fathers of the English Dominican Province, Christian Classics Ethereal Library.

[42] Completed, of course, by *GFO,* in particular by ch. 6, devoted to St. Bonaventure: "The Conversion of the Flesh."

Inchoandum est ab exordio
"We must start from the beginning."

Bonaventure[43]

"I consider a philosophical, or more precisely phenomenological, study of the mystical, moral-theological, and ascetical writings of medieval Scholasticism to be particularly urgent. Only by such paths will we arrive at the vital life of medieval Scholasticism, which so decisively grounded, animated, and invigorated an entire epoch of culture."

Heidegger[44]

---

[43] Bonaventure, *Brev.* Prol. No. 5 (V, 202a), tr. Fr., p. 89

[44] M. Heidegger. *Traité des catégories et de la signification chez Duns Scot* (1915), Paris, Gallimard, 1970, p. 35.

PRELIMINARY MATTER

LETTER FROM MARTIN HEIDEGGER TO A DOCTORAL STUDENT (K. LÖWITH)[1]

"You are preparing to receive the title of 'doctor' at the university. As to what value is accorded to it, how others take it, etc.—I am indifferent to all that; I take the thing as seriously as *I myself* have to…I don't presume to believe that I am doing something comparable (to a great philosopher); that is not even my intention. I simply do *what I must do* and *what I consider to be necessary*, and I do it *as I can*: I do not inflate my philosophical work in view of cultural tasks destined for 'general contemporary relevance'…I work concretely, factually, starting from my *'I am'*—starting with my spiritual origin, factual as such—milieu—cohesions of life, from what is accessible to me from there as living experience in which I live … The fact—which I will mention briefly—that I am a *"Christian theo-logian"* plays a part in this facticity. That implies a radical, determinate concern with the self, a radical, determinate, scientific approach—rigorous objectivity in facticity, which implies *the historical consciousness of the "spiritual story"*—and I am such *in the cohesion of life of the university*. "Philosophizing" is only factually, existentially attached to the university, which is to say that I do not believe that philosophy can *only* exist there, but rather that philosophizing, precisely because of its fundamental, existential meaning, *has in the university a facticity of particular effectuation*, and for this reason its limits and its limitations. This does not exclude the

---

[1] Heidegger, *Lettre du 19 Août 1921*, translated into the French by J. Greisch, *Ontologie et temporalité, Esquisse d'une interprétation intégrale de Sein und Zeit*, Paris, PUF, 1995, pp. 35-36 (my emphases). The present work was, in its first version, a doctoral dissertation defended on October 31, 1998, under the direction of Prof. Jean-Luc Marion at the Université Paris IV-Sorbonne. Whatever might be said of the "rupture with the system of Catholicism" that Heidegger had already largely effected by 1921 (cf. P. Capelle, *Philosophie et théologie dans la pensée de Martin Heidegger*, Paris, Cerf, 1998, §12, pp. 162-170), I have kept this opening letter from Martin Heidegger to Karl Löwith, a *doctoral student* (which of course I, too, once was) in the present work, since it explains, in a very precise manner, the "factual" perspective of my own efforts here.

possibility that a creative "great philosopher" might leave the university, nor does it exclude the possibility that philosophizing at the university might be nothing by pseudo-science, neither philosophy nor science. What is, then, academic philosophy? One can only *demonstrate it by one's life*."

FOREWORD

A NOTE ON THE METHODOLOGY[1]

Phenomenology is not everyone's prerogative—far from it. And yet everyone knows, or thinks he knows, whether he ought to accept or reject it. Even back in 1945, Merleau-Ponty was already blasting the "hasty reader" who wondered "whether a philosophy that cannot manage to define itself really deserves all the *noise* being made about it" and who thus concluded rather dismissively that it must only be a kind of "*myth* or a *mode*." This kind of criticism fails to see that, in Merleau-Ponty's words, "phenomenology may be practiced and recognized as a *way* or a *style*," and that it "exists as *movement* before reaching a complete philosophical consciousness."[2] This phenomenological style or mode has thus far scarcely penetrated the study of medieval philosophy, if at all; and this is paradoxical, for there is no shortage of historical possibilities, as we shall see. Here I will only note those suggested in Brentano's courses on intentionality in Thomas Aquinas, which the young Husserl attended (1884), and those mentioned in the early writings of Martin Heidegger, namely *Duns Scotus's Theory of the Categories and Meaning* (*Die Kategorien- Und Bedeutungslehre des Duns Scotus,* 1915) and the *Philosophical Foundations of Medieval Mysticism* (1918). In a number of my own earlier studies and articles I have attempted to clear the way for a possible encounter between phenomenology and Scholasticism, in which they would ideally be judged merely on the fruits of this exchange, and quite independently of any boundary questions or *a priori* principles. Permit me here to direct the reader to those sources, so that he may fairly

---

[1] At the time of the publication of this book, I wish to point out the happy coincidence of the translation and publication in French of the questions of Bonaventure's *Commentary on the Sentences* (Paris: PUF, Collection Epiméthée). More than fortuitous, this is in reality the fruit of a fertile and stimulating collaboration with their translator, Marc Ozilou. Many thanks are due him for his skill, his friendship, and his faithfulness. We all owe him a great deal; his translations, already numerous, are finally making Bonaventure—usually unknown to the general public—accessible.

[2] M. Merleau-Ponty, *Phénoménologie de la perception*, Paris: Gallimard, 1945, Foreword, p. II (my emphasis). *Phenomenology of Perception*, trans. Donald Landes, New York: Routledge, 2012.

judge the *transformation of that attempt* in the present work—and this, as much to help the book reach its own goal as to raise the stakes more generally: namely, to encourage a renewal in our approach to medieval philosophy today, and to highlight Bonaventure's originality in this debate.[3]

The text before you is meant to stand as an independent work, one that may be approached without any prerequisites. No knowledge of phenomenology or medieval philosophy on the reader's part is presupposed. Focusing solely on the Prologue and Part I of Bonaventure's *Breviloquium* (in which are addressed, respectively, Scripture and its relation to theology, and then the Trinity), this book is the first part of a reflection that should also be developed in a second volume (if I have the luxury of time and the opportunity to undertake it): namely, on the way Bonaventure conceives of the Trinity (*Brev.* I) as unfolding throughout the entirety of the created order, from "the world created by God" (*Brev.* II) through the "last judgment" (*Brev.* VII). The question of "God's entry" (*Brev.* I) suggests how the *way* in which "God enters" both philosophy and theology also determines the mode of His manifestation to man: either directly as Trinity or initially as concept. I will not neglect to note the distance here between the Franciscan Bonaventure and his Dominican contemporary Thomas Aquinas. In this work, however, it would be appropriate neither to revive any polemic between the protagonists (Bonaventure and Aquinas) nor to anticipate the final rehabilitation of the one (the Seraphic Doctor) against the historical omnipresence of the other (the Angelic Doctor). Without being satisfied with asserting the simple "complementarity" of the two perspectives,[4] we should yet be content with attributing *equal* theological importance to Bonaventure and Aquinas. Nor ought this to prevent us from taking stock of the radical divergence of their goals—perhaps even their total incompatibility.

---

[3] See in particular (solely for medieval philosophy) the following: *Vision, excès, et chair: essai de lecture phénoménologique de l'œuvre de saint Bonaventure*, in *Revue des sciences philosophiques et théologiques*, t. 79, No. 1, January 1995, pp. 3-48 (henceforth denoted as RSPT); *Le proemium du Commentaire des Sentences de saint Bonaventure ou l'acte phénoménologique de la perscrutatio*, published in English as *The Phenomenological Act of Perscrutatio in the Proemium of St. Bonaventure's Commentary on the Sentences* in *Medieval Philosophy and Theology*, vol. 2, No. 2, Autumn 2000; *Saint François et saint Dominique, deux manières d'être chrétien au monde*, in *Communio*, No. 113, May-June 1994, p. 59-76 ; *L'alterité angélique ou l'angelologie thomiste au fil des méditations cartésiennes de Husserl*, in *Laval théologique et philosophique*, t. 51, No. 3, Ocobter 1995, pp. 625-646.

[4] Gilson, *La philosophie de saint Bonaventure*. Paris: Vrin, 1924[1] and 1943[2], p. 396 (in particular the work's last sentence).

As for the contents of the present book, I would echo Bonaventure's words in the Prologue to the *Breviloquium*, and say that its shortcomings are due only to the author's inadequacies, and its merits to him whose aid he, with the Seraphic Doctor, would invoke:

if in this treatise … there be anything imperfect, obscure, superfluous, or incorrect, let me be pardoned (*venia concedatur*) on account of my responsibilities (*occupationi*), my lack of time (*et brevitati temporis*), and the poverty of my knowledge (*et pauperculae scientiae*). But if there be anything true (*si quid vero rectum*), then may "to God alone the honor and the glory" be given (*soli Deo honor et Gloria referatur*)[5].

---

[5] Bonaventure, *Brev.* (*Breviloquium*), prol. 6, No. 6 (V, 208b), tr. Fr., (modified) p. 123; the concluding quotation is from 1 Timothy 1:17. My citations of works by Bonaventure will always refer to the critical edition *Doctoris Seraphici S. Bonaventurae, Opera Omnia, ed. Studio et cura PP. Collegii a S. Bonaventura*, Florence, Quaracchi, 1882-1902, 10 volumes. In a reference, e.g. V, 215b, the Roman numeral in parentheses refers to the volume number (Vol. V), the Arabic numeral to the page (p. 215), and the alphabetical letter to the column on that page (col. b). French translations will always be indicated, and sometimes modified, when they exist. I should note that the *Breviloquium*, at least, has appeared in a bilingual edition (in Latin and French) in seven volumes prepared by the Franciscan Brothers of Paris under the title of *Saint Bonaventure: Breviloquium*, Éditions franciscaines, Paris, 1966-67. I will always refer to this edition to indicate, and frequently to revise, the French translation. I would also point out that the work done by the Franciscans at that time—during something of a "Bonaventurian revival" (1965-1970)—allows us to discuss here only the *historical* whys and wherefores of the *Breviloquium* (to which I shall return in the introduction; cf. J.-G. Bougerol, *Le sens du renouveau bonaventurien*, in Études franciscaines, No. 16, 1966, p. 92-100). The introductions and the notes on each of the volumes do indeed succeed, frequently in a very pertinent way, in addressing that first historical objective. My own effort, on the other hand, is to bring to light the specific and problematic logic of this treatise in its very beginnings (the Prologue and Part I), and to show how the question of *God's entry into theology*—as it explicitly fits in there—offers both a possible alternative to the Thomistic approach and a necessary disengagement, in philosophy as in theology, from all purely doctrinal discourse that is not deliberately grounded first in a genuine inquiry that is as much descriptive as it is experiential.

[Translator's note: English citations are my renderings of the Latin and French editions cited above, and of the author's own modifications of the French translations he cites.]

INTRODUCTION

THE *BREVILOQUIUM* AND THE PHENOMENOLOGICAL HYPOTHESIS

Has phenomenology taken a "theological turn"? Interesting though it is to consider, that is not really the essential question.[1] The problem of the relationship between phenomenology and theology must no longer be assessed by recourse to mere *a priori* principles. Rather than constantly sounding the alarm in each camp at the slightest hint of the other's approach, perhaps we should undertake a *joint praxis* of both phenomenology *and* theology. The validity of this hypothesis, I believe, can only be judged *a posteriori*, by its fruits. The profit to be gained from this encounter—if for a moment the parties can agree to step back from their conflicts of principles—would seem to be twofold: theology, on the one hand, might find in phenomenology a *mode* and a *style* adequate to its original object, i.e. a revelation that is not first discursive, but rather descriptive and even corporeal; while phenomenology, on the other hand, might draw from theology, and especially from mysticism, *non-onto-theological* tools and concepts—modes *other* than metaphysical thought that it will certainly seek in vain if it does not first anchor itself in a tradition and instead tries too hard to flirt with the so-called *margins* of philosophy.

On the threshold, hopefully, of this mutual and mutually fruitful engagement, we must return to an earlier encounter between phenomenology and theology, albeit not the first (I have already mentioned the relationship between Husserl and Thomas Aquinas via Brentano). While the young Heidegger was finishing his theological studies and preparing for his habilitation at the University of Freiburg,

---

[1] Cf. D. Janicaud, *Phenomenology and the "Theological Turn"*, trans. Bernard G. Prusak, New York: Fordham UP, 2000, originally published as *Le tournant théologique de la phénoménologie française*, Paris : Éd. de l'Éclat, 1991. I have omitted the qualification "French" above, so as not to reduce a question on which the history and the future of philosophy itself depend to a merely polemical and "hexagonal" problem. [Translator's note: Fondly or otherwise, the French sometimes refer to their country as *l'Hexagone*, in reference to its approximate shape on a map.]

he noted in his *Curriculum vitae* (1915) the strange coincidence that had found thrown together on his desk several works that, over the previous years, he had found important:

> Besides the little *summa* of *Saint Thomas Aquinas* and certain works of *St. Bonaventure*, it was the research of *Edmund Husserl* that was decisive for my academic development.[2]

A) SCHOLASTICISM AND PHENOMENOLOGY

Thomas Aquinas, Bonaventure, and Husserl: could phenomenology perhaps shed some light on Scholasticism, in its origins or at least in its principle representatives, and, in turn, could Scholasticism perhaps do the same for phenomenology? A simple chance occurrence obviously could not justify any such pretension. Nonetheless, the juxtaposition of Husserl (the father of phenomenology) with Bonaventure (a Franciscan) and Thomas Aquinas (a Dominican) should not be seen as mere serendipity. It can be understood if, to take up Heidegger in a new way, we conceived of a deepened study of the Middle Ages that "would consist less in demonstrating the historical relations between different thinkers than in understanding and interpreting the theoretical content of their philosophy by means of modern philosophy."[3] Despite the obvious distances in historical epochs, preoccupations, and beliefs that separate the movements, in this view, there are yet to be explored "latent points of phenomenological consideration within Scholastic thought, and precisely there with the most intensity."[4] Passing beyond the legitimate historical objective—especially in medieval philosophy—something especially relevant to the discourse of descriptivity might appear *phenomenologically*, like a watermark that usually remains invisible, insofar as descriptivity, too, by the treatment of "the thing itself," illuminates the concern of our own preoccupied being. If, then, "in an essential way, phenomenology takes on, in our age, the role of philosophy itself," it requires something remarkable from the point of view of method: "it is less about explaining authors than it is about asking them to tell us

[2] Heidegger, *Curriculum vitae*, in H. Ott, *Martin Heidegger, Eléments pour une biographie*. [*Martin Heidegger: Unterwegs zu einer Biographie*] Paris: Payot, 1990, pp. 90-92 (cit. p. 91, my emphasis).

[3] Heidegger, *Curriculum vitae*, ibid, p. 92.

[4] Heidegger, *Traité des catégories et de la signification chez Duns Scot* (1915), [*Die Kategorien- und Bedeutungslehre des Duns Scotus*], Paris: Gallimard, 1970, p. 32. *Duns Scotus' Theory of the Categories and of Meaning*. Trans. Harold Robbins. Chicago: De Paul University, 1978.

where we are."[5] This is probably true for every thinker, and, I propose, it is particularly so for Bonaventure and his own vision of the world with respect to our time. It is especially through Bonaventure, in fact, owing to his divergence from Thomism, that "another possible departure, still more radical, one that goes as far as decisively altering the very language of metaphysics" (J.-F. Courtine), may be realized—realized, indeed, in a sort of "phenomenological mysticology," conscious both of the possible resources in phenomenology and of the necessity of a contemporary re-interrogation of the theological corpus (E. Martineau).[6]

In recent decades, the encounter of phenomenology *and* theology via medieval philosophy—through, for example, Husserl or Heidegger and Bonaventure or Thomas Aquinas—has not always received the serious attention it merits. This diagnosis seems to be confirmed by the recent publication in the *Gesamtausgabe* of the courses on the "Phenomenology of the Religious Life" (*Phänomenologie des religiösen Lebens*) that Martin Heidegger gave at Freiburg and Marburg (1918-1921).[7] Although it is true that many historical studies, whether by phenomenologists or medievalists, have taken up the task of revealing a more or less explicit relationship between phenomenology and Scholasticism,[8] there is nonetheless no indication that the method of phenomenological inquiry has itself yet worked through the heart of the medieval corpus—if only out of a concern to maintain its strict boundaries and defenses against

[5] Jean-Luc Marion, *Réduction et Donation*, Paris: PUF, 1989, p. 7; and *L'idole et la distance* (1977), Paris: Biblio-essais, 1991, p. 38. *Reduction and Givenness: Investigations of Husserl, Heidegger, and Phenomenology*, trans. Thomas A. Carlson, Evanston, Illinois: Northwestern University Press, 1998; and *The Idol and Distance*, trans. Thomas A. Carlson, New York: Fordham University Press, 2001.

[6] Respectively, Jean-François Courtine, *Suarez et le système de la métaphysique*, Paris: PUF, 1990, pp. 98-99; and Emmanuel Martineau, *Malévitch et la philosophie*, Lausanne: L'Age d'Homme, 1997, p. 13.

[7] Heidegger, *The Phenomenology of Religious Life*, trans. Matthias Fritsch and Jennifer Anna Gosetti-Ferencei, Bloomington, Indiana: Indiana University Press, 2004. Originally *Phänomenologie des religiösen Lebens*, in *Gesamtausgabe*. Frankfurt: Klosterman, 1996, t. 60. See in particular three of the courses published in this volume: (1) *The Philosophical Foundations of Medieval Mysticism* (1918), (2) *Introduction to the Phenomenology of Religion* (winter 1920-21), and (3) *Augustine and Neoplatonism* (summer 1921). A special dossier is devoted to them in *Transversalités, Revue de l'Institut catholique de Paris*. Paris. No. 60. (Oct.-Dec. 1996), pp. 67-112.

[8] For a good introductory guide, see especially Edith Stein, "Husserl's Phenomenology and the Philosophy of St. Thomas Aquinas: Attempt at a Comparison", trans. Mary Catherine Baseheart in her *Persons in the World: Introduction to the Philosophy of Edith Stein*. Dordrecht: Kluwer, 1997. *La phénoménologie de Husserl et la philosophie de saint Thomas d'Aquin, essai de confrontation* (1929), in *Phénoménologie et philosophie chrétienne*. Paris: Cerf, 1987, pp. 31-55.

onto-theology.[9] Considering the number of contemporary studies, at least in France, on Aristotle (P. Aubenque and R. Brague), Descartes (J.-L. Marion), and still others—Leibniz, Spinoza, Schelling, etc.—it seems there is still "nothing more unfashionable than medieval philosophy."[10] Perhaps it is the medieval form of discourse (*lectio, quaestio, disputatio, quodlibet*, article, *summa*, etc.) as well as the directly theological content that it most frequently concerns (Trinity, Creation, sin, Incarnation, grace, sacraments, final ends) that sometimes keep us at a distance. To make the Middle Ages relevant to the present, or at the very least to stop "doing history as if it consisted in brooding over the lives of the dead," is the right move from an historian's perspective, and it is also an *historic* one, for it amounts to a decision no longer to "work on the Middle Ages without letting the Middle Ages work in us."[11]

There are many ways that the Middle Ages can be *brought up to date*, in sense of demonstrating their contemporaneity, and *actualized*, in the sense of developing their potentiality. Two forms of this "updating" or "*aggiornamento*" of medieval philosophy, however, deserve particular attention. The first is the more obvious, but perhaps also the more difficult (at least technically). This is the attempt to show that all contemporary Anglo-Saxon philosophical research in the field of the philosophy of language (the debates surrounding nominalism, the status of logic, etc.) has a medieval pedigree. Here, Proclus, Boethius, Abelard, Bacon, and William of Ockham are still the chief witnesses today.[12] The second type, more recent but probably more widespread, is the return to Rhineland mysticism as the preeminent locus of a sort of non-onto-theological poetics, sometimes even going so far as breaking cleanly with any mode of discourse bound to the classical forms of medieval Scholasticism: and Meister Eckhart is the figurehead of this movement.[13]

[9] On this point, see the very instructive edition of the *Revue thomiste, Saint-Thomas et l'onto-théologie* (Jan.-Mar. 1995). As for the delimitation of onto-theology starting in the Middle Ages, it is "principally valid for *one* of the Latin interpretations of Avicenna which has decisively shaped the Heideggerian vision of metaphysics: Scotism" (cf. A. de Libera, *La philosophie médiévale*. Paris: PUF, 1989, col. *Que sais-je?* No. 1044, pp. 72-73). I would add that this interpretation can point us to Henry of Ghent even more than to Duns Scotus himself (see O. Boulnois, "Quand commence l'onto-théologie? Aristote, Thomas d'Aquin, et Duns Scot." *Revue thomiste*, ibid. pp. 85-108, and especially pp. 106-107: 'Duns Scotus or Henry of Ghent?'

[10] P. Alféri, *Guillaume d'Ockham, Le singulier*. Paris: éd. de Minuit, 1989, p. 7.

[11] De A. Libera, *Penser au Moyen Age*, Paris, Seuil, 1991, p. 25.

[12] See the abundant and recent bibliography compiled by A. de Libera: *La philosophie médiévale*. Paris: PUF, 1993, pp. 498-502.

[13] See, for example, and according to frequently divergent interpretations, the large number of recent French translations and publications of Meister Eckhart. Some are by

Without taking account here of other possible avenues—all of which, however, are important (especially the study of Neo-Platonism, the return to Arab philosophy, and the rediscovery of Jewish philosophy)—I should at least note that these more historical methods will not figure into the line of inquiry that I pursue in this text, either in its intention or in its argumentation. These will instead be more directly and more immediately phenomenological.[14]

It seems to me that Heidegger's mention of Bonaventure—in addition to Thomas Aquinas (an obligatory reference in Freiburg in 1915) and alongside Husserl—is not the result of mere chance or coincidence. For the Seraphic Doctor is unusually well suited to an interpretation of the phenomenological sort, and this, for several reasons. (a) Bonaventure was able to formalize an insight of Francis's which, far from being solely conceptual or linguistic (as was Dominic's tendency), resulted first from a pure and simple descriptivity: the development of a path of conversion, the composition of a "Canticle of the Sun," or better a "Canticle of Creation," and the experience of bodily stigmata. (b) Bonaventure translates this "language of the flesh," which is brought to light in an exemplary way in a Franciscan vision of the world, into a method that measures up to the methodological demands of phenomenology: the act of *perscrutatio* is posited as a way to sound (*ergründen*) the depths of the mysteries. (c) As for the possibility that Bonaventurian theology might offset or transcend metaphysics (at least in the onto-theological sense of the term), there is every indication that this is indeed ultimately the case: (I) first, by the fact that its peculiar phenomenology permits an adequate consideration of God's essence; (II) next, by its account of a divine excess that overflows into human knowing, and by the believer's subsequent conformity to the divine Word, a conformity explained through the doctrine of the spiritual senses; (III) and finally, by the exposition of the opened and stigmatized flesh of Brother Francis, whose passion, like Christ's, both recalls and brings to life a certain inter-corporeity existing between man and God and man and the world.[15]

A. de Libera: *Traité et sermons*, Paris: Garnier-Flammarion, 1993; *Le grain de Sénevé*, Paris: Arfuyen, 1996; *Sur l'humilité*, Paris: Arfuyen, 1998. Others are by P.J. Labarrière (and G. Jarczyk): *Du détachement et autres textes*, Paris: Rivages Poche, 1995; *Le château de l'âme*, Paris: Carnets DDB, 1995; *L'étincelle de l'âme*, Paris: Albin Michel, 1998.

[14] For the different stances that tend to be taken on medieval philosophy today, I refer you to B. Pinchard, "Une nouvelle génération de philosophes face à la pensée médiévale." *Encyclopaedia Universalis, Supplément annuel.* Paris: France S.A., 1990, pp. 452-454.

[15] I draw here on certain conclusions that we have reached in my earlier works. Respectively and in the order listed above: (a) *Communio*, No. 113 (May-June 1994),

Once the possibility of a departure from metaphysics in Bonaventure has been accepted, and even effected—inquiries beyond which medievalists rarely or never venture—we can and should establish, this time theologically, a new type of beginning. And here our watchword should be a line of Hegel's that Heidegger would later cite: "it is *God* who has the most incontestable right to be the starting point."[16]

B) THE QUESTION OF GOD'S ENTRANCE[17]

"Don't you know," Socrates remarks in passing in Book II of the *Republic*, "that the beginning is always the most important thing?"[18] Indeed, the strangest and the most remarkable developments always arise from the beginnings—of a life, a friendship, an exchange, a teaching, or a discourse.[19] Whether we're dealing with "God" (*Gott*) or "the god" (*der Gott*), the "first principle" is no exception to the rule, and in fact thoroughly adheres to it. "*How does God* (or the god) *enter into philosophy?*"[20] This is a decisive line of questioning, if ever there was

---

(b) *Medieval Philosophy and Theology*, vol. 9, No. 2 (Autumn 2000), (c) *Revue des sciences philosophique et théologiques*, t. 79, No. 1 (Jan. 1995).

[16] F. Hegel, *Science de la logique*, Trans. P.J. Labarrière et G. Jarczyk. Paris: Aubier-Montaigne, 1972, t. I, Book I, *Being* (1812), p. 63. Cited by M. Heidegger "Identité et différence, la constitution ontothéologique de la métaphysique" (1957). *Questions I.* Paris: Gallimard, 1968, p. 288.

[17] On the theological origin of this question (which we only address in part here), see my article: E. Falque, "Saint Augustin ou comment Dieu entre en théologie, Lecture critique des livres V-VII du *De Trinitate*." *Nouvelle Revue Théologique*, t. 117, No. 1 (Jan.-Feb. 1995), pp. 84-111 (especially pp. 84-88).

[18] Plato, *République* II, 37a (tr. Fr. Chambry). One will find a judicious analysis of this formula in J. de Gramont, *L'entrée en philosophie, les premiers mots.* Paris: L'Harmattan, 1999, pp. 49-53.

[19] Heidegger. *Discours de Rectorat* (1933), "La puissance du commencement (*Anfang*)"in Écrits politiques 1933-1966. Presentation, translation, and notes by François Fédier. Paris: Gallimard, 1995, p. 103: "the beginning (*Anfang*) *is* again…It exists *before* us…and has gone to make a rupture in our future."

[20] Heidegger, *Identité et différence*, ibid., p. 290. I retain here André Préau's translation by "how does *God* enter philosophy?" A literal translation, however, would demand the following: "how does *the god* (*der Gott*) enter philosophy?" Hence the distance between "*God*" (*Gott*), who, according to Hegel, has "the most incontestable right to be the starting point" and "*the god*" (*der Gott*), who, according to Heidegger, "enters philosophy" (cf. D. Franck, *Nietzsche et l'ombre de Dieu.* Paris: PUF, Epiméthée, 1999, pp. 146-147). However, despite this massive shift, the question remains: can philosophy "grant a visa" or serve as a "place of welcome" in order to permit this entrance of God *himself* into philosophy? The questions demand an urgent response: "the *Trinitarian God*…cannot come to occupy the site that the onto-theological constitution of metaphysics has reserved from

one. It is also one that, if pursued phenomenologically, theology can profitably appropriate. But no sooner does Heidegger raise the question than he immediately circumscribes its answer, confining it, in my opinion wrongly, to philosophy alone:

> We can only reach the bottom of this question if first some space where *God* (or the god) *must arrive* has been sufficiently illuminated: *philosophy* itself.[21]

Without going further into this Heideggerian presupposition that philosophy can pave the way for theology, as if to completely surround the divine presence within it, we should recognize that the question of the *entrance of God* must first of all interrogate theology *theologically*— if not, we risk reducing all theology to mere philosophy. *How did God enter theology—and is he doing so again?* The apparent simplicity of the question must not hide the extreme complexity of the answer. For when God enters theology, he also enters philosophy in a serious way; at least, this has been the case historically. And the *more* he seems to enter theology, the more he really does enter philosophy. When the philosopher (Heidegger?) demands of God, or better of "*the* god" (*der Gott*), that he enter *philosophy*, he in fact is telling him to enter *where* he "*must arrive*" (philosophy itself) and "*in the manner*" in which he must arrive (as *causa sui* or Supreme Being).[22] But when God himself (*Gott*) enters *theology*, he enters first as if not entering at all—or at the very least not *as* some would force him to do. God's entry is not an intrusion, not an act of violence; he enters and reveals himself *theologically* first as Trinity. This is a way that no one could have expected; but, given that it is this way that God is entering, Bonaventure, especially in the *Breviloquium*, prepares for him the only possible route of access.

c) THE CHOICE OF THE *BREVILOQUIUM*

The *Breviloquium*, too, is a beginning, at the very least in the sense that, on the one hand, it has no other aim but to serve as a guide for

---

the very beginning" (D. Franck, ibid., p. 167, my emphasis). Far from any Heideggerian exegesis, which is not the object of the present work, let us only note that Bonaventure's *a priori* acceptance of the Trinity (see below) might serve here as a defense against any attempted reduction of God, either to a simply metaphysical schema (onto-theology) or to a purely numinous sphere (the sacred).

[21] Heidegger, *Identité et différence*, ibid., p. 290.
[22] Heidegger, ibid.

beginners (being something of a handbook for the Franciscan masters charged with teaching in the provincial convents), and that, on the other, it is satisfied with saying "something brief" (*aliquid breviter*), limiting itself to explaining the truths that are most important for faith:

> My brothers have asked me (*rogatus a sociis*) to say something brief (*aliquid breve*), with my own poor and limited knowledge, in a *summa* on the truth of theology. I have submitted to their requests, and have consented to write a *Breviloquium* (*assensi breviloquium quoddam facere*). In it I have treated briefly (*breviter*) not all those truths to be believed, but only the most important to hold (*aliqua magis opportuna*), adding to them such explanations as came to mind while I was writing.[23]

Written in 1257—when Bonaventure found himself between an academic career (he was working on his *Commentary on the Sentences* from 1253 to 1257), pastoral obligations (he served as General of the Franciscan order from 1257 to 1274), and an account of mystical illumination (he wrote the *Itinerarium* in 1259)—the *Breviloquium* came about as something of a transitional or 'borderline' text. (a) Addressed first *ad intra* to his fellow Franciscans, and specifically to teaching brothers (*socii*) in the Franciscan community, the *Breviloquium*'s formal liberties leave behind the many arcane structures of the *Commentary on the Sentences*: as "a summary or a kind of theological study guide for the clerics of the Franciscan School...one must expect neither detail nor the treatment of controversy in the presentation of its arguments."[24] (b) Since it was meant to be taught by other Franciscan masters to all brothers of the order who were ultimately under Bonaventure's care in his capacity as minister general from 1257 on, the *Brief Discourse* was concerned more with making clear the utility of certain theological doctrines (*aliqua magis opportuna*) rather than treating them thoroughly and in all their complexity. (c) Finally, drawn from the experience of Francis and written at the behest of the community, this treatise has the theological ambition to say something (*aliquid dicerem*)—even if only "briefly" (*breviter*) and "with our poor and limited kowledge" (*de paupercula scientiola nostra*)— together with the mystical inspiration which is already present in the prologue to the *Commentary on the Sentences* (1250) and which is found throughout the rest of Bonaventure's corpus, too, all the way from the *Itinerarium* (1259) to the last sermon he delivered at the Second

---

[23] Bonaventure, *Brev.* Prol. 6, No. 5 (V, 208b), Fr. tr. p. 121.

[24] Tr. Mouiren, *Introduction au Breviloquium II, Le monde créature de Dieu.* Paris: Éd. franciscaines, 1967, pp. 13-14.

Council of Lyon (1274).[25] Almost as a concession, some fifty years after he published an account of the *philosophy* of St. Bonaventure (1924), Étienne Gilson declared that "Genuine *supernatural theology*, in the spirit of St. Bonaventure, is the sort found in the *Brief Discourse* (*Breviloquium*) and in the *Collationes in Hexaemeron*. It is in these writings, which in their form are rather free, that the distinctiveness of Bonaventure's teaching becomes apparent."[26]

But the *Breviloquium* is not just a "beginning" work for being (a) free in its theological form, (b) anchored in the pastoral care of novices, and (c) innovative in its indissoluble unity of the theological and mystical. It is also, and above all else, "a beginning" in itself, in the very way in which it teaches us how to begin whenever we are doing theology:

> We must start from the beginning (*inchoandum est ab exordio*). This means means we must approach the *Father* of Lights with pure faith, bending the knee of our heart, so that through the *Son*, in his *Holy Spirit*, He may give us the true knowledge of Jesus Christ and, with this knowledge, His love.[27]

"Start from the beginning"—*inchoandum est ab exordio*: this is probably the foremost imperative of Bonaventurian theology, perhaps the only one. Beginning, at least in theology, means recognizing both spiritually and doctrinally that the theologian cannot begin alone—or better, that some Other (namely, the Father of Lights, through the Son, and in the Holy Spirit) has always *already* begun before I have. Only the theologian who "bends the knees of his heart" (*flectendo genua cordis nostri*)—touching the earth and embracing the humility (*humilitas*) of the man who has fallen to the ground (*humus*)—only he can know (or better, can recognize) the strange privilege of being "lifted up" (*levari*) by an Other. For, in the words of the *Itinerarium*, there is "a higher force that raises us" (*nisi per virtutem superiorem nos elevantem*).[28]

By "starting from the beginning"—*inchoandum est ab exordio*[29]— Bonaventure first effects a double *tour de force* with the intent of revealing a mode of existence for theology that is *a priori* in conformity with

---

[25] An analysis of the organic and indissoluble relationship of the two parts (theological and mystical) of the prologue to the *Commentary on the Sentences* suffices to prove the unity of the theological and the mystical in Bonaventure more generally. See my article in *Medieval Philosophy and Theology* (see Foreword, Note 1).

[26] Gilson, *S. Bonaventura, 1274-1974*. Vol. I, Foreword. Rome: Collegio S. Bonaventura, Grottaferrata, 1974, p. 5 (my emphasis).

[27] Bonaventure, *Brev.* Prol. No. 5 (V, 202a-b), Fr. tr. p. 89.

[28] Bonaventure, *It.* I, 1 (V, 296b), Fr. tr. H. Duméry, *Itinéraire de l'esprit vers Dieu.* Paris: Vrin, 1990, p. 27.

[29] Bonaventure, *Brev.* Prol. No. 5 (V, 210a), Fr. tr. p. 89.

the determination of God as Trinity (Part One). On the one hand, he "transposes" Scripture's descriptive mode into the realm of theological exposition (Ch. I); and on the other, he "reduces" any inquiry about God that would pose questions asking after the *quid* (the *what*) to the sort asking only after the *quomodo* (the *how*) of the potential knowability—even hyper-knowability, in a very Franciscan key—of the divine by man (Ch. II).

"In the beginning"—*in principio*[30]—the theologian also discovers God, already and always there, as just the One whose prerogative alone it is to begin (Part Two). As the origin at work "in its principle" (Ch. III), the divine community gives itself to be "experienced" and "loved"—first of all immanently, by the Persons of the Trinity; and subsequently, through the divine economy, by man (Ch. IV).

Only in this twofold experience does God's Trinitarian being adequately "manifest" and "speak" or "express" itself to man, so that God becomes capable of being received and welcomed (Part Three). He does this on the one hand by giving of himself in such superabundance that the renunciation of his wealth leaves him in real "poverty" (Ch. V). On the other hand, he does it by expressing himself to man in the very specific mode of the "metaphor," making himself close to his creatures without ever ceasing to remain what he is "in himself" (Ch. VI). Creation, finally, does nothing but translate into other terms that which is in reality always already contained in God, almost monadologically, but in an eminently Trinitarian way.[31]

In this sense, the question of *God's entrance into theology* determines not only Bonaventure's *Breviloquium*, but in fact all forms of discourse about God (theo-logy), in which the unique privilege of entering *as God*, which is to say as Trinity, has to be left to God, not to us. This "brief discourse" (*Breviloquium*) nevertheless has the unique virtue of teaching us *how* we must *begin* (in theology), and it stands for this reason as a model for all other works of theology. For, without the sort of beginning that it calls for, there probably would indeed be nothing left of any god before whom it would make sense to "fall to one's knees in awe…play music, pray, sing, and dance," in Heidegger's words.[32]

---

[30] Bonaventure, *Brev.* I, 1, No. 1 (V, 210a), Fr. tr. p. 59.

[31] The hypothesis of a Bonaventurian monadology, to which we shall return (§5c), is formulated by Alain de Libera in *La philosophie médiévale*, Paris: PUF, 1993, p. 405: "with Bonaventure, owing to the fusion of Avicenna and Dionysius, it is the idea of *monadology* that enters the history of philosophy." The idea of monadology, however, enters theology more than it does philosophy for Bonaventure, since, to tell the truth, it makes absolutely no sense outside of the reality of the Trinity that carries it and sustains it.

[32] Heidegger, *Identité et différence*, ibid., p. 306.

In light of the scope of the task and its ambitions, the *Breviloquium* seems to deserve the many accolades that have accrued to it over the centuries: it is a true "bedside book," whose depths one could still sense anew even after thirty years of "frequent reading" (*saepe legendo*) and "rumination on the words themselves" (*saepe ruminando etiam usque ad verba*);[33] it is a "treasure chest" (Scheeben) exhibiting a "power of total synthesis never equaled" (de Lubac);[34] it is "the most beautiful project in sacred hermeneutics that the thirteenth century produced" and, "after the *Itinerarium*, the most exemplary incarnation of Franciscan inspiration"—in fact, a somewhat debatable ranking, in my opinion.[35] But such panegyrics will not be enough to plead its cause. It must be re-examined more closely; and when it is, we will find, I believe, that its insights, as well as the strict development of its themes, rival those of the greatest theological *summae* of its epoch—competitively, at that, and in spite of the obscurity in which the accidents of certain historical turns and doctrinal emphases have managed to leave it.[36]

---

[33] Gerson, *De examination doctrinarum, consid.* 5, cited in S. Bonaventura, *Opera Omnia*, op. cit. (Quaracchi), Prolegomena, c. III (V, XVa-XVIb): "confiteor itaque et ego in insipentia mea…quod a triginta annis et amplius circa volui habere familiares mihi praedictos tractaculos, saepe legendo, saep ruminando, etiam usque ad verba, nedum sententias. Et ecce, hac aetate, hoc otio velut ad votum vix perveni ad initium gustum eorum." On the relationship between Gerson and Bonaventure, see C. Bérubé, *De la philosophie à la sagesse chez saint Bonaventure et Roger Bacon*, Rome, Instituto storico Dei cappuccini, 1976, pp. 312-317: 'Le bonaventurisme anti-scotiste de Gerson'; and P. Glorieux, *Gerson et saint Bonaventure*, in *S. Bonaventura 1274-1974*. Vol. IV. Rome: Collegio S. Bonaventura, Grottaferrata, 1974, pp. 773-791 (especially pp. 785-786 for Gerson's estimation of Bonaventure's *Breviloquium*.

[34] M.J. Scheeben. *Handbuch der Katholischen Dogmatik*. Freiburg: Éd. Freiburg, 1948, t. I, p. 59 (cited by J.G. Bougerol, *Introduction à saint Bonaventure*, Paris: Vrin, 1988, Note 3, p. 196); Henri de Lubac, *Exégèse médiévale: Les quatre sens de l'Écriture*, Paris: Aubier, 1961, t. I, Part 2, p. 425.

[35] M.D. Chenu. *La théologie comme science au XIIIᵉ siècle*. Paris: Bibliothèque thomiste, 1942, 1957, respectively pp. 54, 57.

[36] The allusion to the historical obliteration of Bonaventure's *Breviloquium* by Thomas Aquinas's *Summa theologica* is more than implicit here. Without arbitrarily broaching here the difficult question of a necessary (or anticipated?) replacement of Thomism, I hope at the very least that this study might help end the custom, in philosophy as well as in theology, of citing Bonaventure solely as a hypothetical alternative (even in a non-polemical way) to Thomas Aquinas, and that it might also give some of the requisite evidence necessary for such a recovery by an analysis of the texts themselves.

PART ONE

GOD AND THEOLOGY

CHAPTER I

TOWARD A DESCRIPTIVE THEOLOGY

(Brev. prol.)

The *Breviloquium*, then, is concerned in part with "beginning", with learning how to begin. To judge from the text, nothing, it seems, would serve as a better beginning for a work of theology than a prologue *(prologus)* that sets the stage for everything else by way of genuflection: "I bend my knees *(flecto genua mea)* to the Father of our Lord Jesus Christ, from whom all paternity in heaven and on earth takes its name..."[1] And to *begin well*—at least in the sense of recognizing that one *must* attempt a worthy beginning, and then pulling it off—we must start where God himself, in an act of self-revelation, addresses man: in Scripture. For at the heart of Scripture are the things hidden in the depths of God *(abscondita)*. It is thus these things that the theologian, almost phenomenologically, must make manifest *(manifestare)* or bring to light *(producere in lucem)*:

> Since Scripture *(Scriptura)* conceals multiple meanings under a single letter, he who expounds it must *bring what is hidden to light (abscondita producere in lucem)* and *make manifest (manifestare)* what is thus brought to light, by recourse to other passages whose meanings are more evident.[2]

---

[1] Bonaventure, *Brev.* Prol. No. 1 (V, 201a), Fr. tr. p. 83 (quotation from Ephesians 3:14-19). Cited again, this time in an explicit genuflection of the heart or of the spirit, in *Brev.* Prol. No. 5 (V, 202b), Fr. tr., p. 89: "we must begin in the beginning...bending the knees of our heart *(flectendo genua cordis nostri)*"; and in *Soliloquium*, Prol. No. 1 (VIII, 28a), Fr. tr., V.M. Breton, *Saint Bonaventure.* Paris: Aubier, 1943, p. 275: "let the devoted soul...then bend the knees of the mind *(flectat igitur genua mentis)* before the throne of the Blessed and incomprehensible Trinity."

[2] Bonaventure, *Brev.* Prol. §6, No. 1 (V, 207a-b), Fr. tr. p. 115. On this act of unveiling *(dévoilement – Entbergung)* that the theologian assisted by the Holy Spirit brings about in the act of the *perscrutatio,* see my article in *Medieval Philosophy and Theology.*

In other words, just as phenomenology needs its own method "because phenomena are initially and most frequently not given,"[3] so, too, theology demands *its* own particular mode, since the divine Trinity's divine appearance is not immediately given from itself, but is on the contrary presented through the multiplicity of meanings within Scripture. Right at the threshold of the *Breviloquium* it is thus necessary to define a *method*, called the method of "exposition"—or better, the method of "description"—which finally does not destroy the specificity of divine phenomenality appearing precisely as divine phenomenality, at least in Christianity: the method retains, in other words, its *Trinitarian manifestation*, spelled out in Scripture and relaying to us, at least in our post-lapsarian state, a book of creation that has sometimes become, if not illegible, at least clouded to our eyes.[4]

§1. A *SUMMA* OF REVEALED TRINITARIAN THEOLOGY

A) *Scripture and theology: Trinitarian origins*

According to the *Breviloquium*'s Prologue, the origins of "Scripture," which Bonaventure insists on calling "theology" (*sacra Scriptura quae theologia dicitur*), are to be sought "under the influence of the Most Blessed Trinity": "*ortum Scripturae attendi secundum influentiam beatissimae Trinitatis.*"[5] As I see it, the Trinity thoroughly predetermines the nature of both Scripture *and* theology for Bonaventure, to an extent that is insufficiently appreciated outside of specialized debates on the status of Scriptural theology in his work.[6] To confirm my hypothesis, the Prologue's equation of *sacra Scriptura* and *theologia* is found for a second time in an even more explicitly Trinitarian context right at the beginning

---

[3] Heidegger, *Être et temps* (1927), Paris: Authentica (out of print), §7, p. 36 (German pagination).

[4] On the "clouding" of the book of creation by sin and the necessity of reading the book of Scripture, see Bonaventure, *Hex.* XIII, 12 (V, 390a), Fr. tr. M. Ozilou, *Les six jours de la création*, Paris: Cerf, 1991, pp. 307-308. Text cited and commented on in §12c (below): "The metaphorical truth," especially p. 179 ff.

[5] Bonaventure, *Brev.* Prol. No. 1 (V, 201a), Fr. tr., p. 85.

[6] The question of the status of theology and its relationship to philosophy often remains dissociated from the question of the Trinity, as if theology could be something "in itself"—almost independent of the very thing that is revealed. For analyses that at the very least bracket the one Trinitarian source of Scripture and theology, see, for example, Gilson, *La philosophie de saint Bonaventure*, op. cit., Ch. II, pp. 76-100: "La critique de la philosophie naturelle," and J.G. Bougerol, *Introduction à saint Bonaventure*, Paris: Vrin, 1988, pp. 161-169: "La place de l'Écriture dans la théologie."

of Part I: "Holy Scripture *or* theology (*sacra Scriptura sive theologia*) is the science that gives us sufficient knowledge of the first principle (*de primo principio*)"; and that knowledge recognizes this "first principle as God, both three and one (*de primo principio scilicet de Deo trino et uno*).[7]

The claim that the Trinity alone accounts for the equivalence of Scripture and theology in Bonaventure prohibits us from considering them either in a simple identity or in pure opposition: both originally find in their Trinitarian source, and only there, the community to which they both belong, as well as the principle of their differentiation. In this sense, contrary to the conclusions suggested in many exegeses of Bonaventure, we should be content neither with affirming that "we can infer nothing about the relationship between these two terms" (Bougerol) nor with placing them unilaterally "alongside" each other according to a methodological difference supposedly capable of safeguarding the identity of their contents (Tavard).[8] Only the affirmation of a *Trinitarian a priori*, rarely invoked for this distinction, can provide its key and hold together in a single stroke—*sacra Scriptura sive (dicitur) theologia*—the assertions in the Prologue (no. 1) and Part I (*Brev.* I, 1, no. 2), and thus also maintain the unity of the whole text. The recourse, indeed the return, to Scripture and theology toward the end of the Prologue, and thus on the threshold of the exposition on the Trinity in Part I, can be explained by the *common* return to their shared and exclusive origin—the Trinity. For, in the formulation of the opening of the treatise on the Trinity, "theology speaks 'princepally'[9] of the first principle, of God three and one" (*Brev.* I, 1, no. 1). This corresponds to the introduction to the subject in the Prologue, which claims that "the origins of Scripture are to be sought under the influence of the Most Blessed Trinity" (Prol. no. 1). Both formulations take the absolute fontality of the Trinity as the principle of both theology (*Brev.* I) and Scripture (Prologue). As I shall show, in contrast to the various—and false—*a posteriori* dichotomies between the theological and the Scriptural, these approaches manage to express, in an original and exemplary way, *the* mode of proceeding (*modus procedendi*) proper to Scripture as a style that also conforms to *its* mode of teaching (*modus*

---

[7] Bonaventure, *Brev.* I, 1, no. 1 (V, 210a), Fr. tr. p. 61: adequation of Scripture and theology (with parallels in the Prologue: Prol. No. 1 [V, 201a], Fr. tr. p. 85 and Prol. 6, no. 6 [V, 208b], Fr. tr. p. 123); and *Brev.* I, 1, no. 1 (V, 210a) Fr. tr. p. 59: equivalence of the first principle and the one and triune God.

[8] See respectively J.G. Bougerol, *Introduction au prologue du Breviloquium*, éd. francicscaines (*Brev.* prol.), op. cit., p. 76; and G.H. Tavard, *La théologie d'après le Bréviloque de saint Bonaventure*, in *Année théologique*, 1949, NO. 10, pp. 201-214 (especially p. 210).

[9] Bonaventure's word is *principaliter*; see §1b, below, for the rendering 'princepally'.

exponendi), in which theology, too, shares. In these reciprocal exchanges of the Scriptural and the theological, the purely *descriptive* ambition of the one and the *expository* ambition of the other both become clear by means of a mode of descriptivity and performativity that, once again, permits the possibility of a phenomenological rereading.[10]

B) THE BREVILOQUIUM: A SUMMA OF REVEALED THEOLOGY

Much has been written on the Scripture-theology relation, with regard as much to its form as to its content, at the heart of the Prologue (especially in the last four paragraphs). Bonaventure exegetes are divided into three different interpretative camps. First, there are those who say it treats Scripture as revealed wisdom and distinguishes Scripture from—indeed, opposes it to—theology as a human science (e.g. Bougerol). Second, there are those who claim it highlights the specificity and importance of the Scriptural method but yet laments its alleged absence from theological exposition (Tavard). Third, there are those who argue—and I believe this to be the most fruitful hypothesis—that behind the dichotomy is in fact an accident of the circumstances of the text's composition, for it may be that Bonaventure started out by using one of his academic lectures (from the beginning of the Prologue to Prol. 6,3) to which he then added an introduction properly speaking on the other (Prol. 6, 4-6) (Bérubé).[11]

---

[10] I shall return, where appropriate, to this sort of implicit correspondence. Let us only note here the reference to Bonaventure: *Brev.* Prol. §5, (V, 206b-207a), Fr. tr., p. 111-115 (Holy Scripture's mode of proceeding); and *Brev.* Prol., §6 (V, 207a-208b), Fr. tr., pp. 115-123 (the mode of teaching Holy Scripture).

[11] Respectively, Bougerol, *Introduction au prologue du Breviloquium, Brev.* prol., pp. 78-79; Tavard, *La théologie d'après le Bréviloque de saint Bonaventure*; Bérubé, *De la philosophie à la sagesse chez saint Bonaventure et Roger Bacon,* Rome: Istituto storico Dei cappuccini, 1976, pp. 117-130 (especially pp. 119-120 and pp. 123-125). One will find beyond these many historical and textual commentaries on the editorial stages of the composition of the *Breviloquium*'s prologue in M. Ozilou, *Un Deutero-Bonaventure: la symbolica theologica de Richard Rufus de Cornouailles.* Thesis for Section V of the École Pratique des Hautes Études. Paris: 1990, vol. I, esp. Note 4, pp. VIII-IX (speaking of a revision or reorganization more than a collage), and pp. LXII-LXVII (on the link between the prologue of Bonaventure's *Breviloquium* and Richard Rufus of Cornwall. In the hopes and expectations of the publication of this text—as well as of the same author's master's thesis on *L'herméneutique de saint Bonaventure* and a DEA thesis on *Le De Trinitate de saint Augustin dans le commentaire des Sentences de saint Bonaventure* (taken, respectively, in 1993 and 1994 at the Institut catholique de Paris)—let this note be for me an occasion to thank once again someone who, since that time, has become a friend and who, over many long hours, has been able to guide me by his warm advice without holding back anything of his immense knowledge of Bonaventure's corpus.

Whether there is some theological motive, or some Scriptural imperative, or some quirk of composition, the debate might distract us and draw us into a discussion in which the deficiencies in form from the very beginning might by used to undermine its reliability and utility. This, at least, would explain its omission, at least historically, from the standard lists of theological reference books (cf. *above*, note 5, p. 27). As such, it would be easy to prefer, as many historians and theologians tend to do, the more emphatically mystical *Itinerarium* as Bonaventure's principal contribution, and then to leave to Thomas Aquinas the task or the honor of pulling off a true "summary" (*summa*), he being the only real authority (*auctoritas*) capable of bearing the weight of this charge. Nonetheless, and paradoxically, the Franciscan master's aim as expressed in the Prologue of the *Breviloquium* was the very same as Thomas's:

> This doctrine [the plan of salvation], as much in the writings of the saints as in those of the doctors of the Church, is transmitted in a manner so diffuse that for those who come to Holy Scripture to understand it, it cannot be understood at all—because of which young theologians (*novi theologi*) frequently have an aversion to Holy Scripture itself (...). My brothers have asked me to say *something brief* (*aliquid breve*), with my own poor and limited knowledge, in a *summa* on the truth of theology. I have submitted to their requests, and have consented to write a *Breviloquium.*[12]

I can probably do no more than merely emphasize here that the project of a summary of theology (*summa theologiae*) was not the privilege of Thomas Aquinas alone, that others before him had already blazed the trail (Alexander of Hales, for example, and Albert the Great), and that Bonaventure was following the same course. For of the goals set by both Thomas and Bonaventure in the Prologues to their respective *summae* (the *Breviloquium* in 1257, and the *Prima pars* of Thomas's *Summa theologica* in 1268), it was only really Bonaventure who managed to achieve his—a fact not without a certain irony, considering the history of theology from those days to our own. And yet Thomas Aquinas promised to do much the same thing as Bonaventure, just as explicitly and in very similar terms:

> The doctor of Catholic truth ought not only to teach those who are most advanced, but also to instruct *beginners* (*incipientes*) ... Our intent in this book is thus to treat of whatever belongs to

---

[12] Bonaventure, *Brev.* Prol. 6, No. 5 (V, 208b), Fr. tr. p. 121.

the Christian religion, in a manner suited to the instruction of beginners ... We shall try, trusting in God's help, to set forth whatever is included in sacred doctrine as *briefly* (*breviter*) and *clearly* (*ac dilucide*) as the matter itself may allow.[13]

In light of the intentions set forth in the two prologues, it would be an understatement to claim that it was Bonaventure, not Thomas Aquinas, who really kept his word. In fact, their goals are so similar that one wonders whether they didn't make some sort of pact (before their respective appointments as masters in the Faculty of Theology at Paris?) to undertake the same kind of project someday. Even the word choices are similar: to write "something brief" (*aliquid breve*—Bonaventure) or "briefly" (*breviter*—Thomas) for "young theologians" (*novi theologi*—Bonaventure) or "beginners" (*incipientes*—Thomas). Be that as it may, consider the weight of the *five hundred twelve* questions of the *Summa theologica* (not including the supplement) against the *seventy-two* chapters of the *Breviloquium* (the biblical numerical symbolism is not to be neglected here) as evidence: Bonaventure succeeds, at least formally, where the Aquinas fails. The differences in the scope and contents of the works are explainable, first of all, by a difference in method—and on this point, once more, we will be able to see just how original and how important is the approach that St. Bonaventure brings to bear in the *Breviloquium*, both in his conclusions and in how he arrives at them.

For Bonaventure, as I have said, it is the Trinity in Itself and in Itself alone, that, like a unifying axis keeping together the spokes of a vast wheel, holds together the whole of Scripture *and* theology, and indeed the totality of Creation in general. Hans Urs von Balthasar, commenting on Bonaventure, underscores the fact that "in appearing in the world (by Creation and the Incarnation of Christ), the Trinity truly opens itself and reveals that it is the foundation and the *a priori* of all terrestrial reality."[14] In other words, to cite only the *Breviloquium*'s introduction to the subject (Brev. I, 1), theology treats, as I would render it, "princepally (*principaliter* [Fr.: *principiellement*]) of the first principle, of God three and one"—not in the sense that the Trinity is its chief and principal subject, i.e. simply its most important concept, which a translation by the more standard "principally" [*principalement*] might wrongly suggest. Rather, the point here is that Trinity precedes and governs all things *as* the *principal*, i.e. as *princeps*, Who is also the *principium* of things: for,

[13] Thomas Aquinas, *Summa Theologica*, Biblioteca de autores cristianos, Madrid, 1978, Ia., Prologus, p. 3, Fr. tr. *Somme théologique*. Paris : Cerf, 1984, vol. I, p. 153.
[14] Hans Urs von Balthasar, *La gloire et la croix*. Paris: Aubier, 1972, t. II, Styles I (monograph on Bonaventure), p. 238.

as in the well-known polysemy of the Greek *archê*, the Trinity both first creates and then rules over everything—every doctrine in theology, every creature in the world. This is what the opening of this whole first part of the *Breviloquium* is about. The reference to the Prologue of John seems so clear that it should be emphasized in the translation of this first line of Part One, at least allusively: "*in the beginning* (*in principio*), it must be understood that…"[15] The Trinitarian *a priori* in Bonaventure must be understood first in a transcendental sense as "a unity that precedes all the data of intuition, a unity by relation to which the representation of the object is possible."[16] And this is true not only of the relationship between Scripture and theology but also of the whole method of theology itself.

Considering both its form and its content, the Prologue presents a twofold challenge. First, it does have an integral unity of its own, and should not be chopped up. Second, it likewise stands in an integral, organic relationship with the rest of the work. If it is divided—in itself, or from the rest of the *Breviloquium*—there is a real risk that, at least methodologically, we will read a rupture into Bonaventure's account of what is really an organic union of the Scriptural and the theological. It is in fact a union that constitutes the very heart of the text. Bonaventure's project of a summary (*summa*) of theology (*Brev.* Prol. 6 no. 5), immediately repeated (albeit only partially) in the title of the first chapter on the Trinity,[17] can thus already be seen in the Prologue. And

---

[15] Bonaventure, *Brev.* I, 1, no. 1, (V, 210a), Fr. tr. (modified) p. 59. The translation of the first phrase must in fact be corrected on two points in order not to change its meaning, and with it, the aim of the *Breviloquium* in general: by (a) translating *principaliter* by 'princepally' [*Fr. principiellement*] and not by 'principally' [*Fr. principalement*] and (b) rendering the parallelism with the Prologue of the Gospel of St. John by opening the text with "in the beginning" (and not by "one must understand in order to begin," which omits the ontological perspective for the merely chronological point of view). Translating *principaliter* by *princepally* [*principiellement*] (as one might speak of a school principal) is incidentally justified and confirmed by studies in the usage of medieval Latin. See A Blaise, *Lexicon latinitatis medii aevi*, Tournhout, Brepols, Corpus christianorum, 1896, pp. 732-733 (art. "*princeps*" and "*principale*") and A. Dauzat, *Nouveau dictionnaire étymologique*. Paris: Larousse, 1964, p. 602 (art. "principal") [Tr. note: Hoping to avoid the ambiguities of the already-existent *principalement,* which serves as the adverb for both *principal* and *principe,* much as *principally* does for the English cognates *principal* and *principle,* Falque uses *principiellement* to correspond to *principal,* in the sense of one who is first, i.e. who enjoys pride of place and is in a position of authority, and leaves *principalement* to convey the sense of *principe*. To retain the precision of the French and while drawing out the connection to the Latin *princeps* alongside the more obvious connotations of primacy, we have rendered *principiellement* as *princepally*.]

[16] E. Kant, *Critique de la raison pure* (1781). Paris: PUF, 1980, Fr. tr. Tremesaygues-Pacaud, pp. 120-121 (defintion of transcendental aperception).

[17] Bonaventure, *Brev.* I, 1 (V, 210a): "Les sept parties de la théologie *dans une somme* [On the Seven Parts of Theology *in a Summary*]" (*De illis septem de quibus est theologia*

yet some insist on calling it a "treatise written according to the theology of Scripture that was dominant at the time" (Bordoy-Torrents) or a discrete "academic lecture on Scripture" (Bérubé),[18] as if it one could really separate the Prologue from the rest of the work and from theology itself, despite Bonaventure's own words:

> Holy Scripture describes (*describit*) the contents of the whole universe as in a sort of summary (*quasi in quadam summa*), and by this we can understand its breadth.[19]

We know that the form called the *summa*, which originally meant only a work of synthesis, also had encyclopedic and pedagogical ambitions in the thirteenth century: the former in its ordering of subjects and the latter in its adaptation for students. I would say that the very fact that these are clearly present in the *Breviloquium*'s Prologue, as we have seen, should justify putting it in the same class as Thomas's *Summa theologica*, rather than his *Compendium theologiae*, to which it is more often compared.[20] One way that Bonaventure's approach is original here is that he does not restrict the use of the term *summa* to theology alone, though he certainly uses it in this sense, too (cf. the title of *Brev.* I, 1); rather, he goes further, extending the sense of *summa* beyond theology to Scripture itself, as well as to the entire universe: Scripture, recall, "describes the contents of the whole universe (*totius universi continentiam*) as in a sort of summary (*quasi quadam in summa*)."[21] The *Breviloquium* is thus a "*summa*" not only in that it is a "summary" and exposition of a set of theological principles, but also in that it claims that "the whole universe"—and with it, Scripture, in our post-lapsarian state—depends on the Trinity as its unique source and principle, and always *leads back* to the Trinity by embracing it in its totality (see below, p. 74 *sq.*).

---

in summa)." The French translation (p. 59) by "Les sept parties de la théologie" loses the general aim of the *Breviloquium* insofar as it omits any mention or any reference to the project of a *summa*.

[18] Respectively, P.M. Bordoy-Torrents. "Téchnicas divergentes en la redaccion del *Breviloquio* de S. Bonaventura," in *Ciencia Tomista* (1940), pp. 442-451 (cited by Bérubé, Note 46, p. 118); and Bérubé, *De la philosophie à la sagesse…*, op. cit., pp. 119-120 and pp. 126-130.

[19] Bonaventure, *Brev.* Prol. No. 3 (V, 201b), Fr. tr. (modified), p. 87.

[20] M.D. Chenu. *Introduction à l'étude de saint Thomas d'Aquin.* Paris: Vrin, 1950, 1993 (5th ed.), Note 2, p. 256.

[21] Bonaventure, *Brev.* Prol. No. 3 (V, 202a), Fr. tr. p. 87.

c) CAPAX TRINITATIS AND CAPACITAS HUMANA

Yet the ambitious project of extending the notion of *summa* from theology to Scripture and to the whole universe—or better, the project of *leading the summa back* into these domains—must not exceed the limitations of our own humanity. Rather, it must conform to the first imperative of all Scriptural discourse: to proceed "according to the constraints of human capacity" (*ut sic progressus sacrae Scripturae attendatur secundum exigentiam capacitatis humanae*).[22] Both the *summa* of Scripture, too, as I will show (§5c), and the *summa* of theology constitute "a most noble mirror (*tanquam speculum quoddam nobilissimum*) in which ... [all things] are destined to be described (*in quo nata est describi*)".[23] For on the one hand, they refuse to say anything univocally, because of the wealth of meaning to be found in Scripture and of the limitations of human reason (*capacitas*); and, on the other hand, they nonetheless endeavor to transmit something of a message that always extends beyond our reason's limits (*exigentia*). A theological hermeneutic, then, has the task of discerning just what the polysemic contents of Scripture are, and of rationally setting their bounds. These, in turn, must be grounded (a) in the constraint or *need* of passing on to man the divine excess and simultaneously (b) in the pursuit of a *capacity* adequate to receive it. Now, the rational spirit or mind that is "close to God" (*prope Deum*) in this sense is only "capable of God" (*capacem Dei*) by virtue of its own powers—see here the general conclusion of the *Breviloquium* (*Brev.* VII, 7)—to the extent that it is also "capable of the Most Blessed Trinity itself" (*capacem ipsius beatissimae Trinitatis*), whose image it bears. Thus, for Bonaventure, there is no *active capacity* in the man who seeks God (*capacitas humana*) that does not at the same time suppose the believer's preliminary transformation according to a *passive capacity*, a kind of structure of *welcoming*, that leaves him apt to receive the revealed Trinity itself (*capax Trinitatis*).[24]

The Seraphic Doctor insists on this primary theological criterion of "the constraints of human capacity" (*secundum exigentiam capacitatis humanae*), invoking it twice on the threshold of the Prologue of the

---

[22] Bonaventure, *Brev.* prol. no. 3 (V, 202a). Two occurrences in the same paragraph: "*secundum exigentiam capacitatis humanae*" (Fr. tr. p. 87) and "*sic exigebat conditio capacitatis humanae*" (Fr. tr. p. 89).

[23] Ibid.

[24] Bonaventure, *Brev.* VII, 7 ("la gloire du paradis"), No. 3 (V, 289b), Fr. tr., p. 111-113: "Now in his power, God created the rational mind, close to God (*prope Deum*), capable of God (*capacem Dei*), capable of the Most Blessed Trinity itself (*capacem ipsius beatissimae Trinitatis*) in accordance with the innate dynamism of the image."

Breviloquium (No. 3). There is thus every indication that the (*descriptive*) *summa of Scripture* here, drawn directly from the Trinity (Prol. No. 3), is also to be understood as the *summa of theology*, as the end of the prologue (Prol. 6, No. 5) and the title of the first chapter of the treatise on the Trinity (*Brev.* I, 1) both suggest. The project of a *summa* is thus not limited to the mere "breadth" of Scripture (*De latitudine sacrae scripturae*), which here means only the relationship between the Old and New Testaments and their respective books.[25] The *descriptive* ambition of Scripture—here extended by Bonaventure to cover the whole of theology—also covers the entire course of history and its seven ages (length), the celestial hierarchies (height), and divine judgment (depth):

> Holy Scripture *describes* (*describit*) the contents of the whole universe as in a sort of *summa* (…); it *describes* (*describit*) the unfolding of the course of time (…); it *describes* (*describit*) the excellence of those who are ultimately to be saved (…); it *describes* (*describit*) the misery of those who will be damned…[26]

§2. DESCRIPTIO AND EXPOSITIO

A) SCRIPTURAL DESCRIPTIO

To describe—*describere*: this seems to be the sole imperative of the art of Scripture. And yet it is an all-encompassing one, for it covers the entire economy of salvation (from the creation of the world to its redemption). "Holy Scripture thus *describes* the whole universe (*sic describit totum universum*)," Bonaventure ultimately insists by way of synthesis, here refuting any who would continue to seek causes or explanations where the intent is to depict the totality of the created world through the use of prophecies, psalms, proverbs, and parables.[27] This is not to say that the philosophical use of reason should be rejected. Each discipline has its own task: where philosophy "treats of the true in pure speculation" (*agit de vero nuda speculatione considerato*), Scripture exposes "the truth of morals" (*de veritate morum*).[28] But in reality, theology, the only "perfect wisdom" (*sapientia perfecta*) and the repository of "perfect taste" (*sapor perfectus*), "begins where philosophical knowledge ends"—in the double sense of completion and the exhaustion that is implied when philosophy

---

[25] Bonaventure, *Brev.* Prol. 1, No. 1-4 (V, 202b-203b), Fr. tr. pp. 91-95.

[26] Bonaventure, *Brev.* Prol. No. 3 (V, 201b), Fr. tr. p. 87.

[27] Bonaventure, *Brev.*, Prol. No. 3 (V, 201b), Fr. tr. p. 87.

[28] Bonaventure, *Brev.*, Prol. 1, No. 2 (V, 203a), Fr. tr. p. 93.

achieves its own end: *sapientia perfecta…incipit…ubi terminatur cognitio philosophica.*[29] In other words, the clean rupture or the collaboration between philosophy and theology—insofar as theology, "as if setting up a ladder" (*quasi scalam erigit*) to reach from earth to heaven, subjects to itself and then assimilates philosophical knowledge of the natures of things (*theologia substernens sibi philosophicam cognitionem et assumens de naturis rerum*)[30]—demands that the *proximity of Scripture and theology* be considered more fundamental than *the distance between theology and philosophy*. It must be affirmed, as Étienne Gilson recognized over the course of the fifty years (1924 to 1974) following his early work *La philosophie de saint Bonaventure*, that "this attempt [viz. his own earlier book] to define St. Bonaventure as a philosopher has distorted his thought in no small way."[31] What historians have considered many times by invoking "the illusion of the separated philosophy"[32] has wrongly diverted their attention from the Seraphic Doctor's properly *positive* aim: the truth of a theology that is "anchored" (in Scripture).

In my opinion, there is a gulf between philosophy and theology only because no distance, at least no methodological one, can exist between theology and Scripture. For theology derives its method from Scripture, according to Bonaventure, at least in the *Breviloquium*: when Scripture describes (*describit*) the whole universe "as in a sort of summary," the resulting *description* is only ever recorded "to the extent that this knowledge is expedient for salvation" (*quantum expedit de ipso habere notitiam ad salutem*)—and in this Scripture (and theology) distinguishes itself from philosophy.[33] Thus, from two things, one: for theology either meets this criterion of utility for salvation and derives both its method and its aim directly from Scripture, as called for in the *Breviloquium*, or else it works—as in the *Proemium* of the *Commentary on the Sentences*— to move what is to be believed toward the rationality of the what can be understood "by the addition of reason" (*per additionem rationis*), in

---

[29] Bonaventure, *Brev.*, I, 1, No. 3 (V, 210a-b), Fr. tr. p. 61.

[30] Bonaventure, *Brev.*, Prol. 3, No. 2 (V, 205a), Fr. tr. p. 103.

[31] Gilson, *S. Bonaventura, 1274-1974*, op. cit., Foreword, p. 2.

[32] Gilson, *La philosophie de saint Bonaventure*, op. cit., p. 33. On the rightful opposition of Bonaventure to Thomas Aquinas, i.e. *not* according to the ends they were pursuing (salvation) but only according to the means of getting there that they proposed (philosophical knowledge or Scripture alone), see in particular p. 99 of the same work: "St. Bonaventure's thought is visibly animated by an inspiration quite different (from that of St. Thomas Aquinas). It is clear that to Bonaventure's eyes reason is not competent in its own domain if it does not keep its gaze fixed on truths which it cannot determine. Practically, for us there is no longer any domain proper to reason, and thus St. Bonaventure turns his back on *the separated philosophy* of modern times" (my emphasis).

[33] Bonaventure, *Brev.*, Prol. No. 3 (V, 201b-202a), Fr. tr. p. 87.

which case, theology requires some autonomy of its own, relying more on reason, as Augustine demands, than on authority.[34] And of these two possibilities, the overall project of the *Breviloquium*, inasmuch as it refers explicitly to the truth of theology (*de veritate theologiae*), makes its choice explicit: the criterion of "the knowledge necessary for salvation" (*notitiam ad salutem*) proper to Scripture, and not the addition of some reason supposedly appropriated by theology, is to serve as the right prism for its purposes and ends, and, like diffracting light that passes through a crystal renders its spectrum visible, so, too, theology itself is "diffracted" by Scripture. Let us recall again the scope of the theological project at stake here (cf. above, p. 24):

> My brothers have asked me to say something brief, with my own poor and limited knowledge, in a *summa* on the truth of theology. I have submitted to their requests, and have consented to write a *Breviloquium*. In it I have treated briefly not of all those truths to be believed (*non omnia*), but only of the most import-ant to hold (*sed aliqua magis opportuna ad tenendum*), adding to them such explanations as came to mind while I was writing.[35]

One can immediately see why "the knowledge sufficient for man here below according to what is necessary for salvation" (*secundum quod est necessarium ad salutem*) can justly be called "Holy Scripture *or* theology" (*sacra scriptura sive theologia*).[36] Far from being some insignificant or abstract unity, this equivalence denotes in reality what serves as the very organizing principle of the work's theological subject matter: the truths

---

[34] Bonaventure, *I Sent.*, *Proem.*, quaest. poem. q. 1, concl. (I, 7b): "the subject to which all things are led back as to the universal whole…we can also give it a unique term: the believable (*credibile*) inasmuch as it passes toward the reason of the intielligible (*prout tamen transit in rationem intelligibilis*), and this by the addition of reason (*et hoc per ad-ditionem rationis*). Properly speaking, such is the subject of this book, and of theology." Gloss of a citation of Augustine, *De utilitate credendi*, Fr. tr. *L'utilité de croire*, Paris: DDB, B.A. No. 8, 1951, XI, 25, p. 269: "thus, understanding is the affair of reason (*quod intel-ligimus igitur debemus rationi*); believing, of authority (*quod credimus auctoritati*); preju-dice, of error (*quod opinamus errori*). But understanding never comes without believing, nor does prejudice, whereas believing is not always understanding and prejudice never is." Cited, in part at least, by Bonaventure, *Brev.* I, 1, No. 4 (V, 210b), Fr. tr. p. 63. See, on this point, my article on the *proemium* of Bonaventure's *Commentary on the Sentences* in *Medieval Philosophy and Theology*..

[35] Bonaventure, *Brev.* Prol. 6, No. 5 (V, 208b), Fr. tr. p. 121.

[36] Bonaventure, *Brev.* I, 1, No. 2 (V, 210a), Fr. tr. p. 61 with its equivalent in the Prologue, No. 1 (V, 201a), Fr. tr. p. 85: "Sacred Scripture, which is called theology" (*sacra scriptura quae theologia dicitur*).

"most important to hold for the faith"[37] (*magis opportuna ad tenendum*), and not "all those to be believed" (*non omnia*). Thus, for an example to which I shall later return (in §5 and §6), we find from the very beginning of the *Breviloquium* that it is free of any proofs for the existence of God or any kind of treatise '*De Deo uno*' (as if independent of the Trinity). Just as "the origin of Scripture is not in human inquiry (*non est per humanam investigationem*) but in the divine revelation (*sed per divinam revelationem*) which pours forth from the Father of Lights ... and through His Son, Jesus Christ, and which flows into us through the Holy Spirit,"[38] theology cannot speak "princepally" (*principaliter*) of the first principle other than "as the God Who is three and one" (*de primo principio, scilicet de Deo trino et uno*).[39] Furthermore, one cannot "enter into the knowledge of Scripture" (*in sacram Scripturam ingrediatur agnoscendam*) "without first having faith in Christ infused in him"[40] anymore than "theological discourse" (*theologia sermo*) can "treat of God and the first principle" (*de Deo et de primo principio*) without "showing thereby that the truth of Holy Scripture comes from God" (*a Deo*), "treats of God" (*de Deo*), "is in accordance with God" (*secundum Deum*), "and has God as its end" (*propter Deum*)."[41] For Bonaventure, theology is therefore not (as has sometimes been affirmed with respect to the *Breviloquium*, and wrongly, in my opinion), "the work of man,"[42] but on the contrary attests in faith—*ut sic ostenderem*—to the *revealed* truth of the provenance, conformity, object and finality of Scripture in the very being of God. Scripture can thus be called theology in the *Breviloquium* insofar as one (theology) expounds in a "single" (*una*) and "ordered" (*ordinata*) manner precisely what the other (Scripture) attests and guarantees in its divine origin and end.[43] Responding to the "aversion" that the new theologians seem to be have to Sacred Scripture (*exhorrent*), which dogmatic theology presents as "uncertain" (*incertam*) and "disorderly" (*inordinatam*)— even as an obscure "subject" or "forest," in the Latin wordplay (*silvam opacam*)— Bonaventure attempts in the *Breviloquium* first to find the path (or the journey—*Itinerarium*) that guides Scripture *and* theology in step, though each in its own way:[44] "The Prologue to the *Breviloquium*,"

---

[37] Bonaventure, *Brev.* Prol. 6, No. 5 (V, 208b), Fr. tr. p. 121.

[38] Bonaventure, *Brev.* Prol. No. 2 (V, 201a), Fr. tr. p. 85.

[39] Bonaventure, *Brev.* I, 1, No. 1 (V, 210a), Fr. tr. p. 59.

[40] Bonaventure, *Brev.* Prol. No. 2 (V, 201a), Fr. tr. p. 85.

[41] Bonaventure, *Brev.* Prol. 6, No. 6 (V, 208b), Fr. tr. pp. 121-123.

[42] J.-G. Bougerol, *Introduction au prologue du Breviloquium*, Brev. Prol. p. 78.

[43] Bonaventure, *Brev.* Prol. 6, No. 6 (V, 208b), Fr. tr. p. 123.

[44] Bonaventure, *Brev.* Prol. 6, No. 5 (V, 208b), Fr. tr. p. 121. The forest (*silva*) of Sacred Scripture is mentioned twice in the *Breviloquium*'s prologue (Prol. 6, No. 4 and No. 5, Fr. tr. pp. 119 and 121). The amphibology of the term *silva* in Latin—meaning

as Hans Urs von Balthasar says, "chooses the same text to explain the essence of revelation and of theology ... Theology takes as its point of departure not human inquiry, but the divine revelation that emanates from the Father of Lights."[45]

From the point of view of the believer, then, it is *the analogy of faith*, in the name of which *all* of the Scriptural and theological illuminations throughout the *Breviloquium* are drawn, that responds to the theological stance of a Trinitarian *a priori* that organizes and unifies doctrinal knowledge in a sort of *summa*:

> faith ... is itself the stabilizing foundation and the gate of entry for *all* supernatural illuminations (*omnium supernaturalium illuminationum*). The wisdom that is given to us by God must be determined according to the measure of our faith (*secundum ... mensuram fidei*).[46]

Scripture, like the theology that expounds it, "*condescends* to each mind" (*omni intellectui condescendat*), albeit in a different way (cf. pp. 43-45). Likewise, God's "benevolent condescension" (*dignativa condescensio*) and his "condescending benevolence" (*et condescensiva dignatio*) constitute at once the summit and the climax of the whole *Breviloquium* (below, §10).[47] Despite what many commentators have claimed, the fact that Bonaventure's *summa* of theology is indelibly and intentionally grounded in faith alone, without "the addition of reason" (*per additionem rationis*) and with only the aim of setting down "the knowledge necessary for salvation," amounts to more than a pure and simple reprise or synthesis, successful or not, of the *Commentary on the Sentences*.[48] When compared to the *Sentences*, the *Brief Discourse* reveals

not only the *forest* made of trees and foliage but also the *subject matter* of a work—might also lead us to believe here that for Bonaventure the first thing to be done in theology is to organize the "subject matter" of Sacred Scripture, apparently obscure (*silva opaca*), for it had not yet been made one (*una*), certain (*certa*), and ordered (*ordinata*) by theology. Such will be the sole task, and the justification, of theological work as the *Breviloquium* defines it.

[45] H.U. von Balthasar, *La gloire et la croix*, op. cit., p. 242.

[46] Bonaventure, *Brev.* Prol. No. 2 (V, 201b), Fr. tr. p. 85.

[47] Bonaventure, *Brev.* Prol. 4, No. 3 (V, 206a), Fr. tr. p. 107 (Scripture's condescension to each mind); and *Brev.* V, 1, No. 2 (V, 252a), Fr. tr. p. 29 (benevolent condescension and condescending benevolence).

[48] This opinion is unanimously (or almost unanimously) shared by all exegetes of St. Bonaventure. See, for example, Bougerol, *Introduction au prologue du Breviloquium*, op. cit., pro. p. 24-25: "the doctrine that we will find in this book *does not differ* from that found in the *Commentary on the Sentences*, because these two works were written contemporaneously...Most of the time, the *Breviloquium* simply *condenses* the magisterial

certain silences and topical choices that must be interrogated, silences which the novelty of the *Breviloquium*'s theological project will allow us to understand. Thus, for example, I will show (§5) that although there is a real absence of any proof of the existence of God from the *Breviloquium*, this absence is a sign of his hyper-presence, and is far from indicating the contrary. Beyond the simple hypothesis that the Prologue consists of a "collage" of a university lecture and a proper introduction (Bérubé), we can speak here of a "re-collage," or better a "revision" or "reconfiguration" of the two components, each as a function of the other and each starting with its own presuppositions. Since the *Breviloquium* purports to be a "*summa*" (Prol. 6, No. 5 and the title of *Brev.* I, 1) and claims to treat only of "the most important" truths (Prol. 6, No. 5), it begins with the recognition that the Scriptures describe the contents of the whole universe "as in a sort of *summa*" (Prol. No. 3) according to the extent to which this knowledge appears "necessary for salvation" (Prol. No. 3).[49] The academic discussion of Scripture (from the beginning of the Prologue to Prol. 6 No. 3), defining the criteria for the most important truths, runs through the whole theological project of the *Brief Discourse*; the introduction properly speaking (Prol. 6, No. 4-6), taking up the classic aim of a *summa* of theology, then plants the seeds of some preliminary considerations on Scripture, which again, emphatically, has itself been declared "a sort of *summa*" in its description of the universe.[50]

---

teachings [of the *Commentary on the Sentences*] in *the same terms*. Where different terms are used, it is in order to expose *the same doctrine*" (my emphasis). This had already been plainly affirmed in the same author's *Introduction à l'étude de saint Bonaventure*, Paris, Desclée, 1961, p. 162: "the fundamental position remains the same." The alleged exception of Tavard, emphasized by the same author (*ibid.*, Note 2, p. 162), is in reality no such thing, since the article of Tavard's that is cited there, "La théologie d'après le Bréviloque de saint Bonaventure," in *Année théologique*, No. 10 (1949), pp. 201-214, concludes with the non-differentiation of the *Breviloquium* and the *Commentary on the Sentences*. Cf. p. 214 "on the nature of theology, the *Breviloquium* adds nothing to what Bonaventure had written in his *Commentary on the Sentences*." We will emphasize here, on the other hand, the remarkable exception of Camille Bérubé, *De la philosophie à la sagesse...*, op. cit., p. 130: "from this rapid analysis of the salient points of the prologue and the whole of the *Breviloquium*, it would seem that this treatise supposes a notion of theology that can in no way be superimposed onto that of the *Commentary on the Sentences*."

[49] Bonaventure, see respectively *Brev.* Prol. 6, No. 5 (V, 208b), Fr. tr. p. 121 and *Brev.* I, 1 (V, 210a), Fr. tr. p. 59 (incomplete translation of the title) for theology as *summa* and *Brev.* Prol. No. 3 (V, 201b), Fr. tr. p. 87 for Scripture as *summa*; see the same references for the criterion of *useful or necessary truths* applied on the one hand to theology (Prol. 6, No. 5) and on the other to Scripture (Prol. No. 3).

[50] I borrow the idea (although without developing it) of a "reshuffle," rather than a collage, of two originally distinct pieces in the Prologue of the *Breviloquium* from Ozilou, *Un deutero-Bonaventure...*, op. cit., Note 4, p. IX.

The aim of Scripture (the necessary truths) is thus the vision of theology, and the intention of theology (to establish a summary) is the reality of Scripture. It is this reciprocal proximity and fertility of Scriptural wisdom and theological wisdom that, in a state of rupture or collaboration with philosophical science, now demands we find the intersection of their methods—and it is precisely here that both paradoxically lend themselves to the same phenomenological (and theological) project: to "return to the things themselves."

B) THEOLOGICAL EXPOSITIO

As we have seen, Scripture uses all the dimensions in the way it *describes* (*describit*): the contents of the universe (breadth); the course of time, unfolding in seven ages (length); the excellence of the saved (height); and the misery of the damned (depth). These *descriptions* of the totality of the world and of the beings in it (*totum universum*) are of interest to Bonaventure's project only since the knowledge they contain is "necessary for salvation" (*de ipso habere notitiam ad salutem*).[51] It is Scripture's descriptive *ambition* that will be of chief interest here, more than what it actually describes, for it is this ambition, this purpose that the Seraphic Doctor transposes onto theology itself. After describing the four dimensions of Scripture starting with a commentary on the *Letter to the Ephesians* (3:14-19), Bonaventure concludes his Prologue by distinguishing, on the one hand, sacred Scripture's "mode of proceeding" (Prol. 5: *De modo procedendi ipsius sacrae Scripturae*) from, on the other, its "mode of teaching" (Prol. 6: *De modo exponendi sacram Scripturam*).[52] Having also already admitted the basic equivalence of Scripture and theology (*sacra Scriptura sive theologia*) by virtue of their common foundation in the Trinitary as their source (cf. pp. 32-33), it becomes possible to consider the basis of their distinction as well as the fruit that their interaction may bear.

Bonaventure first presents Scripture's mode of proceeding as unique in its genre (*unus est communis modus procedendi, authenticus videlicet*). This, in my opinion, precludes the possibility of speaking for any allegedly plural *modes* of proceeding in Holy Scripture.[53] To sacred

---

[51] Bonaventure, *Brev.* Prol. No. 3 (V, 201b-202a), Fr. tr. p. 87.

[52] Bonaventure, *Brev.* Prol. 5 (V, 206b-207a), Fr. tr. pp. 111-115 and *Brev.* Prol. 6 (V, 207a, 208b), Fr. tr. pp. 115-123.

[53] (a) In paragraph 5 of the Prologue, *de modo procedendi* designates *the* mode of proceeding that is proper to Scripture, and not its various modes—which is very neatly clarified by No. 1 (Fr. tr. p. 11) in speaking of "a single mode of proceeding" (*unus*

Scipture's *one mode* of proceeding, one the other hand, there are then added many rhetorical forms and literary devices—narration, precepts, prohibitions, exhortations, sermons, threats, examples, promises, devotions, and so on.[54] The *quid* of Scriptural processes (what they are) is thus not the equivalent of their unique *quomodo* (the "how" mode, the mode *according to* or *by* which they are). The use of different approaches demands that we define that "single mode of proceeding"—shared in common by the whole set of Scripture's stylistic approaches (narration, precepts, prohibitions, etc.)—that Bonaventure here designates as the "authentic mode" (*unus est communis modus procedendi, authenticus videlicet*); and this single mode occurs only where the *descriptio*, as I shall show, constitutes at the same time both the exegetical key and the principle of its movement into theological *expositio*.[55] The *authenticity* of Scripture comes from its Author, and from Him alone—the Trinitarian God. This God is never deceptive, as Bonaventure explains, sometimes echoing Augustine and Descartes:

> There is no person who both cannot err of and knows not even how to do so, except for God and the Holy Spirit (*nullus autem est qui falli non possit et fallere nesciat nisi Deus et Spiritus sanctus*). Thus, in order that Holy Scripture might be perfectly authentic in its own way (*perfecte authentica*), it has not been handed down by human inquiry, but by divine revelation (*non per humanam investigationem est tradita, sed per revelationem divinam*).[56]

The God who is not deceptive, the God who is the guarantor of the authenticity of Scripture rather than of any hypothetical, sustainable evidence of the *cogito*, thus shows himself—as Trinity—to be the *author* of the Holy Scriptures, in and by his Holy Spirit (*Deus et Spiritus Sanctus*). Scripture's only true mode of proceeding comes about less from the various literary devices, genres, and rhetorical forms—which could be the artifice of human inquiry and invention, transmitted by humans alone (*per humanam investigationem*)—than from the divine revelation

---

est communis modus procedendi), even though it uses different literary devices [*procédés*] (narratives, precepts, prohibitions); (b) similarly, in paragraph 6 (Fr. tr. p. 115), *de modo exponendi* cannot be translated by something like "how to teach"—this expression would both lose the parallelism with the *modo procedendi* and restrain exposition to a strictly didactic function, which in fact, in my opinion, it largely transcends, designating instead the modality proper to all of theology in general.

[54] Bonaventure, *Brev.* Prol. No. 5, No. 1-2 (V, 206b-207a), Fr. tr. p. 111.
[55] Ibid.
[56] Bonaventure, *Brev.* Prol. 5, No. 3 (V, 207a), Fr. tr. (modified) p. 113.

that begets and sustains it. The "how" (*quomodo*) that is revealed again comes to take precedent over the *quid* of the revelations. The same is true of theology, and not only of Sacred Scripture, in its mode of exposition (*modus exponendi*).

In keeping with the priority given in medieval times to the *lectio*— here meaning less the solitary and quasi-monastic reading of texts than their primary mode of public exposition, i.e. in a lesson or a lecture[57]— the Seraphic Doctor writes that *reading Scripture for oneself*, to the point of "committing to memory (*commendet memoriae*) the text and the letter of the Bible by assiduous reading," is just as easy and (just as necessary as a prerequisite) as the *work of exposition* of Scripture that must follow the reading is difficult and comes as a result of theological wisdom.[58] Bonaventure and Thomas Aquinas were both pained to see theologians-in-training getting lost in "the forest of the Holy Scriptures"; for both of them, it is the highest task of the *expositor* (the one who expounds or explains Scripture) to give definitive answers when anything is called into question.[59] The mission of the *theologian-expositor* is thus clearly delimited by Bonaventure, according to a mode of understanding (*intelligi*) and exposition (*exponi*) which is proper to him:

> [his task is] to bring what is hidden [i.e. in Scripture] to light (*abscondita producere in lucem*) and to make manifest what is thus brought to light (*et illam eductam manifestare*), by recourse to other passages whose meanings are more evident (*per aliam Scripturam magis patentem*).[60]

We must thus distinguish the mode of proceeding (*modus procedendi*) proper to Scripture from the mode of expounding Scripture (*modus exponendi*) that is proper to the theologian: what the one (Scripture) *describes* in various ways—by narration, precepts, exhortations, etc.—the

---

[57] Chenu, *Introduction à l'étude de saint Thomas d'Aquin*, op. cit. p. 67-71: the procedures of exposition (the *lectio*).

[58] Bonaventure, *Brev.* Prol. 6, No. 1 (V, 207b), Fr. tr. p. 115.

[59] Bonaventure, *Brev.* Prol. 6, No. 4 (V, 208a), Fr. tr. p. 119.

[60] Bonaventure, *Brev.* Prol. 6, No. 1 (V, 208a), Fr. tr. p. 115. I do not take up here the doctrine of the "mystical senses" (*Brev.* Prol. 4 [V, 205b-206b], Fr. tr. p. 105-111) in which this theological method is rooted, the work having already been done in a remarkable way, à l'appui de Bonaventure lui-même, by Henri de Lubac, *Exégèse médiévale*, Paris: Aubier, 1959-1964, t. II (and especially pp. 263-270). I shall only show here how the exposition, the establishment of order, and the interpretation of what remains hidden in Scripture (*abscondita*) properly defines Bonaventure's theological method as we have defined it, starting from the Prologue of the *Commentary on the Sentences* as an "act of *perscrutatio*." See again my article in *Medieval Philosophy and Theology*.

other (theology) *exposits* and *makes manifest* by rendering the first clearer and more ordered.

For Bonaventure, and thus for the whole *Breviloquium*, theology cannot (or can no longer) *primarily* use narrations, precepts, prohibitions, or exhortations. This set of literary devices, a set which in its form alone belongs to Scripture and is addressed above all to the inclination of the will (*inclinationem voluntatis*), is distinct from theology, since the latter is turned first toward the intellect or pure contemplation (*nudam considerationem*), to which end it makes use of argument, reasoning, and definition.[61] Precisely on this point the *Breviloquium* is neither simply a Scriptural commentary nor merely a Sunday homily.

c) The descriptio-expositio chiasmus

Even if, however—and herein lies the originality of Bonaventure's *summa theologica*—the stylistic processes are different, theology nonetheless inherits from Scripture *its own* unique (and "authentic") mode of proceeding. Argumentative synthesis is *revealed* to the theologian just as much as Scripture is to the prophet, though the theologian is dependent on the prophet and also makes use of argument, reasoning, and definition where the prophet does not. Theology is all the more opposed to the natural light of philosophy here, in that it is illumined more by the supernatural light of Scripture:

> Theology (*theologia*), as a science founded on faith and *revealed* by the Holy Spirit (*tanquam scientia supra fidem fundata et per Spiritum sanctum revelata*) treats of things relevant to grace, to the vision of glory, and to eternal wisdom.[62]

Squarely rejecting a definition of theology as a science that is the "work of man," as I have said,[63] Bonaventure here defines the conditions of a "Scripture-theology"[64] that would be able to enflame not only the theologian's desire but also "the desire of all Christians" (*inflammari debet desiderium omnium Christianorum*)[65]—depending on whether it is ordered toward the inclination of the will (Scripture) or toward the contemplation of the intellect (theology). This twofold capacity, totally

---

[61] Bonaventure, *Brev.* Prol. 5, No. 2 (V, 206b), Fr. tr. p. 111.

[62] Bonaventure, *Brev.* Prol. 3, No. 2 (V, 205a), Fr. tr. p. 103.

[63] Bougerol, *Introduction au prologue du Breviloquium*, op. cit., Prol., p. 78.

[64] Bérubé, *De la philosophie à la sagesse*, op. cit., p. 124.

[65] Bonaventure, *Brev.* I, 1, No. 3 (V, 210b), Fr. tr. p. 63.

specific to a theology that is directly and immediately revealed by the Holy Spirit (*per Spiritum sanctum revelata*) to the theologian just as Scripture was to its human authors, demands of theology itself that it somehow bring about a conversion in its own methods. The aim is not to recast them in the very molds of the modes of proceeding that are proper to Scripture (narration, precepts, prohibitions)—far from it. Rather, the point is instead for them to be conformed analogically to Scripture's mode of being in its own uncompromising submission to the same revealed given:

> As Scripture has a special mode of proceeding (*haec specialem habet modum procedendi*), it ought to be understood (*intelligi*) and exposited (*exponendi*) in a special way *according to its mode of proceeding* (*iuxta suum procedendi modum*).[66]

Scripture's special mode of proceeding—its real mode, the mode of description—is thus in some way exported into the theological mode of comprehension (*intelligi*) and exposition (*exponendi*). And here Bonaventurian theology, seeking as it does to comprehend and explain, has as its one goal "to observe (*ut attendat*) *how* Scripture describes (*quomodo Scriptura describat*)."[67] The *quomodo* of a theology that understands and exposits by using argumentation, reasoning, and definition takes its cues from Scripture's own *quomodo*, the way in which it recounts, exhorts, promises, forbids, and so on. But both Scriptural descriptivity and theological exposition always fundamentally describe *the same thing*, under the *one and only modality* of revelation: as an hermeneutic or explanatory model, "what should be believed, as a thing that can be understood" (*credibile ut intelligibile*) is superimposed onto "what should be believed, as a thing that can be believed" (*credibile ut credibile*), the latter wholly contained in the canonical books (*Old* and *New Testaments*). That which is "believable insofar as understandable" is treated in the books of expositors (*in libris expositorum*)—which should be understood not only as the works of the learned teachers or doctors (*doctorum*) but also the works of the saints (*sanctorum*), above all those of the Fathers of the Church, but also in hagiographies, which mysticism sometimes turns into proper works of theology (in particular for Francis

---

[66] Bonaventure, *Brev.* Prol. 6, No. 1 (V, 207a), Fr. tr. p. 115.

[67] Bonaventure, *Brev.* Prol. 6, No. 4 (V, 208a), Fr. tr. p. 119. Scriptural description of the origin, development, and the end of the two hosts that contend with each other (good and evil), throughout the whole universe.

of Assisi).[68] The point of all this is that we are to find in theology, with the means proper to it, a type of discourse that, like Scripture's, bends under the weight (*kabôd*) of revelation just enough to take on its form. This is what the narrations, precepts, exhortations, promises, prayers, and praise found in the books of the Scriptural canon do; and similarly, in a theological key this time, the teachings of the saints and the doctors (*doctrina in scriptis sanctorum et doctorum*), too, will be reexamined, expounded, and applied in the *Breviloquium*.

There, instead of the formal structure based on questions (*quaestiones*) and responses (*responsiones*) that undergirds most of the scholastic *Commentaries on the Sentences* and *Summae theologicae*, the Seraphic Doctor intentionally adopts a model of theological exposition (*expositio*) derived partly from Scriptural descriptivity (*descriptio*) and partly, although in a different manner (recall the distinction between prophet and theologian), from the *same* given that Scripture receives—always Trinitarian, always revealed. Thus, one will find none of the famous medieval argumentative formulae here: neither objections (*ad oppositum*), nor 'on-the-other-hands', (*sed contra*), nor responses (*respondeo*), nor fundamentals (*fundamenta*), nor solutions (*solutiones oppositorum*) in this *Brief Discourse*. Instead, Bonaventure gives us only the formulation of a "statement" of something that is to be believed or understood (*hoc tenendum—intelligendum—est*), and then an "explanation" of it (*ratio autem ad intelligentiam praedictorum haec est...*).[69] The formula *hoc tenendum est, quod* ("we should hold this truth, namely, that, etc.") recurs in several close variations in each chapter of the *Breviloquium*, and each time the section that follows it elucidates and clarifies the statement's contents. Always remaining within the faith, the *Breviloquium* does not seek reasons *for* belief; it only presents reasons *from* belief, so to speak. And this is why the *expositor* of Scripture—the theologian who explains and understands (*intelligi et exponi*)—must "bring to light what is hidden" (*abscondita producere in lucem*), the hidden meaning, "and make it manifest" (*manifestare*).[70] This is also why the first part of the *Breviloquium* starts by *stating* "what must be held" (*quid tenendum est*) on the subject of the Trinity (*Brev.* I, 2) *before elucidating* it by "the sound

---

[68] Bonaventure, *Brev.* Prol. 6, No. 4 (V, 210a), Fr. tr. p. 63 for the distinction of "believable as believable" and "believable as understandable"; and *Brev.* Prol. 6, No. 5 (V, 208b), Fr. tr. p. 121 for the theology of the doctors and the saints (see Bougerol, *Introduction au prologue du Breviloquim*, op. cit., Note 11, p. 21).

[69] This is a recurrent structure that undergirds the mode of exposition of each chapter in the *Breviloquium*, except for the Prologue (although most of the time the "*hoc tenendum—intelligendum—est*" of the statement is merely presupposed and not explicit).

[70] Bonaventure, *Brev.* Prol. 6, No. 1 (V, 207b), Fr. tr. p. 115.

understanding of this belief" (*de istius fidei intelligentia sana, Brev.* I, 3) and *expressing* it in its catholic form (*de istius fideis expressione catholica, Brev.* I, 4).[71] Furthermore, while theology does *not* take up Scripture's various literary devices (narration, precepts, prohibitions, etc.) and instead only its "unique mode of proceeding" (a pure description starting from a revealed Trinitarian given), Scripture, to have any hope of being understood, needs the knowledge that only theology can supply:

> to understand Scripture (*ad quam quidem intelligendam*) we must know the principle of things (*oportet nosse rerum principium*), God; the creation of those things; their fall; their redemption ...[72]

Far from any binary opposition, what we see between Scripture and theology is a relationship of complementarity, an irreducible chiasmus: theology takes from Scripture its unique mode of proceeding (description), and Scripture takes from theology the keys to its own intelligibility (exposition or "bringing to light"). Here we run into Paul Ricœur's basic claim that there is a hermeneutic circle of belief and its theological exposition, a notion drawn from Augustine and Anselm of Canterbury: "We must understand in order to believe, but we must believe in order to understand."[73]

§3. PERFORMATIVITY AND DESCRIPTIVITY

A) THE HERMENEUTIC CIRCLE

This is a very *non*-"vicious circle" (*circulus vitiosus*)—it is a virtuous circle, even—of meaning and its comprehension, the theological provenance of which Heidegger himself explicitly recognized.[74] It does not turn the modality of theological discourse into a mediation of Scripture, as if it were not itself revealed and could be reduced to being a

---

[71] Bonaventure, *Brev.* I, 2-4, respective chapters titles (V, 210-212), Fr. tr. p. 65, 71, 75.

[72] Bonaventure, *Brev.* Prol. 6 No. 4 (V, 208a-b), Fr. tr. p.121.

[73] P. Ricœur. *Finitude et culpabilité*, t. II, *La symbolique du mal*. Paris: Aubier, 1960, p. 326 ('Le symbole donne à penser').

[74] Heidegger, *Sein und Zeit*, op. cit. §32 (Understanding and Explaining), pp. 152-153: the non-vicious circle; and *D'un entretien de la parole* (*Entre un Japonais et un qui demande*), in *Acheminement vers la parole* (1959). Paris: Gallimard, 1976, p. 95 : the theological origins of the notion of hermeneutics.

purely human undertaking. Instead, it makes the modality that is proper to theological discourse a "second immediacy" or a "second naïveté." In this conception, even though we must believe to understand (the role of Scripture), we should also understand in order to believe (the role of theology), supposing that the goal is to explain what it is that Scripture teaches.[75] "It is crucial," Heidegger stresses, "not to leave the circle, but rather to enter it in the right way."[76] It is not enough to say nice things about the *Breviloquium*'s Prologue and its study of the four senses of Scripture (Prol. 4): for instance, that it outlines "the most beautiful vision of sacred hermeneutics that came out of the thirteenth century."[77] What is true of Scripture (and can justly be said of Origen's *Peri archon*[78]), according to Bonaventure, must *originally* apply to the status of theology, too. The four senses of Scripture in its *depth* (literal, allegorical, tropological, and anagogical) must be all the more foundational for Scriptural theology, Bonaventure holds, because the *form* of theology is derived from the mode of unveiling found in Biblical hermeneutics and yet in its *content* theology simultaneously explains Scripture in accordance with its own principles. In this sense, Scripture and theology refer to one and the same Word of God, according to the *one* (descriptive) *mode of proceeding* of the Trinitarian revelation, a mode which is, however, formalized by the use of *several* different and complementary *processes* (examples vs. arguments, promises vs. reasoning, devotions vs. definitions, etc.).[79] This is because for God, *speaking*—in a sort of strangely contemporary performativity, addressed here as much to the prophet as to the theologian—is identical to *acting*, to *doing*:

> God speaks not only by words (*non tanquam loquitur per verba*),
> but also by deeds (*verum etiam per facta*). For to speak, for Him,

---

[75] Ricœur, *Finitude et culpabilité*, op. cit., p. 327: the circle of comprehension and interpretation.

[76] Heidegger, *Sein und Zeit*, op. cit., (Fr. trans. Martineau), §32, p. 153 (German pagination).

[77] Chenu, *La théologie comme science eu XIIIᵉ siècle*. Paris: Bibliothèque thomiste No. 33, 1957 (3rd), p. 54.

[78] Origen, *Peri Archôn* (*Treatise on the Principles*). Sources chrétiennes No. 286, Book IV (cf. H. de Lubac, *Histoire et esprit, l'intelligence de l'*Écriture d'après Origène. Paris: Aubier, 1950. The convergence of the nascent study of hermeneutics and the exegetical problematic of the meanings of Scripture had already been shown by W. Dilthey in *Origines et développement de l'herméneutique*, in *Le monde et l'Esprit* (1900). Paris: Aubier-Montaigne, 1947, t. I.

[79] Bonaventure, *Brev*. Prol. 5, No. 2 (V, 206b), Fr. tr. p. 111.

is to do, and to do is to speak (*quia ipsius* dicere *facere est, et ipsius* facere *dicere*).[80]

B) *A PERFORMATIVE THEOLOGY*

Speaking is doing, and doing is speaking (*dicere facere est, et facere dicere*)—we might see here an indication of "*how to do things with words.*" For it is in Bonaventure that Austin's performativity paradoxically finds its most explicit and most paradigmatic formulation, when he applies it to the Scriptural mode of revelation that theology, too, takes on.[81] In this Trinitarian theological hermeneutic, the Word of the Father will first of all be the Son, less in what he says than in his very person, being the Word made flesh. But because the wisdom of God is wrapped (*involutus*) in the humble figures of Scripture "as Christ was wrapped in swaddling clothes" (*sicut Christus fuit paniculis involutus*), it falls to the theologian to reveal the meaning of Scripture as well as of the universe itself, precisely because God speaks in it.[82] The flesh of the word—Scripture *or* (*sive*, so the disjunction is not exclusive) theology—is inscribed within a text that needs to be interpreted (*hermeneuein*); and its inscription there comes both before and concurrent with the incarnation of the Word of the flesh in history.[83] Bonaventure's account of the seven ages (from Adam to the final resurrection) and the three epochs (the first under the law of nature, the second under the written law, and the last under the law of grace) that describe the *length* of Holy Scripture (*Brev.* Prol. 2), beyond introducing an original theology of history (as has already been demonstrated elsewhere[84]), also invites us to discern the meter of a well-wrought *poem* and the project of an integral *summary*, as much Scriptural as theological, in Scripture's description of the whole universe:

> Thus the whole world is described (*describitur*) by Scripture in a most orderly sequence ... like the beauty of a well-constructed poem (*ad modum cuiusdam pulcherrimi carminis ordinati*) ... As

[80] Bonaventure, *Brev.* Prol. 4, No. 4 (V, 206a), Fr. tr. p. 109.

[81] J. Austin. *How to Do Things with Words* (1962), Fr. tr. *Quand dire, c'est faire*. Paris: Seuil, 1970. This formula is anticipated in Bonaventure's statement at *Brev.* Prol. 4, No. 4 (V, 206a), Fr. tr. p. 109.

[82] Bonaventure, *Brev.* Prol. 4, No. 4 (V, 206a), Fr. tr., p. 109. Reference to Luke 2:7.

[83] Cf. my article, *RSPT*, (above, Note 0, p. 00), third part, pp. 34-47: "La chair ou l'en-deçà de la métaphysique."

[84] J. Ratzinger, *La théologie de l'histoire de saint Bonaventure* (1959). Paris: PUF, 1988 (esp. §4: on the central form of Bonaventure's theology of history, the double schema of seven ages, pp. 17-23).

no one can see the beauty of a poem unless he beholds it in its entirety (*sicut nullus potest videre pulchritudinem carminis, nisi aspectus eius feratur super totum versum*), so likewise no one may see the beauty of the order and the governance of the universe unless he contemplate it in its totality (*nisi eam totam speculetur*).[85]

c) A DESCRIPTIVE THEOLOGY

It is ultimately wrong to speak of a "technique" or a "method" of reduction in Bonaventure.[86] Far from any logical procedure by which, in something like the Cartesian method, the mind turns from itself toward itself, Bonaventure's redirection from all things and from the self toward the Trinitarian God actually designates a "rule of life" (*ordinem vivendi*). To take up the Heideggerian metaphor of the retreat or the backtracking, this is a rule according to which "the mode of the movement of thought and the long path to travel" are even more important than *what* is thought or traveled.[87] To pursue the hypothesis of reciprocal fruitfulness, the Bonaventurian reduction can, like Merleau-Pontian phenomenology, be "practiced and recognized as a manner or style; it exists as a movement before achieving a complete philosophical consciousness."[88] Scriptural or theological discourse only orders life (*ordo vivendi*) insomuch as it also supplies a "reason for living" (*ratio vivendi*) that can also be a reason for *dying*—contrary to the mathematical or philosophical *logos*, which, for its part, can never justify such reasons:

one would consider the geometer foolish (*stultus*) who would suffer death (*subire mortem*) in order to defend the conclusion of a theorem. The truly faithful person (*verus fidelis*), on the other hand, even should he possess all philosophical knowledge, would rather lose it all than be ignorant of a single article of faith, so

[85] Bonaventure, *Brev.* Prol. 2, No. 4 (V, 204b), Fr. tr. p. 101.

[86] For example, G.H. Allard. *La technique de la "Reductio" chez Bonaventure.* In *S. Bonaventura 1274-1974*. Vol. II. Rome: Collegio S. Bonaventura, Grottaferrata, 1974, pp. 395-416. On this point, see Ozilou's judicious comment in his introduction to and translation of St. Bonaventure's *I Sent.*, d. 42-44, in *La puissance et son ombre* (ed. O. Boulnois). Paris: Aubier, 1994, Note 2, pp. 171-172.

[87] Bonaventure, *De reductione artium ad theologiam*, §17 (V, 323b), Fr. tr. *Les six lumières de la connaissance humaine.* Paris: Éd. franciscaines, 1971, p. 75: "If we imagine discourse itself, we see there a rule of life (*ordinem vivendi*)"; and Heidegger, *Identité et différence*, in *Questions I*, op. cit., p. 284.

[88] M. Merleau-Ponty, *Phénoménologie de la perception*, op. cit., p. II (phenomenology itself being here the subject of the proposition in this phrase of Merleau-Ponty's).

attached is he to the truth that he believes (*adeo adhaerat veritate creditae*).[89]

By "method," the Bonaventurian reduction understands not some artifice of the theologian, but instead the word's etymological meaning (*meta-hodos*): a route to be followed and a path to be climbed toward its original source—a "hodology" rather than an ontology (S. Breton). It is a path to be traveled "until," according to the last words of the *Breviloquium*, "I enter into the joy of my Lord, the God who is Three and One" (*qui est trinus et unus Deus*).[90] The hermeneutic circle of Scripture and theology is grounded in this act of return: theology receives from Scripture its unique mode of proceeding (Trinitarian revelation), and in return gives to Scripture the keys to its intelligibility (Trinity, Creation, Fall, Redemption, etc.) because theological discourse (*theologia sermo*) "resolves all things into God" (*Omnia resolvit in Deum*) even while "the truth of Sacred Scripture (*veritatem sacrae Scripturae*) comes from God (*esse a Deo*), treats of God (*de Deo*), is in conformity with God (*secundum Deum*) and has God as its end (*et propter Deum*)."[91] The suspension proper to the phenomenologist in his method of (Bonaventurian?) reduction, to which I shall return (§5), is thus seen to lead back to the one Trinitarian God—the true source from which it came and for which it was from the beginning seeking to find an adequate mode of discourse. To hope to arrive one day at this end, and to be completely dependent on it, it was once again necessary to define, besides the diverse literary devices (examples vs. arguments, promises vs. reasoning, etc.), a single mode of proceeding common to both Scripture and theology: the *description* or the *exposition* that begins from the Trinitarian given revealed *a priori* in the act of faith. Scripture describes (*describit*) the totality of the universe, and theology understands and explains (*intelligit et exponit*) what Scripture describes, but in both there is the same desire to return, in

---

[89] Bonaventure, *III Sent.*, d. 23, a.1. q.4, concl. (III, 481b-482a). The idea had already been developed in *I Sent*, proem. q. 3, concl. (I, 13b): "for the knowledge that Christ has died for us (*nam haec cognitio quod Christus pro nobis mortuus est*), and other similar truths…moves us to love; whereas the proposition, 'the diagonal is incommensurable with the square' (*quod diameter est asymeter costae*) does not produce any such effect (*non sic ista*).'"

[90] Bonaventure, *Brev.* VII, No. 9 (V, 291b), Fr. tr., p. 127. On the meaning of method (*metha-hodos*) from an etymological and phenomenological point of view, see Marion, *Réduction et donation*. Paris: PUF, 1989, II. 2, pp. 70-79: the method of ontology (esp. p. 71 and p. 75); and on the distinction between "hodology" and "ontology," see S. Breton, *Deux mystiques de l'excès: J.-J. Surin et Maître Eckart*. Paris: Cerf, 1985, Cogitatio fidei, No. 135, III, 2, pp. 177-191: 'les voies de la mystique' (esp. p. 189).

[91] Bonaventure, *Brev.* Prol. 6, No. 6 (V, 208b), Fr. tr., pp. 121-123.

theology as well as in exegesis, to *God himself*, who remains the unique
source for each. Far from presenting causal explanations concerned with
the *quid*, or analyses taking the form of the disputes addressing the *quis*
in the *Commentaries on the Sentences*, just as in the *Summae Theologica*,
the *Breviloquium* (in its form and in its foundation) thus responds to,
probably in an original fashion, and I would dare say, in a theological
anticipation of, the methodological imperative established by Maurice
Merleau-Ponty, here following Husserl, to determine the entirety of the
phenomenological approach:

> phenomenology is concerned with description, not with expla-
> nation or analysis. This primary constraint, which Husserl gave
> to a nascent phenomenology, either to become a descriptive psy-
> chology or to *return to the things themselves*, is first of all the
> disavowal of science.[92]

Simultaneously hermeneutic, descriptive, and performative, the
Bonaventurian theology of the *Breviloquium*, starting from the Prologue
(*prologus*), gives itself the means to welcome God truly, to welcome
Him as He is in Himself: that is to say as the Trinity (*Trinitas*), whom
Scripture "describes" (*describit*) and theology "exposits" (*exponit*)—always
"in conformity with the constraints of human capacity" (*secundum
exigentiam capacitates humanae*). Therefore, when the *Trinitarian God*
"enters into theology," he claims not only, in the guise of a pure and
simple Absolute, "the most incontestable right to be the starting point"
(Hegel), but also, as Trinity, the most incontestable right to craft a mode
of discourse that befits him: first, in the descriptivity (*descriptio*) in which
he is revealed according to the same mode as in Scripture; and second, in
the explanation (*expositio*) of the hidden meaning of this same descriptive
revelation, of which theology, for its part, is made the interpreter. Against
all theological ambitions in the form of *quid*—always desperately lost
in the impossible quest for the proof (or definition) of the divine—
the Franciscan Doctor opposes, as I shall show (§5b), a sort of hyper-
knowability of God who gives himself to man to the extent that man
finally renounces the attempt to "seize" God (*capere*) and instead learns,
in a new way, to receive or accept him (*accipere*). *Nemo capit nisi qui
accipit*: "only he who receives, takes [*nul ne prend sinon celui qui reçoit*]"

---

[92] M. Merleau-Ponty, *Phénoménologie de la perception*, op. cit., p. II. First definition
of phenomenology as a "descriptive theory" in Husserl, E., *Idées directrices pour une phénoménologie* (1913), *Ideen I*. Paris: Gallimard, 1950, §75, pp. 238-241.

(*Itinerarium*).[93] This formulation, all the more striking for the fact that it is an intentional departure from its Biblical inspiration—"no one *knows* (*nemo scit*) but him who receives" (Acts 2:17)—thus summarizes, in the very beginning, the whole of Bonaventurian thought. Passing from purely and simply setting the bounds of descriptive theology (Prologue) and moving on to prepare the way for God's entry into a theology that is at last exclusively Trinitarian (*Brev.* I), Bonaventure sets up the first principle (*primum principium*)—namely, the God who is three and one (*Deus trinus et unus*)—as the *princepal* subject (*principaliter*) of which the seven parts of the *Breviloquium* treat, as in a single stroke:

in the beginning (*in principio*), we must understand that sacred doctrine (*sacra doctrina*), that is to say theology (*videlicet theologia*), which speaks *princepally* (*principaliter*) of the first principle—God three and one (*scilicet de Deo trino et uno*)—treats in its universality (*in universe*) of seven subjects.[94]

---

[93] Bonaventure, *It.* IV, 3 (V, 306b), Fr. tr. *Itinéraire de l'esprit vers Dieu* (trad. H. Duméry). Paris: Vrin, 1990, p. 75: the translation "que personne n'atteint sans un don [no one obtains without a gift]" loses, in my opinion, some of the original force of the expression, substantializing – in the concept of the gift – that which first of all gives itself to be seen in terms of "taking" and "receiving."

[94] Bonaventure, *Brev.* I, 1, No. 1 (V, 210a), Fr. tr. (modified) p. 59. All the other parts of the *Breviloquium*—Creation (*Brev.* II), sin (*Brev.* III), Incarnation (*Brev.* IV), grace (*Brev.* V), sacraments (*Brev.* VI), and the Last Judgment (*Brev.* VII)—thus depend directly on the first part, which we are studying here—the Trinity (*Brev.* I)—and are in fact really only the latter's development "in its universality" (*in universo*).

CHAPTER II

HOW GOD ENTERS THEOLOGY

(Brev. I, 1-2)

How did God enter theology, and is he entering once again? I have answered
this provocative question by saying that he enters it first of all as if not
entering it at all—or at the very least not entering in the *way* one would
like to force him to do. In this sense, the "descriptive theology" that
Bonaventure sets forth starting from the Prologue of the *Breviloquium*
(see Ch. I of this volume) prepares the way for the Triune God's entry
that will do violence neither to Scriptural revelation nor to theological
exposition. Even better, we may say that this descriptive theology
frames the threshold of the *Brief Discourse* like a portico: the Trinitarian
mystery is not—or is no longer—depicted on the pediment overhead in
a substantification or objectification of the divine. For in the history of
theology there is no shortage of risks in reifying God; there is a certain
justice in Heidegger's portrayal of philosophy as a kind of host while
theology arrives as a mere guest, free to act only insofar as it abides by
philosophy's house rules. Here Bonaventure departs from Augustine,
who, in his *De Trinitate*, invariably explains the category of *relation*
(Book V) by recourse to the schema of *substance* (Book VII), as I have
shown elsewhere.[1] Bonaventure, for once moving away from his famous
fidelity to Augustine, rejects, or at least nuances, this kind of one-sided
substantification of the Three Persons of the Trinity in the One of their
substance. The divergence in their answers, as I will show, can already be
seen in the gulf that separates the questions that prompted them. Tracing
the movement will take us from the *quid* to the *quomodo*.

As Théodore de Régnon emphasized in 1892, and in spite of the
numerous "Thomistic reactions" since then, "the theological line stretching
from Richard of St. Victor to Alexander of Hales and *Bonaventure*
takes us more toward the oriental conceptuality of the Greek Fathers
than the more commonly known and purely Latin line running from

---

[1] Falque, *Saint Augustin ou comment Dieu entre en théologie, Lecture critique des livres
V-VII du De Trinitate*, in *Nouvelle Revue Théologique*, 117.1 (1995), pp. 84-111.

Augustine to Anselm and Thomas Aquinas."[2] The schematic aspect of this division, which various theological studies of the twentieth century—including the very most recent—have justly attempted to correct, must nonetheless not occlude what it gets right.[3] We should not let the almost exclusively Thomistic focus of a book called *The Creative Trinity* (G. Emery) obscure the fact that another work—similar in name, and even perhaps more radical—was published first, and was concerned with a study of Bonaventure alone (L. Mathieu).[4] With or without any doctrinal rapprochement between Bonaventure and Thomas Aquinas, probably "as fallacious as it was inevitable," in the words of Étienne Gilson, the divergence of their respective theses stems more from a divergence in their respective problematics than from an internal conflict inherent in the thinkers themselves.[5]

We must still take a "step backwards" (*Schritt zurück*) toward the "source" of Bonaventure's interrogation so that, according to "a mode of movement of thought" and by "a long path to travel," we might really discover the originality of its *questioning being*—demanding that we somehow "leave behind what philosophers have considered so far."[6] Far from any "absurd originality" in an undisciplined quest for

---

[2] Th. De Régnon. Études de théologie positive, second series (Scholastic theories). Paris: 1892, p. VIII. On this opposition between two irreducible lines of Trinitarian theology, see (from the same author) t. II (ibid.), pp. 128-129 (the two sources of these theories) and t. III, third series, on Greek theories of the divine processions, pp. 559-566 ("Résumé historique, Orient / Occident"). For the schema of the two models (linear for the Greeks and triangular for the Latins), see t. I (exposé of dogma) pp. 339-340, and t. III (Greek theories) p. 242. For Bonaventure's attachment to the theology of the Fathers, see especially t. II (Scholastic theories), article III, pp. 447-458: "La métaphysique dionysienne (chez saint Bonaventure)."

[3] The employment of this division in Trinitarian theology (Greek and Latin) can be read already in A. Malet. *Personne et amour dans la théologie trinitaire de saint Thomas d'Aquin*. Paris: Vrin, 1956 (esp. p. 11 and following).

[4] L. Mathieu. *La Trinité créatrice d'après saint Bonaventure*. Paris: Éd. franciscaines, 1992, and Emery, G. *La Trinité créatrice, Trinité et cré*ation dans les commentaires aux Sentences de Thomas d'Aquin et de ses précurseurs Albert le Grand et Bonaventure. Paris: Vrin, 1995.

[5] Gilson. *La philosophie de saint Bonaventure*, op. cit., p. 189. The divergence in *points of view*, largely demonstrated by this medievalist, nonetheless demands, in my opinion, that we pose a divergence *in views*. To affirm that "the philosophy of St. Thomas and that of St. Bonaventure complement each other as the two most universal interpretations of Christianity" (p. 396) may amount to giving too much to each of them. Far from constituting a totality, these two ways instead diverge so much from each other that we ought rather to choose one—not *against* the other, since they do not meet, but *alongside* the other, i.e. on a radically different path (*itinerarium*).

[6] Heidegger. *La constitution onto-théologique de la métaphysique* (1957), in *Questions I*, op. cit., p. 284.

novelty, Bonaventure's *genius* in Trinitarian theology is "exemplary," in
my opinion, because he fixes the rules for the entry *of* God into theology
at the threshold of the *Breviloquium* (*Brev.* I., 1-2) without denaturing
him either as a phenomenon that is always giving itself "of itself and
starting from itself" (Heidegger) or as "objective evidence from which
the phenomenon itself emanates and shines forth" (Balthasar).[7] Rather
than trying to conceive of *something different*—Bonaventure's fidelity to
the theological tradition and his strict submission to *auctoritas* are well
known—the Seraphic Doctor proposes that we conceive of *the same things
in a different way*. Thence the importance of interrogating Bonaventure's
corpus in a way that—like Heidegger's method, and thus neither centered
solely on "what is in question," i.e. the questioned (*Gefragtes*), nor on that
to which the question is posed, i.e. the interrogated (*Befragtes*)—seeks
instead to reveal the very meaning of the question as such, which is to
say as the *meaning* and the *manner* of proceeding with the inquiry—the
asked (*Erfragtes*).[8]

To elucidate the originality of the Bonaventurian interrogation of
the Trinity, or better that of its answer, we have to situate it relative to
other types of possible interrogations with respect to the determination
of the "three" (Persons) of the Trinity. Not simply raising the question of
"*what* they are" (*quid tres sunt*), as in Augustine and Thomas Aquinas,
or the question of "*who* they are" (*quis designatur*), as in Richard of St.
Victor and Alexander of Hales, Bonaventure this time poses a question
no less original and paradigmatic for its very naïveté: he asks "*how* they
are" (*qualiter sunt*).[9] Thus he anticipates a type of questioning opened

---

[7] One will have noted the obvious allusion to the Kantian duality of the "absurd orig-
inality" and the "exemplary originality." See Kant. *Critique de la faculté de juger* (1790).
Paris: Vrin, 1982, §46, pp. 138-139: "the *beaux arts* are the arts of the mind." As for the
Heideggerian definition of the "phenomenon" and its relation to the "objective evidence"
of Balthasar, see Heidegger, Être et temps, op. cit., §7, p. 34 (German pagination) and
Balthasar, *La gloire et la croix*, Paris: Aubier, 1965, t. I (Apparition), p. 392.

[8] For this tripartite phenomenological division of the question, where the path traveled (*itinerarium*) counts more than the result obtained, see Heidegger, *Sein und Zeit*,
introduction, §2, pp. 5-8 (German pagination): "the formal structure of the question of
being"; Marion, *Réduction et donation*. Paris: PUF, 1989, §6: "la réduction redoublée – le
Dasein," pp. 104-110 (police metaphor on p. 106); and Greisch, *Ontologie et temporalité,
Esquisse d'une interprétation intégrale de Sein und Zeit*. Paris: PUF, pp. 76-80: triangle of
the question (esp. pp. 77-78).

[9] Bonaventure, *Brev.* I, 2 (V, 210, b), Fr. tr. p. 65 (we will return to this in §5c):
"on the subject of the Trinity, there are three points to be considered: *how* (*qualiter*) the
unity of substance and of nature accord with the plurality of persons; *how* (*qualiter*) it
accords with the plurality of apparitions; and *how* (*qualiter*) it accords with the plurality
of appropriations."

by phenomenology, and thereby permits, once again, an attempt at a phenomenological interpretation of his theology:

> phenomenological expression signifies primarily a methodological concept. It does not characterize the *real quid* of the objects of philosophical inquiry, but rather their *how*.[10]

§4. THE END OF THE EMPIRE OF THE *TI ESTI*

A) QUID

Frequently, if not always, the aporia of an answer comes from the inadequacy of the question posed. Such was probably also the case, as I have emphasized, with the aporia inherent in Augustine's *De Trinitate*, where the type of questioning is itself sufficient to explain how substance subsumes relations:[11]

> Incidentally, when we ask "*three of what?*" (*quid tres*), the human word falls short. We may well answer: three persons, but that is less to say what it is than to remain with nothing to say.[12]

The only possible answer to this question, posed in the form of a *quid*—three of what? (*quid tres*)—was a *quidditas* or *quiddity*, or rather a "sub-stantiality" (since Thomas Aquinas, following Aristotle's lead, would later distinguish the two),[13] the tenacity of which could only be assured by the substance: "if there is no substance, there is nothing called person

---

in the relative sense."[14] The three Persons of the Trinity thus amount to being so much *quid*, marked by the seal of the *ousia*, probably designating so many modalities of "presence and constancy in the sense of dwelling."[15] In this sense, to say "*which ones* these three are" (*quid tria*)—or *who* they are—amounts to the same thing as explaining "*what* they are" (*quid tres*): "if one speaks of three persons or of three substances, this is not to be understood as a diversity of essences; it is rather an attempt to answer in a single word this question: *what* these three are or *what kind* these are—as three (*quid tres, vel quid tria*)."[16] For the bishop of Hippo, who found himself in a real theological battle, the affirmation of an equality of Persons, necessary in the struggle against Arianism, nevertheless does not permit us to infer some final primacy that the unity of natures might enjoy over the distinction of the hypostases. Going beyond these historical perspectives and justifications, it is most astonishing to discover this same type of substantializing inquiry in Trinitarian theology centuries later and from the pen of a thinker who unilaterally made theology the authority (i.e. over philosophy). For Thomas Aquinas went as far as dispelling the ambiguity, still tacit in Augustine, of the *nature* (*natura*) of the three Persons of the Trinity by means of the definitely 'presentifying' notion of the *suppositum*:

> the question *quid?* refers sometimes to the *nature* (*natura*) expressed by the definition, as when we ask: *Quid sit homo?* (What is man?) and answer: a mortal rational animal. Sometimes it refers to the *suppositum*, as when we ask, *Quid natat in mari?* (What swims in the sea?) and answer: a fish. And it is *in this latter sense* that the question, *Three of what?* has been answered thus: three Persons.[17]

To say in this sense with Michel Corbin that "we can no longer (today) simply repeat the Trinitarian discourse of Thomas Aquinas" is first to recognize with him that Aquinas, at least on the subject of the Trinity, remains a "prisoner of the Arian problematic," and that it is this line of questioning that still forces him to privilege the pure equality of

---

[14] Augustine, ibid., L. VII, I, 2, p. 511.

[15] Heidegger, *La métaphysique en tant qu'histoire de l'être*, in *Nietzsche II* (1961). Paris: Gallimard, 1971, pp. 321-329: "quiddity and quoddity in the beginning of the essence of the Metaphysics" (cit. p. 324).

[16] Augustine, *De Trinitate*, op. cit., B.A. vol. 16, L. VIII, prol., p. 25 (trans. modified).

[17] Thomas Aquinas, *Summa Theologica*, op. cit. (Biblioteca de Autores Cristianos), Ia, q.29, a.4, ad.2, pp. 225-226, Fr. tr. *Somme théologique*, op. cit. (Cerf), t. I, p. 373.

substances over the actual plurality of persons.[18] Beyond repeating the Augustinian duality of the *esse* and the *operari* by the binary of the *ad intra* and the *ad extra*—which one would seek in vain in Bonaventure (§6)—Thomistic Trinitarian theology already erects its own fortress, in my opinion, as soon as it gets tangled up in a line of questioning in the form of *quid*. It is precisely just this philosophy, and probably also just this Trinitarian theology, that, as the "empire of the *ti esti*," must be abandoned today. We ought to emphasize here, with Jacques Derrida, that "more seriously, in asking *what is it?*...we subject the question... to an ontological schema; we claim to assign it...a place, fundamental or regional, in an ontology. That would be a classical approach...[with] philosophy as the empire of the *ti esti*."[19] Setting himself neither against Thomas nor Thomism, certainly, but merely operating in *another* type of discourse and pursuing a fruitful alternative, Bonaventure gives us, if not the means to liberate ourselves from this empire, at least the premises of another possible "path" (*Itinerarium*). From the Thomas Aquinas who is sometimes rediscovered today, in a second degree, as "non-onto-theo-logical" (Marion), we must also go back toward his irreducible *other*, Bonaventure: for, in the sense of onto-theo-logy, Bonaventure is primarily non-metaphysical, as attested by his categorical rejection of all metaphysical thought that is not from the very beginning primarily Trinitarian:[20]

> the *metaphysician* may well rise to this Being insofar as he has the notions of principle, means, and final end, but he cannot do it with the notions of Father, Son, and Holy Spirit ... But when

---

[18] M. Corbin. *Essai sur le mystère trinitaire.* Paris: Association André Robert, 1980, respectively pp. 41 and 49. Cited, although in a more nuanced way but not more obvious way, in the same author's *La Trinité ou l'excès de Dieu.* Paris: Cerf, 1997, pp. 54-55.

[19] J. Derrida. *La voix et le phénomène* (1967). Paris: PUF, 1983, pp. 25-26: a critique of the dominance of *ti esti* addressing the question of the sign, which we extend here to all interrogation of the Trinity in theology.

[20] For the demonstration of the non-metaphysical (or non-onto-theo-logical) meaning of Bonaventure's corpus, see my article in the RSPT, pp. 20—25: "Le dépassement de la métaphysique: l'excès de donation du Père." As for the impossibility of assigning Thomas Aquinas in toto to onto-theo-logy—which would seem first of all to imply Jean-Luc Marion in *Dieu sans l'être* (Paris, PUF, 1982, Ch. III, 3, pp. 109-123: "l'Être ou (le) Bien")—see (from the same author) the "retraction" in *Saint Thomas et l'onto-théo-logie,* in *Revue thomiste* (Jan.-Mar. 1995), p. 59. This retraction suffices to indicate that any prize for originality in Bonaventure cannot be exclusively won for or against Thomas Aquinas. Saint Thomas—but not Thomism—also avoids, as such, the hypothesis of onto-theo-lo-gy. There can thus be no question here of blaming the Angelic Doctor or of setting him up against the Seraphic Doctor. Their "divergent views" alone must be (fully) emphasized here..

he considers this being as the exemplar of all things, *he does not share it with anyone* and he is a *true metaphysician (et verus est metaphysicus)*.[21]

b) Quis

Characterizing an exclusively Trinitarian metaphysics as the only "true metaphysics" demands that we move the question from the *what* of the three of the Trinity toward a type of interrogation capable of preparing an entry *for God* into theology. And it must be an entry that will not distort him on his way in. Just as in the history of philosophy the genealogical question legitimately supplanted, in Nietszche, the purely ontic inquiries of his predecessors,[22] so, too—and, paradoxically, ahead of its time—the *De Trinitate* by Richard of St. Victor, Bonaventure's precursor, definitively liberated Trinitarian theology from the Augustinian substantialism that was later confirmed again by Thomas Aquinas. The *quid sit* of the Trinitarian question gives way to its *quis sit*: thus, to the "*what it is (per quid)* that is asked of a common property (animal, man, horse)" is added, in the words of Richard of St. Victor, word for word, the "*who it is (per quis)* that is asked of a singular property (Mathew, Bartholomew, the father or the son of a given man...)."[23] The new question (new at least with respect to the Latin theological tradition) of the *quis* of the three of the Trinity—and with it, the notion of alterity (otherness) in God—had just taken the baton from that unilateral question of its *quid* and of the pure commonness of being:

> when we say three persons, what do we mean if not *three some-ones (tres aliquos)*? ... Assuredly, wherever there are three persons, it is necessary that the first be *someone*, that the second be *some-one else*, and that the third be *still another someone (ut alius aliquis sit iste, alius aliquis sit ille et alius qui est tertius ab utroque)*.[24]

---

[21] Bonaventure, *Hexaemeron* I, 13 (V, 331b), Fr. tr. M. Ozilou, *Les six jours de la création*. Paris: Cerf/Desclée, pp. 107-108. For commentary on this central text of Bonaventure's, see my article in RSPT, pp. 13-14, "le choix du Bonum"; and pp. 20-25, "le dépassement de la métaphysique."

[22] F. Nietzsche. *Généalogie de la morale* (1887). Paris: Gallimard, 1971, Foreword, §6, p. 220.

[23] Richard of St. Victor. *De Trinitate*. Sources chrétiennes, No. 63, Paris: Cerf, 1958, L. IV, c. VII, p. 245.

[24] Ibid., L. IV, c. VIII-IX, pp. 247-249.

"O my God ... you have called me by my name ... and behold, all of a sudden you are *someone!*"[25] Paul Claudel's *Third Ode* ("Magnificat") resonates with Richard of St. Victor's affirmation of the Trinity's three *quis* in a very interesting theological key. For it goes without saying that if the plurality that Richard identifies in the persons does not coincide with any plurality of substances in God,[26] it nevertheless remains the case that, for the first time in Latin Trinitarian dogmatics, 'person' designates less *what* the hypostasis *is* (a question of *quid*) than whom it *identifies*, in the sense of linking it to its origin or relations (a question of *quis*). According to Richard, the "principle of the essence" of God (*ratio essentiae*), which produces his unity, is distinct from the "principle of obtainment" or "of the origin" of his Persons (*ratio obtinentiae*), which produces his plurality—or better his *alterity* in himself. Father and Son no longer share only some sort of "this" and "that" (*aliud et aliud*), of which the communion of love would constitute *another this*, i.e. the Holy Spirit; rather, they live together in a genuine alterity of "him" and "him" (*alium et alium*), and the third Person here not only constitutes the link tying the first two together but also amounts to the fruit of their common fertility:[27]

in our rational nature, the distinction between *this* and *that* (*aliud et aliud*) is the fact of the *diversity* of substances (*diversitats substantiarum*); the distinction between *him* and *him* (*alium et alium*) is the fact of the *alterity* of the persons (*alteritas personarum*). On the other hand, in the divine nature who is Supreme Wisdom, we find this alterity (*istam alteritatem*), but not at all the aforesaid diversity (*nec tamen antedictam diversitatem*).[28]

---

[25] P. Claudel, *Cinq grandes odes*, in Œuvre poétique. Paris: Gallimard, Pléiade, 1967, *Troisième ode, Magnificat*, p. 249 (my emphasis).

[26] Ibid., c. VIII, p. 247: the statement "there are as many substances as there are persons (*quot sunt personae, tot sunt substantiae*)" is valid for humans, but not God.

[27] We will later return to the originality of Richard's investigation in the context of its relation to Bonaventure (§9). As an appetizer, consult the very old, but no less suggestive, analysis of Th. de Regnon, Études de théologie positive sur la sainte Trinité, op. cit. (1892), t. II, p. 235-335; as well as G. Salet, *Introduction au De Trinitate de Richard de Saint-Victor*, Sources chrétiennes (No. 63), op. cit. (1958), pp. 7-48.

[28] Richard of St. Victor, op. cit., L. IV, c. IX, p. 249. As for the meaning of the word "obtainment" in expressing the reason of the origin, see Richard of St. Victor's own justification for it, ibid., p. 253: "I know that the word *obtention* (*obtinentia*) is hardly fitting...Here, by the word *obtainment*, I mean *the manner by which one obtains* what one is substantially or what one has by nature."

The alterity of the Persons—*alteritas personarum*—discovered here
in God accords very closely with the contemporary philosophical and
perhaps also the theological vocabulary of the alterity to the self or to the
being-other in the self: it is a type of conceptuality long present in the
theological tradition, but one that is frequently, if not always, obscured
by Trinitarian dogma.[29] We must not forget this as we attempt to read in
Bonaventure the idea of an "*in-common in God,*" the premises of which
are revealed by the reworking of the perichoresis into a circumin*cessio*,
and not the circumin*sessio* of Thomas (§9).

c) Quomodo

The multiple references in Bonaventure's Trinitarian theology to the
De Trinitate of Richard of St. Victor, as well as the recent study of their
rapprochement (R. Javelet), will suffice to indicate the close convergence
of the two—even without taking into account the many indirect
influences of the latter on the former, especially through Alexander of
Hales.[30] But the justifiable prolixity of historical studies of the parallels and
convergences (the distinction of the Persons by their origin, condilection,
the primacy of the personal mode over the community of essence, etc.)[31]
has nonetheless failed to explain the type of questioning that is proper to

[29] Today historical and social considerations seem to take primacy in Trinitarian
studies. For the strictly historical perspective, see for example Forte, B. *La Trinité comme
histoire*. Paris: 1989, pp. 166-193: "l'origine trinitaire de l'histoire"; and for the social
perspective, see Moltmann, J. *Trinité et royaume de Dieu*. Paris: Cerf, Cogitatio fidei, No.
123, 1984. One will nonetheless find a detailed analysis of the limits and the stakes of the
application of the intersubjective schema, and thus of alterity, in the Trinity in Margerie,
B. de. *La Trinité chrétienne dans l'histoire*. Paris: Beauchesne, 1975, Ch. VIII, pp. 367-
420: "intersubjectivité et amitié familiales, intersubjectivité ecclésiale, intrasubjectivité
personnelle."

[30] R. Javelet. *Saint Bonaventure et Richard de Saint-Victor*, in *Bonaventuriana I*, Paris,
1988, pp. 63-96. Bonaventure refers to Richard seventeen times in the first book of the
Commentary on the Sentences alone, and four times in Part I of the *Breviloquium*. Cf. *Index
locorum sanctorum patrum* of the Quaracchi edition (X, 277) and Notes 5, 15, 16, and 24
of the French edition of the first volume of the *Breviloquium* (op. cit.). On this point one
could profitably compare Bonaventure, *De mysterio Trinitatis*, q. III-VIII (V, 68-115) and
Richard of St. Victor, *De Trinitate*, op. cit., L. III, c. 10, pp. 182-185. Beyond the Javelet
article already cited, one could also consult Bougerol on this question in *Introduction à
l'étude de saint Bonaventure*. Paris, Desclée, 1961, pp. 78-79; M.J. Gelot, *Les doctrines
psychologiques de Richard de Saint-Victor sur la processsion du Saint Esprit et leur influence
sur Bonaventure*, Tunis, 1938; and finally, O. Gonzales, *Sobre las fuentes de Ricardo de San
Victor y su influjo en San Bonaventura*, in *Ciudad de Dios*, No. 176 (1963), pp. 567-602.

[31] Cf. Mathieu, introduction to Part I of the *Breviloquium*, *La Trinité de Dieu*, op.
cit., pp. 7-48 (respectively pp. 13, 17, and 40).

Richard's analysis as well as the adaption that Bonaventure makes of the Master of St. Victor.

After an introductory chapter that lays out the seven parts of theology, and accordingly of the *Breviloquium*, the treatise on the Trinity (*Brev.* I) opens with a triple interrogation that structures it in form and content from one end to the other:

> on the subject of the Trinity of God, three points are to be considered: *how* (*qualiter*) the unity of substance and of nature accords with the plurality of persons, *how* (*qualiter*) it accords with the plurality of acts of appearing (*pluralitate apparitionum*), and *how* (*qualiter*) it accords with the plurality of appropriations.[32]

The originality of Bonaventure's starting point in Trinitarian theology has often rightly been observed in the absence from his works of any '*De Deo bono*' (of the sort that one finds in both Augustine and in Alexander of Hales' *summa*) and of any '*De Deo uno*' (as would appear, for example, in the *Summa Theologica* of Thomas Aquinas).[33] This deliberate, twofold silence in the very foundation of his Trinitarian theology should not obscure the Seraphic Doctor's eminently positive approach, with its aim of *describing* the modality of Trinity's appearing in the unity and the plurality of the Persons. A triple "*how*" (*qualiter*) of the unity and plurality in God (persons: Ch. II-IV; acts of appearing: Ch. V; appropriations: Ch. VI) thus guides the whole structure of this first part of the *Breviloquium*. Neither the *quid* (Augustine, Thomas) nor the *who* (Richard) is to guide the inquiry from now on, but rather the *quomodo*—or better, the *qualiter* insofar as it indicates the "manner" or the "style" of the divine appearance more than the means of its manifestation.[34] Why this shift, and how to make sense of it?

---

[32] Bonaventure, *Brev.* I, 2, No. 1 (V, 210b), Fr. tr. p. 65.

[33] See, respectively, Augustine, *De natura boni*, B.A No. 1; Alexander of Hales, *Summa Theologica*, Quarrachi, 1924, Ia, No. 102-122 (I, 160-192): "De bonitate divinae naturae"; and Thomas Aquinas, *Summa Theologica*, Ia, q.2-26: "De Deo uno seu de essentia divina."

[34] In the adverbs "how" and "*comment*" in English and French, respectively, the modality of usage (by what manner) is not distinguished from the utilization (by what means). Latin, for its part, uses *quomodo* to indicate the modality, but never to signify the means (there having recourse to the ablative): *quo-modo* thus signifies only "by what mode" or "by what manner." Furthermore, Latin adds another nuance—one that is sometimes found in Bonaventure—in distinguishing between *quomodo* and *qualiter*. Whereas *quomodo* indicates man's ethical way of relating to the world—"how to live" (*quomodo vivendum*)—*qualiter* is focused more on the modality of man's relationship to the divine or to transcendence—"how we are to cling to God" (*qualiter est Deo adhaerendum*). Thus,

The historical and doctrinal debates surrounding the Fourth Lateran Council (1215), as well as the theological responses that it engendered—especially in Alexander of Hales and later in Bonaventure—give us the precise reason. Explicitly condemning the tritheistic tendency of the Cistercian abbot Joachim de Fiore, this council also opposed the Trinitarian doctrine of Richard of St. Victor. According to Richard's teaching—as the magisterial text put it—the Father was said to "transfer his substance to the Son in begetting him, as if giving it to the Son without retaining it for himself."[35] At the heart of this debate was a formulation, certainly ambiguous, by Richard of St. Victor that said that "the substance [of the Father] begets the substance [of the Son] (*substantia genuit substantium*)"—just as for him, as for many of the Greek Fathers, wisdom begets wisdom.[36] Despite the fact that Richard did neatly distinguish "essence" from "substance" in God—such that the gift of the substance really would not signify any corresponding loss of essence—it is nonetheless important to emphasize here just how much the Trinitarian inquiry in the form of *quis* cannot help but lead at least to certain misunderstandings, if not *aporiai*.[37] Indeed, there is a great risk of losing the unity of God's essence by dwelling too much on the identity proper to each Person in him. And the history of theology is full of thinkers who have followed this line of thought to its necessary conclusion in some form of tritheism (Arius, Roscelin, Joachim de Fiore).

---

for example, the third part of the *Breviloquium* attempts to "understand how—*qualiter*—the corruption of sin has entered the world" (*qualiter corruptela peccati introivit in mundum*)—*qualiter* appearing since sin directly implies the modality of a human rupture with God (*Brev.* III, 2, No. 1 [V, 231b], Fr. tr. p. 57). The exemplary form of the nuance between *quomodo* and *qualiter* is found in the *De Reductione artium ad theologiam* I, No. 5 (V, 321b), Fr. tr. op. cit. (Éd. franciscaines), p. 61: "the moral meaning of Scripture teaches us how to live (*quomodo vivendum sit*) and the anagogical meaning teaches us how to cling to God (*qualiter est Deo adhaerendum*)." The use of the term *qualiter* rather than *quomodo* in the first part of the *Breviloquium* thus reinforces the idea that Bonaventure is aiming first at the *a priori* relationship of man to God (anagogical sense—*qualiter*), who alone can determine any utility for his own life (moral sense—*quomodo*).

[35] Fourth Lateran Council (1215), in Denzinger, H. *Enchiridion symbolorum, definitionum et declarationum de rebus fidei et morum*, Fribourg, 1967, No. 805; cited by Dumeige, G., *La foi catholique*, Paris, éd. de l'Orante, 1975, No. 225, p. 120: "the error of Abbot Joachim."

[36] Richard of St. Victor, *De Trinitate*, op. cit., L. VI, c. XXII, p. 445 (as well as the complementary note of G. Salet, pp. 504-507: "substantia genita").

[37] We will not return here to the necessity of recovering Richard from the judgment of a council that too immediately identified essence with substance in a doctrine that nonetheless clearly distinguished them. See on this point Salet's note (cit.) as well as the excellent updates by Th. de Regnon, Études de théologie positive sur la sainte Trinité, op. cit., t. II (Scholastic theories), pp. 252-262 (Richard of St. Victor) and pp. 352-355 (Hugh of St. Victor).

Hence the legitimacy of the pronouncement at the Fourth Lateran Council (1215): "although the Father, Son and Spirit are different, they are not different realities."[38]

Though Bonaventure's teacher, Alexander of Hales, retained the necessity of Trinitarian interrogation in the form of *quid* (Augustine, Thomas) and of *who* (Richard), I would dare say that his phenomenological merit was that he managed to "suspend" the one-sidedly ontic and genealogical goal of his predecessors so as to consider the three of the Trinity only according to their *how* (*quomodo*), or their *modalities of appearing*—a lesson that will keep the entirety of Bonaventure's seraphic and Franciscan theology wholly oriented, as we will see (§11), toward the paradigmatic appearance of the Trinity at the heart of the sensible:

> there are three manners of speaking (*triplicem modum dicendi*) of God corresponding to three questions: *Quid? Quis? Quodmodo?* ... To the question *Quid* corresponds the common nature (*ipsam naturam communem*). Thus, the answer to the question *what is the Father (quid est Pater)?*" is God or the Deity. To the question *Quis* corresponds the possessor of the nature (*habentem naturam*) under a distinct and incommunicable property, and this possessor is called a person ... Thus, to the question *who is it?* we answer: the Father, the Son, or the Holy Spirit. Finally there is *mode* of possessing the nature (*modus habendi naturam*), i.e. to what relationship or order the question *Quomodo* corresponds. Thus, to the question, *how is the Father related to the Son (quomodo se habet Pater ad Filium)?* we answer: as begetting (*ut generans*), because begetter and begotten indicate a relation in the order of nature. And so we seek in this way: by the question *Quid*, the divine essence itself (*ipsa divina essentia*); by the question *Quis*, the person himself (*ipsa persona*); and by the question *Quomodo* the notional relations (*ipsae habitudines notionales*) that distinguish the persons.[39]

This excerpt on divine and intra-Trinitarian generation from Alexander of Hales' *Summa Theologica*—the question is *an generare vel generari sint*

---

[38] Fourth Lateran Council, in Denzinger, *Enchiridion symbolorum...* op. cit., No. 805; cited by Dumeige, *La foi catholique*, op. cit., No. 224, p. 120: "the error of Abbot Joachim." Citation from Gregory Nazianzen, *Epist. (1) ad Cledonium*, PG 37, 179.

[39] Alexander of Hales, *Summa Theologica*, studio et cura PP. Collegii S. Bonaventurae. Florence: Quaracchi, 1924, Ia, q. 42, membr. 3, q.1, c.3, a.1, sol. (No. 297, I, 424b). A translation (cited and modified here) and a brief commentary on this text can be found in Th. de Regnon, Études de théologie positive... (1892), op. cit., t. II (Scholastic theories), pp. 353-354.

essentiae vel personae—is remarkable as much for its density as for its precision. It steers the whole Trinitarian inquiry toward the *quomodo*, i.e. toward what Scholastic theology conceptually calls "notions" (*notiones*) or "notional relations": innascibility (unbegottenness), paternity, filiation (sonship), spiration, and procession.[40] This is not an attempt to reject inquiries into the essence (*quid*) or the persons (*quis*), but it does insist that the persons really only relate to the essence through the consideration of their origin or provenance. Richard had already indicated as much when he made the distinction in God between the "mode of being" (*modum essendi*) of the essence and the "mode of obtaining the being" of the persons (*modum obtinendi*); after him Alexander would refer to this as "the mode of possession of the nature" (*modus habendi naturam*) for the hypostases. It is a question of *quomodo*, i.e. *quo-modo*—by what mode, by what way, or in what manner.[41]

The gulf between Bonaventure and Thomas in their reactions to Alexander's view on this point remains obvious here, less in the content of their responses—which once again eschews a summary opposition of the two—than in the particular *ways* in which they approach the determination of persons by their origin. While Aquinas seeks in the five notions a "proper formal notion by which to know a divine person" (*quod est propria ratio cognoscendi divinam personam*), the Seraphic Doctor shows on the contrary that is by these very relations and notions that the divine hypostases "make themselves known to us" (*innotescunt nobis*). Where the one seeks to determine *what* God *is in himself*—albeit in the relations to the origin—the other, using the same concepts, but turning them away from all autarchy and orienting them toward man, makes clear *how* he appears *to us*.[42]

§5. PERFORMING A REDUCTION

The whole first part of the *Breviloquium* attests thus to the shift, first in Hales, from the *quis* toward the *quomodo* of the three persons of the

---

[40] Five notions (*notiones*) explicitly cited by Bonaventure, *Brev.* I, 3, No. 5 (V, 212a), Fr. tr. p. 73.

[41] A parallel with Richard of St. Victor, *De Trinitate*, op. cit. L. IV, c. 11, p. 253 (distinction examined earlier). The direct and explicit criticism of Joachim of Fiore and of the danger of tritheism in the same text of Alexander of Hales's *Summa Theologica* (ibid., No. 297, I, 424b) confirms that in fact we are leaving behind the aporia of the *quis* by introducing the *quomodo*—which sometimes becomes *qualiter* in Bonaventure (as we have seen)—of the divine persons' act of appearing.

[42] Thomas Aquinas, *S. Th.*, Ia, q. 32, a. 3, resp. ("utrum sint quinque notiones"), Fr. tr. (Cerf), t. I, p. 391; and Bonaventure, *Brev.* I, 3, No. 5 (V, 212a), Fr. tr. p. 73.

Trinity, a shift that came after Richard of St. Victor had himself moved the *quid* of Augustine—later taken up again by Thomas Aquinas—toward the *quis*. The reason for this shift, which can be discerned in Alexander of Hales as he grappled with the decisions of the Fourth Lateran Council, finds in Bonaventure, and in him alone, its fullest development and expression. The Seraphic Doctor not only picks up the Trinitarian inquiry in the form of *quomodo* from his master, Alexander, he makes it *the* operative rule of his whole theology.

Much has been written of the so-called "method" or "technique" of Bonaventure's *reductio*— philosophically conferring on it either a transcendental meaning of the Kantian sort or a dialectic meaning of the Hegelian. For some, it means first, like the Thomistic *resolutio*, "the very method of transcendental reflection" (Chenu) or the act by which "the truth of a judgment is derived by proceeding from condition to condition until one reaches the principles that ground the judgment" (Gilson);[43] for others, who rightly distinguish it from the *resolutio*, either it always leads "from a negative pole to a positive pole" (Allard) or it assumes a "coincidence of opposites" at the foundation of all divine theophanies (Cousins, Prunières).[44] Besides such readings, the interpretation of the *quomodo* as the *a priori* modality of Bonaventure's Trinitarian discourse mandates and sanctions an interpretation of the *reductio* along lines that, if not directly Husserlian, are at least phenomenological. Some writers have already noted the homology of the phenomenological *epochê*—translated by the term "reduction" (*Reduktion*)—and the Bonaventurian *reductio*. But a simply homonymy of terms does not suffice to demonstrate a synonymy of principles, as the author who observed it rightly emphasizes (R. Russo); again, we must start with the significations themselves (concepts) to find any possible convergence of the signifiers (words).[45] Perhaps there was, after all, more than mere serendipity at work when

[43] Chenu, *Introduction à l'étude de saint Thomas d'Aquin* (1950), Paris: Vrin, 1993, p. 162; Gilson, *La philosophie de saint Bonaventure*, op. cit., p. 319.

[44] Allard, *La technique de la "Reductio" chez Bonaventure*, in *S. Bonaventura 1274-1974*. Rome: Grottaferrata, t. II, p. 395-416 (passage cited on p. 399 and pp. 413-416 for the distinction between *reductio* and *resolutio*); Cousins, E. *La Coïncidentia oppositorum dans la théologie de Bonaventure*, in *Actes du Colloque S. Bonaventure 9-12 Sept. 1968*, Orsay, Supplément Études franciscaines, 1968, t. XVIII, pp. 15-31 (see above all pp. 16-18); Prunières, L. *La problématique de saint Bonaventure ou la coïncidentia oppositorum*, in Études franciscaines, 1971, t. XXI, No. 59, pp. 263-272 (esp. pp. 267-268, "réduction au tout intégral").

[45] R. Russo. "Riduzione bonaventuriana e riduzione husserliana." *Miscellanea francescana*. Rome: 1975, pp. 733-744, esp. p. 734: "Ora, il termine 'riduzione,' ricorrente nel linguaggio di san Bonaventura comme in quell di Husserl, sembra in punto di convergenza non meramente verbale tra i due pensatori."

the young Heidegger claimed in his *Curriculum vitae* (1915) to have studied Bonaventure *and* Husserl simultaneously?

The term *reductio* in Bonaventure is found in both the title of one of his famous university lectures, *De reductione artium ad theologiam* (1255), as well as in the central argument of the first lesson of the *Collationes in Hexaëmeron* (1273), where *all things*, including the true metaphysician (I, 13), are led back to Christ as center and mediator (*medium*).[46] But the very movement of the *reductio*, which leaves its imprint on the whole of Bonaventure's theology and lends it much of its originality, can be found first in the fifth part of the *Breviloquium*—the treatise on the grace of the Holy Spirit—which, if not the heart of the text, can yet be considered its most decisive moment:

> whoever possesses those qualities [rightness of choice and the tranquility of joy] is *led directly back* to God (*immediate ad Deum reducitur*), just as he is immediately conformed to him (*immediate ei conformatur*)...In this [i.e. by grace], the work emanating from God *returns* to God (*opus emanans a Deo revertatur in Deum*) in whom, in the manner of a circle grasped in thought (*ad modum circuli intelligibilis*), the end of all reasonable minds is attained.[47]

For Bonaventure, reducing first means allowing oneself to be *led back* in order to make a return (*reducere*), or to turn (*revertere*), toward God: the sections on the Trinity (I), Creation (II), and the Incarnation (IV), which indicate the descending approach of God toward man, up to and including the detour through sin (III), are followed by those on grace (V), the sacraments (VI), and the last judgment (VII), which show instead the way of ascent, or the movement of man's return toward God. We should nonetheless add another sense to this ordinary meaning of the "reduction" as a redirection and a returning (indeed, a conversion)— closer this time to the phenomenological *epoché*, even as we move ahead beyond the 'portico' of the *Breviloquium* (Prologue) to its *De Trinitate*

---

[46] Bonaventure, *De reductione artium ad theologiam*, No. 7 (V, 322a), Fr. tr. P. Michaud-Quantin, *Les six lumières de la connaissance*, Paris: Éd. franciscaines, 1971, p. 63 (in my opinion, the title is a somewhat unfortunate translation, in spite of its historical justifications [Introduction, pp. 7-10], since it omits the term "reduction" entirely); and *Collationes in Hexaemeron* I, 10-39 (V, 330b-335b), Fr. tr. M. Ozilou, *Les six jours de la création*, Paris: Cerf, 1991, pp. 105-124. For an argued exposition on the "reduction" and commentary relevant to this passage, see Gerken, A. *La théologie du Verbe*. Paris: Éd. franciscaines, 1970, respectively pp. 151-165 and pp. 379-397.

[47] Bonaventure, *Brev.* V, 1, No. 3 and No. 6 (V, 252b and 253a), Fr. tr. p. 31 and p. 33.

Dei (*Brev.* I). Three specific traits characterize *God's entrance*, which is above all Trinitarian, *into theology*, and they are also precisely those of the method of phenomenological reduction: (a) the suspension or the bracketing of any judgment about of the existence of God; (b) the assertion of a mode of knowing adequate to the object sought; (c) and the evaluation of a mode of appearing as such (*quomodo*), i.e. independent of the what (*quid*) and of the who (*quis*).[48] Saying that God appears as Trinity in the world, without explaining or analyzing the reasons for his appearance—such will thus be the double originality, at once Theological *and* phenomenological, of the Bonaventurian approach.[49] Letting *God enter theology* will amount to making God himself appear as *the thing itself*, which is to say, in a specifically Christian theology, as Father, Son, and Holy Spirit.

A) REDUCING AND PROVING GOD

Is it necessary to prove the existence of God? The question is somewhat jarring in the context of an era that had just seen a proof by an appeal to his essence (Anselm of Canterbury's ontological argument) and which would soon see a demonstration from his effects (the "five ways" of Thomas Aquinas).[50] Bonaventure himself is not an exception to the rule: "Is the divine being real, so that one cannot think that he is not?" he wonders in the *Commentary on the Sentences*, following Anselm.[51] Without pursuing an argument that has already been very well treated elsewhere (Gilson), let us note that Bonaventure is here doing nothing but stripping Anselm's ontological argument in order to reduce to its most

---

[48] See, respectively, for each of these traits of the phenomenological reduction (a) Husserl, *Ideen I* (1913), Paris, Gallimard, 1950, §32: "the phenomenological *epoché*"; (b) Marion, *Le phénomène saturé*, in *Phénoménologie et théologie*, Paris, Criterion, 1992, pp. 79-128 (RSPT, pp. 16-20: the *excessus* as mode of knowing); (c) Heidegger, *Sein und Zeit*, op. cit., §7, p. 27 (German pagination): definition of the methodological concept of phenomenology as an investigation of the phenomenon in its *how* and not is its *quid real* (referring to Husserl, *Ideen I*, ibid., §132, p. 444: the object in its how—*das Objekt im Wie*).

[49] See M. Merleau-Ponty, *Phénoménologie de la perception*, op. cit., Foreword, p. II: "in phenomenology, the point is to describe, and not to explain or analyze."

[50] Anselm of Canterbury. *Proslogion*. Paris: Cerf, 1986, Fr. tr. M. Corbin, t. I, Ch. II-III, pp. 244-249: *quod vere sit Deus/quod non possit cogitari non esse*; Thomas Aquinas. *Summa Theologica*, Ia., q.2 a. 3, Fr. tr. (Cerf), pp. 171-173: "utrum Deus sit."

[51] Bonaventure, *I Sent.*, d. 8, p. I, a. 1, q. 2 (I, 153-155): *utrum divinum esse sitadeo verum, quod non possit cogitari non esse.*

simple, tautological expression: "*si Deus est, Deus est.*"[52] He also gives it
a positive or cataphatic formulation that is absent—or nearly so—from
Anselm's argumentation. Whether the argument is conceptual or beyond
the concept (Jean-Luc Marion), for Anselm, the "*id quo majus nihil
cogitari potest*" in fact just means the *negative name* or the *limit* beyond
which God, the unthinkable, becomes, properly speaking, thinkable—
or better, that which gives *itself* to be thought: no longer as idol, but
as an icon of God (Barth and Marion).[53] Furthermore, Bonaventure
the Franciscan, abandoning once again all dispute on the threshold of
the discourse, allows God himself to appear immediately, and sees in his
temporal and spatial omnipresence the sole legitimate foundation of the
Anselmian argument (in reality, Anselm seems not to have held this, but
the Seraphic Doctor himself seems to conceal the interpretive shift):

> now, God is always and everywhere (*semper et ubique*), and abso-
> lutely always and everywhere (*et totus semper et ubique*); for this
> reason one cannot think that he is not (*ideo non potest cogitare
> non esse*). This is the reason that Anselm gives in his book against
> the fool.[54]

Whereas the fool (*insipiens*) of Anselm's *Proslogion*, in some kind of
incomprehension, admits that he does not grasp divine ubiquity—"*if*
you are everywhere, *why* do I not see you present everywhere (*si autem
ubique es, cur non video praesentem*)?"[55]—Bonaventure's *Commentary on
the Sentences* (*I Sent.* d. 8, p. I, a. 1, q. 2) in fact radically changes the terms
when contemplating the "e-vidence" (*ex-videre*) of God, in the sense of his
self-manifestation to man: *since* you are everywhere, *how* could I ever *not*
see you present everywhere?[56] The shift from Anselm to the Bonaventure
is obvious: the initial affirmation of the divine omnipresence against the

[52] Bonaventure, *De mysterio trinitatis*, q. 1, a. 1, No. 29 (V, 48a): "si Deus est, Deus
est; sed antecedens est adeo verum, quod non potest cogitari non esse; ergo Deum esse
verum indubitabile." Cited and commented on by Gilson, *La philosophie de saint Bonaventure*, op. cit., pp. 108-112.

[53] K. Barth. *Fides quaerens intellectum, la preuve de l'existence de Dieu*. Neuchâtel:
Delachaux-Niestlé, 1958; Corbin, M. *Introduction à l'œuvre de saint Anselme de Cantor-
bery*, Paris, Cerf, 1992, pp. 183-203: the two epiphanies of God; Marion, *L'argument
relève-t-il de l'ontologie*, in *Questions cartésiennes, méthodes et métaphysique*, Paris, PUF,
1991, pp. 221-258.

[54] Bonaventure, *I Sent.*, d. 8, p. I, a. 1, q. 2, concl. (I, 154b).

[55] Anselm of Canterbury. *Proslogion*. Paris: Cerf, 1986, Fr. tr. M. Corbin, Ch. I, p.
239.

[56] Bonaventure, *I Sent.*, d. 8, p. I, a. 1, q. 2, concl. (I, 154b): "Deus autem est semper
et ubique et totus semper et ubique: ideo non potest cogitari non esse."

inanity of the hypothesis of his potential absence (were such omnipresence to be rejected) gives way to a transformation of the *quid* into the *quomodo*; the *why* of the causal interrogation (Anselm) is replaced by the *how* of the evidence of the *Canticle of Creation* (Francis)—with Bonaventure feigning, however, to have found the latter in Anselm ("this is the reason that Anselm gives…"). The immediate evidence of the presence of God, for Bonaventure, always differs in some manner from the deductive evidence of Anselm.[57] But this is one of the Seraphic Doctor's ways of pouring new wine into old skins—or even making entirely new wine while pretending to keep pouring the old.

Since it stands in implicit but direct dialogue with the fool of Anselm's *Proslogion*, and by virtue of a programmatic schema stipulated in the *Sentences* (*I Sent.* d. 8), the question of the *God's entrance into theology* in Bonaventure, too, may seem to proceed through a demonstration of God's existence—even though it is taken as self-evident. However, the only possible reading of the *Breviloquium* must rather infer the opposite. The total absence of any ontological proof—in fact, the total lack of any proof for the existence of God, in the whole of this *Brief Summary* of theology—indicates instead what the Seraphic Doctor saw any deductive and demonstrative attempt to understand God as utter nonsense. And yet it would be wrong to suggest that Bonaventure succumbs here to any kind of Franciscan pseudo-fideism, which was in fact quite alien to him. For Bonaventure, "the *habitus* of faith," and the God who is experienced, always remain explicitly *compatible* (*compati*) with "the form of knowledge" in which God is demonstrated and understood.[58] Avoiding arbitrary and false dichotomies (e.g. faith/science), the complete silence of the treatise on the Trinity (*Brev.* I) on the ontological proof of God must first be understood theologically, and in the context of the whole of Bonaventure's corpus, as trying to tell us something crucial. Why say anything of a proof that, in itself, seems to say everything—even if it means that the Anselmian argument has to be entirely restructured for it to signify the thoroughly Franciscan omnipresence of God in his creatures?

---

[57] Gilson, *La philosophie de saint Bonaventure*, op. cit., p. 109 (without showing, however, this interpretive shift from Anselm's *Proslogion* to dist. 8 Bonaventure's *Commentary on the Sentences*).

[58] Bonaventure, *III Sent.*, d. 24, a. 2, q. 3 (III, 523a): "concerning the *habitus* of faith (*habitum fidei*) and the mode of knowing considered here (*talem modum sciendi*), we must manage to understand that they can remain *compatibles* (*compati*) at the same time in the same man and with respect to the same object." A (French) translation and commentary on this question in the *Commentary on the Sentences* ("utrum fides sit de his, de quiubus habetur cognitio scientialis") can be found in Bougerol, *Introduction à l'étude de saint Bonaventure*, Paris, Desclée, 1961, pp. 105-115.

Neither (a) the occasion of the *Breviloquium*'s composition nor (b) the abstract division of the ontological argument and the explanation of the Trinity will suffice in themselves to justify this silence. (a) As for the circumstances of the editing and publication of the *Breviloquium* (1257), it is known that the work was written at the behest of some of the brothers (*socii*) of the Order of Friars Minor, who begged their master to prepare something brief (*aliquid breve*) with the end of teaching it themselves, in the various provinces, to their own students of theology. Thus, one of Bonaventure's criteria was to include only the truths most important for the faith (*opportuna ad tenendum*).[59] This, initially at least, could justify this absence: what use is it, after all, for the believer to have a proof drawn up for the existence of the divine being, when it is only the Trinity who saves, and not the demonstration of its existence? Such is the stance taken from the beginning of our discussion of the Trinity (*Brev.* I), which, as it demands above all the salvation of the human race, at first glance makes the absence of any proof of the existence of God understandable:

> Holy Scripture or theology is the science that gives us the knowl-
> edge of the first principle sufficient (*sufficientem notitiam*) for
> man here below, according to what is necessary for his salvation
> (*secundum quod est necessariumn ad salutem*).[60]

But the mere fact of being addressed to those already convinced—the brothers or *socii*[61]—does not justify in itself this *demonstrative* silence (at once manifest and of the order of demonstration). How could the *Breviloquium* neglect a proof for God's existence, when such efforts elsewhere amounted to masterpieces of Scholastic theological argumentation at its best, and yet at the same time carefully attending elsewhere to arguments that are even more complicated (the theory of divine appropriations, for example)? (b) It is claimed—and this is the second argument, after the circumstances of the work's composition—that the ontological proof is about the essence and not the Trinity, and that from reasoning about the essence to the revelation of the Trinity there is no movement that is *per se* required. Besides the depth of the objection—incidentally, an entirely banal observation, since no one in Scholastic theology (not Anselm, not Bonaventure, and not Thomas) ever claimed to have deduced the Trinity from the ontological argument, but only the existence of God—"the beyond" of the concept that Anselm was aiming for in the essence of God could then at least lead to the

---

[59] Bonaventure, *Brev.*, Prol. 6, No. 5 (V, 208b), Fr. tr. p. 121.
[60] Bonaventure, *Brev.* I, c. 1, No. 2 (V, 210a), Fr. tr. p. 61.
[61] Bonaventure, *Brev.* Prol. 6, No. 5 (V, 208b), Fr. tr. p. 121.

portico of the mystery of the Trinity: put simply, the Prologue of the *Breviloquium* supplies *its* ontological proof. This is a new objection that is all the more powerful for the fact that the *reportatio* of 1254 in the *De mysterio Trinitatis*, three years before the *Breviloquium* (1257), finds its support precisely in this proof in order to introduce the Trinitarian mystery:

> having posited (*suppositum*) that in truth God cannot be doubt-
> ed, it is consequently fitting to ask (*quaeritur consequenter*)
> whether one can truly *believe* in the triune God.[62]

Besides the injunction to follow a structure dictated by the "quodlibetical" disputes of the Middle Ages,[63] an inherent convergence with the ontological proof would demand at least a review of that argument—but precisely this is absent from the *Breviloquium*.

It is Bonaventure's *De mysterio Trinitatis* that, in its account different, this time, from Thomas Aquinas, provides the key to the absence of proofs in the *Breviloquium*, an absence which, in reality, signals the hyper-presence of the Trinitarian manifestation. To say that God exists, for Bonaventure, is to show that his existence cannot be doubted: *non est dubitabile Deum esse.*[64] In other words, and in a pre-Cartesian move that is yet much closer to the *cogitatio* of the *Meditations on First Philosophy* than to the Anselmian ontological argument, the undoubtable divine points less to the divine essence itself than to the impossibility that the believer who is blessed with sound understanding (*intelligentia sana*) could consider it to be nonexistent. If all *dubitatio* about God results from a defect in reason with respect to the evidence for his existence (*ratio evidentiae*)—that is, his existence either in itself, from the point of view of the proofs that demonstrate it, or relative to the knowledge that we have of it[65]—then only the criticism of the knowing subject (*ex parte cognoscentis*) contains Bonaventure's true theme:

> one can, however (*tamen*), doubt his existence on the part of the
> knowing subject (*ex parte cognoscentis*), i.e. because of a defect
> (*defectum*) in the act either of his apprehension (*vel apprehensio*)

---

[62] Bonaventure, *De mysterio Trinitatis*, q. 1, a. 2 (V, 51a).

[63] Chenu, *Introduction* à l'étude de saint Thomas d'Aquin (1950), Paris, Vrin, 1993, Ch. IX, pp. 241-246.

[64] Bonaventure, *De mysterio Trinitatis*, q. 1, a. 1, concl. (V, 49a).

[65] Bonaventure, ibid.: "*non est dubitabile, Deum esse, si dubitabile intelligitur aliquod verum, cui deficit ratio evidentia sive in se, sive in comparatione ad medium probans, sive in comparatione ad intellectum apprehensivum.*"

or of his questioning (*vel conferendi*) or of his analysis (*vel resol-vendi*).[66]

All the dissociations and all the positions that Bonaventure takes—frequently implicitly—are here taken up in a certain way with seeing or striving for God. Just as the distinction between the *oculus* and the *aspectus* determines the dichotomy of the Being and the Good in the *Itinerarium*,[67] so here the believing subject's intention toward God moves the Anselmian ontological argument of internal perfection from the concept to the subject who conceives of it. Where the proof once signified an *in itself* of the concept, it now becomes essentially a sign indicating a *for us* of his act of appearing: my thought—if it is not guilty of any defects in its mode of apprehension, its line of questioning, or its analysis—cannot reasonably doubt the existence of God, and even less the reality of his manifestation to me.

Étienne Gilson rightly shows, against the claims of the publishers of the *Quaracchi* editions of Bonaventure's texts, that one cannot assimilate Bonaventure's *verum indubitabile* too readily into the *per se notum* of Thomas Aquinas.[68] Yet, while it is true that one cannot simply assimilate the two, at the same time one must not oppose them—if not in their content, then at least in their respective goals, i.e. the essence of God: for whereas the *known by itself* of Thomas remains the norm, and the *to us* the admission of a defect in our knowledge, the "true undoubtable" for Bonaventure instead consecrates God's *to us* as the *in himself* that is most proper to him, since there is no *in himself* of his being outside of his givenness to man—at least for that which man can receive of him.

Indeed, taking up Aristotle again, and contrary to Bonaventure (below, §5b), Aquinas justifies in the *Summa Theologica* the recourse to several proofs of the existence of God by the distinction between the *in himself* of God and the *to us* of his knowledge. Because God in himself (*per se*) is not known to us (*nobis*), his existence must be demonstrated (*indiget demonstrari*), this time starting from what is more immediately known to us (*quoad nos*): his effects (movement, efficiency, necessity, degrees of being, and finality). Paradoxically integrating, like Bonaventure, the dimension of the *to us* from the proofs of the existence of God—an

---

[66] Ibid. Gilson cites this and comments on it (*La philosophie de saint Bonaventure*, op. cit., pp. 117-118), but does not notice how much taking the knowing subject into account in the intentional aim of God designates at the same time, for Bonaventure, and as the negation of his *in himself* as a repercussion.

[67] RSPT, pp. 6-15: (I) the hypothesis of a phenomenology of the gaze (*regard*).

[68] Gilson, *La philosophie de saint Bonaventure*, op. cit., Note 2, p. 117. Cf. Thomas Aquinas, *Summa Theologica*, Ia., q. 2, a. 1: "utrum Dum esse sit per se notum."

integration which does not necessitate *a priori* the Anselmian reading of the argument—Thomas has no less need of that dimension to consign the *in himself* of the ontological proof to the unknowable: the *to us* of the five ways of showing the existence of God by his effects ends up locking the ontological argument (initially at least) within an unfathomable *in himself*. Hence the explicit reference and the separation of the proof by effects (q. 2 a. 3) from the ontological proof—or from its Thomistic variation (q.3 a. 4):

> God is indeed his own existence, as will be shown below (*ut infra patebit*) (q.3 a.4). But as we do not know of God what he is (*quid est*), this proposition is not evident to us (*non est nobis per se nota*), but rather needs to be demonstrated (*sed indiget demonstrari*) by the things that are better known to us (*magis nota quoad nos*), though less known in their nature (*minus nota quoad naturam*)—namely, by [God's] effects (*par effectus*).[69]

Given the supposedly self-evident necessity (in Thomism) of giving the ontological proof a preamble involving proof by effects, one might be surprised to find nothing of the sort in the Seraphic Doctor—all the more since this theological starting point in the divine works seems, at first glance, to be eminently Franciscan. The reason is that the use of the proof, even more than the type of approach, in my opinion, separates the two theologians. Neither Bonaventure nor Thomas balks at either starting with Creation and being thence elevated to God (the ascendant approach of the five ways of the *Summa Theologica* or the global movement of the *Breviloquium*) or proceeding from the opposite direction, starting with the Divine Being himself and returning thence to Creation (the

---

[69] Thomas Aquinas, *Summa Theologica*, Ia., q.2, a.1 resp., Fr. tr. (slightly modified), *Somme théologique*, op. cit. (Cerf), t. I, p. 170. Our interpretation of these two articles of the *Prima pars* of the *Summa Theologica* (q.2 a. 1 and q.3 a.4), however, raises two difficulties: (I) it supposes that one might read in the Thomistic formula *Deus est suum esse* (God is his own being) a form or a version of Anselm's ontological argument, and (II) it implies that the link that Thomas establishes between the five ways (q.2) and the proof by the simplicity of essence (q. 3) in reality remain only verbal. Without getting involved here in a debate on Thomistic exegesis, which is not my purpose in this work, let me only note (a) that, for the first justification, the term *esse*—sometimes translated into French as existence in editions printed by Cerf (e.g. q.3 a. 4: y a-t-il en Dieu composition de l'essence (*essentia*) et de l'existence (*esse*)?]—is always drawn from the *essentia*, as in Anselm, despite its possible distinction from *existentia* (movement from q.3 a.3 to q.3 a.4, respectively); and (b) that, for the second justification, Thomas makes no explicit reference to the five ways (q.2 a.3) as soon as he embarks upon his argument about the simplicity of God (q.3).

descendant approach found in the structures of both the *Summa Theologica* and the *Breviloquium*). The final question instead requires asking whether God, starting with his effects or with an ontological proof, actually needs to be demonstrated (*indiget demonstrari*)—which Thomas, for his part, expressly affirms in both cases and which Bonaventure, on the contrary, intentionally rejects by his silence (or his *epochē*)—at least in the *Breviloquium*. Contrary to the Seraphic Doctor's view (below, §5b), for Aquinas a demonstration of God's existence can only be legitimate insofar as the affirmation of his existence does not come from itself—or better, only insofar as its *in itself* (*per se*) does not designate identically and immediately a *to us* (*nobis*). To say with Gilson, and with several caveats, that "the two philosophers are not answering the same question,"[70] will probably not (or no longer) suffice—even if the unjustified *Diktat* establishing Thomas Aquinas as the sole and exclusive norm of all scholastic philosophy has expired. We must again follow the hypothesis to its conclusion and accept, finally, that a *plurality of points of view* may also engender a real *diversity of views*—a conclusion, incidentally, that the Parisian disputes of the 1270s certainly support.[71]

In Bonaventure, the "proof" for the existence of God, or his self-manifestation to man (*ex-videre*), says not only that this existence is evident *in itself* (as an axiom is with respect to a theorem) and that it therefore does not need to be demonstrated, but also that *in himself* God *is* just as much as he *is* first of all *to us*. For Bonaventure, God is not *proved* first by *his* nature (Anselm) or *his* effects (Thomas)—even if that risks seeming to render any proof null and void, as an overly immediate interpretation of the absence of demonstrations in the *Breviloquium* might falsely suggest. On the contrary, God is (and only is) *seen in the* nature. Where some seek "proofs" (Anselm) or at the very least "ways"

---

[70] Gilson, *La philosophie de saint Bonaventure*, op. cit., Note 2, p. 117.

[71] Gilson seems to have perceived this *distance between their views* in the retraction he announced in 1974 (*S. Bonaventura 1274-1974*, op. cit., t. I, Foreword, p. II), some fifty years after the publication of his *La philosophie de saint Bonaventure*: "animated by good intentions, this attempt to define St. Bonaventure as a *philosopher* (1923) nonetheless gravely *distorted* his character" (my emphasis). As for the Parisian debate of 1270, see above all Weber, E.H., *Dialogue et dissensions entre saint Bonaventure et saint Thomas d'Aquin à Paris (1252-1273)*, Paris, Vrin, 1974. This imposing work, full of information, only ever seems to reveal Bonaventure's originality in order to show how this same originality had already been assumed by Thomas—perhaps another way of suppressing in advance this so-called specificity (cf., for example, "by way of conclusion," p. 499). For a glimpse onto this debate—a debate that Bonaventure tried to end in 1273, and one often wrongly called the "Battle of the *Hexaemeron*—that, if not more objective, is at least more Bonaventurian, see Ozilou, *Introduction aux six jours de la création de saint Bonaventure*, Paris, Desclée/Cerf, 1991, pp. 12-26: "la vocation bonaventurienne" and " le testament inachevé."

(Thomas), Bonaventure only ever discovers traces or "vestiges" of God's *presence*—evident in himself and manifest to us.[72] Here we can see one last difference between Bonaventure and Dionysius the Pseudo-Areopagite: Bonaventure achieves the "bracketing" or the "suspension" of the question of the *quid* of the existence of God *not* by ignorance of his nature, but by its supreme and explosive visibility in the midst of the created world.

B) *THE HYPER-KNOWABILITY OF THE DIVINE*

Despite the sly allusion by which Bonaventure suggests a precedent in Anselm of Canterbury, in reality the fullest evidence (*ex-videre*) that he finds for the "*id quo majus nihil cogitari potest*"—evidence which comes without proof, and which is strictly theophanic—is supplied simply by the total omnipresence of God, in accord with the theology underlying the *Canticle of Creation*. The Divine and Trinitarian Being is not first of all, for the theologian and disciple of Francis, the supremely unknowable so familiar from the Pseudo-Dionysius. Hence the pressing need to mediate the opposition, or at the very least the divergence, between Bonaventure and Thomas Aquinas by their respective recourse to Dionysius:[73] Dionysian theology's apophaticism suffers from a kind of evasion within the "superessential Trinity,"[74] which is quite opposed, in my opinion, to the earthiness of Bonaventure's Franciscanism. Hardly unknowable, even in the sense of Dionysian knowledge of the unknowable, God is instead for Bonaventure—from the very first book of his *Commentary on the Sentences* (d.3)—first of all a "supremely knowable" being (*summe cognoscibilis*), not only in himself (*in se*) but also to us (*nobis*). Failure to know this "supremely knowable" being is due more to the defects of our intellects than to the learned ignorance of the concept:

> God in himself (*in se*) is supremely knowable (*summe cognoscobi-lis*), and he is supremely knowable to us (*nobis*); if he were not, it

---

[72] On this symptomatic opposition of the ways (*viae*) and the vestiges (*vestigia*), it is worth comparing Thomas Aquinas, *S.th.* Ia., q.2, a.3 with Bonaventure, *Itinerarium*, c.2, no.1.

[73] Hypothesis suggested by Weber, *Dialogue et dissensions entre saint Bonaventure et saint Thomas d'Aquin à Paris (1252-1273)*, ibid., pp. 489-490.

[74] Dionysius, *Mystical Theology*, I, 1, 3, in Œuvres complètes du Pseudo-Denys l'Aréopagite. Trans. M. de Gandillac. Paris: Aubier-Montaigne, pp. 177-183.

would simply be because of the defects of our intellect (*defectus ex parte intellectus nostri*).[75]

Bonaventure presents the knowledge of God along the lines of an Augustinian illuminism that is simultaneously pushed to its limits and extended from the faculties of the soul to the whole of Creation. This knowledge is like a ray of light (*lux*), for it, too, only completely attains its end when it reaches us (*etiam nobis*). Like the radiance that is at its brightest when it allows itself to be possessed and reflected in a receiving other, so God in his very being (*quantum est de se*) is fully knowable (*clarissime cognoscibilis*), in a paradoxical reversal, only when he also offers himself as such—that is to say so as to be known—by a creature (*Deus sit cognoscibilis a creatura*).[76] Bonaventure anticipates Bultmann in asserting the primacy of what is knowable of the Divine Being to us (*nobis*) over what is knowable about him in himself (*in se*); we can read this primacy in the *Trinitarian a priori* (cf. p. 35), even before any praise for Creation, which in fact always remains within the Trinity and becomes its final reflection.[77] Indeed, the first part of the *Breviloquium* (*Brev.* I, 3) emphasizes, apart from any consideration of Creation (*Brev.* II), the fact that "the divine hypostases *make themselves known to us*" (*innotescunt nobis*) by their relations (paternity, filiation, spiration, procession).[78] Far from any division between the immanent Trinity and the economic Trinity—between the divine life *ad intra* and the expansive donation *ad extra* (below, §6)—the "*to us*" (*nobis*) of the supremely knowable in itself (*in se*) of the divine thus signals, in an exemplary way, the truly Franciscan character of Bonaventure's Trinitarian God: it is "*in the name of the Holy Trinity*" alone (*in sanctae Trinitatis nomine*) that Francis—according to Bonaventure's *Legenda maior*, albeit contrary to the *Vita prima* (and *secunda*) of Thomas of Celano—three times opens the Gospel and understands that he is to pass from the *imitatio Christi* in his actions to the *conformatio* in his passion (the stigmata). According to the *Itinerarium*, too, pilgrim man is to turn himself toward the mercy

---

[75] Bonaventure, *I Sent.*, d.3, p. I, a. un., q.1, concl. (I, 69a): "utrum Deus sit cognoscibilis a creatura."

[76] Bonaventure, ibid. (I, 69a): "dicendum quod Deus in se tanquam summa lux est summe cognoscibilis; et tanquam lux summe intellectum nostrum complens, et quantum est de se esset summe cognoscibilis etiam nobis…Concedendae sunt igitur rationes, quod Deus sit cognoscibilis, quantum est de se…"

[77] On the primacy of the "to us" over the "in itself" in theology, see in particular R. Bultmann. *Le Dieu proche et lointain*, in *Jésus, mythologie et démythologisation* (1926), Paris, Seuil, 1968, pp. 123-181 (and esp. pp. 172-173: "le point de vue du spectateur abandonné").

[78] Bonaventure, *Brev.* I, 3, No. 5 (V, 212a), Fr. tr. p. 73.

seat where Christ sits regnant (*respice in propitiatorium*) *and toward the Trinity within him*, just when he reaches, or has almost reached, the end of his ascent to God.[79]

This Bonaventurian "*to us*" (*nobis*) in the act of knowing the divine "*in itself*" (*in se*) demands a mode of apprehension adequate not only to the essence of God, but also to his omnipresence in the created order and in us ourselves—an omnipresence that we have already seen in Bonaventure's surreptitious distortion of the Anselmian argument, which he eases away from its originally ontological meaning. Still arguing in favor of this divine hyper-knowability but this time centering it more on the very act of knowing than on the "*to us*" of its orientation, the Seraphic Doctor distinguishes in an almost pre-Cartesian manner between two types of knowledge—the one apprehensive and the other comprehensive:

> apprehensive knowledge (*cognitio par apprehensionem*) consists in the manifestation of the truth of the thing known (*in manifestatione veritatis rei cognitae*); comprehensive knowledge (*cognitio comprehensionis*) consists in the inclusion of the whole (*in inclusione totalitatis*).[80]

Bonaventure's *solution* (*ad primum*) responds explicitly to the Dionysian objection that claims it is impossible for a creature "either to speak of or to understand God."[81] For if, in Bonaventure's telling, man indeed could not manage to aim *comprehensively* at God insofar as this mode of knowing would presuppose an impossible "relation of equality" between the knowing subject and the known object (*proportio aequalitas*), he can nevertheless touch and grasp God *apprehensively*—or better, let himself be grasped by God—insofar as a "relation of harmony" is now established from his soul to the divine nature (*proportio convenientiae*): to

---

[79] Bonaventure, *Legenda maior*, c. 13, No. 2 (VIII, 542b), Fr. tr. D. Vorreux, in *Saint François d'Assise, Documents,* Paris, Éd. franciscaines, 1968, p. 681 (cited in *Vie de saint François d'Assise,* Éd. franciscaines, 1968, p. 137) ; and *Itinerarium* VI, 6 (V, 311b), Fr. tr. (Vrin), p. 99. For the comparison of Bonaventure's *Legenda maior* with Thomas of Celano's *Vita prima*—where the mention of the Trinity does not come into the act of interrogating the Gospel; it is Bonaventure who introduces it—see Thomas of Celano, *Vita prima*, II, 2, No. 93, in *Saint François d'Assise, Documents*, ibid., p. 272 (as well as the comparative table on p. 1482).

[80] Bonaventure, *I Sent.*, d. 3, p. I, a.un., q.1, ad.1 (I, 69a): "cognitio per apprehensionem consistit in manifestatione veritatis rei cognitate; cognitio vero comprehensionis consistit in inclusione totalitatis."

[81] *Ibid.*, arg. 1 (ad oppositum) (I, 67a) : "Circa primum, quod non sit Deus cognoscibilis a creatura, ostenditur (1) per auctoritatem Dionysii *De Divinis Nominibus* (c. 1): Deum neque dicere neque intelligere possibile est."

the very point that the soul, as the image and likeness of God, becomes supremely capable of receiving God's very nature (*anima maxime est capax Dei per assimilationem, quia est imago et similitudo Dei*).[82] Recall here Descartes's comment to Father Mersenne in the letter of May 27, 1630, and his famous distinction between knowing and understanding: Descartes may just as well be speaking of Bonaventure's apprehensive knowledge of God as of a mountain when he claims that "I may well touch it with my hands but I cannot embrace it as we might a tree, or some other thing that did not exceed the breadth of our arms."[83] One would think that Descartes himself, in his attempt to "go it alone" and re-found theology against (and with) Scholasticism—that is to say, the Thomism still dominant at the time—was no stranger to the subtle distinctions made by the Seraphic Doctor and Augustine before him.[84]

Reduction in the phenomenological sense of the term, or Bonaventure's "bracketing" of any proof of the existence of God at the threshold of the *Breviloquium* (*Brev.* I) does not exclusively indicate a pure and simple absence justified either by the mere circumstances of the work's editorial history (destined, as it was, *ad intra*, for the friars) or by crude distinctions (between the essence and the Trinity, for example). Just as in a phenomenological reduction the *epochalization* of the world signifies neither its negation nor its placement in doubt, but rather only its suspension or "putting out of play,"[85] so Bonaventure's silence in the *Breviloquium* with respect to the proofs of God's existence is meant neither to suppress them nor to enlist them in his cause—since, on the contrary, their indubitability to us can be seen only as soon as we give ourselves over to them (*non est dubitabile Deum esse*). Rather, the suspension of any demonstrative approach consists in affirming here that God's omnipresence to the believing subject is such that it designates for him precisely the irreducible and inseparable residue of his *ego*. Nothing

---

[82] *Ibid.*, ad. 1 (I, 69a): on the *capax Trinitatis* and the *capacitas humana* (above, §1c).

[83] Descartes, *Lettre au Père Mersenne du 27 Mai 1630* (on the creation of eternal truths), in Œuvres complètes, Paris, Vrin, 1996, ed. C. Adam and P. Tannery, t. I, p. 151.

[84] This implicit relationship between Bonaventure and Descartes with respect to apprehensive knowledge is at least emphasized, but not developed, by Gilson in *La philosophie de saint Bonaventure*, op. cit., Note 2, p. 103. More originally, we can relate this distinction to Augustine himself: *De videndo Deo*, Fr. tr. *Sur la manière dont Dieu peut être vu*, Letter 147 (to Pauline), in Œuvres complètes de saint Augustin, Paris, Vives, 1870, t. 5, Ch.IX, 21, p. 286: "it has never been given to anyone to see the fullness of God, whether by the eyes of the body or those of the spirit. Seeing is indeed one thing (*aliud est enim videre*), and understanding everything by seeing is another (*aliud est totum videndo comprehendere*)."

[85] Husserl, *Ideen I* (1913), op. cit., Gallimard, §32, pp. 101-104: "l'épochè phénoménologique" (cit. p. 102).

remains, indeed, at the end of the reduction or the suspension of every proof for the existence of God, except precisely God himself—the God who is tried and tested, not indemonstrable, dying for whom without proof is itself enough to show how self-evident he is.[86]

In the *phenomenological reduction* indicated by the demonstrative silence of the entrance of God in the *Breviloquium*, Bonaventure thus does not admit—as Husserl does—a *transcendental reduction* intending to suspend any of God's transcendence not "given in an immediate unity with the reduced conscience."[87] Instead, there is all the more reason that God—not as an object of demonstration, but as *Trinity*, inscribed in the heart of the world (below, §11)—actually cannot be reduced because on the one hand he is always already there and immediately present to my consciousness in his omnipresence to me; and the fact that, on the other hand, as with the pure "me," there remains no distance between God and my *ego* that would allow any suspension of that sort. The fact that the starting points of the Bonaventurian *reductio* and of the Husserlian *epochê* are identical thus in no way implies the convergence of their destinations. Far from it. The difference of aims or ends between the two types of reduction can be seen, in my opinion, if not in a reworking of transcendence, at least in the rejection of any suspension of God himself (transcendental reduction)—constituting in its own right Bonaventure's theological act relative to Husserl's phenomenological gesture.[88]

c) THE MONADOLOGICAL HYPOTHESIS

The God who is reduced or suspended in his proofs at the beginning of the *Breviloquium* indicates another (non-metaphysical) face of God, this time an irreducible residue, because it is more intimate to me than I am myself—*interior intimo meo*, in Augustine's words, or *intimior intimo*

---

[86] Bonaventure, *III Sent.*, d. 23, a.1, q. 4 ("*utrum fides sit certior wuam scientia*"), concl. 3 (III, 481b-482a) : "one would deem foolish (*stultus*) the geometer who chose to die (*auderet subire mortem*) for the conclusion of a theorem…"

[87] Husserl, *Ideen I*, op. cit., §58, pp. 191-195: "la transcendance de Dieu mise hors circuit" (cit p. 191).

[88] R. Russo. "Riduzione bonaventuriana e riduzione husserliana," op. cit., p. 744: the hypothesis of a restructuring of transcendence from Bonaventure to Husserl—*transcendence of immanence* in the former and *immanence of transcendence* in the latter—could, in my opinion, once again lose Seraphic theology in a mysticism of the flight from the world and from pure transcendence, probably contrary to the Franciscan spirit and to its attachment to the earth (cf. RSPT, pp. 5-6 and pp. 33-34: "le refus d'une transcendance surplomb [Bonaventure et Merleau-Ponty]").

meo in Bonaventure's adaptation: namely, the Trinitarian God.[89] In no way contrary to the demonstrative ambition in a crude dualism between the essence and the Trinity, any proof of the existence of God in the presence-to-itself of the divine becomes obsolete, not by virtue of some regrettable absence but rather by its absolute presence. The existence of God goes undemonstrated in the *Breviloquium* not because it is indemonstrable, but because it is always already hyper-proven and hyper-known as soon as the question of the *quomodo* of the three of the Trinity—or better of the *qualiter*—supplants that of their *quis* and their *quid* (*Brev.* I, 2). Furthermore, the attempt at a demonstration that is found elsewhere in Bonaventure's corpus, as we have seen (*I Sent. d. 8* and *De myst. tr. q. 1*), already supposed his existence, in that the very act of demonstration could be engendered silently, yet without ever being said according to the order of proof (*ordo probandi*), by the work of the Trinitarian persons at the very heart of the believing subject: "our experience of the existence of God is the very condition for the inference by which we claim to establish it."[90] The Trinitarian persons are thus all the more presupposed in their creative work for the fact that, from the very first lines of the *Breviloquium* onward, God's hyper-knowability is established as soon as the believer finds it, without constructing it, in his soul, in which "the whole world is inscribed, or better described" (*below*). In this sense, as if to distance himself anew, the Franciscan Bonaventure explicitly refuses to be satisfied only with the Augustinian introspection taken up precisely by Husserl at the conclusion of his *Cartesian Meditations*: "'noli foras ire,' Augustine says, 'in te redi, in interiore homine habitat veritas.'"[91] To the Augustinian and Husserlian ban on studying the external (*noli foras ire*), Bonaventure

---

[89] Augustine, *Confessiones*, III, 6, 11, Fr. tr. *Confessions*, Paris, DDB, B.A No. 13, 1962, p. 383. The shift from the *interior* to the *intimior* occurs at least twice in Bonaventure, precisely in order to indicate how much less it is a question of being opposed to the figure of a superior God (*superior*) than it is of a God who is purely exterior (*exterior*). Cf. *I Sent.*, d. 1, a. 3, q. 2, concl. (I, 41a): "God alone, by virtue of his supreme simplicity and his pure spirituality, penetrates the soul (*illabitur animae*), to such a point that he dwells within the soul according to truth (*ita quod secundum veritatem est in anima*) and dwells *more intimately* in the soul than it itself (*et intimior animae quam ipsa sibi*)"; or again, *II Sent.*, d. 8, a. un. q. 3, concl. (II, 227a): "Because only God is superior (*superior*) to the spirit of man [Augustine], in all that is *highest* (*secundum sui supremum*), only God can be *intimate* with the spirit (*solus Deus potest menti esse intimus*)."

[90] Gilson, *La philosophie de saint Bonaventure*, op. cit., p. 108.

[91] Husserl, *Méditations cartésiennes* (1929), Paris, Vrin, 1980, last sentence of the fifth meditation, p. 134. Citation of Augustine, *De vera religione*, Fr. tr. (modified) *La vraie religion*, Paris, DDB, B.A. vol. 8, 1951, No. 39, 72, pp. 129-131 (reflection of the interior man): "recognize, then, what is supreme harmony (*recognosce igitur quae sit summa convenientia*). Do not go out (*noli foras ire*); look within yourself (*in teipsum redi*): it is within man (*in interiore homine*) that the truth dwells (*habitat veritas*)."

opposes a desire of the soul (*vult anima*) which, returning within finds inscribed in itself only the irreducible opacity of the *exterior*. The detour toward things (*ad res*) immediately coincides thus with a return to the self (*in se*) in which the whole world is and remains engraved:

> when it is turned toward the world (*ut convertitur ad res*), the innate vision of the intellect is thus the truth. And the soul desires (*vult anima*) that the whole world be inscribed in it (*totum mundum describi in se*).[92]

In Bonaventure, the soul—which, in Augustine, always sees only "*as* in a mirror" (*tanquam per speculum*) or "*through* a mirror" (*per speculum*), though in anticipation of the final face-to-face encounter (1 Cor. 13:12)[93]—sees also, and above all, in conformity with the famous distinction in the *Itinerarium*, *in* a mirror (*in speculo*).[94] Better, the mirror which in Book XV of the *De Trinitate* of the Bishop of Hippo only ever indicates a single image of the soul in a structure of referral—"they do not see that this very mirror that they see is a mirror, in other words an image (*esse speculum, id est, imaginem*)"[95]—really amounts to the soul's very being (*fit speculum*) in the Seraphic Doctor's *Hexaemeron*:

> when the soul sees all these objects (its powers and its works), in returning to itself, it *becomes a mirror* (*fit speculum*), very beautiful and pure, in which it sees all that is radiant and beautiful (*quidquid est fulgoris et pulchritudinis*), in the same manner as one sees an image in a polished mirror.[96]

For Bonaventure, "the mirror is not only a *means* of knowing, it is *the very being* of the soul."[97] In contemplating itself and the created world at once, the soul *is made into* or *becomes* a mirror: *fit speculum*. Without

---

[92] Bonaventure, *Hex.*, col. IV, 6 (V, 349b), Fr. tr. Ozilou, *Les six jours de la création*, op. cit., pp. 174-175. The opposition between Bonaventure and Augustine on this point is briefly suggested by Russo, op. cit., p. 741.

[93] Augustine, *De Trinitate*, B.A No. 16, op. cit., L.XV, respectively 8, 14 (p. 457) and 12, 21 (p. 477).

[94] Bonaventure, *It.* I, 5, (V, 297b), Fr. tr. Duméry, Paris, Vrin, 1990, p. 31. For an interpretation of this text, see RSPT, pp. 10-11: "l'enjeu d'un regard, le passage du *per* au *in*."

[95] Augustine, *De Trinitate*, op. cit., L.XV, 24, 44, p. 541.

[96] Bonaventure, *Hex.*, col. V, No. 25 (V, 358a), Fr. tr. (slightly modified), *Les six jours de la création*, op. cit., p. 204.

[97] Ozilou, *Le De Trinitate de saint Augustin dans le Commentaire des Sentences de saint Bonaventure*, (unpublished), pp. 57-59.

ever escaping the thickness of the created world (which thickness
is so Franciscan, after all), or fleeing into some kind of defensive and
smothering mysticism, the soul's being-as-mirror finds in itself—or better
discovers itself as—the radiance of the world (*fulgor*) and the beauty of
God (*pulchritudo*).[98] One can rightly speak here of the "Bonaventurian
monadology, which is without a pre-established harmony." [99] In my
opinion, this is so not just in the sense in which the totality of the world
is reflected and expressed in the soul, but also and above all insofar as the
operation of the reduction—not only as renewal but also as suspension
(especially of the proofs of the existence of God)—demands that we
maintain the intimate union of God himself and his Trinitarian work
with the believing *ego* as a final, irreducible, and non-suspending residue.
Prior to the terror of the Pascal's freethinker before the infinite, but
after the theological rigor of Alain de Lille's *more geometrico*, God, for
Bonaventure, is "wholly within and wholly beyond all things (*totum
intra omnia et totum extra*)" only insofar as, in the soul's ultimate act
of *re-flection* and admiration in itself, this "intelligible sphere of which
the center is everywhere and the circumference nowhere" (Alain de Lille,
Rule 7) implies less a naïve dissemination of the divine in the created
world than a primary and exclusive nourishment by a natural Trinitarian
insemination in *myself*.[100]

> What is admirable in the sun or discoverable in the moon, as
> we have already noted, is in fact neither the sun nor the moon
> in their respective substances as located in existence, but the act
> by which the believer can see in them the divine presence sup-
> porting them and being manifest in them as the Most Blessed

---

[98] The two senses of the "Theological aesthetic"—formal beauty (*pulchritudo*) and
radiance (*fulgor*)—are explicitly examined by Hans Urs von Balthasar, *La gloire et la croix*,
op. cit., t. I (Apparitions), p. 17.

[99] Balthasar, *La gloire et la croix*, op. cit., t. II, 1 (Styles), monograph on Bonaven-
ture, p. 304. See also Ozilou, *Introduction aux six jours de la création*, op. cit., pp. 48-50:
"Monadology." Let us note that this "monadological hypothesis" is the same one that
Alain de Libera maintains in *La philosophie médiévale*, Paris, PUF, 1993, p. 405: "with
Bonaventure, thanks to the fusion of Avicenna and Dionysius, *the idea of monadology*
enters the history of philosophy" (my emphasis).

[100] Bonaventure, *It.*, V, 8 (V 310a), Fr. tr. pp. 89-91; and Alain de Lille, *Theologicae
regulae*, Patrologie latine, Migne, 1855, vol. 210, col. 627, reg. VII: "Deus est sphaera
intelligibilis, cuius centrum est ubique et circumferentia nusquam." The wonder and admiration before the infinity of God in the cosmos that the Cistercian Alain de Lille and
the Franciscan Bonaventure share is far from the "therapy by terror" that Blaise Pascal
would develop for the libertine, with the support of this same formula. See Pascal, *Pensées*,
B. 72/L. 199: the disproportion of man; and Carraud, V. *Pascal et la philosophie*, Paris,
PUF, 1992, §30, p. 403-422: "terror as anti-contemplation."

Trinity. This operation by which the world, for a time at least, is deliberately declared without value, or better beyond all value (bracketed), paradoxically establishes a community of nature between the phenomenological *epoché* and the Christian experience of the conversion of the senses.[101]

Thus, it is only by the Trinitarian presence intimately offered to my *ego* that the phenomenological hypothesis of a possible "departure from metaphysics" is revealed, precisely because the originary to which it opens does not yield in any way to the imperatives of causality (*causa sui*)— imperatives which, most of the time, conceal the effort "at work" under the deceptive mask of pure efficiency.

---

[101] RSPT, pp. 31-32.

PART TWO

GOD IN THE BEGINNING

CHAPTER III

THE ORIGIN AT WORK *IN* THE WORK
(*Brev.* I, 3-4)

For Bonaventure, God's entrance into theology is first of all defined by the strict delimitation of a "descriptive theology" that takes the passage from (Scriptural) *descriptio* to (theological) *expositio* as the true mode of all discourse about God and his exemplary performativity (as we saw in Ch. I). What's more, this entrance next suspends or "reduces" any statement of God's nature in the form of *quid* and definitively liberates his *quomodo* in rejecting both the presumed necessity of proving the existence of God and the alleged privilege of his unknowability; man's hyper-cognition of God is drawn directly from the monadological inscription in his soul (Ch. II). The relationship of *God to theology* (Part One) is thus given the lineaments of a doctrine that finally lets God be God—which is to say it lets him reveal himself first, and primarily, as Trinity. Once it is established, then, that a certain kind of discourse about God—or better, one starting with God (*theo*-logy)—is possible, at least with respect to his act of revelation (Part One), we must again examine how the One who enters theology, or rather who agrees to take his place there, remains precisely the One whom Scripture says *begins* (Part Two)—for if we do not, we risk either turning this into a new idol or getting lost forever within a total muteness on the subject. In other words, according to Hans Urs von Balthasar's theological modalities, "the subjective evidence" of revelation, which is to say the delimitation of the anthropological conditions of its reception (Part One), must here give way to its "objective evidence," namely to the "evidence that emanates and shines forth from the phenomenon itself, and not that which has as its base the satisfaction of the needs of the subject" (Part Two).[1]

"Starting from the beginning" (*inchoandum est ab exordio*)[2] requires that first of all we "bend the knees of our heart" before the Father of Lights—and this is crucial, for here we recognize that *God* is the one

---

[1] H.-U. von Balthasar, *La Gloire et la Croix*, op. cit., t. I (*Apparition*), p. 392.

[2] Bonaventure, *Brev.* Prol. No. 5 (V, 202a), Fr. tr. p. 89. Cited as an epigraph in the present work and initially explained in the introduction.

who begins, not us.[3] This imperative, posited at the beginning of the *Breviloquium* as the very principle of any study of the Holy Scriptures that is to be fruitful and complete, establishes the rigor of any theological exercise. This, in a new way, argues in favor of the profound formal unity of *sacra Scriptura* and *theologia*:

> theology (*theologia*), and it alone, is thus the perfect science, *because it begins from the beginning* (*quia incipit a primo*), which is the first principle (*quod est primum principium*).[4]

For Bonaventure, as a genuflection of the mind and a conceptual recognition, the *primum principium* immediately means the Trinitarian God before whom we are to kneel. In the beginning (*in principio*)—in the *Breviloquium* as in the Prologue of the Gospel of St. John, as well as in the opening of the *Itinerarium*—the future teacher to whom the manual is addressed must understand (*intelligere*) theology as the study of that which treats "princepally" (*principaliter*) of the first principle, God three and one (*de primo principio scilicet de Deo trino et uno*).[5] This basic fact of pure exposition or of the first principle's deployment in its *primarily* Trinitarian dimension undergirds Part One of the *Breviloquium* so fundamentally that it returns recurrently as a *Leitmotiv* at the beginning of every *explanation* or *explication* in each chapter, or nearly so: "*because he is the first principle*" (*quia primum principium*), God is "absolutely simple" (c. 3), "perfect to the highest degree" (c. 4), "immense and limitless" (c. 5), "noble and perfect" (c. 6), "powerful, with a pure and simple might" (c. 7), "possessing a simple and perfect knowledge" (c. 8), and "of a supremely noble will" (c. 9).[6] *Primacy* and *principiality* [*principialité*][7] (*primum – principium*) are joined together

---

[3] Ibid.

[4] Bonaventure, *Brev.* I, 1, No. 2 (V, 210a), Fr. tr., p. 61. The formula certainly evokes its equivalent, "inchoandum est ab exordio."

[5] Bonaventure, *Brev.* I, 1, No. 1 (V, 210a), Fr. tr. p. 59. See also *It.* Prol. No. 1 (V, 295a), Fr. tr. Duméry (modified), Vrin, 1990, p. 21: "In the beginning (*in principio*), I invoke the first principle (*primum principium*) from which every illumination comes, the Father of Lights, author of all the wonders of nature and all the perfections of grace."

[6] See, respectively, the very beginning of each explanation (Ch. 3-9): *Brev.* I, 3, No. 2 (V, 211b), Fr. tr. p. 71; *Brev.* I, 4, No. 2 (V, 212b), Fr. tr. p. 77; *Brev.* I, 5, No. 2 (V, 214a), Fr. tr. p. 87; *Brev.* I, 6, No. 2 (V, 215a), Fr. tr. p. 95; *Brev.* I, 7, No. 2 (V, 216a), Fr. tr. p. 99; *Brev.* I, 8, No. 4 (V, 216b-217a), Fr. tr., p. 107; *Brev.* I, 9, No. 4 (V, 218a), Fr. tr., p. 115.

[7] [Tr. n.: With *principialité*, Falque invents a substantive in part to distinguish it from the French *principauté*, like our *principality*, which nowadays has chiefly political connations. *Principialité* is introduced to distance the notion from these while retaining both the sense of a ruling primacy and a foundation].

to affirm the Trinity as the ultimate source both of all theology and of Scripture (*above*, §1). The rules of this Trinitarian stance, however, also establish its limits: nothing, indeed, can ensure either that *principiality* does not force a return toward a pure, metaphysical causalism by which the first principle "produces its effects" as well as itself (*Causa sui*), nor that primacy does not lead to the establishment of the kind of inequality between God and his creatures such that every attempted overture or condescension (*condescensio*) of the divine toward the world would, in itself, make the act of condescension pointless. We must now attempt to define the meaning, and the interplay, of primacy and *principiality* in the *primum principium* (Ch. III). The Trinity's circumincession is only made visible and thinkable when it opens itself in its own manifestation—to man, and within the whole world created through him (Ch. IV-V).

§6. FROM THE DEPARTURE FROM METAPHYSICS TO THE CREATIVE TRINITY

A) PRINCIPIALITY AND CAUSALITY: BEYOND METAPHYSICS

In Trinitarian theology, unlike in the metaphysical prism often wrongly imposed on it, *being a principle* for God never signifies the "production of an exterior effect"—which, to follow Aristotle, implies only efficient causality.[8] Such, according to Thomas Aquinas, here legitimately converting Aristotelianism to Christianity, was precisely the common error of Arius and Sabellius: "they took procession (*processionem*) in the sense of a movement toward something external (*secundum quod est aliquid extra*), and consequently neither of them posited the procession within God himself (*unde neuter posuit processionem in ipso Deo*)."[9] No interpretation of a causal scheme, so important to Aristotelianism, is appropriate for speaking of God himself—even be it only in a purely immanent fashion, as with the *primum principium* in the Angelic Doctor (cf. the metaphor of the architect).[10]

Studying the notion of the principle for itself in the *Commentary on the Sentences*—*utrum nomen principium in divinis personaliter sive notionaliter accipi possit* (*I Sent.* d. 29)—Bonaventure, for his part,

---

[8] Aristotle, *Metaphysics*, Fr. tr. Tricot, Paris, Vrin, t. I, Delta 2, 1013a. 30, p. 248.

[9] Thomas Aquinas, *S.th.*, Ia., q. 27, a.1, resp., Fr. tr. (Cerf) t. I, p. 353.

[10] *Ibid.*, ad.3, Fr. tr. p. 354: "But God, who is the first principle of things, is to created things as the architect is to his works (*Deus autem qui est primum principium rerum, comparatur ad res creatas ut artifex ad artificiata*)."

anticipates the Thomistic objection, and decisively keeps any form of causalism far away from the Trinity. This he does in an original way:

> the doctrine of the 'principle' (*ratio principii*) pertains to God principally [*principalement*] for what concerns the person of the Father; but neither the idea of cause and effect (*non autem ratio nec causae et effectus*), nor that of prior and posterior (*nec prioris et posterioris*), nor that of the beginning and that which is begun (*nec initii et initiati*), nor that of the end and that which leads there (*nec finis et eius quod est ad finem*) can be related to the same.[11]

By virtue of the Father's primacy, which we will have to return to later (§7), the unique sense of divine principiality in Bonaventure is maintained here only as the source or fontality of the principle (*archê*): "in God is the true origin and emanation (*vera origo sive emanatio*), not only real (*non tantum vera*) but also totally complete (*sed etiam completissima*)."[12] Particularly with respect to Dionysius, the proximity of the Bonaventurian *principium* and the *archê* of the Greek Fathers, always at once the source and origin of all things and of itself, has often, and rightly, been noted.[13] It has not been sufficiently observed, however, just how much the *principium* whose support Bonaventure invokes, like the *aitia* that Dionysius makes use of, "does not correspond to Greek thought as such"—which we should understand here to mean the Aristotelian schema of the four causes.[14] Dionysius does indeed move a substantial distance away from Aristotle's causal scheme, as far, in fact (although for other reasons), as the distance that separates Bonaventure from St. Thomas Aquinas on the question. It is not that the Angelic Doctor forces efficient causality back into God; I have just noted his rejection of both Arianism and Sabellianism. Rather, *principiality* in Thomas—without being itself

---

[11] Bonaventure, *I Sent.*, d. 29, a.1, q.1 concl. (I, 509a).

[12] *Ibid.*

[13] Dionysius the Areopagite, *The Divine Names (Noms divins)*, ch. 2, §7, in Œuvres Complètes, Fr. tr. M. de Gandillac, p. 85: divinity "in the original state" or "fontal state" (*pêgaia theotês*). On the relationship between Bonaventure and the Greek Fathers, see Th. de Regnon, Études de théologie positive sur la sainte Trinité, op. cit., t. II, pp. 450-451 ("Une métaphysique dynamique") and t. III, p. 162-165 ("le nom de principe"); O. Gonzales, *Misterio trinitari y existencia humana*, Madrid, Rialp S.A., 1966, pp. 217-219 ; Mathieu, *La Trinité créatrice d'après saint Bonaventure*, op. cit., pp. 184-190 ("Le Père créature"); Bougerol, *Saint Bonaventure et le pseudo-Deny l'Aréopagite*, in *Saint Bonaventure, Études sur les sources de sa pensée*, Northampton, Variorum Reprints, 1989, p. 118.

[14] Marion, *L'idole et la distance* (1977). Paris: Biblio-essais, 1991, §14 ("la requête du Requisit"), p. 199.

an intra-divine cause—nonetheless remains in its movement the *cause of primacy* (§7). To put it in Martin Heidegger's phenomenological terms—and only to mention him here—this cause could well reduce both Creation and God himself to the status of a "thing" or "product" if it does not stay within what is opened by the origin "at work *in* the work": for "we are not yet thinking decisively enough about the essence of acting (*das Wesen des Handelns*)," as the Freiburg philosopher underscores in the introduction to his *Letter on Humanism*:

> Action is only known as the production of an effect (*nur als Bewirken einer Wirkung*) of which the reality is appreciated according to the utility that it offers. But the essence of action is the completing (*das Vollbringen*). To complete means: to unfold something in the fullness of its essence, to reach this fullness, *producere*. Nothing can properly be completed but that which already is.[15]

"Principle, because first" (*principium quia primum*), says Bonaventure—thus establishing the originarity of that which is opened as the sole source of primacy—while Thomas Aquinas, as I will show (§7), instead sets up God as "first, because principle" (*primum quia principium*). This is another way to make principiality a kind of causality: not of itself, but of primacy itself—something that spills out over the structure of the whole creative act, which is now divided into a life *ad intra* and in a departure from the self *ad extra*. We must reexamine what Bonaventure says, redundant or not, about *the primacy of primacy* precisely in order to be able to escape the aporia engendered by the causality of the principle.

b) PRIMACY AND GOODNESS: TOWARD AN AFFIRMATIVE THEOLOGY

The absence of any proof for the existence of God at the beginning of the *Breviloquium* (§5) has already convinced us to pass through the Trinity *first*, since theology expounds what Scripture describes (§3). The proximity mentioned between the Bonaventurian *principium* and the Dionysian *archê* should, in all logic, necessarily take us toward the affirmation of a *De Bono* as much in conformity with the *De bonitate divinae naturae* of Alexandre de Hales as with the axiom, drawn from

---

[15] Heidegger, respectively *L'origine de l'œuvre d'art*, in *Chemins qui ne mènent nulle part*. Paris: Idées-Gallimard, 1962, pp. 27-29 (where he distinguishes between the thing, the product, and the work); and *Lettre sur l'humanisme*, Paris, Aubier (Fr.-Ger. bilingual edition), 1964, p. 27.

Dionysius, of the *bonum diffusivum sui*.[16] This necessity is all the more obvious, in my opinion, for the fact that between the names of Being and the Good in the *Itinerarium*, Bonaventure explicitly "chooses the (Trinitarian) good" for reasons that are at once theological and mystical.[17] Now, the absence of any consideration of the goodness of God in the *Breviloquium*—confirmed by the recurrence of the Dionysian axiom throughout Bonaventure's corpus[18] and even including the opening to the *Commentary on the Sentences*—resonates in the theologian's ears even more forcefully than the silence of the proofs: what does the *Breviloquium*, with its strict criterion of the truths that are most important for salvation (§5), tell us of this God whose goodness is so great (*summa bonitas*) that it seeks to communicate itself (*se communicare*) in such a way that in it and from it a plurality of divine Persons is begotten?[19] Recalling once again the distance and the difference between the goals of the *Commentary on the Sentences* and those of the *Breviloquium*, the consideration of *primacy* alone (without *goodness*) in our "*summa theologica*" demands that it be weighed simultaneously against the Halesian idea of goodness *and* the Dionysian idea of the good that diffuses from itself. Only in this way can we evaluate the originality that it claims and the "overcoming" that it effects.

"Reproducing his master's theory," Théodore de Regnon writes, "Bonaventure substitutes for the concept of goodness the concept of primacy"—and in my opinion he makes this even more evident in the *Breviloquium* by omitting any consideration of the *bonum*.[20] Whereas his master, Alexander of Hales, finds "in perfection, goodness, power, and charity" the notion of *number* in God, and "in his goodness the *principal* reason for this number (*ex parte bonitatis est sicut principalis ratio*

---

[16] Alexander of Hales, *Summa theologica*, Ia., q. 45, membr.5: "goodness as principle of the processions" (translated and with commentary by Th. de Regnon, Études de théologie positive, op. cit. t. II, pp. 407-421 [esp. pp. 419-421]). On the Dionysian axiom of the "*Bonum diffusivum sui*"—incidentally, neither formulated as such nor applied to the divine persons by Dionysius—see Mathieu, *La Trinité créatrice d'après saint Bonaventure*. Paris: Éd. franciscaines, 1992, p. 19-27: "Le Bien, nom propre de Dieu."

[17] RSPT, pp. 12-15: "Le choix du bonum: raisons théologiques et mystiques."

[18] Bougerol, *Saint Bonaventure et le pseudo-Denys l'Aréopagite*, op. cit. (Variorum Reprints), p. 81: summary of twenty-six explicit citations, in chronological order, of the Dionysian axiom of the "*Bonum diffusivum sui*" in Bonaventure's corpus—and none in the *Breviloquium*.

[19] Bonaventure, *I Sent.*, d.2, a.un., q.2, f.1 (I, 53a): "si [Deus] est summa bonitas, cum bonitatis sit summe se communicare…ergo necesse est plures esse personas."

[20] Th. de Regnon, Études de théologie positive sur la sainte Trinité, op. cit., t. II, p. 466 (fruitful hypothesis of a substitution of primacy for goodness in Bonaventure, but unfortunately scarcely developped in that work to truly be demonstrated).

illius numeri),"[21] Bonaventure, at least initially on the threshold of the *Commentary on the Sentences*, adds the original and remarkable quality of "supreme primacy" (*summa primitas*) to the supreme beatitude (*summa beatitudo*) of God containing his "supreme goodness" (*summa bonitas*):

> to show the plurality of persons, we must presuppose in God four things: first, that there is in him supreme beatitude (*summa beatitudo*); second, supreme perfection (*summa perfectio*); third, supreme simplicity (*summa simplicitas*); and fourth, *supreme primacy* (*summa primitas*).[22]

Primacy, in the *Commentary on the Sentences*, indicates here a twofold fecundity—of the Father relative to the other persons of the Trinity, and of the divine essence with respect to creation.[23] The principle's double fontality is at once *notional* and essential, and, as the *creative Trinity*, is particularly definitive for Bonaventurian theology (below, §6); nevertheless, it must not mask the distance between the Bonaventurian *primum principium* and the Dionysian *bonum diffusivum sui*, as relayed here by Alexander of Hales. The primacy of the principle is presented for the first and only only time (but is it treated fully?) in the first part of the *Breviloquium*, in the form of the *unbegottenness* of the Father (*Brev.* I, 3). Without going deeper at this point into the use of the figure of the Father as a "quest for the origin" (§7), let me just note that right away the paternal unbegottenness of God—etymologically indicating the fact that the Father was "not born" (with Augustine's appropriate safeguards against the Arian *aggenêtos*)[24]—not only reveals that he is without an origin, as negative theology does, insofar as he is the "principle without principle" (*principium non de principio*) of which nothing can be said other than that

---

[21] Alexander of Hales, *Summa theologica*, studio et cura PP. Collegii S. Bonaventurae, Florence, Quaracchi, 1924, Ia., q. 45, membr.5, resolutio: "numeri ratio in divinis est ex parte perfectionis bonitatis, virtutis et charitatis: sed *principalius ex parte bonitatis*" (our emhasis).

[22] Bonaventure, *I Sent.*, d.2, a.un.q.2. fund. (I, 53a), with the justification of the conversion of supreme blessedness into supreme goodness, which Dionysius and then Alexander (ibid.) both take up.

[23] Bonaventure, *I Sent.*, d.2, a. un., q.2, f.3 (I, 53b): "ergo sicut essentia divina, quia prima, est principium aliarum essentiarum, sic persona Patris, cum sit prima, quia a nullo, est principium et habet fecunditatem respectu personarum." See also *De myst. tr.* q.8, No. 7 (V, 115b), even more explicit in speaking of a twofold fontality: "haec autem *fontalis* quodam modo origo est *alterius fontalis*. Quia enim Pater producit Filium et per Filium et cum Filio producit spiritum sanctum; ido Deus Pater per Filium cum Spiritu sancto est principium omnium creaturorum."

[24] Augustine, *De Trinitate*, op. cit., L. V, 6, 7-7, 8 (B.A No. 15), pp. 435-443: the term "unbegotten" (*De ingenito*).

he *is not such* that one could express him;[25] unbegottenness also reveals him, in an eminently *affirmative* way, as absolute primacy (*primitas*) and the source, the font (*fons*) of the other divine persons:

> unbegottenness designates the Father negatively (*per modum negationis*), but consequently it does so affirmatively (*licet ex consequenti per modum positionis*), because it supposes a fountain-like fullness (*plenitudo fontalis*) in the Father.[26]

In Bonaventure's thought, the *negative mode* (*modum negationis*) as original privation or as principle without principle gives way, as an attestation of the Trinitarian self in a singular and personal identity, to a new *positive mode*, or better an *affirmative mode* (*modum positionis*): the Father is the overflowing source of all fullness or plenitude (*plenitudo fontalis*)—first for his own Son and, with him, for the Holy Spirit.[27] The whole grandeur of Bonaventure's Trinitarian schema lies not simply in the fact that it sets up an end to the Aristotelian regression toward an infinity of causes—albeit by substituting the figure identified with the Father for that of the prime mover or the pure act.[28] Even more it amounts to affirmatively making what is *first* into the source and origin of everything and of itself, the *first* principle (*primum principium*) on which all things positively and nobly depend, and which they claim as their own cause, like so many vassals happy to submit to their king: the *Commentary on the Sentences* says that "not to have an origin (*non esse ab alio*) is to be first (*est esse primum*); and primacy is a *noble position* (*et primitas est nobilis positio*)."[29]

Just as the hyper-knowledge of God revealed to man forbids us to take refuge in some kind of un-knowing, or in a learned ignorance (§5), so, too, the absolute primacy of the Father at the heart of the Trinity, in

---

[25] Bonaventure, *Brev.* I, 3, No. 7 (V, 212a), p. 73: "it is characteristic of the Father to be innascible or unbegotten (*innascibilem sive ingenitum*), to be the principle without principle (*esse principium non de principio*), and to be Father (*et esse Patrem*)."

[26] Bonaventure, *Brev.* I, 3, No. 7 (V, 212a), Fr. tr. (modified) p. 73.

[27] The formula *modus positionis* must be translated, in my opinion, by "mode of affirmation" rather than by "mode of position" or "positive sense" (tr. L. Mathieu), at the very least in the sense that Bonaventure's affirmative or cataphatic theology, in an original break with Dionysius's negative or apophatic theology, must never be confused with anything like a "positive theology" inherited from 19th-century positivism, something diametrically opposed to the true sense of Bonaventure's "descriptivity."

[28] On the infinite regression of causes and the necessity of stopping it by the prime mover or the pure act, see Aristotle, *Metaphysics*, Lambda, 7, 1072a.20-25, tr. Tricot (Vrin, 1981), t. II, p. 675.

[29] Bonaventure, *I Sent.*, d. 27, p. I, a.un., q.2, ad.3 (I, 470a).

my opinion, makes Bonaventure's an eminently "*affirmative*" theology, one "*of positing*" (*modum positionis*)—cataphatic and not primarily apophatic. This does not mean that the Seraphic Doctor was unaware of the negative way of theology, or avoided it; far from it, for this is exactly what he follows on the path of the *Itinerarium*, and there again with explicit reference to Dionysius;[30] rather, it means only that the act of conceptually analyzing the divine determinations, because of the divine's neutrality with respect to the determination of the persons, does not express everything about the nature of God. The work of negation effaces the idol that we ourselves make of this nature, and even makes way for the icon that we receive from it.[31] Yet of itself it never discovers or liberates the form of an *economic* and *differentiated* Trinity, which is given to be seen only starting from the fontality of the Father.

In this sense, far from affirming (in a Thomistic move that would be closer to Dionysius than to the Bonaventure) that with the concept of unbegottenness "Bonaventure desperately attempts to find a positive aspect in a negative concept to prove his theory" (Malet), we would instead do well to recognize that "the Trinity, according to the Seraphic Doctor, is no longer, as it was in Dionysius, something totally distant and unknowable...but rather the foundation and the *a priori* of all terrestrial reality" (Balthasar).[32] What we are here calling *affirmative theology*—the theology "of positing" (*modus positionis*) or of "noble affirmation" (*nobilis positio*)—does not deny the work of negation, but it nonetheless finally refuses to found all revealed theology on the latter. Certainly, only by misunderstanding the meaning of negative theology in Dionysius could we claim to ground an absolute on it: "the meaning of negation does not, above all, mean that negation has the last word in the discourse on God."[33] Yet it remains the case that the practice of this unfathomable Dionysian obscurity commits the essential character of the divine and its superessential Trinity to an absolute; the humanly untraversable distance from this absolute to man actually creates, for the Bonaventurian, a *proximity* between the two, albeit one that only God can cross. Bonaventure's opposition to Dionysius on this point, as well as the Seraphic Doctor's eminently Franciscan inspiration, leads one to believe that God's proximity to man somehow always overcomes the distance between them. God, *as God*, within the Trinity, crosses the

---

[30] Bonaventure, *It.* VII, No. 5 (V, 323a), Fr. tr. Duméry, op. cit., p. 105

[31] See Marion, *L'idole et la distance*, op. cit. (Biblio-essais), Ch. IV, pp. 177-243: "la distance du requisit et le discours de louange: Denys."

[32] A. Malet, *Personne et Amour dans la théologie trinitaire de saint Thomas d'Aquin*, op. cit. (Vrin, 1956), p. 158; and von Balthasar, *La gloire et la croix*, op. cit., Styles II, p. 238.

[33] Marion, *L'idole et la distance*, op. cit. (Biblio/Essais), pp. 185-186.

distance from Father to Son, thereby reconnecting, in the one incarnate Word, the simultaneously particular and universal forms of the Son of Man and of every man. The "running within God [*course en Dieu*]" (*intra Deum currunt*) that Bonaventure discerns in the form of the good angels[34] first implies that God's own "running"—of himself, by himself, and in himself—already crosses, and abolishes, any distance between him and the heart of his created order. The course along which God "runs" to man in his condescension (*condescensio*) thus supposes, and presupposes, "running" within God himself, ever satisfied, as Trinity, to join in himself the three of the Trinity in one and the same nature. God *runs within himself* in order to *run toward man*, because "whatever has been said of creation," to take up the famous Bonaventurian adage (as reformulated by Hans Urs von Balthasar), "applies *first of all* in the heart of God."[35]

c) THE TRINITY AS MAKER (FABRICATRIX): THE "PRIMUM DIFFUSIVUM SUI"

The purely *economic* perspective of a *differentiated* Trinity, rightly noted by exegetes of Bonaventure as being absent from the Dionysian corpus,[36] makes the Franciscan master's studies both original and relevant. The *notional* and intra-Trinitarian primacy of the Father over the Son and the Spirit is the only guarantee and foundation for the *essential* and creative primacy of God over the world:

> insofar as primacy (*primum*) means the lack of personal origin (*privatio originis personalis*), it belongs to the only unbegotten person, the *Father*, in whom fountain-like fullness (*plenitudo fontalis*) is found producing the *Son* and the *Spirit*. But this fon-

---

[34] Bonaventure, *Brev.* II, 8, No. 2 (V, 226a), Fr. tr. p. 99: "in contemplating God face to face, wherever they are sent, it is always in God that the [good] angels run (*quocumque mittantur, intra Deum currunt*)."

[35] Balthasar, *La gloire et la croix*, op. cit., Styles II, p. 262 (my emphasis). The presupposition of *God's running in God* (*Brev.* prol. and *Brev.* I) on *God's running toward man and Creation in general* (*Brev.* II-VII) thus fully justifies our endeavor here to show that while "God enters theology" (cf. the present study on the Prologue and Part One of theology), it is also and immediately the whole of Creation that enters, stays, and returns to him from the "creaturely world of God" (*Brev.* II) until the "Last Judgment" (*Brev.* VII). Hence the idea for a second volume that would complete this present work on Bonaventure, which we hope will come someday, tentatively entitled "Saint Bonaventure and the Ontology of the Sensible: The *Breviloquium* as a *Summa* of Theology (*Brev.* II-VII)."

[36] For example, Bougerol, *Saint Bonaventure et le Pseudo-Deny l'Aréopagite*, in *Saint Bonaventure, Études sur les sources de sa pensée*, Variorum Reprints, Northampton, 1989, pp. 117-118; and Gonzales, *Misterio trinitario y existencia humana*, op. cit., pp. 204-209.

tality is somehow at the origin of *another fontality* (*alterius fon-talitatis*): because the Father brings forth the Son, and by the Son and with the Son brings forth the Holy Spirit, God the Father by the Son and with the Spirit is *the principle of all creatures* (*est principium omnium creaturorum*).[37]

The expression "creative Trinity," or better "the Trinity as maker," which is so clearly present implicitly even though textually so rarely explicit in Bonaventure's corpus, finds in the *Breviloquium* its original and exemplary theological formulation, for in one fell swoop—the assertion of *notional* and *essential* primacy—*both* the Trinity (*Brev.* I) *and* Creation (*Brev.* II) "diffuse" themselves: "the creation of the world is like a book in which the *Trinity as Maker* (*Trinitas fabricatrix*) shines forth, is represented, and is read," to which point I shall return in the conclusion.[38] Far from any false Heideggerian identification, for once, of creative hylomorphism with some theology of *making* as "production" and "construction"[39]—and despite its nominal relation with the term *Trinitas fabricatrix*—the Trinity remains "Maker," for Bonaventure only insofar as it binds and relates the multiple production sites in the world, like so many subsidiaries of the one divine Maker. If "all creatures look back to their Creator, on whom they depend (*omnes creaturae respectum habeant et dependentiam ad suum Creatorem*)," in the words of the *Breviloquium*, and if the world itself must be thought of as "a creature [of God]" (*de creatura mundi*),[40] it is because every creature and the totality of the world reproduce or express precisely that which *is always already expressed* or *made manifest* in the immense workshop of God (below, §11). Nothing is made in this world that is not also and already made in God (except sin); creatures, for their part, can thus only ever *re*-produce. But,

---

[37] Bonaventure, *De myst. Tr.*, q.8, ad. 7 (V, 115b), passage translated and with commentary by Mathieu, *Introduction au Breviloquium (première partie)*, pp. 22-23.

[38] Bonaventure, *Brev.* II, 12, No. 1 (230a), Fr. tr. (modified) p. 123 (sole occurrence of the *Trinitas fabricatrix* according to Hamesse, J. *Thesaurus Bonaventurianus, Concordance et Indices*, Louvain, CETEDOC, 1975, t. II [*Breviloquium*], p. 118). A genealogy of the expression *Trinitas fabricatrix*, moreover, permits us to establish a relationship that runs from Augustine (*De vera religione* VII, 13) to Bernard of Clairvaux, cited by Alexander of Hales (*Glossa* in *I Sent.*, d.3, c. 1, §9). One finds the explicit citation, futhermore, in Peter Lombard's *Book of Sentences* itself, where he cites the Venerable Bede (*Sentences*, L.II, d.8, c.4, No. 3, Collegii Bonaventurae; Grottaferrata, 1971, p. 370). On the different relationships and the textual rarity of the expression, see in particular Mathieu, *La Trinité créatrice*, op. citl, p. 11; and Emery, G. *La Trinité créatrice*, op. cit., Note 1, p. 9.

[39] Heidegger, *L'origine de l'œuvre d'art*, in *Chemins...*, op. cit., pp. 28-29: "all beings as something *created*; let us understand here: *made*" (my emphasis).

[40] Bonaventure, respectively *Brev.* II, 12 No. 2 (V, 230a), Fr. tr., p. 124 and *Brev.* II, 1, No. 1 (V, 219a), Fr. tr. p. 55.

diametrically opposed to a world constructed by some grand clockmaker, the *divine workshop*, on the contrary, impresses on all things *its* brand— leaving its trace (*vestigium*) on each of them and thereby making manifest its ultimate and sole origin.

And, in Bonaventure, the Father's primacy plays such a guiding role that it contains in itself alone the whole Trinity, transcendentally making it possible: "his primacy not only does not exclude the Trinity (*primitas non solum non excludit trinitatem*), it actually includes it (*verum etiam includit*)."[41] The Trinity's inclusion within the primacy of the Father, however, does not mean that the *plurality* of divine persons is absorbed in an ever-higher *unity*; on the contrary, "it is precisely the unity of God that the philosopher does not know at the very moment when he proves its necessity, since he believes he is reasoning about a pure unity when he is reasoning in fact about a Trinity."[42] In the *Breviloquium*, there *cannot* be a direct affirmation of the principle of the Trinity by the Dionysian "*bonum diffusivum sui*," any more than there can be any hypothetical Plotinian "*unum diffusivum sui*" to hold together the divine persons in a diffuse unity—this time in the sense of a neutral dissipation.[43] Only a "*primum diffusivum sui*," in its very originality, can make sense of the entirety of Bonaventure's Trinitarian movement, which is precisely expressed by this axiom: "the more something is *first* (*quanto aliquid prius*), the more *fruitful* it is and the more it is the *principle of other things* (*tanto fecundius est et aliorum principium*)."[44] This hypothesis of the absolute fecundity of primacy, drawn from the *Liber de Causis*, still attributed to Aristotle at the time of the preparation of the first book of the *Commentary on the Sentences* (1253-1257), is the foundation of the entire movement of the *Breviloquium*.[45] Shorn of all truths not immediately important to hold

---

[41] Bonaventure, *De myst. tr.*, q.8, concl. (V, 114b): statement of the conclusion.

[42] Gilson, *La philosophie de saint Bonaventure*, op. cit., p. 92.

[43] The hypothesis of the *unum diffusivum sui* is examined and rejected, rightly, by J. Peghaire in *L'axiome Bonum diffusivum sui dans le néoplatonisme et le thomisme*, in *Revue de l'Université d'Ottawa*, 1932, No. 2, p. 6. A discussion of this critique and Marie-Dom-inique Chenu's confirmation of it (*a théologie au XIIᵉ siècle*, op. cit., p. 132) can be found in Mathieu, *La Trinité créatrice*, op. cit., pp. 26-27.

[44] Bonaventure, *I Sent.*, d.2, a.un., q.2 (V, 53a).

[45] It is well known that only with Thomas Aquinas and the translation by William of Moerbeke that Proclus—or even more precisely, as we know now, an Arabizing adaptation of Proclus's *Elements of Theology*—could be identified as the true source of the *Liber de Causis*. See on this point A. de Libera, *La philosophie médiévale*, op. cit., pp. 78-81: "Proclus et le 'Livre du bien pur'" ; as well as, from the same author, *Notice sur le Livre des causes*, in *Philosophes et philosophies*, Paris, Nathan, 1992, t.I, p. 206. Bonaventure, for his part, cites the *Liber de Causis* no fewer than forty times, using the translation of Gérard de Crémone (cf. Bougerol, *Introduction à l'étude de saint Bonaventure*, op. cit., p. 67).

for faith (*magis opportuna ad tenendum*), the *Brief Discourse* explicitly dissociates primacy and goodness so as retain only one formula, of a Proclusian appearance, as the single point of departure for any sound understanding (*sana intelligentia*) of faith in the Trinity:

> the first and sovereign principle, *by the mere fact that it is first* (*hoc ipso quod primum*), is most simple.[46]

Reducible neither to Dionysian agathology nor to Plotinian henology, then, Bonaventure's Trinitarian doctrine nonetheless retains the idea of diffusion from Dionysius, and the hypothesis of a single fontal principle from Plotinus. Yet this double heritage does not force him to bow under the yoke imposed by the Arabizing author of the *Book of Causes*—as if it agreed, so to speak, to return its primacy to *the primacy* only in order to adapt Greek polytheism to Islamic monotheism.[47] On the contrary, the import of Bonaventure's *Brief Summary* of theology—it, too, published via Christendom's confrontation with Islam, but not addressed apologetically against it (recall the criterion of the "truths important for the faith")—amounts to a liberation from any neutral essentiality of the divine, which allows for the positing of the plurality of divine persons as *a priori* and self-evident: "since the unity of his nature has been saved (*salva unitate naturae*)," says the *Breviloquium*, "there are perfect modes of emanation in the first principle (*primum principium*)."[48] Far removed from the ancient struggles against Arianism and Greek polytheism, the unity of God's nature no longer needs *to be saved* inasmuch as to Bonaventure it no longer seems to be threatened. Whereas God's oneness has been "saved," the plurality of persons that distinguishes the Christian God must, on the other hand, be shown: hence the necessity of the crucial description of their modes of emanation (*modi emanandi*) which, by the double movement of generation and spiration, properly constitute the essence of Christianity.

---

[46] Bonaventure, *Brev.* I, 3, No. 2, (V, 211b), Fr. tr. p. 71. The statement of the (at least so-called) Proclusian equation "*quanto prius...tanto fecundius*" in Pattin, A. *Liber de causis*, in *Tijdschrift voor Filosophie*, No. 28, 1966, prop. 1 and prop. 17. For its roots, consult Proclus, *Eléments de théologie*, Fr. tr. J. Trouillard, Paris, Aubier, 1965, prop 1 (p. 61) and prop. 17 (pp. 71-72); as well as P. Magnard (ed.), *La demeure de l'être, autour d'un anonyme*, Paris, Vrin, 1990.

[47] This is a contemporary and univocal thesis among exegetes of the *Liber de causis*, for whom this work is first a "synthesizing text" (cf. A. de Libera, *La philosophie médiévale*, op. cit., p. 79). It is probably valid, in my opinion, with respect to the meaning and historic destiny of the text itself, but not for all of the readings that it eventually came to see, especially that of Bonaventure.

[48] Bonaventure, *Brev.* I, 3, No. 2 (V, 211b), Fr. tr. p. 71.

§7. THE SEARCH FOR AN ORIGIN

What is ultimately at stake remains the question of how to *name* the divine, not through its metaphysical aspects but primarily through its personal and Trinitarian properties,. It is what Bonaventure is trying to address throughout the whole of his corpus, but particularly in the *Breviloquium*. It is probably also this that, paradoxically, lends it its surprising relevance today. For Bonaventure—at the heart of the Franciscan awakening and the mystical experience of God that is offered to every human being, but especially to the "simple ones"—defining God in his essence or demonstrating him in his existence will certainly not be enough, for these efforts amount to so many statements that nevertheless retain a meaning as much as they also beg, as things interrogated, to be situated philosophically with respect to the limits that they exhibit (above, §5). The contemporary Christian theologian, grappling with an over-celebrated return of the religious, as we have observed in the Heideggerian figure of "the god" (*der Gott*) who enters philosophy, can no longer allow the *holy* identity of the Trinitarian God to dissolve into the merely *sacred* dimension of the divine god. The necessary abandonment of the neutrality of the divine is effected here, in the Christian framework, only by the *personal* and *Trinitarian* naming of the divine hypostases: the Father, the Son, and the Holy Spirit. In Bonaventure's view, invoking the *ego sum qui sum* alone is not enough to give us the *proper name* of the Christian God—thus preemptively cutting short a debate on the "metaphysics of Exodus"[49] that has sometimes been even more fruitful in theology than in philosophy. The Old Testament's naming of God as Being (Ex. 3:14) must give way to the New Testament's naming of God as Good: "no one is good but God alone" (Lk. 18:19).[50] And as if to confirm evangelically this rightly agathological stance, the theological and mystical *choice* of the *good*, a choice characteristic of the "true metaphysician," according to Bonaventure,[51] is rooted in the last words

---

[49] Beyond the numerous discussions that this kind of debate has sometimes aroused, the clearest expression of the "metaphysics of Exodus" and of the "Christian philosophy" that is bound to it can be found in Gilson, *L'esprit de la philosophie médiévale*, Paris, Vrin, 1932, t.I, pp. 54-56.

[50] Bonaventure, *It.* V, 2 (V, 308b), Fr. tr., *Itinéraire de l'esprit vers Dieu*, op. cit. (Vrin), p. 85 (cf. RSPT, pp. 12-15: "Les deux noms de Dieu [Être et Bien]" and "Le choix du *bonum*").

[51] Bonaventure, *Hex.* I, 13 (V, 331b), Fr. tr. *Les six jours de la création*, op. cit. (Cerf), p. 108 (cf. RSPT, p. 14).

of the resurrected Son to his disciples, cited explicitly in the *Itinerarium* (Mt. 28:19): "Go, then, make disciples of all nations, baptizing them in the name of the *Father*, of the *Son*, and of the *Holy Spirit* (*baptizantes eos in nomine Patriis, et Filii, et Spiritus sancti*)."[52]

To *name* the Father, the Son, and the Holy Spirit explicitly and before all else: such is thus the task and the essential goal of the *Breviloquium*, even more than it is of the *Itinerarium* (for the ascendant and mystical approach of the latter exhibits the Trinitarian *a priori* and the fontality of the Father less clearly than when they are theologically posited and showcased in the former). The primacy that is notional (Father—Son—Holy Spirit) and the primacy that is essential (God—creatures), or better the primacy that is essential *because* it is notional, in that everything is produced in an exemplary way in God, thus define the conditions of a departure from the *aporias* of neutrality: those of times gone by, e.g. Jewish or Islamic monotheism, and probably those of today, e.g. certain "anonymous" reliefs of onto-theo-logy (the Other, the sacred, or *différance*).[53] In other words—and this is a conviction I cannot develop further in this context—nothing will move beyond ontological difference *if it does not permit itself to be moved first by an Other*. Again, the presence of this Other must be recognized and accepted, an Other so singular in his personal nomination—Father, Son, and Holy Spirit—that he is furthermore addressed intentionally to each person in his proper and definite humanity.[54] *Primacy* thus becomes the key word in theology, and *alterity* in philosophy, as soon as causality's ambitions for control are replaced by the indispensable originality of the principle that is considered to be such solely by virtue of its primacy.

A) PRIMACY AND PRINCEPALITY

---

[52] Bonaventure, *It.* V, 2 (V, 308b), Fr. tr. p. 83: explicit citation of Mt. 28:19 (Father, Son, Holy Spirit) after the citation of God as Being (Ex. 3:14) and God as Good (Lk. 18:19).

[53] J.-L. Marion, *L'idole et la distance*, op. cit. (Biblio-essais), §17 (distance and difference) and §18 (the differing other): emphasis on the respective neutralities of the dimension of the sacred (Heidegger), the face of the Other (Lévinas), and of the operation of the "différ*ance*" (Derrida); and the necessity of moving to a properly Christian perspective through the dimension of the profundity discerned in the Trinity (§19: the fourth dimension).

[54] RSPT, pp. 20-25: "le dépassement de la métaphysique: l'excès de la donation du Père."

Following the Aristotelian problematic that identifies the *principle* with what is *first* (*cum idem sit primum et principium*),[55] two ways determine, according to Bonaventure, what it means for something to *be first*: a thing is "either first because it is the principle (*aut ideo est primum quia principium*), or the other way around (*aut e converso*) [i.e. a thing is the principle because it is first]."[56] With regard to this possibility of reversing the relation of principality to primacy later developed by Thomas Aquinas (below, §7c), and because what is "first" (*primum*) must always stay so even up through its relation to the principle, the Seraphic Doctor explicitly and deliberately opts for the latter choice (i.e., the other way around—a thing is principle because it is first):

> it is obvious that the notion of first principle is fitting *by- the very fact that it is first* (*quia est primum*); thus, it has this through itself (*ideo per se hoc habet*). And it is clear that thought rests in the first principle, *not because it is a principle* (*non quia principium*), *but because it is first* (*sed primum*). And it is obvious that this is a noble condition (*conditio nobilitatis*).[57]

Principium   quia   primum—"principle,   because   first":   this characteristically Bonaventurian formula is calling for a fresh theological re-evaluation of the meaning of the Father's absolute primacy over all things, an evaluation touching the very principle itself. God's primacy always stays first in Bonaventure only to the extent that his essence— like the origin of the work of art in Heidegger (*Vom Ursprung des Kunstwerkes*)—is opened and revealed through the bringing to light of his manner of appearance (*quomodo*) and his mode of origination.[58] Of the three modes of differentiation in God that we can find in the *Breviloquium* (*Brev.* I, 4)—by origin (the modes of being or emanating), by attributes (the modes of being in relation), and by connotations (the modes in which we conceive of God)—only the first difference (by origin) is explicitly called "greater" (*maior*), and here it means that which is "among the *supposita*" (*est enim in suppositis*) such that "one is not [i.e.

---

[55] Aristotle, *Metaphysics*, (Paris, Vrin, 1981, p. 245), Delta, 1, 1012b.35: "The principle (*archê*) is said first of the initial term of a thing's movement."

[56] Bonaventure, *I Sent.*, d.27, p. I, a.un. q.2, ad. 3 (I, 472a): "utrum generatio sit ratio paternitatis, an e converso."

[57] Ibid.

[58] Heidegger, *L'origine de l'œuvre d'art*, in *Chemins...* op. cit., p. 13 (first part of the text): "origin (*Ursprung*) means here *starting from what*, and *that by which* the thing is what it is, and *how* it is" (my emphasis).

cannot be] said of the other" (*ita quod unum non dicitur de altero*).[59] In other words, only the modes of being or emanating—namely, the *relation to the origin*—determine the true personal identity, which is to say the particularity, of the Father, of the Son, and of the Holy Spirit. Here an original way, and a specifically Christian way, is then opened to us to depart with Bonaventure from the meaningless neutrality of the divine.

Among these modes, generation and procession (or aspiration)—one according to nature and the other according to will—explicitly identify the persons of the Son and Holy Spirit in their common dependence on a unique source.[60] But what of the first hypostasis—the Father—who, "producing first (*primo producentem*), does not emanate from any other (*ab alio non emanare*)"?[61] Does it suffice to establish his person as principle (*principium*) to assure him a primacy that is all the more aloof as it rules, in its very non-appearing (*inapparition*), over all that dares take the risk of appearing, from the Father's own Son to the most ephemeral creature? Does not the absolute fontality of the first hypostasis imply this exemplary primacy (*primum*) that appears all the more *itself* for *giving itself to be seen* more legibly in a second who is yet equal to him, as the passage "whoever has seen me has seen the Father—*qui videt me, videt et Patrem*" suggests (Jn. 14:9)?

Following Bonaventure, it would be worth daring to consider a surprising remark from John Paul II. Rightly overwhelmed by the iconographic genius written into the ceiling of the Sistine Chapel, he says: "With great audacity, Michelangelo transfers Adam's visible and corporal beauty *into the invisible Creator himself*. We find ourselves facing what is probably an unusual boldness in art, since the visibility characteristic of man is imposed on the invisible God. Might this not be blasphemy? Yet it is difficult not to recognize in this visible and humanized Creator the God clothed in infinite majesty."[62] This is what the Franciscan John J. Coughlin, appealing to the historico-theological hypothesis of an explicit cross-fertilization of the Sistine Chapel's fresco and Bonaventure's doctrinal project, suggests somewhat differently:

---

[59] Bonaventure, *Brev.* I, 4, No. 6 (V, 213b), Fr. tr. p. 83 (with the complementary note at No. 21, p. 129).

[60] Bonaventure, *Brev.* I, 3, No. 2 (V, 211b), Fr. tr. p. 71.

[61] Bonaventure, *Brev.* I, 3, No. 3 (V, 212a), Fr. tr. pp. 71-73.

[62] John Paul II, *Homélie du 8 Avril 1994 pour l'inauguration de la restauration des fresques de Michel-Ange dans la Chapelle Sixtine*, in *La Chapelle Sixtine, sanctuaire pour la théologie du corps humain*, Éditions du Vatican, pp.28-30 (homily reproduced at the end of the volume).

the theological vision of the Sistine Chapel begins with three scenes, in each one of which Michelangelo has given the central role to the *Father and Creator*. When he separates the light from the darkness, fixes the stars, and creates the animals, the Father-Creator is the only and incontestable master of the universe ... *Saint Bonaventure* and *Michelangelo* seem to attribute a certain *primacy* to the Father. In this regard, Bonaventure's understanding of God differs somewhat from that of St. Augustine and St. Thomas Aquinas. These latter had emphasized the *equality* of the three persons of the Trinity. While affirming the equality of the three *distinct* persons of the one God, Bonaventure highlights the Father as the *source* of all life."[63]

B) PATERNITY, BEGETTING, AND SIMILITUDE

Besides asserting the primacy of the *first* over the principle (*supra*), Bonaventure, once again, and in advance of Thomas Aquinas (below, §7c), effects a second reversal by which God no longer "begets because he is the Father," and so to speak *in himself*, as if without his Son (*quia Pater est, generat*), but is rather "the Father because he begets": in this way of looking at it, he exists only in the act of begetting a Son (*Pater quia generat*):

> there is another opinion that says that God is Father because he begets (*quod ideo est pater quia generat*). And this is well stated (*et quod illud sit bene dictum*) ... For it is clear that the origin is the reason for existence of the relation (*origo est ratio habitudinis*), and that the relation is not the reason for the existence of the origin (*non habitudo ratio originis est*). This is why divine generation is the reason for the paternity's being (*et ideo generatio est ratio paternitatis*), and not the other way around (*non e converso*).[64]

Invoking generation as the reason for the existence of paternity amounts first to recognizing, very sensibly, that there is no paternity in

---

[63] John J. Coughlin. *La théologie franciscaine de la chapelle Sixtine*, in *Pierre d'Angle* (the review of the monastic fraternity of the Apostolic Monks of the Parish of St. John of Malta), Aix-en-Provence, No. 3, 1997, pp. 127-137 (cit p. 130 [my emphasis]).

[64] Bonaventure, *I Sent.* d. 27, p. I a.un. q.2, concl. (I, 469b). The translation of *ratio* by "reason for being [*raison d'être*]" (of relation, of the origin, or of paternity) and not simply by "reason" is meant to emphasize here its explanatory and ontological character, rather than its simply and purely epistemological dimension.

God—and, for that matter, probably not in man, either—apart from the very act of begetting a Son: the *origin* (the act of begetting) explains the *relation* (being Father), and not the other way around (*non e converso*). In short, for Bonaventure there is no Father without the Son: "that which is given," to cite an adage of Claude Bruaire's *ontodology*, "is *nothing* before being given, and independent of the *fact* of the gift."[65] The reason is that, going beyond its apparent banality, this expression is really not a self-evident one: must there not indeed always *already* be an (artistic) origin *in* the work, or a (potential) father *in* the son, even before any act producing them? Or, on the other hand, can we say that there is an artist only in the *act* of creation, and a Father only in the *movement* of begetting? In other words, does *the origin to the work* signify the origin *of* the work—as the artist might divest himself of his painting, even while leaving on it his mark or signature—or, on the other hand, does it imply even more the work *of* the origin—like the painter who never sees his painting's completion on the canvas as it is offered to the eyes of an astonished spectator, or like the father who only reveals his generosity when he is turned upside down by the reunion with the son who once was lost but now is found (Lk. 15:20)? The answer finally depends on what the work or the Son actually *is*, and on the line that binds them to their origins.

The artist and the Father, or better the artist as the Father (with the only difference being the exteriority of the work in aesthetics), *conceive*, whether we are talking about works of art or of procreation.[66] But *conceiving*, in Latin (*concipere*) as in French and English, is itself understood in two ways: either as an act of intellection—as an architect conceives his project even before its realization—or as an act of begetting—as parents conceive a child in embryogenesis. Thus in Trinitarian theology Bonaventure, too, distinguishes in the relation of the Father to the Son between the simple "speaking to self" (*loqui ad se*) as the *conceived word* that is intelligible in itself (*verbum conceptum*) and the "speaking to another" (*loqui ad alterum*) as the *word proclaimed* distinctly to another (*verbum prolatum*). Bonaventure is here following Augustine and Anselm, but he clearly favors the second sense.[67] Without denying the "speaking to self"—the

---

[65] C. Bruaire. *L'Être et l'Esprit*, Paris, PUF, 1983, Ch. III, 1, pp. 51-64: "ontodology" (cit. p. 53, original emphasis).

[66] The aesthetic formulation of the conception, or better the begetting, of the Son as "work" of the Father is suggested by Hans Urs von Balthasar, *La Gloire et la Croix*, t. II (Styles), op. cit. p. 264.

[67] Bonaventure, *I Sent.*, d. 27, p. II, a.un. q.1, concl. (I, 482b): "speaking (*loqui*) is understood in two ways: either to oneself and in oneself (*ad se, id est apud se*), or to another (*ad alterum*). Speaking to oneself (*loqui ad se*) means nothing other than conceiving something mentally...this is what we call the conceived word (*verbum conceptum*). Speaking to another (*loqui ad alterum*) *expresses* the mind's conception and the proclaimed word

mental word—the Seraphic Doctor nonetheless sides with the "speaking to another" in God—the proclaimed word. This stance is novel, and with it he explicitly responds to the possible disputes that separate him as much from the Bishop of Hippo as from the Abbot of Bec. Neither the modes of knowing or of conceiving in the artist, nor the work's manifest or proclaimed act of appearing, will suffice to express the act of begetting (or of creation) of one by the other—any more than separate considerations of the "in itself" of the Father and of the Son can convey the particularity of their filiality and paternity. Again one must introduce there the very act of conception (*conceptum*) as a "proclamation" or an "expression" of another in oneself and similar to oneself, to whom all is yet given or returned, as if it were paradoxically—although it never is—beyond the self and different from the self:

> as has been said, the Father begat a Son who is coeternal with him, and he has proclaimed his likeness (*et dixit similitudinem suam*); and consequently he has expressed all his power (*et per consequens expressit omnia, quae potuit*).[68]

As we also find in Hilary of Poitiers, the Son-Word is this "expressed similitude" (*similitudo expressa*), but in the *Breviloquium* he is considered even more as an "*expressive* similitude" (*similitudo expressiva*), meaning that this similitude makes visible in the very act of filiation the *how*

(*verbum prolatum*) corresponds to this speech." For background on this distinction between the "mental word" and the "proclaimed word," see Augustine, *De Trinitate*, op. cit. (B.A No. 16), L.XV, X, 17-19, pp. 465-471 and Anselm, *Monologion*, Paris, Cerf, 1986, Fr. tr. M. Corbin, c. 10, pp. 79-83. Bonaventure nonetheless distinguishes himself from these two, who require the proclaimed Word only as a foil for the mental Word, which they explicitly prefer. See, for example, Augustine, ibid. (L.XV, c.10, 19), p. 469: "anyone (*quisquis*) can understand what the word is, not only before its sounds are heard aloud, but even before the mind produces the images of these sounds within it"; and Anselm, ibid., (Ch. 10), chapter title, p. 79: "That this reason is a certain word (expressing) things in the same way an artisan *first* speaks what he is going to make *to himself* (*prius apud se*)" (my emphasis).

[68] Bonaventure, *Hex.* I, 16 (V, 332a), Fr. tr., *Les six jours de la création*, op. cit., p. 110. For a hypothetical interpretation of the Trinity on the model of "oneself as another" (Ricœur), I refer you to my work *Le Passeur de Gethsemani, Angoisse, souffrance, et mort: lecture existentielle et phénoménologique*, Paris, Cerf, cool. " La nuit surveillée," Jan. 1999, pp. 130-131. As for the historical sources of the *verbum prolatum* in Bonaventure (especially with respect to the mention of the Stoic "*logos prophorikos*"), see Mathieu, *La Trinité créatrice*, op. cit., pp. 137-144: "Le Verbe du Père." On the justification of the interpretation of the *expressio* in terms of conception or begetting, see Gilson, *La philosophie de saint Bonaventure*, op. cit., p. 123-124.

(*quomodo*) of the divine paternal being, who is always begetting.[69] Like Maurice Merleau-Ponty's "conquering speech"—permitting ourselves another detour through phenomenology—the Son "causes the meaning to be" that is given by the Father, yet without making it known exclusively in a complex of significations already instituted by a supreme principle, as if independent of the Son. Far from any intellectualism that might separate them, the Word that is *uttered* or *brought to the fore* (*pro-latum*) expresses the Father here almost aesthetically, in that he shows him *as* his work—or better *as working*—rather than *in* his work: "the Father is the foundation, and the Son is the manifestation; the Father is the content, while the Son is the form…[and] the two are one in the beautiful."[70] There is thus not only "community of being" but also "community of doing" from the Father to the Son, completing here our Merleau-Pontian exercise: not a succession of actions but the expression of a "style" or of a "word being born" and causing a world to arise—in other words, the Trinity in labor, as is still visible today: "the whole creation is groaning" (Rom. 8:22).[71]

In addition to the Son's intellectual and co-natural conformity and similitude (*similitudo*) to the Father, there is the other expressed similitude, namely, the expressive and hypostatic similitude that properly designates the Son as the Father's *work* or *begetting*.[72] Paul Claudel's claim that "we are not born alone" or that "every birth is a co-birth" holds first for God himself—and only subsequently for man.[73] Besides the necessary, if peculiar fact of the equality in God between the begetter and the begotten (recall the struggle against Arianism), the Son is somehow *born* of the Father in the heart of the Trinity just as the work of art suddenly arises from within the artist and causes him or her to *be* an artist solely in his or her act of bringing the work forth. Bonaventure's choice of the God who is "*Father because he begets*" (*Pater quia generat*)—and not

---

[69] Bonaventure, *Brev.* I, 3 No. 8 (V, 212a), Fr. tr. p. 75: "Image (*imago*) means person as expressed similitude, Word (*Verbum*) as expressive similitude, and Son (*filius*) as hypostatic similitude."

[70] H.-U. von Balthasar, *La Gloire et la Croix*, t.I (Apparition), op. cit., p. 518.

[71] Merleau-Ponty, *La perception d'autrui et le dialogue*, in *La prose du monde* (1969), Paris, Tel/Gallimard, 1992, p. 196 (the conquering word instituting a language), p. 195 (the community of doing and not solely of being in the word's expressive work), and p. 198 (the community of doing as the imposition of a common style).

[72] Bonaventure, *Brev.* I, 3, No. 8 (V, 212a), Fr. tr., p. 75.

[73] P. Claudel. *Traité de la co-naissance au monde et de soi-même*, in *Art poétique*, published in Œuvre poétique, Paris, Gallimard, Pléiade, 1957, p. 149. [Tr. n.: there is some French wordplay here in Claudel's claim that "*toute naissance est une co-naissance.*" *Naissance* is birth, and *co-* has the same sense as a prefix in French as it does in English (*cum / con / with*), but *connaissance* means knowledge.]

begetter because he is in himself Father, as if he could be Father without his Son (below, §7)—opens up a theological aesthetic, later rediscovered by Hans Urs von Balthasar and discernible (in part, at least, though in different terms) in Heidegger's account of the relation of the artist to his work: "when the work of art in itself arises, then a World is opened over which it permanently reigns."[74] Like the artist or the poet, when the Son, who is the begotten (but not created) work, issues forth from the Father, the world *worked* by the Father is forever held open in the Son.

Without ever ceasing to proclaim his Son or to place him in the world, the Father reveals, by the Son's natural sonship, and as if in counter-relief, the adoptive paternity that he accords to every man. Thus, even before all creation, the Son, even though not incarnate, exists no less as Son by the single begetting act of the Father: and the Father, the original, arch-foundation of God in God, remains Father only in unceasingly proclaiming his own Son and (in so doing) also the world in him:

> if in God there is perfect fecundity, God *is always begetting* (*semper ergo generat*); but he begets none other than the Son (*sed non generat alium nisi Filium*). Thus the Son is *always being begotten* (*ergo Filius semper generatur*).[75]

It would be wrong to reproach Bonaventure for "preventing this expressionism from leading to its end the immanence that it implies."[76] That would only be possible if we failed to take sufficient notice of the movement of immanence within the doctrine of the Trinity, which it deploys both in the assumption of all things *into* God and in surpassing the trivial opposition of the within (*ad intra*) and the without (*ad extra*), for the world of man also designates the world of God: it is even carried by the Son. But far from any Spinozist horizontalism that would identify God with nature (*Deus sive natura*),[77] emanation for Bonaventure does

---

[74] M. Heidegger, *L'origine de l'œuvre d'art*, in *Chemins...* op. citl, p. 47. For the theological aesthetic and its definition (though of course no direct parallel is established with Heidegger here), see Hans Urs von Balthasar, *La Gloire et la Croix*, op. cit., t. I, Apparition, p. 32: "theological aesthetic" and "aesthetic theology."

[75] Bonaventure, *I Sent.*, d.9, a.un., q.4, arg.4 (I, 186b): "utrum generatio Filii terminata sit." This perspective of a perpetual begetting of the Son by the Father is today better known through Meister Eckhart, but in fact it comes from Bonaventure. Cf. Eckhart, Sermon No. 6, in *Trinité et sermons*, Fr. tr. A. de Libera, Paris, Garnier-Flammarion, No. 703, 1995, p. 263.

[76] G. Deleuze. *Spinoza et le problème de l'expression*, Paris, Minuit, 1967, pp. 163-164.

[77] Baruch Spinoza, *Ethics*, Fr. tr. Paris, Vrin, 1983, t. II, Part IV, Preface, pp. 4-5.

not prevent immanence from finding refuge in transcendence.[78] It indicates on the contrary the movement by which God's world is identical to the world of creatures (*Deus sive natura*), though only in the sense in which the Son born of the Father first of all bears within himself the totality of the world, almost as if carrying a fetus. The neutral Spinozist good of the *Deus sive natura* is thus replaced with the good that is called Trinitarian: *Pater, Filius, et Spiritus Sanctus*—at the heart of which the entirety of creation and God himself are constantly at work, as in the labor of childbirth.

Just as God is "principle because first" (*principium quia primum*) for Bonaventure—and not the opposite (*non e converso*)—so, too, is he "Father because he begets" (*pater quia generat*)—and not the opposite (*non e converso*). The great originality of Bonaventure's Trinitarian theology probably consists in this double formulation of a single utterance at the heart of a crucial question in the first book of the *Commentary on the Sentences*, which is posed as *utrum generatio sit ratio paternitatis, an e converso*.[79] It is only this absolute primacy of the *first* over the principle and the total and permanent *donation* of the Father in the Son whom he is "always" (*semper*) generating, and of the world in him, that accounts for the very identity of the *holy* God and makes possible—in anticipation of the incarnation—the opening of the whole of the Trinitarian being to man's *habitaculum*, his dwelling place: the sensible world.[80] The origin is thus *at work in the work* for Bonaventure not as *origin of the work* but as *work of the origin* in the sense that only the origin of the Father makes of God the one who completely and firstly gives himself to his Son in who the entirety of the world is held. Exercizing and retaining his paternity, the origin of the Father has no other task than to open himself continually toward his Son, and by him to "establish a world": "to establish," means—returning in a new way to Heidegger, though

---

[78] Deleuze, *Spinoza et le problème de l'expression*, op. cit., p. 164: "The idea of expression is found to be suppressed as soon as it is raised. The reason is that the themes of creation or emanation cannot forego some minimal amount of transcendence, which prevents expressionism from proceeding to the very end of the immanence that it implies."

[79] Bonaventure, *I Sent.*, d.27, p. I, a.un., q.2 (I, 468-472). See, respectively, concl. (I, 469a) for the expression "*pater quia generat*"; ad.3 (I, 472a) for the formula "*principium quia primum*"; likewise ad.3 (I, 470) for the previously noted mention of the innascibility of the Father as a "noble position" (*nobilis positio*) in the passage from the negative to the positive.

[80] Hence the desire I have already expressed to compose a second volume that would complete this first work on Bonaventure, constrained as it is to focus solely on the Prologue and Part I of the *Breviloquium*, and which would be entitled "Saint Bonaventure and the Ontology of the Sensible: The *Breviloquium* as a *Summa* of Theology (*Brev.* II-VII)."

rejecting the unilateral dimension of the *sacred* god—not to "arrange something somewhere" but "to set up in order to dedicate and glorify" the work, and to hold it in "what is opened by its presence."[81]

c) THE THOMISTIC REVERSAL[82]

With regard to this double conceptual primacy—of the first over the principle and of begetting over paternity—Thomas, for his part, strangely reverses Bonaventure's very terms, word for word.[83]

(a) God, in the first place, is not "principle because he is first" (*prinicipium quia primum*) but rather "first because he is principle" (*primum quia principium*)—the "first one" (*unum primum*) being immediately and surreptitiously pushed into—indeed swallowed up in— the Peripatetic demands of the "one principle" (*unum principium*): "just as (*sicut*) in every genus one must posit *a first thing* (*oportet ponere unum primum*), so (*ita*) in God one must posit *some one principle* (*oportet ponere unum principium*) which is not from another and which is thus said to be unbegotten."[84] This explicit shift from primacy toward principality is in fact grounded, as if in advance, in Thomas Aquinas's intentional twofold rejection of part of the distinctive character of Bonaventurian theology: it is a rejection of the anti-Dionysian and characteristically Franciscan assertion of an "affirmative" or "positive theology" (*modus positionis*), and a rejection of the anti-Aristotelian and more Plotinian establishment of a fontal plenitude or source of fullness (*plenitudo fontalis*) not as "principle of the origin" (*principium originis*) but as origin of the principle in its absolute primacy:

> according to some [Bonaventure?], the innascibility meant by *unbegotten*, in the sense in which this attribute is proper to the

---

[81] Heidegger, *L'origine de l'œuvre d'art*, in *Chemins...* op. cit., pp. 46-47: "To be a work thus means: to set up a world."

[82] [Tr. n.: As the afterword discusses, the author's thoughts on the subject evolved somewhat in the years following this book's first publication. One will find, in the following sources proof of an evolution, even a turn towards Thomas Aquinas by the author: "Limite theologique et finitude phenomenologique chez Thomas d'Aquin" *Revue des sciences philosophiques et theologiques* 92/3 (2008), 527-556 (http://www.cairn.info/resume. php?ID_ARTICLE=RSPT_923_0527#hit1), *God, the Flesh and the Other* Ch. 7 et *Passer le Rubicon* (Par. 17 , Ch. 5.)

[83] One will find the lineaments of this double reversal in Th. de Regnon, Études de théologie positive sur la sainte Trinité, op. cit., t. II, pp. 455-458 (*principium quia primum*) and pp. 480-484 (*ideo Pater quia generat*).

[84] Thomas Aquinas, *S.th.*, Ia, q.33, a.4, ad.4, Fr. tr. (modified) (Cerf), t. I, p. 398.

Father, *is not a simple negation* (*non dicitur tantum negative*), but instead either includes the two aspects just identified (namely, that the Father is from no one, and that He is the principle of all others), or it evokes universal authority (*universalem auctoritatem*), or again his fontal plenitude as the source of all (*vel etiam fontalem plenitudinem*). *But, this does not seem correct* (*sed hoc non videtur verum*) … For, God being Source and *Author* (*fontalis et auctoritas*) means nothing other than for him to be the *principle of the origin* (*principium originis*).[85]

Having thus rejected the superiority of affirmation over negation and the primacy of the origin over the principle, Thomas somehow pushes back the origin of the principle over the principle of the origin (*principium originis*)—to the point of giving as the sole reason for its fountain-like character (*fontalitas*) only the principle (of the origin) that is its cause, and no longer its original act of self-begetting that puts it in motion: there is no source without a "source point" for the Angelic Doctor—even if emphasizing it hides the stream that issues forth from it. I note this opposition here only to bring to light the originality of the one (Bonaventure) without yet compromising the better-known grandeur of the other (Thomas); let me only add that Bonaventure's emphasis on *the origin at work in the work* makes the *work of the origin* all the more manifest than Thomas's *origin of the work*, in the opposite way, manages to do.

(b) As for the Father—still considering the differences between Thomistic and Bonaventurian theology—far from signifying precisely the flux that is given even in his *visibility* by the expressed work that is his Son, in Thomas the Father ends up as the static and enclosed pole in his *invisibility* (to which point I shall return in §11b) from which everything else is begotten and drawn. God is thus no longer "Father because he begets" (*pater quia generat*) and thus solely by virtue of his eternal generation of the Son, but on the contrary, "begetter because he is Father": "since he is a subsistent person," says Thomas, "we must reverse the formula (*oportet e converso*) and say—*because he is the Father, he begets* (*quia Pater est, generat*).[86] Thus, contrary to Bonaventure's account, the *relation* (being Father) becomes the reason for the *origin* (the act of begetting) from the moment when, according to a substantializing or presentifying logic confirmed by the editors of the *Summa Theologica*, one cannot reasonably conceive "that a person exists by the act, as

---

[85] Thomas Aquinas, *S.th.*, Ia, q.40, a.4, ad.1, Fr. tr. (Cerf), t. I, p. 397.

[86] Thomas Aquinas, *S.th.*, Ia, q.40, a.4, ad.1, Fr. tr. (modified) (Cerf), t. I, p. 438.

characteristic as it may be, that the person produces, because *to act it must first exist*" (our emphasis).[87] In short, as a "subsistent person," and in spite of the counterbalance that the notion of relation provides, the Father, if "orphaned" by his Son, would nonetheless paradoxically remain Father in order to retain himself in and from himself, in this hypostatic function:

> under the constituting aspect of the person of the Father, the re-
> lation must be *presupposed* in the notional act, as the person who
> acts is *presupposed* in his action (*sicut persona agens praeintelligitur
> actioni*).[88]

Rather than seeing *the work of the origin* and *the opening of the world* that it establishes in its self-begetting, Thomistic theology is anchored instead more in the *origin of the work* and the *principal mandate* of the entire created world that it governs. As principle of the origin (*principium originis*), God, in Thomas and in an Aristotelian way, always remains "first *principle*" in the initial sense of the "starting point of a thing's movement," and not "*first* principle," according to a very Dionysian tradition, as "superessential fecundity from which all paternity, in heaven and on earth, receives its being and its name."[89] The hypothesis mentioned elsewhere of a passage from technical control to mystical detachment in Bonaventure[90] finds an exemplary expression in the Trinitarian theology that lies at the heart of the gulf between the Seraphic and Angelic Doctors. It is not that Thomas, as I have said above,, considers intra-divine generation as a formal cause—far from it. But inasmuch as the very idea of fontality or of originality in God can always be led back to a principle of the origin (*principium originis*) by which the very one who brings forth or produces (i.e. the Father-principle) grounds his origin-hood not in begetting a Son, but on the contrary first in that he maintains himself in himself and by himself—as if independent of his Son. Diametrically opposed to Bonaventure's Trinitarian *a priori* is that which "everyone calls God" (*quod omnes dicunt Deum*), found at the end of each of Thomas Aquinas's

---

[87] J.-H. Nicolas, note on the *Summa Theologica* (Ia., q.40,a.4), op. cit. (Cerf), t. I, Note 7, p. 438.

[88] Thomas Aquinas, *S.th.,* Ia, q.40, a.4, resp., Fr. tr. (Cerf), p. 437 (my emphasis).

[89] Respectively, Aristotle, *Metaphysics*, Delta c.1, 1012b.34, op. cit. (Fr. tr. Tricot), t.I, p. 245: first definition of the *archê*; and Dionysius the Areopagite, *The Divine Names*, c.1, §4, 592a., in Œuvres complètes, op. cit., (Fr. tr. M. de Gandillac), p. 71: definition of the Trinity as superessential fecundity.

[90] RSPT, p. 31-34: "l'*epochê* sur le sensible: de l'emprise technique à la déprise mystique."

ways of reaching God's existence: it never designates the Trinitarian and specifically Christian relation of the Father to the Son, but rather only the first principle, the cause of all things as of himself (prime mover, first efficient cause, necessary Being, cause of perfection, and final end).[91] The *actuation* of the principle takes precedent over the *action* of begetting; the principle prefers to keep to himself rather than to empty himself (*kenosis*) immediately and constantly in another: it is an opposition between the metaphor of the "wellspring of grace" (Bonaventure) and the model of the "instrumental efficiency of the productionary type" (Thomas) that will also spill out elsewhere in the *Breviloquium* in its treatment of sacramental theology.[92]

Aquinas's work cannot be counted among the neutral theologies, for the Trinity itself is certainly there (q. 27-43), albeit in a different manner and only once the preamble of the *De Deo uno* is completed (q. 2-26). Nonetheless the project of the *Summa Theologica* considered broadly justifies this placement of the Thomistic account of Trinitarian action in opposition to the Bonaventurian perspective, insofar as it splits or at least runs the "risk of a disjunction" between the immanent Trinity (*ad intra*) and the economic Trinity (*ad extra*).[93] Precisely because the principle (*principium*) could, however, once again falsely hold the place of origin and be honored illegitimately by the displacement of the first (*primum*), Bonaventure deliberately presents the continued work of the unique *primacy* of God in opposition to the pure *principiality* of a divine "in itself":

---

[91] Thomas Aquinas, *S. Th.*, Ia, q. 2, a.3, resp., Fr. tr. (Cerf), t. I, pp. 172-173; and Marion, *L'idole et la distance*, op. cit., Biblio-essais, §2, pp. 24-28: "le Dieu de l'on-to-théologie" (the arbitrary character of the implicit consensus of that which "everyone calls God" and a critique of the tactical procedure of Thomism's five ways).

[92] Bonaventure, *Brev.* VI, 1, No. 5 (V, 265b), Fr. tr. p. 45: "it is not that grace is contained (*contineatur*) in them [viz. in the sacraments as *receptacles* and *causes* of grace] substantially (*substantialiter*), or that is produced causally (*nec causaliter*). These terms [*receptacles* and *causes*] come to them from the fact that it is in them and through them that, by a divine decree, on must *draw* grace (*oporteat hauriri*)." One will easily oppose here the Bonaventurian schema, with an "easy etiquette," of "occasional causality" (Mathieu, *Introduction au Brev. Vi,* ibid., p. 21) against the "schema of a productionist type of representation" developed by Thomas Aquinas in his clear movement from "dispositive causality" to "instrumental causality" (cf. Chauvet, L.-M., *Symbole et sacrement, une relecture sacramentelle de l'existence chrétienne*, Paris, Cerf, Cogitatio fidei No. 144, 1990, respectively pp. 26 and 21-25).

[93] M. Corbin, *Essai sur le mystère trinitaire*, Cahier de l'Institut catholique de Paris (1980), op. cit., pp. 29-31.

since the diffusion is supremely actual…God is always begetting (*semper generat*), has always begotten (*semper generavit*), and will beget forever (*semper generabit*).[94]

It is probably for this reason that, in his "Remarks on the Dogmatic Treatise 'De Trinitate' " (1967), Karl Rahner gives priority to the Seraphic Doctor instead of the Angelic Doctor, mentioning Bonaventure as the author of the Latin and Western theological tradition who best illustrates the axiom of the complete identity of the economic Trinity and the immanent Trinity, a theme Rahner picks up later in his *Foundations of Christian Faith* (1976).[95]

"No one *takes* except the one who receives (*nemo capit nisi qui accipit*)."[96] This paradigmatic statement, which, we have seen, already delimits the right relation of the theologian to the divine being in welcoming rather than circumscribing him, holds first of all for God himself: because the Father affirmatively gives and gives *himself* (*modus positionis*), as fountain-like fullness, the overflowing wellspring, he needs his Son as the receiver who alone is capable of integrally welcoming him in the excess of his giving.[97] And if theology, according to the *Breviloquium*, "*not only* treats of the creative God (*non tantum agit de Deo creatore*) *but also* of Creation and the creature (*sed etiam de creatione et creatura*),"[98] the reason is that the abundant givenness of the Father that is totally transmitted to his Son likewise specifies him who offers himself to a creature; this creature, however, in its finitude, can in turn only receive him imperfectly and incompletely.[99] The entirety of the Trinitarian movement of Bonaventure's theology is thus always opened toward "the world as the Creation of God" (*de creatura mundi*):[100] the

[94] Bonaventure, *Hex.* XI, 11, (V, 381b), Fr. tr. *Les six jours de la création*, op. cit., p. 282.

[95] K. Rahner, *Quelques remarques sur le traité dogmatique De Trinitate*, in Écrits théologiques, t.8, Paris, DDB, 1967, pp. 107-140, esp. pp. 112-113: "In the doctrine of creation, one can scarcely find today any mention of the Trinity (in contrast to older theology, e.g. in Bonaventure). It is thought that this silence is in fact legitimate, because the divine works *ad extra* are 'done in common' such that the world as creation cannot fundamentally present in itself any true sign of the intra-divine life of the Trinity." For the axiom of the identity of the economic Trinity and the immanent Trinity, see (from the same author) *Traité fondamentale de la foi* (1976), Paris, Centurion, 1983, pp. 160-162: "The history of the economic Trinity of salvation history *is* the immanent Trinity."

[96] Bonaventure, *It.* IV, 3 (V, 306b), Fr. tr. (modified) Duméry, p. 75.

[97] RSPT, pp. 20-25: "Le dépassement de la métaphysique: l'excès de la donation du Père."

[98] Bonaventure, *Brev.* I, 1, No. 2 (V, 210bb), Fr. tr. p. 61.

[99] RSPT, pp. 20-25 (ibid.), esp. pp. 21-22.

[100] Bonaventure, *Brev.* II, 1, No. 1 (V, 219a), Fr. tr. p. 55.

notional primacy of the Father relative to the Son and to the Spirit, in first pouring itself out in itself, has no other end but to pour itself out at the same time in an *essential* primacy with respect to the created world. In order to make visible this givenness of the Trinitarian being, whose simultaneously begetting and creating act is revealed as always exceeding and overflowing itself (going as far as necessarily self-emptying in its manifestation or mission), we should (a) take stock of how God "senses himself" or is auto-affective as Trinity by also letting himself be sensed by the believer (§8); and (b) define the proper modalities of this divine *"in-common"* such that from the sovereign love of "the lover" (*amans*) communicated to "the beloved" (*dilectum*) there also issues forth "another loved together" (*condilectum*) as a *community* at the source of every giving act (§9).

CHAPTER IV

THE "IN-COMMON" OF GOD
(*Brev.* I, 2)

A strictly linear order, following the *Breviloquium* step by step, would logically demand that we move from "the origin at work *in* the work" (Ch. III of this volume, *Brev.* I, 3-4) to its "Trinitarian manifestation" (Ch. V, *Brev.* I, 5). But this analysis would fail to take account, first of all, of the believer's own "sense of God," which is necessary for receiving any such manifestation of the Trinity, and, second of all, of the "divine community," or the love shared amongst the persons of the Trinity, the love by which they give their respective selves (*Brev.* I, 2). Thus, moving from the radical primacy of the Father (*Brev.* I, 3-4) back to the intimate sense of the divine circumincession (*Brev.* I, 2) does not imply a regressive movement through the text. It only means accepting theologically that the three persons of the Trinity might be said to be simultaneous and *in common* in the act of revelation, even if the third, the Holy Spirit, only comes into play starting from the consideration of the first two, the Father and the Son (§7). The "sense of God" takes place at the heart of this double examination (§8): first, in that the Father and the Son are themselves self-affective in a Trinitarian way, i.e. in a community of love and life, only in as much as they spirate the Holy Spirit together; and second, in that man only senses God to the extent that the Trinity itself "is sensed" and thus offers to the believer a *way of sensing* [*sentir*], or better of "re-affection" [*re(s)-sentir*]—if not *as* the Trinity does, at least *with* it.

§8. THE SENSE OF GOD

The first task that the *Breviloquium* sets out to accomplish is explaining "what is to be held and believed" (*hoc tenendum est*) about the Trinity of persons and the unity of essence (*Brev.* I, 2), a task it sets for itself from its opening, even before any "sound understanding" (*intelligentia sana*) of this faith in the Trinity (*Brev.* I, 3).[1] The reason is that the internal structure of each of its chapters, which draws a distinction between the utterance that must be believed (*hoc tenendum—intellegendum—est*) and the way it is "made explicit" (*ratio autem ad intelligentiam...*), spills over onto the structure of the whole exposition on the Trinity, which treats first of what should be believed (*Brev.* I, 2) and then of what should be understood (*Brev.* I, 3). Thus, we must first of all consider the Trinity from the point of view of faith, which some will call, in a very Bernardian vein, an "argument from piety" (*argumentum ex pietate*) (*Brev.* I, 2). Then, secondly, we will have to examine the meaning of a sound understanding of this faith—involving what are usually called "necessary reasons" of a rather more Anselmian sort (*rationes necessarias*) (*Brev.* I, 3). This two-pronged line of argumentation, which has already undergone historical examination,[2] covers the whole of the *Breviloquium* and demands (*dictat*) that its reader receive, before undertaking any theological work, a "sense of God" (*sentire de Deo*) so elevated and so pious that it even defines his very *style* or his *way of being*—permitting him to auto-affect himself through the Trinitarian mystery and the movement of circumincession:

> *in order* for our faith to have a *supremely elevated and pious* sense of God (*ut altissime et piissime sentiat*), God supremely communicates himself by eternally having a beloved (*dilectum*) and an-other-loved-together (*condilectum*), and hence God is One and Three.[3]

---

[1] Bonaventure, *Brev.* I, 2 (V, 210a), Fr. tr. p. 65: "Quid tenendum est de Trinitate personarum et unitate esentiae," and *Brev.* I, 3 (V, 211b), Fr. tr. p. 71: "De istius intelligentia sana."

[2] See especially Bougerol, *Introduction à l'étude de saint Bonaventure*, op. cit. (Desclée), pp. 122-127.

[3] Bonaventure, *Brev.* I, 2, No. 3 (V, 211a), Fr. tr. (modified) p. 67: I have modified the translation here of the first proposition, which in my opinion gives the wrong meaning. To translate *ut altissime et piissime sentiat* by "having thus a most high and most pious sense of God" (Mathieu) suggests a causal and inverted relationship of the sense or experience of faith and of the divine *condilectio*: it is not, as we shall see, *because* the believer has a most high and most pious sense of God that the latter communicates himself to him; rather, it is *in order* to confer on him a most high and most pious sense that God communicates himself to the believer. For Bonaventure, divine donation always takes priority, and is always at the root of any exercise of faith. [Tr. n.: the English translation in *The Works of St. Bonaventure* vol. IX (ed. Dominic Monti. NY: Franciscan Institute, 2005), translates the latin *sentire* as "to conceive": "Since faith is the source of our worship of God and the foundation of that doctrine which is in accord with piety, it dictates that we should conceive God in the most elevated and loving manner" (30). The French *sentir* means "to smell, to feel, to be aware of, to appreciate," as well as "to sense." It is usually translated into English here as "to sense" or "to feel," but the proximity of

A) NECESSARY REASONS AND THE ARGUMENT FROM PIETY

"Right faith" (*recta fides*) or "sound faith" (*sana fides*) is thus that which "dictates what must be held" (*hoc dictat esse tenendum*) on the subject of the Blessed Trinity.[4] In this *hoc tenendum* of the faith we can discern the whole originality of Bonaventure's exposition of theology, in particular with respect to Anselm and Richard of St. Victor: although the explanation of "necessary reasons" could be justly said to distinguish the theological tradition running from Anselm to Bonaventure (and sometimes against or apart from the way of "natural reason" privileged by Thomism),[5] the argument from piety that serves as its foundation rightly confers on Bonaventure's theology a humility in reason that probably also constitutes one of the originalities of his Franciscan project. Ever since Anselm and Richard of St. Victor, the term "necessary reasons" has usually been applied to the *rational* development or exposition of the mystery of salvation, starting from which, in virtue of right rationality, *faith alone* ratifies a certain type of *certitude* in the general comprehension of the economy of salvation: "it seems altogether impossible," Richard writes, here following Anselm, "that everything necessary [for the salvation of the human race] should not have a necessary reason [in theology or in the comprehension of this salvation]"—"*videtur autem omnino impossibile omne necessarium esse necessaria ratione carere.*"[6] Hence, against Hugh of St. Victor—though the latter was his master—Richard's radical rejection of the quadripartite division established in Hugh's *De Sacramentis* between reasons that are "necessary or proceed from reason" (*ex ratione*), affirmations that are "probable or in accordance with reason" (*secundum rationem*), propositions that are "admirable or beyond reason" (*supra rationem*), and statements that are "unbelievable or contrary to reason"

---

sense as "feeling" and sense as "meaning," and hence in relation to understanding should be kept in mind.]

[4] Bonaventure, *Brev.* I, 2, No. 2 (V, 210b-211a), Fr. tr. p. 65.

[5] Seen in particular (for the Anselmian roots of this conception and their legacy) R. Roques. *La méthode du Cur Deus homo de saint Anselme de Cantorbéry*, in *Structures théologiques, De la gnose à Richard de Saint-Victor*, Paris, éd. de la Bibliothèque de l'École des Hautes Études, 1962, pp. 243-293. As for Thomas Aquinas's reluctance to explain the Trinity by the argument from necessary reasons, see especially his response to Richard of St. Victor, *S.th.* Ia q. 32, a. 1, ad.2: "Given the Trinity, one can find fitting reasons (*congruunt huiusmodi rationes*); but these reasons do not suffice by themselves (*non sufficienter*) to demonstrate the Trinity of persons.

[6] Richard of St. Victor, *De Trinitate*, op. cit., (Cerf), L.I, c.4, 892c, p. 71 (as well as the note on pp. 465-468 on the meaning of necessary reasons in Richard).

(*contra rationem*).[7] *All* truths pertaining to the salvation of the human race *must*, in Richard's view as in Anselm's, correspond only to the first category—necessary reasons: "our aim in this book [*De Trinitate*] will be to present for the support of our faith reasons not only probable (*non modo probabiles*), but also necessary (*verum etiam necessarias rationes*)."[8]

Bonaventure's originality in this debate is not limited to the development of necessary reasons, which, as was shown elsewhere, provide the framework for the movement of the whole of the *Breviloquium*.[9] His special contribution amounts to establishing these necessary reasons themselves on the faith, not only as a principle of rationality (as Anselm and Richard did), but as "doctrine that accords with piety" (*secundum pietatem est doctrina*). Retaining, with Anselm, the demands of a rationality in faith, Bonaventure nonetheless grounds it, with Bernard of Clairvaux, on an attitude of *piety*, which alone can supply its key. Faith "demands," *dictat* in the *Breviloquium*'s words—like the *dictatio* of angelic knowledge so close in this regard to "divine sensing" (*It*. IV, 4)— the practice of a "sense of God" (*de Deo est sentiendum*) in which piety itself is founded (*fundamentum*) or rooted:

> faith, since it is the principle of the worship of God and the foundation of doctrine in accord with piety (*fundamentum eius quae secundum pietatem est doctrinae*), demands (*dictat*) that we have a most high and most pious *sense* of God (*de Deo esse sentiendum altissime et piissime*).[10]

What is called the "argument from piety" (*argumentum ex pietate*)— or rather what was given that name, probably wrongly, in spite of its rightful discovery (Guardini)—does not, properly speaking, constitute an argument.[11] Neither a purely rational aim nor a strictly exterior devotion, the "doctrine of piety" to which the experience of the divine belongs here (*de Deo sentiendum*) instead first implies the believer's *interior attitude*

---

[7] Hugh of St. Victor, *De Sacramentis christinae fidei*, Patrologie latine, Migne, 1854, vol. 176, Lib. I, part III, Ch. 30, col. 231: "alia enim sunt…ex ratione, alia secundum rationem, alia supra rationem, et praeter haec quae sunt contra rationem. Ex ratione sunt necessaria, secundum rationem sunt probabilia, supra rationem mirabilia, contra rationem incredibilia."

[8] Richard of St. Victor, *De Trinitate*, op. cit. (Cerf), L.I, c.4, 892c., p. 71.

[9] Bougerol, *Introduction générale au Breviloquium*, in *Brev*. prol. pp. 40-43 (where he rightly moves beyond Anselm's argument from necessary reasons by way of Bonaventure's analogy of faith).

[10] Bonaventure, *Brev, Brev*. I, 2, No. 3 (211a), Fr. tr. p. 67.

[11] R. Guardini, *Das Argumentum ex pietate beim hl. Bonaventura und Anselm Dezenzbeweis*, in *Theologie und Glaube*, Paderborn, No. 14, 1922, pp. 156-165.

(*sensus interior*), a *way of understanding* (*intelligendo*) *or of striving for God* [*de viser Dieu*]:[12] he must be an "adorer of God" (*cultorem Dei*), as the third lesson on the *Seven Gifts of the Holy Spirit* emphasizes, in order to "sense God (*sentire de Deo*) with reverence and fear (*cum reverentia et timore*)."[13] The "gift of piety" (*de dono pietatis*), by a blossoming of faith, leads the believer toward God as "all things tend naturally to their origins" (*naturaliter quaelibet res tendit ad suam originem*)—or better, as "the tree is united with its root" (*arbor continuatur cum radice*).[14] "Sensing God" (*sentire de Deo*), to put it in phenomenological terms, can first be "recognized as a *way* or a *style* ... before reaching a complete philosophical consciousness."[15] And the human being contemplates the mystery of the Trinity precisely, and paradoxically, by experiencing a *sensing* [*sentir*] of it (*sentiendum esse*)—or better, simply a "re-affection" [*re(s)-sentir*] even before any attempt to translate it into a *logos*.

For the believer to have a "sense of God" (*sentire de Deo*), as a dancer might be said to possess a "sense of rhythm," nevertheless does not yet mean here (in *Brev.* I) the sensory and fleshly incorporation of man in God (*sentire*)—which Bonaventure will later envision in an original way with his doctrine of the spiritual senses, but only after treating of the "incarnation of the Word" (*Brev.* IV).[16] In the kind of *sensing of God* that is in question here, only *feeling* or *affect* (*affectus*), and not the five senses converted in the crucible of faith (*sensus spirituales*), shows itself to be the privileged place of the human soul; it is here that all our affections, up to their culmination (*apex affectus*), are transformed by God:

---

[12] Bonaventure (or better the Pseudo-Bonaventure), *Commentarius in librum Sapientiae*, c.I, vers.1 (VI, 111a): "Monet autem ad bene sentiendum et sensu exteriore pie divinas Scripturas legendo, et sensu interiore pie intelligendo."

[13] Bonaventure, *Collationes de Donis Spiritus Sancti*, Fr. tr. Ozilou, *Les sept dons du Saint-Esprit*, Paris, Cerf, col. *Sagesse chrétienne*, 1997, third lectur, (The Gift of Piety), No. 5 (V, 469a), p. 74. As for the general meaning given to gift of piety in Bonaventure, see J.F. Bonnefoy. *Le Saint-Esprit et ses dons selon saint Bonaventure*, Paris, Vrin, 1929, pp. 144-151.

[14] Ibid.

[15] Definition of phenomenology as "style" cited in the Foreword of the present work, which I note again here in order to clarify the mode of being of the "sense or experience of God" for the believer (cf. Merleau-Ponty, *Phénoménologie de la perception*, op. cit., p. II).

[16] Bonaventure, *Brev.* V [The Grace of the Holy Spirit], 6, No. 6-7 (V, 259b-260a), Fr. tr. pp. 73-75: the twelve fruits of the Spirit and the five spiritual senses; and for commentary, see RSPT, pp. 25-34: "Extase et sens spirituels." The distinction between "sensing" by the organs of the body united to the soul and the "sense of God" experienced by the believer (*sentire de Deo*) is furthermore confirmed by Bougerol in *Lexique saint Bonaventure*, éd. franciscaines, Paris, 1969, p. 118: "Sentire."

in order to be perfect, in this passage [of the soul into excess (*ad excessum*)] one must leave behind (*relinquantur*) all the operations of the intellect, and the whole apex of affection (*apex affectus totus*) must be transported and transformed in God (*et transferatur et transformetur in Deum*).[17]

As the unitive power of the soul, before any differentiation of its functions (sensation, sentimental affectivity, act of intellection, etc), the *affectus* by which the believer senses "in accord with God" (*sentire de Deo*) is not opposed here to the *intellectus*; far from it. It precedes it only insofar as this "divine feeling" always goes ahead of its "articulation" or its "theology"—just as for Bonaventure, as a good mystic, a true "experiential knowledge of God" (*cognitio experimentalis*) necessarily precedes its rational formulation.[18] Thus, Jacques-Guy Bougerol says that "for Bonaventure, sensing God is at once believing in his existence and sensing his presence in an act that is as intellectual as it is affective."[19] The believer's feeling for God thus shows that the essential part of the Trinity's indwelling in its adorers does not consist first in its objectification in a purely theoretical knowledge or in a strictly empirical experience—not even one starting from necessary reasons. To experience God, or to sense in accord with God (*sentire de Deo*), refers on the contrary and above all else to an experience immanent to oneself—a sort of "auto-affection" by

---

[17] Bonaventure, *It.* VII, No. 4 (V, 312b) Fr. tr. (modified) op. cit. (Duméry), p. 103. Note 3, p. 103 rightly distinguishes the *affectus* from pure and simple sentimental affectivity. As for the distinction between "excess" (*excessus*) and "ecstasy" (*extasis*) that Duméry does not perceive here, see RSPT, pp. 26-31: "L'impossible identification: sens spirituels et ravissement extatique" (esp. p. 29).

[18] Bonaventure, *III Sent.*, d.24, dub.IV, resp. (III, 531a) : "Augustine speaks of the *experiential knowledge* (*loquitur de cognitione experimentali*) that we have of God, either in heaven or on earth…To whomever would object that he is knowable neither on earth nor in heaven, we respond that this is to be understood *above all* (*immo*) for our knowledge on earth. For this latter knows by degrees…We know God finally [in the last degree] by the soul's intimate union with him (*per intimam Dei unionem Dei et animae*), according to the Apostle's words: 'The man who unites himself to God becomes one spirit with him' (1 Cor. 6:17). And *the most excellent knowledge* (*et haec est cognitio excellentissima*), as Dionysius teaches, is that which resides in ecstatic love and which rises above the knowledge of faith that is common to all."

[19] Bougerol, *Sur le sens de Dieu*, in Études franciscaines, No. 14 (June 1964), pp. 23-30 (cit. p. 28, my emphasis). The Bonaventure exegete rightly adds the "affective" dimension of the sense and experience of the divine here, which Gilson does not notice here but which he nonetheless examines in his comments on the three meanings of *sentire* (but not the *sentire de Deo*) in Bonaventure: (a) to confirm the presence of a thing; (b) to know its particular nature; (c) and the faculty of sensing (cf. *La philosophie de saint Bonaventure*, op. cit. p. 281).

which "the living I," to put it again in phenomenological terms, "does not have an intentional aim, does not see, but feels."[20] Far from any sensation—the Word not yet being incarnate—the presence to self of the uncreated Trinity is experienced first of all as a "primitive sensing" or a feeling by which I cannot and must not detach myself from what I feel. The "sensing of God" (*de Deo esse sentiendum*) thus becomes "most high and most pious" in the *Breviloquium*, since it relates to—or better, by the sole intent of faith, adheres to—the Trinity: most high (*altissime*) in the necessity of believing that "God can communicate himself in the best way" (*posset se summe communicare*), and most pious (*piissime*) in the obligation to reject any god who, "though able to share himself, would not wish to" (*quod posset et nollet*).[21]

Besides the urgent necessity, taken up here from Richard of St. Victor, of holding together potential (power) and generosity (power and desire) in God,[22] this amphibology of the divine experience designates two particular modalities of believer's divine end, in that he submits himself, by his act of faith, to the specifically Christian "power" and "desire" of the Trinity's self-communication. Like the suspension of any objective statement in the form of *quid* on the Trinity (above, §4)—and extending it here, but this time from the believing subject's point of view—the "sense of God" contained in the doctrine of (or the argument from) piety indicates to the worshiper how he ought to sense God (honor, veneration, and praise), precisely in order to reveal to him how (*quomodo*) the Trinity itself remains the sole foundation of his faith:

> having the sense of God (*de Deo sentire*) amounts most of all to honoring him, venerating him, and praising him. Through this is revealed (*et ex hoc apparet*) *how* the faith in the Trinity (*fides Trinitatis*) is the foundation (*fundamentum*) and the root (*radix*) of divine worship and of the whole Christian religion (*et totius christianae religionis*).[23]

---

[20] M. Henry, respectively *L'essence de la manifestation*, Paris, PUF, 1965, t. I §31 and 36 (for auto-affection) and *Généalogie de la psychanalyse*, Paris, PUF, 1985, p. 29 (for primitive sensing and the *videre videor* in Descartes).

[21] Bonaventure, *Brev.* I, 2, No. 3 (V, 211a), Fr. tr. p. 67.

[22] Richard of St. Victor, *De Trinitate*, L. III, c.4, op. cit. (Cerf) pp. 175-177.

[23] Bonaventure, *De Mysterio Trinitatis*, q. 1, a.2, concl. (V, 55b-56a).

B) THE SENSE OF GOD, AND TRINITARIAN AUTO-AFFECTION

The "perfect sense of God" (*perfectus Dei sensus*) from the point of view of the faith—which is to say, one starting from a divine donation that is total and without reserve and by which God not only "can" but "wants" to communicate himself—thus invites us to "contemplate" the Holy Trinity (*facit nos contemplari*), to honor it, to venerate it, and to praise it, and takes us, still from the perspective of the believing subject, as far as associating it with a "tranquil state" (*statum quietum*) and a "joyful excess" (*excessum iucundum*).[24] There is thus no exceptional, mystical ecstasy, or divine rapture (*raptus*) in the "feeling of God" (*sentire de Deo*), but only the ordinariness of the Trinity, which gives itself to the faithful so that, in the movement of divine circumincession and in the unity of the human *affectus*, they might sense [*sente*] or "re-affect" [*re(s)-sente*] *as* the Trinity does, and *with* the Trinity.[25] It is for this reason that, for example, the author of the *Book of Wisdom* demands that his disciple be wed to the "sensing of the Lord" (*sentite de Domino*) in his good deeds (Ws. 1:1), or again that Paul advises the Philippians to have precisely the same "mind" or "attitude" in them (*sentite in vobis*) as that which is in Christ Jesus (Ph. 2:5).[26] It is thus probably *in order to* confer on faith "a sense of God" (*ut sentiat*) that, according to the *Breviloquium*, the Trinity "communicates itself in the best way" (*se summe communicare*) to man— and not the reverse: "faith in the Trinity" (*fides Trinitatis*)[27] indicates more the movement by which the Trinity bestows faith than it does a simple "natural" adhesion of the Christian to his dogma, even though it is manifestly essential to his doctrine. The community in God remains in service to communion with man, and the practice of faith in the act of piety only holds them together because God himself shares with man at

---

[24] Bonaventure, *Hex.* XXIII, 27 (V, 449a), Fr. tr. Ozilou, p. 507: "in the West we find the perfect sense of God (*est perfectus Dei sensus*), which teaches us contemplation (*et hic sensus facit noc contemplari*); with it is associated a state of tranquility and joyous excess (*et comites habet statum quietum et excessum iucundum*)."

[25] The meaning of *sentire* as "experiencing in oneself" or "having the experience of," here understood with respect to the Trinity, is found in Latin since the third century, starting with Novatien, *De Trinitate*, VIII (P.L.III): "every human soul senses God (*quem [Deum] mens omnis humana sentit*), even if it cannot express it (*etiamsi non exprimit*)." Cited by Blaise, A. *Dictionnaire latin-français des auteurs chrétiens*, Turnhout, Brepols, 1954¹, 1967², p. 735 col.a: art. "sentio."

[26] Vulgate, *op. cit. Vetus Testamentum* (Wisdom 1:1), p. 742: "sentite de Domino in bonitate, et in simplicitate cordis quaerite illum"; and *Novum Testamentum* (Ph. 2:5), p. 213: "hoc enim sentite in vobis, quod et in Christo Jesu."

[27] Titles of *Brev.* I, 3 (*De istius fidei intelligentia sana*) and *Brev.* I, 4 (*De istius fidei expressione catholica*).

least piety, if not faith—which latter point, however, has become one of the major themes of contemporary theology (cf. Balthasar).[28]

Better, "although (*quamquam*) God himself possesses all the noblest properties," according to the *Collations on the Seven Gifts of the Holy Spirit*, "he is nonetheless *most excellent* in the property of piety" (*excellentissimum tamen est in ista proprietate, scilicet pietatis*)."[29] As the *exemplary principle*, then, the Trinity paradoxically reveals itself in a final reflection or "re-flexion," or return to itself, as the place of God's sensing [*sentir*] or "re-affection" [*re(s)-sentir*] of himself—that of God by God. The piety practiced by the believer in his experience of the divine, then, belongs specifically to the movement of the Holy Trinity itself, which confers this piety on man with the Trinity's own feeling. Put differently, and more trivially, man only senses "in accord with God" (*sentire de Deo*) because God first senses and experiences *himself*—which alone is precisely what makes possible the discernment of all "Life" (purely divine or properly human) as an expression and auto-affection of the Trinity in itself.[30] "The book of *life* (*liber vitae*)," as Bonaventure writes in the *De Mysterio Trinitatis*,

> explicitly and expressly bears by itself and in itself irrefutable witness to the eternal Trinity (*testimonium irrefragibile Trinitati aeternae*) for those who see the face of God revealed (*revelata facie*) in the glory of their heavenly homeland (*in patria*) while still living here below (*in via*), according to their capacity to receive this light (*secundum influentiam lucis cuius capax est anima in statu viae*).[31]

Jacques-Guy Bougerol says that "Bonaventure uses the term *book of life* because it in some way shows that *God gives himself of himself in the*

---

[28] Balthasar, *La foi du Christ*, Paris, Cerf, col. Foi Vivante, 1994, pp. 13-79. The perspective of "Christ's faith" is obviously absent in Bonaventure, for whom faith, as in all medieval theology, primarily designates at least negatively a privation of supernatural light, of which Christ constitutes the exemplary exception. On this point, see for example *III Sent.* d. 24, a.2, q.3, concl. (III, 522b): "scientia apertae comprehensionis non compatitur secundum fidem."

[29] Bonaventure, *Collationes de Donis Spiritus Sancti*, col. III, No. 11 (V, 470b-471a), Fr. tr. (ibid.), p. 80.

[30] Cf. Henry, *C'est moi la vérité*, Paris, Seuil, 1996, p. 47: definition of (divine) Life as "auto-affection" or "self-revelation." A directly Trinitarian translation of this can be found in my book *Le passeur de Gethsémani...*, op. cit. pp. 132-133: "destitution and auto-affection."

[31] Bonaventure, *De myst. tr.*, q.1, a.2 ("utrum Deum esse trinum sit verum credibile"), concl. (V, 55b-56a).

intimacy of our selves by the fact that life is the light illuminating each man who comes into this world."[32] By this double auto-affection of God by God, *in himself* and *in man*, the praying worshiper comes to espouse the *style* or *way* in which God auto-affects himself in his own mode of feeling—revealed in his Trinitarian cirucmincession and all the more obvious for making himself *"feel incarnate being"* in the Word made flesh and *"sensibly perceived"* by the operation of the conversion of the senses.[33]

All divine experience, then, always presupposes a divine "in-common" or "being-with" by which its very being is nourished by this community where a lover (*amans*), a beloved (*dilectum*), and another-loved-together (*condilectum*) circulate together. Far from being denied by the *manner* of (and not by the argument from) piety, the "necessary" reasons, become all the more necessary for Bonaventure because they are first rooted in God himself, who inscribes them in the depths of the believer's faith. As a tiny receptacle for a piety that in reality does not belong to him, the believer who senses God (*sentire de Deo*) reminds us, always implicitly, as if in counter-relief, and contrary to any rational dialectic separated from a true Trinitarian *affectus*, that "no one knows what is in God (*quae sunt Dei nemo scit*) but the Spirit of God (*nisi spiritus Dei*)" (1 Cor. 2:11).[34] This divine *perscrutatio*, offered to man as a pneumatological deepening of the "secrets and depths of God,"[35] invites theologians to interrogate the meaning of this divine community, in which the Holy Spirit both opens and sustains the binding link (*nexus*) between the members—for he himself *is* this link, which we *receive* and in which we share.

c) The Divine Being-with

"The Father loves *himself* (*amat se pater*), the Son loves *himself* (*amat se Filius*), and each loves the other (*et alter alterum...*): it is absolutely

---

[32] Bougerol, *Sur le sens de Dieu*, op. cit. p. 24. As for the general meaning of "book of life," esp. in the *Breviloquium*, see Bonaventure, *Brev.* VII, 1, NO. 3 (V, 282a), Fr. tr., p. 59; and for commentary, Rauch, W. *Das Buch Gottes*, München, Max Hueber Verlag, 1961, S.239-256: "Das Buch des Lebens."

[33] RSPT, pp. 25-34: "Extase et sens spirituels." The almost carnal "sensing" or "experiencing" (*sentire*) of God in the conversion of the senses (*Brev.* V, 6) can thus also be understood as a sort of Incarnation in the Word made flesh (*Brev.* IV) of the "sense of God" (*sentire de Deo*) that is experienced in the soul's contact with the Trinity.

[34] Quoted by Bonaventure, *It.* IV, 8 (V, 308a), Fr. tr. p. 81.

[35] Bonaventure, *I Sent.*, *Proemium* (I, 5b): "ille enim est praecipuus *perscrutatior* secretorum et profundorum, secundum quod dicitur primae ad Corinthios secundo: *Spiritus omnia perscrutatior, etiam profunda Dei*" (1 Cor. 2:10). See on this point my article "Le *proemium* du *Commentaire des Sentences* ou l'acte phénoménologique de la *perscrutatio* chez saint Bonaventure."

the same one who loves and is loved (*omnino idipsum*) in the Father and in the Son."[36] This statement of Anselm's, which Bonaventure explicitly denounces on account of the fact that the love of self (each loves *himself*) always precedes the love of the other in the identity of their common love (each loves the other), highlights the advance that Bonaventure's treatment of the Trinity would later make in claiming that the act of loving is immediately and exclusively directed to the love of the other:

> the love which is the Holy Spirit does not proceed from the Father insofar as the Father loves himself (*non procedit a Patre, in quantum amat se*), nor from the Son insofar as the Son loves himself (*nec a Filio in quantum amat se*), but insofar as each loves the other (*sed in quantum unus amat alterum*).[37]

The opposition could not be clearer, in spite of a certain psychologism necessary at least for its pedagogical value: either the Holy Spirit is born first of all from the *love of self*—with each divine person loving himself first, and his love then being shared with another by loving him—or he proceeds from the persons' *mutual love*—with one loving the other precisely in renouncing his own self-love. These two teachings, derived from the two opposing interpretations of the *De Trinitate* of Augustine that Peter Lombard's *Sentences* offered to medieval students of theology,[38] certainly present "two irreducible types of Trinitarian theology": one founded on the individual and psychological analogy of the mind (*mens*) knowing and loving itself in its nature, the other on the social and amical analogy of the exchange of friendship (*amicitia*) between two persons or between two spouses.[39] Everything depends, then, on what "to love" really means—in theology as in phenomenology.[40] Bonaventure, for one, opts deliberately for the second model, the social and amorous analogy, as the *Breviloquium* attests in exemplary fashion:

[36] Anselm of Canterbury, *Monologion*, op. §51, Fr. tr. M. Corbin, t.I, p. 161: "That each is loved by and loves the other with an equal love."

[37] Bonaventure, *I Sent.*, d.13, a.un., q.1, f.4 (I, 231a).

[38] Peter Lombard, *Sententiae in IV Libris distinctae*, Spicilegium bonaventurianum, Grottaferrata, 1971, Liber I, dist. 10, t. I, pp. 110-114.

[39] T.L. Pénido. *Gloses sur la procession d'amour dans la Trinité*, in *Ephemerides theologicae Lovanienses*, t. XIV, 1937, pp. 33-66 (passage cited p. 48).

[40] For what is of phenomenological relevance here, we lean here on Lévinas, E. *Totalité et infini, Essai sur l'extériorité* (1971), Paris, Biblio-essais, 1992, first part, pp. 21-108: "The same and the other"; as well as Marion, *L'intentionnalité de l'amour (en hommage à Emmanuel Lévinas)*, in *Prolégomènes à la charité*, Paris, éd. La Différenc, 1986, pp. 91-120.

God supremely communicates himself by eternally having a beloved (*dilectus*) and another-loved-together (*condilectus*).[41]

Moreover, as we have just seen, divine affection as defined here
has no other end but to offer itself to man, insofar as it appears first
to the believer only *in order* to confer on his faith a "sense of God" (*ut
sentiat*). The fact that there is an act of begetting in God satisfies not
only the requirements of communicability (God "can" communicate
himself and "wants" to do so [see above]), but also opens the path toward
a community at the heart of which man himself can take (his) part—
though always through the Son of Man. That by which we sense God,
and which makes him sense *himself* first, takes priority in the community
of love that makes him knowable. In this context, Bonaventure draws on
St. John: "he who does not love does not know God, since God is love
(*quoniam Deus caritas est*)" (1 Jn. 4:8).[42]

The love by which we love ourselves is thus always somehow, although
to a lesser measure, the love by which God loves *himself*—precisely the
love in which we are also, in some way, integrated into the movement of
his Trinitarian circumincession:

the Holy Spirit is the love (*dilectio*) by which the Father and the
Son love each other (*se invicem*) and love *us* (*nos diligunt*).[43]

In other words, it is because God loves himself and experiences
himself as "love" (*caritas*) in the motion of the Trinity that he can be
re-affected [*re(s)-sentir*] by humanity in humanity's own mode of loving
itself.[44] In short, instead of loving himself first for himself, he loves

---

[41] Bonaventure, *Brev.* I, 2, No. 3 (V, 211a), Fr. tr. p. 67.

[42] Passage cited and discussed by Bonaventure, *Collationes in Ioannem*, col. 52, No.
4 (VI, 602a).

[43] Bonaventure, *I Sent.* d. 10, dub. 3 (I, 206a). In this formula, Bonaventure considers only the love by which God loves himself and us. It is thus a question there of the
uncreated *habitus* of charity or of the Holy Spirit, even though, from the human point
of view, we can only love God through a created *habitus*. See on this point Bonaventure's
long discussion on the Lombard's perspective, *I Sent.*, d. 17, p. I, a.un., q.1 (I, 292-
296): "utrum praeter caritatem increatem poni debeat habitus caritatis creatus"; as well as
Mathieu's commentary on this difficulty in *La Trinité créatrice d'après saint Bonaventure*,
op. cit. pp. 265-269.

[44] We will return later to the different meanings of *caritas* in Bonaventure in the
distinction between *erôs* and *agapê* (below, §9b). Tr. N.: *ressentir* in French can be simply
"to feel," but *re-* also retains the Latinate sense also found in English of a repetition.
Re(s)-sentir is meant to convey two meanings: *ressentir*, "to feel (again)" and "to feel the
res, the 'thing' the 'reality'," namely, God. Re(s)-sentir stands for the repetition of God's
auto-affection on the human plane, in humanity and for humanity, but also, at the same

himself paradoxically first *for us*—allowing us to participate in the *way* or the *style* in which he loves himself. Using a psychologism inherited from Richard of St. Victor, Bonaventure does need the model of human love to represent the Trinity: not, however, to extrapolate from it (as Richard did), but on the contrary to show how the human model is able to express itself beginning only with the *exemplar* that is God himself. In other words, man cannot and must not love himself other than in the manner in which God loves himself—and not the other way around. Several forms of love are thus to be distinguished here, at least in God, according to Bonaventure—and of which the degrees grow in proportion to the forgetfulness of self in the donation to another: "reflexive love" (*dilectio reflexa*), "in which it is me whom I love" (*qua me diligo*); "mutual love" (*dilectio connexiva*), "in which I love another" (*qua alterum diligo*); and the "charitable love" (*dilectio caritativa*), which "knows a Beloved and a Co-Beloved" (*quae habet dilectum et condilectum*). This last form of love, the Seraphic Doctor adds, "is more perfect than the two others" (*perfectior ceteris est*); "it is thus found in God" (*ergo haec est in divinis*).[45]

Developed consistently from the first book of the *Commentary on the Sentences* (d. 10) through the *Hexaemeron* (XI, 12) and, in passing, in the *Breviloquium* (I, 2) and the *Itinerarium* (VI, 2), the thesis that Bonaventure inherits from Richard of St. Victor (below, §9c) of charitable love or condilection—by which the Father and the Son together know a "Co-Beloved" (*con-dilectum*)—very clearly supplies, for Bonaventure, the key to opening the Trinitarian structure to the sensible world, thus avoiding the dual pitfalls, which are also henceforth to be stigmatized, of divine autarky in the love of self and of splitting the *esse* from the *operari* in the donation to the other. Richard, the chief author of this thesis, thus ends up supplying the lineaments of a true *intentionality of love in God*, precisely, as will be shown, proceeding from an interrogation of scholastic theology (in particular of Anselm and Thomas Aquinas), such that, in order to form a divine community of love, it will suffice neither (a) to love oneself, nor (b) to love another in oneself, nor again (c) to love oneself in the other.[46]

---

time, in and for God: humanity's experience of itself and of God through that experience is a share in God's Trinitarian affectivity. Hence re(s)-sentir as "re-affection." Its consonance with "auto-affection" should be underlined.

[45] Bonaventure, *Hex.* XI, 12 (V, 382a), Fr. tr. Ozilous, op. cit., p. 283.

[46] I transpose here, in an immediately theological and Trinitarian context, the categories of an autistic account of love ("loving the other in me") and a self-idolatrous account of love ("loving myself in the other"), which Jean-Luc Marion develops in *L'intentionnalité de l'amour*, in *Prolégomènes à la charité*, op. cit., pp. 91-120 (esp. pp. 95-98): "l'autisme amoureux."

§9. CONDILECTION OR ANTI-JEALOUSY IN GOD

A) THE IMPASSES OF LOVE

(a) All theologians, including those who tend to privilege the love of self over the love of the other, agree in emphasizing that it obviously is not enough for the divine persons to love themselves in the same way in order to make sense of the triune God: if the Father loves *himself* and the Son loves *himself*, "*each loves the other*," Anselm insists.[47] Self-love or "reflexive love" (*dilectio reflexa*) is necessarily accompanied by mutual love or "connective love" (*dilectio connexiva*), at the risk, on the other hand, of getting lost as love. The constitution of a designated alterity does, in fact, make the act of loving more than a simple desire; it always addresses an injunction to someone (*alicui*), in the very relation of donor to receiver. As Thomas says,

> to love is nothing other than to desire the good for someone (*amare nihil aliud sit quam velle bonum alicui*).[48]

In this sense, the difficulty of explaining the Trinity no longer lies in explaining the love of the first person (the Father) for the second (the Son): whereas the *origin at work in the act* determined the relation of expression of the Father to the Son (§7), only the procession of the third (the Holy Spirit)—or "charitable love" (*dilectio caritativa*)—can meet the demands of a delimitation of an *"in-common" of God* in which the believer, too, participates by his divine sense (§8).

(b) Can the procession of the third person, then, be freed of the simple relational mutuality of the first and the second? In other words, is it still enough here, as it was for Anselm, to posit the absolute identity of a single love (*omnino idipsum*) of the Father and the Son in order to form their community *as* a community, in the Holy Spirit? The question is a serious one: it forces us to look closely not only at the Trinity but rather at *all* alterity, all otherness, once (as we have seen) the equality of the divine persons and the identity of their nature are admitted or "saved" (*salva*). Indeed, the whole paradox of the Trinity in God, as of alterity in man, consists precisely in the fact that for there to be *two* persons, there must in fact be at least *three*. This point takes us away from Anselm's Trinity,

---

[47] Anselm of Canterbury, *Monologion*, op. cit., §51, Fr. tr. Corbin, t.I, p. 161.
[48] Thomas Aquinas, *S.th.* Ia., q.20, a.2, resp., Fr. tr. (modified) (Cerf), t. I, p. 310.

where the identity of the love of self and the love of the other are what make up the community of the Trinity; and it likewise takes us away from Husserl's constitution of alterity, too, where it is only the goal of a *common world* (*Vergemeinschaft*) that opens the way to an encounter of the *ego* and the *alter ego*, in virtue of which they do not obscure or plunge each other into a total estrangement.[49] For Husserl, however, the aim of the other in man, like the other in God for Anselm, amounts only to "loving the other in oneself"—which Jean-Luc Marion stigmatizes in the human subject as "amorous autism."[50] In fact, whether I reduce the other to just the lived experiences of my consciousness (Husserl), or whether the Father and the Son only love each other in the love of themselves and the identity of the each person's nature (Anselm), it is always—in the human mode as in the divine—*my* love that I love: "I see not him, but the sum of the lived experiences [the loved love (*amare amabat*), I would dare to add here in an Augustinian vein], of which he is only the occasional cause and of which my consciousness is the real measure."[51] Only the loving subject and his love of self are established on a single norm of all love—and this in proportion to his unique capacity to love. Anselm asks:

> what is then the grandeur of this supereminent love that *in this way is common* (*sic communis*) to the Father and to the Son? But if he loves *himself* (*se diligit*) as much as he remembers *himself* and recognizes *himself* (*sui neminit et se intelligit*), if he remembers *himself* and recognizes how great *his* essence is … *his* love (*amor eius*) is assuredly as great *as he himself* (*ipse*) is great.[52]

Thus, Anselm declares self-love—or better, the love of *the* self or of *oneself*—to be the only norm in loving. Love that is common (*sic communis*) to the lover and the beloved finds the reason for its existence in the self's capacity to reflect *itself* (*ipse*) and *its own love* (*amor eius*). The Father and the Son love *themselves* not first by a common attraction toward another or a third (the Holy Spirit), but only, and in order of

---

[49] Husserl, *Méditations cartésiennes* (1929), Paris, Vrin, 1980, §55, pp. 102-109 (esp. p. 102) : the community of monads and the first form of objectivity. For the possibility of a theological reinterpretation of the phenomenological schema of the community of monads, see my article *L'altérité angélique ou l'angélologie thomiste au fil des Méditations cartésiennes de Husserl*, in *Laval théologique et philosophique* (Oct. 1995), t.51, No. 3, pp. 625-646 (esp. pp. 641-646: "Vers un monde commun de l'ange à l'homme").

[50] Marion, *L'intentionnalité de l'amour*, op. cit., pp. 95-98.

[51] Ibid., p. 97.

[52] Anselm of Canterbury, *Monologion*, Fr. tr. Corbin, Paris, Cerf, 1986, t.I, §52, p. 161.

priority, in the recognition of their common essence. The *other* is thus always reduced to *the same*—in the double sense of the identity of nature and of the banality of repetition—in first loving only in himself.[53] In phenomenology (Levinas) and in Trinitarian theology (Bonaventure) the other cannot and must not end up in the sphere of the *same*. Would leaving behind the *aporias* of the *same* amount only to inverting the terms radically, i.e. by loving oneself in the other more than loving the other in oneself, and by preferring the reflected image of one's own love in the other over the image of the other imprisoned in oneself?

(c) In Thomas, loving love in loving *oneself* first, as in Anselm, and the other *next*, will probably no longer suffice to constitute a community of intra-divine love. Loving is in reality always addressed to *someone* (*alicui*), as we have followed Thomas in observing, and no one truly loves in this sense, since, in a purely anonymous fashion, he only loves love – like a pure will that appropriates its object to itself and only loves withn itself. For Thomas, then, far from any appropriation of the other into the self, true divine love actually means "the *relation* of the Father to the Son (*habitudo Patris ad Filium*), and conversely (*et e converso*), as the relation of the lover to the beloved (*ut amantis ad amatum*)."[54] One would certainly be wrong, following a somewhat arbitrary separation of the "static character of peripatetic metaphysics" from the "dynamic character of Dionysian metaphyics," not to see first in Aquinas the properly "ecstatic" dimension of the reciprocal love of the Father for the Son (*ad Filium*) in the Holy Spirit.[55] It remains the case, however, that this ecstasy somehow always has its wings clipped in Aquinas, who deliberately forces all *notional* reciprocity of the Father and Son back to the *essential* love of self that is always supposed to be its foundation:

> it is *not only his Son* (*non solum Filium*) whom the Father loves by the Holy Spirit, but also *himself* (*sed etiam se*) and us (*et nos*).[56]

Thus, although Thomas follows Bonaventure (and Dionysius) in affirming an ecstatic love of the Father and of the Son, his line of thinking nevertheless always redirects, in an Anselmian way, the ecstatic movement from the affirmation of the divine persons to the prioritized

---

[53] We take up here again Lévinas's famous categories of the critique of metaphysics. See Lévinas, *Totalité et infini*, op. cit., pp. 21-208 (and esp. pp. 33-34): "Le même et l'autre."

[54] Thomas Aquinas, *S.th.* Ia, q.37 a.1 ad.3, Fr. tr. (modified) (Cerf), t.I, p. 415.

[55] Th. de Regnon, Études de théologie positive sur la sainte Trinité, op. cit., t. II, pp. 448-451.

[56] Thomas Aquinas, *S.th.*, Ia, q.37 a.2, ad.3, Fr. tr. (Cerf), t.I, p. 417.

love of their essence. Let me dare to transpose here certain philosophical categories onto schemas that are above all theological, and to say that a certain form of *auto-idolatry*—in which it is only myself that I love in the other (Thomas)—follows from an *autistic love*—by which it is only *within myself* that I love the other (Anselm).[57] So, when, the Father first loves the Son by the Holy Spirit *essentially* (*Pater et Filius se Spiritu Sancto*), he loves himself, as I have said—since the loving is addressed to someone (*alicui*) and does not merely love the identity and the community of love (Anselm)—but he only loves inasmuch as his love reflects first the *me* of his own *essence* (*essentia sua*) as found in his beloved:

> if loving (*diligere*) is taken as an essential attribute, it means that the Father and the Son love each other, not by the Holy Spirit (*non diligunt se Spiritu Sancto*), but rather *by their own essence* (*se essentia sua*).[58]

Because "the beloved is in the loving as the known is in the knowing," according to an obvious representative or intellective reduction of the other to the same in Thomas (*amatum dicitur esse in amante sicut et intellectum in intelligente*), the name of Love (*amor*) properly describes (*proprium nomen*) the Holy Spirit.[59] The gift (*donum*) thus proceeds from love but does not produce it. In fact, Love is "the principle of free givenness" (*ratio autem gratuitae donationis est amor*), in precisely the sense in which love *is* or *makes* the gift, more than that the gift *gives* love.[60]

B) EROS AND AGAPÊ

In his *Commentary on the Sentences*, on the other hand, Bonaventure slights essential love by describing what it "merely" (*sed solum*) amounts to being, and in so doing implicitly prefers notional love:

---

[57] For the meaning of auto-idolatry as love of oneself in the other, see Marion, *L'intentionnalité de l'amour*, op. cit., pp. 96-97.

[58] Thomas Aquinas, *S.th.* Ia., q.37 a.2, resp., Fr. tr. (Cerf), t.I, p. 416.

[59] Thomas Aquinas, *S.th.* Ia., q.37 a.1, resp., Fr. tr. (Cerf), t.I, p. 414.

[60] Thomas Aquinas, *S.th.* Ia q.38 a.2 ("utrum Donum sit proprium nomen Spiritus Sancti"), resp., Fr. tr. (Cerf), t. I, p. 419. On Aquinas's exemplary reversal of the primacy of the gift over love in Bonaventure (where a subsistent Love now takes priority over the gift), see Bonnefoy's valuable analysis in *Le Saint-Esprit et ses dons selon saint Bonaventure*, op. cit., pp. 28-35.

essential love does not indicate a *movement proceeding out from the lover* (*non dicit egressum ab amante*), but only (*sed solum*) a deference of the will (*complacentiam voluntatis*) by which each person loves and is loved.[61]

Although Bonaventure would preserve here a certain form of essential love in God, the divine persons are bound primarily by the mode of the will—thus forbidding, in a very Franciscan line of thought, any identification of the act of loving and the act of knowing. The Father and the Son are essentially united to each other first by "deference" (*complacentia*) in the sense in which one necessarily *wants* that which the other also *wants*. Only an amorous tendency, the reciprocal ecstasy of the lover toward the beloved, can in reality make sense of this union of wills. Notional love (of persons between each other) thus grounds essential love (each person's love of self), and the departure from the self toward the other is here such that the motive of desire (*desiderium*), or the dimension of *eros*, initiates also in God the chain of love:

> desire (*desiderium*) has as its principal object that which moves or excites it the most (*quod maxime ipsum movet*); now, that which moves it the most (*maxime autem movet*) is that which it loves the most (*quod maxime amatur*).[62]

The tension from the beloved toward the lover and from the lover toward the beloved is thus that which, in God as in humanity that carries his image in tending toward him, "excites and moves him the most" or "puts him in motion" (*maxime movet*). The love of the Father and the Son, far from being satisfied with their static mutuality, grows instead in proportion to their propensity to tend toward each other. Here, desire pours forth into another and produces love, not the opposite. Instead of a conception in which love *is* or *makes* the gift, here the gift *gives* love. There is no *subsistent Love*, in Bonaventure, apart from the Gift that gives it: "whereas the name of Gift is posterior to that of Love in Thomistic exposition, it is anterior to it in the Bonaventurian system."[63]

Because God, in himself, is defined above all as a desiring being in his tendency toward another, no man is his image if he does not also ready himself to become a "man of desire" (*vir desideriorum*)—like the prophet

---

[61] Bonaventure, *I Sent.*, d.10, a.2, q.1, ad.4 (I, 201b).

[62] Bonaventure, *It.* III, 4 (V, 305a), Fr. tr. Duméry, p. 69. This is a formula of desire that is first applied to man insofar as he tends toward God, but it also befits God himself, insofar as it is in this very way that man bears God's image. (ibid.).

[63] Bonnefoy, *Le Saint-Esprit et ses dons selon saint Bonaventure*, op. cit., p. 34.

Daniel.[64] In man as in God, no pure love can be satisfied with a kind of indifference toward its object, an indifference by which love amounts to a fiction. The purity of divine love implies its total gratuity and its absolute superabundance rather than some probably inconceivable detachment: "the opposition frequently raised between *eros* and *agapê* thus indicates above all a misunderstanding that sterilizes them both: benevolence (*agapê*) only loves if its detachment does not make it indifferent, but rather transfers it toward what it desires (*eros*).[65]

Only the univocity of love in God, in the impossible separation of *eros* and *agapê*, frees any schema of the Trinity from both its latent autism (loving the other in oneself) and its closeted auto-idolatry (loving oneself in the other). Assured first, and principally, of the real identity of the forms of divine love in the act of their motion (*una et eadem in affectione*), Bonaventure goes on to distinguish, strictly notionally (*ratione*), several forms of divine love: love (*amor*), dilection (*dilectio*), and charity (*caritas*).[66] Far from any sort of divine impassability, the Father in this sense *wants* to beget the Son, the Son *wants* to spirate the Spirit (with his Father), and the whole entire Trinity *wants* to pour itself out into Creation. The superabundance of this metaphysical Desire— that which "tends toward something completely other" and never "revels" or "delights" in the poverty of need—belongs first to God himself: the "desire for the invisible" paradoxically *makes visible*, in my opinion, the dimension of desire, in particular when it presents itself in the very depths of Trinitarian auto-donation or self-giving, which is to say in a Christian way, and no longer a strictly Judaic one (Levinas).[67]

---

[64] Bonaventure, *It.* Prol. No. 3 (V, 296a), Fr. tr. Duméry, p. 23: "furthermore, in order to be made apt to contemplate God and in order to reach the fullness of ecstasy, one must be, like Daniel, a man of desire (*vir desideriorum*)" (a reference to Dn. 9:23).

[65] Marion, "Ni passion, ni vertu," in the journal *Autrement*, Série Morales, No. 11 (Apr. 1993), La charité, pp. 240-243 (cit. p. 242). A restatement of the necessity of the univocity of love can be found again, albeit in a paradoxically less theological and Trinitarian way, in the same author's "*La connaissance de la charité*," in Communio, t. XIX, No. 6 (Nov.-Dec. 1994), pp. 27-42.

[66] Bonaventure, *I Sent.*, d. 10, dub. 1 (I, 205a): "love (*amor*), dilection (*dilectio*) and charity (*caritas*) are distinguished according to their concept (*ratione*), although they might be said to be one and the same thing according to affection (*quamvis enim de una et eadem possint dici in affectione*)." From the mere perspective of reason, Bonaventure thus distinguishes love (*amor*) as "the adhesion of the affect to the beloved" (*affectus ahesionem respectu amati*); dilection (*dilectio*) as that which "adds the character of choice" (*hoc addit electionem*); and charity (*caritas*) as that which "adds its great nobility" (*addit magnam appretationem*).

[67] Lévinas, *Totalité et infini*, op. cit. (Biblio-essais), pp. 21-24: "Désir de l'invisible" (the opening of the work). The category of the "superabundance of desire" as opposed to the "indigence of need" obviously stems, as so often with Lévinas, from the Biblical cor-

Neither pure love of oneself, nor love of the other in oneself (Anselm), nor love of oneself in the other (Thomas): none of these three modes of Trinitarian loving are appropriate, at least from Bonaventure's perspective, to form the *how* (*qualiter*) of divine circumincession, nor to make any sense of it. Beyond the urgent necessity of first interrogating the love in God in order to be able to understand the love in man—since the entirety of Creation is contained and reflected in his mirror (*in speculo*) (cf. p. 77)—we must find a new way to interrogate his *condilectum*, or the Co-Beloved through whom he forms a community, senses and experiences himself as such, and communicates to us his divine awareness (*Brev.* I, 2).

c) From "Common Friend" to "Loving-in-common"

It is well known that *condilectio* is a neologism that was invented by Richard of St. Victor. Its original meaning is the "joy for God," but it also implies the extreme difficulty for humans to share the mutual love that *two* have for each other with a *third*:

> when a being gives his love to another, and when he loves this other exclusively, there is *dilection* (*dilectio*) but not condilection (*sed condilectio non est*)…There is rightly said to be *condilection* (*condilectio autem jure dicitur*) when two who are in love then love a third in a concord of dilection (*concorditer diligitur*), in a sociality of love (*socialiter amatur*) and when the affections of the first two are unified in the conflagration of love that they have for the third.[68]

Here, truly loving in God is no longer the pure love of self, nor is it the love of the self in the other, nor love of the other in the self; it is rather an interweaving of the aims of the love of self and the love of the other, such that their sharing with a third becomes the indication of the superabundance of their common love. We can discern a *haecceity*, a "thisness" or "particular character," of divine love in the distinction of

---

pus. A particularly Christian and Trinitarian perspective, however, permits us to integrate the dimension of metaphysical desire into God himself (in the relationship of the Father to the Son, spirating the Holy Spirit), and thus not limiting it to the relationship between God and Creation alone (in the interpretation of the account in *Genesis*, for example). For a discussion of the impossibility of incorporating Lévinas's thought too immediately into Christian theology, see my work *Le Passeur de Gethsémani*, op. cit., pp.131-133 ("Altérité et fraternité") and pp. 167-169 ("L'insubstituable substitution").

[68] Richard of St. Victor, *De Trinitate*, op. cit. (Cerf), L. III, c.19, 927b, Fr. tr. (modified), p. 209. For the particularly and specifically Ricardian origin of this neologism, see Note 2, p. 192: "The word *condilectus*, which seems to be a creation of Richard's…"

persons—as of human love in the necessity of alterity or otherness—all the more clearly in Trinitarian theology by the fact that the Father and the Son, exulting in joy without holding back any of their glory, draw from the weight of this glory (*kabôd*) to share themselves with a third.[69] Whereas in autistic love, as in auto-idolatrous love, *one* was always confused with the *two* in the reciprocal identity of the self and the other, sharing the love with a third who is beloved definitively removes any claim that egoism might have, be it human or divine, to present itself as the sole donating or giving source of the love. The *I-Thou* of the Father and the Son—to put it in Martin Buber's terms, applied here to the Christian Trinity—is answered by the *We* of the Holy Spirit, who alone grounds it and makes the reciprocity toward a third shine forth, again and always contained in God himself.[70]

Encountering this demanding, and almost impossible, sharing of a third love—Sartre's *No Exit*, incidentally, makes the difficulty of this sharing sufficiently clear—some occasionally claim that it is an anthropomorphic tendency that transposes this scheme of strictly infra-human amity onto the divine Trinity, "as if a divine egoism made the least sense(!)"[71] On this view we should have to thank Thomas for "taking reciprocity from the notional level back to the essential level," thereby definitively barring the "dangerous path" of Ricardian anthropomorphism and conferring on the love of the divine self the kind of purity that would make this love attract all things to itself, without itself ever being lost or

---

[69] I permit myself here a free—and theological—interpretation of the theme of the "invisible insubstitutable" developed by Jean-Luc Marion, *L'intentionnalité de l'amour*, in *Prolégomènes à la charité*, op. cit., pp. 118-120. However, where the author sees the gazes meeting, somewhere always invisible to everyone else, as the key to an intentionality of love (p.107), I hold instead, at least where Trinitarian love is concerned, that the particular characteristic of the sharing of love between the lover and the beloved amounts to showing the mutual play of the gaze and the counter-gaze of the lovers *to* the friend.

[70] M. Buber. *I and Thou*, Fr. tr. *Le Je et le Tu*, Paris, Aubier-Montaigne, 1981; as well as Emmanuel Lévinas's criticism on the necessity of the opening of the *I-Thou* to a *You* "as the form of a Totally Other who surpasses man" (Lévinas, *Martin Buber et la théorie de la connaissance*, in *Noms propres* [1976], Paris, Biblio-essais, 1987, pp. 23-43 [cit. p. 39]). Without denying this necessity of the two (*I-Thou*) to be opened to a third (*You*), totally in conformity with the aim of Richard of St. Victor, Christian Trinitarian theology nonetheless possesses the specific characteristic of integrating this triangular relationship, which in Lévinas is only posited in the relationship of man (and the other man) to God, into a *We*, i.e. *into God himself* and *into man*, who, in the Word, is always given shelter in God. For a careful reinterpretation of Buber's dialogical structure in the context of the Trinity, see H.U. von Balthasar, *La Théologique* (*Theologik*), t. II, *Vérité de Dieu* (1985), Bruxelles, Culture et vérité, 1995, pp. 53-56.

[71] Pénido, *Gloses sur la procession d'amour dans la Trinité*, in *Ephemerides theologicae Lovanienses*, t. XIV, 1937, pp. 33-66 (cit. p. 61).

forgotten in the other.[72] This is an all the more original and foundational move, according to one interpretation, for the fact that it deliberately counters the hypothesis formulated by his own master, Albert the Great, according to whom "even if the essence did not unite the Father and the Son, they would be bound by affection."[73]

But what Thomas uses here to attack Richard as well as Bonaventure makes, in my opinion, a better shield than sword. Just as the Seraphic Doctor refuses to lose the "for us" of divine knowledge in pure *unknowing* (as if the analogical *unlikeness* of man and God always had to take priority over their likeness [§5b]), so here the similarities of the amorous experiences of man and God takes primacy over their possible differences (although one would also have share divine love to understand, at the heart of this *exemplar*, the role of human love in it, too). To accuse Bonaventure of anthropomorphism, e.g. in a Thomistic line of criticism, respects neither the divergence of his views from Aquinas nor his strongest theological effort. Beyond the necessary reservations that help to correct some excessively immediate transpositions from human love to divine love (Richard), does it not in fact properly belong to the God of the Christians, and even more as he is transmitted in a Franciscan experience, to be precisely, and in the right sense of the term, *anthropo-morphic*—i.e. does it not belong to the Christian God to be anthropomorphic only by the Trinity's choice, alone among all the gods, to be a Christ who truly takes on "*human form*"? No one could really object to the false accusations of anthropomorphism if the much-maligned argument of the love shared with a third (*condilectio*), in man as in God, did not proclaim from its heights the basis of a truth that is Biblical before all else. With or without moralizing speculations, the venom of sin in the book of Genesis consists entirely, and before all else, in the jealousy of the serpent alone: "I want to be God *because* God is defined as he who does not want me to be like him … It is thus a matter of taking the place of God after the declaration that he wanted to occupy his divinity alone."[74] Because sin is defined as the incapacity, or better the refusal, to share love, the perfect charity in God demanded very precisely what in my opinion is the opposite: that

---

[72] Pénido, ibid., pp. 49-51 and pp. 60-6,1 (for the insistent denunciation of Ricardo-Bonaventurian anthropomorphism: a "disconcerting," "dangerous," "heavy," "hazy" anthropomorphism; and p. 61 (for the love of self as the answer to anthropomorphic tendencies).

[73] Pénido, ibid., p. 61 (citation of Albertus Magnus but without precise reference); and p. 62 (justification of the Thomistic condemnation of anthropomorphism by the twofold affirmation of the primacy of the love of God for himself and of the leading back (*réconduction*) of the reciprocity of the notional plane to the essential plane).

[74] P. Beauchamp. *L'un et l'autre Testament*, Paris, Seuil, t. 2, ch. 3 ("L'homme, la femme, le serpent").

"another be associated with the dilection which is shown to him" (*exhibitae sibi dilectionis consortem requirit*)—thus containing, in its very nature, the antidote to the venom of sin, namely sharing the love of a third against the rivalry of jealousy. In God, the supreme grandeur (*maximum*) of the reciprocal love of the Father and the Son in their common donation to the Holy Spirit amounts, in Richard's telling, not only to "undergoing" or "suffering" (*pati*) a community in love, but again to "accepting" or "embracing" it (*suscipere*)—indeed "desiring" it (*ex desiderio requirere*).[75]

Thus, in spite of some rather hasty interpretations, there is nothing here that permits us to affirm, at least from the point of view of Bonaventure's corpus, that "it is precisely this notion of the common friend that Bonaventure will reject."[76] The very expression "common friend," used in translations of Richard, really conveys nothing more than the same *condilectus* already encountered on many occasions in Bonaventure. It is thus necessary to preserve for it, at least textually, a *definite* meaning.[77] This step back is justified, first by the fact that Bonaventure's *condilectus*—namely, as Richard says, the common friend (*condilectum*) of the lover (*amans*) and the beloved (*dilectum*)—probably designates less the one who is loved in common (the friend) and rather the Father's and the Son's *common act of loving*—their "Co-*Loving*" or their "*loving*-another-together." In Bonaventure, the community of a love that has no other inclination but to share with a third the modality of its own Loving-in-common replaces Richard's community of a Beloved or a friend that arrives as if in addition to the first two.[78] The Holy Spirit or the friend is not added, for the Seraphic Doctor, as a third and in an extrinsic and derived manner to the self-being of the Father and of

---

[75] Richard of St. Victor, *De Trinitate*, op. cit. L. III, c.9, 923a p. 193 (condilection as association with a third) and 922b p. 193 (divine desire of a community of love).

[76] B. de Margerie, *La Trinité chrétienne dans l'histoire*, op. cit. pp. 419-420 (incidentally without reference to Bonaventure, and thus unable to justify this).

[77] For Bonaventure, see the many references already cited, *I Sent.* d.10, *Hex.* XI, 12, *Brev.* I, 2, *It.* VI, 2. They find all their roots in Richard of St. Victor, *De Trinitate*, op. cit., (Cerf), L. III, c.11, 923a p. 193: "those who thus are loved supremely, and who deserve to be, must each claim, with a shared desire, a common friend who belongs to them (*ut pari voto condilectum requierat*)." In light of these many occurrences, it is surprising that there is no reference to the *condilectio* in the article "*dilectio*" of the *Lexique saint Bonaventure* (ed. Bougerol), op. cit., p. 55.

[78] If the translation of *condilectus* by "common friend" is not deemed fitting in Bonaventure, as it is in Richard of St. Victor, it is less to deny his very reality than to indicate the *act* of loving that produces him more than the *being* thus brought forth. One could thus somehow make more *active* the usual translations of *condilectus*, e.g. "Co-Be-*loved* (Co-Bien-*Aimé*)" in Duméry (*It.* p. 93) and Ozilou (*Hex.* p. 283) or "Another-*loved*-together" in Mathieu (*Brev.* I, p. 67) by insisting more on the gerundive that produces them: "Co-*Loving*" or "*Loving*-Another-together."

the Son or of their amorous community. Contrary to the illusion of
pure isolation as a merely negative mode of community, the *Co-Loving*
(*condilectum*) is instead somehow always there already—"with" the
Father and the Son (*Mitsein*)—just as, phenomenologically speaking, the
term *the Others* "does not mean 'all the other people outside of myself...
but rather those among whom one is also oneself.'"[79] In other words, the
being is *in common* at the heart of a human community (as of a divine
community), not in the sense that the community belongs to the beings
that compose it as one of their properties, but on the contrary only
inasmuch as the community, and it alone, constitutes their very mode of
being, the one most proper to them: "the community of being—and not
the being of the community—is that of which it is always the question,"
in phenomenology as well as, in my opinion, in Trinitarian theology.[80]

The world of God, like that of *Dasein*, is established immediately in
a "common world" (*Mitwelt*) in the sense that the Trinitarian community
properly constitutes it before even existing—and even in order to
exist—in giving itself *in* itself or *to* itself. The *divine being-with*, or the
in-common in God, and this alone, creates in the *Breviloquium* the *how*
(*qualiter*) of the Trinity's being. The Trinity here satisfies the demands of
communicability (*diffusio*) only by first meeting the requirements of the
community (*condilectio*):

> *by the very fact* (*ac per hoc*) that He communicates himself in the
> best way (*Deum se summe communicare*) by eternally having a be-
> loved (*dilectum*) and a Co-Loving (*condilectum*), God is Triune
> and One (*Deum unum et trinum*).[81]

The originality of Bonaventure's Trinitarian *a priori* (cf. p. 35), related
as much to Dionysius the Areopagite as to Richard of St. Victor, consists
in this redirection of the *diffusio* to the *condilectio*. With respect to the
first, Dionysius, he reminds the reader of the necessary rootedness of all
creative diffusion in a Trinitarian communion:

> If there were not a Beloved (*dilectus*) and a Co-Beloved (*condi-
> lectus*), God would not be the supreme good, since he would not

---

[79] Heidegger, *Sein und Zeit*, op. cit., Fr. tr. Martineau, §26 (the being-there-with
others and the quotidian being-there) [l'être-là-avec des autres et l'être-là quotidien], p.
118 (German pagination).

[80] J.-L. Nancy. *La communauté désœuvrée*, Paris, Christian Bourgois, col. Détroits,
1986, Part 4, ("De l'être en commun"), p. 202 (attempt to reinterpret the Heideggerian
Mitsein [l'être-en-commun]).

[81] Bonaventure, *Brev.*, I, 2, No. 3 (V, 211a), Fr. tr. (modified) p. 67.

pour himself out in the most complete way (*quia non summe diffunderet*).[82]

As for the second, Richard, Bonaventure warns of the danger of deducing divine love from the characteristics of human love alone, which wrongly reifies the properly divine ambition of the *loving*-in-common in an all-too-human substantification of the form of the *friend*:

> the conditions of pure love (*amor purus*) [the term attributed here to Richard by Bonaventure] do not designate a mode of loving with respect to love (*non dicunt modum amandi circa amorem*), but rather indicate a mode of emanating or proceeding from the origin relative to the persons (*sed dicunt modum emanandi sive originis circa personas*).[83]

This affirmation of the divine persons and of their amorous community always takes precedent, according to Bonaventure, over both the act of diffusion (Dionysius) and the accomplishment of the communion (Richard). The community is thus first drawn, in the words of the *Itinerarium*, from an "ineffable co-intimacy" (*summam cointimitatem*) by virtue of which "each person is necessarily in the others (*qua unus est in altero*) by a close circumincession (*per summam circumincessionem*)."[84] In this incessant co-presence of one to the other, the Father, the Son, and the Holy Spirit do not *sit* together with or beside each other (*circum-in-sedere*), but rather *compenetrate each other* in the progress or movement of circulation from one to another (*circum-in-cedere*)—thereby marking more the provenance of their journey than the place of their activity:

> circumincession is the term (*vocatur circumincessio*) for that by which one person is said to be in another and vice versa (*quod unus est in alio et e converso*); and this belongs properly and perfectly to God alone since circumincession (*circumincessio*) posits at once distinction and unity in the essence (*in essendo ponit distinctionem simul et unitatem*).[85]

Remaining oneself while in movement (distinction by origin) and nonetheless always passing through the other when the persons coincide

---

[82] Bonaventure, *It.* VI, 2 (V, 210b), Fr. tr. (modified) p. 93

[83] Bonaventure, *I Sent.*, d.10, a.1, q.3, ad.4 (I, 199a).

[84] Bonaventure, *It.* VI, 2 (V, 311a), Fr. tr. p. 95.

[85] Bonaventure, *I Sent.*, d.19, p. I, a.un., q.4 (*utrum in divinis sit aequalitas circumincessione*), concl. (I, 349a).

with and encounter one another (unity by substance): this is the force that the incessant motion of Bonaventurian circumincession provides, all the more centripetal as centrifugal. Writing before the Council of Florence (1439), which relied more on a kind of textbook Thomism than on the writings of Thomas himself when it definitively re-spelled circumin*cession* (*circumincessio*) as circumin*session* (*circuminsessio*)— thereby resolutely marking the primacy of divine session (*in-sedere*) over the movement of the persons' compenetration (*in-cedere*)—Bonaventure managed to build, in this transcription of perichoresis by *circumincessio*, a final rampart against all reification or immobilization of the divine persons.[86] At the heart of the co-intimacy (*cointimitas*) of the persons between themselves, each divine person is somehow "oneself as another" in his Trinitarian encounters (Ricœur): "each in the other and with the other"—*unus in altero et cum alio*.[87] As I have already emphasized—but with a more *static* intention (both by the monadological hypothesis [§5c] and that of the proximity of man to God [§6b])—the "running of the angels in God" (*intra Deum currunt*) during their substantiation (*Brev.* II, 8) expresses well here an authentic *flow* of God within himself, in the incessant movement of his perichoresis, which proceeds from the Father toward the Son, and with them, together toward the Holy Spirit (cf. p. 88).[88] The somewhat *choreographic* movement of their shared dance (*peri-choreô*) or their progress together (*circum-in-cedere*) describes in the

---

[86] The Greek origin of Bonaventurian circumincession can be discerned in Burgundio of Pisa's Latin rendering of *perichoresis* by *circumincessio* in his 12th-century translation of John Damascene. See John Damascene, *De Fide orthodoxa, Versions of Burgundio and Cebarnus,* Louvain-Nauwelaerts, The Franciscan Institute, 1955, I, 8 (De sancta Trinitate), 829a [290], p. 45: "Pater, Filius, et Spiritus Sanctus uniuntur enim, ut diximus, non ut confundatur, sed ut habeantur in invicem *circumincessionem* habeant, sine omni congregatione et commassatione." As for the general movement from circumincession in Bonaventure (*circum-in-cedere*) to circuminsession (*circum-in-sedere*) in the Council of Florence, see Mathieu, art. *circumincessio* in *Lexique saint Bonaventure*, op. cit., Éd. franciscaines, p. 33 as well as B. de Margerie, *La Trinité chrétienne dans l'histoire*, op. cit., pp. 249-250.

[87] Bonaventure, *It.* VI, 2 (V, 311a), Fr. tr. (Duméry) p. 95: "there results from this an ineffable co-intimacy (*summam cointimitatem*) by virtue of which each person is necessarily in the others (*in altero*) by a total circumincession (*per summam circumincessionem*) and each acts in concert with the others (*cum alio*) in the indivisible and total unity of substance, power, and action that is the Blessed Trinity." For the possibility of a Trinitarian reinterpretation of "oneself as another" (P. Ricœur, *Soi-même comme un autre*, Paris, Seuil, 1990, and esp. pp. 380-393: "l'altérité d'autrui"), see my work *Le Passeur de Gethsémani*, op. cit., pp. 130-131: "Soi-même comme un autre."

[88] Bonaventure, *Brev.* II, 8, No. 2 (V, 226a), Fr. tr. p. 99: "for in contemplating God face to face, wherever they are sent, it is always in God that they are running (*intra Deum currunt*)."

last instance the "how (*qualiter*) of the accord in God of the unity of substance with the plurality of personnes."[89] *How* they are when they live together (*quomodo/qualiter ... vivendum*)—and no longer solely *what* they do when they diffuse (Dionysius), nor *who* they are when they love each other (Richard) becomes thus the final question of Bonaventurian Trinitarian auto-affection—the very same of which our faith also, as we have shown (§8b), experiences a very high and very devout *sense*.

In Bonaventure, setting aside any objections of anachronism, this common living of the three persons of the Trinity (*convivendum*)—like the "intersubjective sphere of belonging" in Husserl—can probably also be discerned as "a community (*Gemeinschaft*) that constitutes, by its common intentionality, one and the same world."[90] Witness Bonaventure's use of the example of spouses to speak of the Trinity, whose social community of life somehow makes sense of the conjugal fruit of the procreative act:

> one can find an example (*autem exemplum potest poni*) [of the love in God (*dilectio in divinis*)] in the created love by which husband and wife love each other (*quo sponsus et sponsa se diligunt*). They love each other indeed with a social love (*amore sociali*) to the end of *living together* (*ad convivendum*); and they love each other, besides this (*ulterius*), with a conjugal love (*amore coniugali*) in order to *procreate offspring* (*ad prolem procreandam*).[91]

There are certainly elements of this familial metaphor, used for making sense of the Trinity in Augustine's *De Trinitate*. The model's inadequacy before the reality of the divine nature, however, ultimately demands that it be rejected: how to understand in the strict meaning of the terms, a Father and a Son spirating the Spirit as spouses procreate a child without making of him (the Spirit) precisely the son that he is not; and how, on the other hand, to speak of a Son spirating the Spirit in the way of a procreative source without consecrating himself (the Son) as the father, or mother, that he, too, is not?[92] This considerable objection,

---

[89] Bonaventure, *Brev.* I, 2, No. 1 (V, 210b), Fr. tr. p. 65.

[90] E. Husserl, *Méditations cartésiennes*, op. cit. (Vrin), Fifth Meditation, §49: "Esquisse préalable de l'explicitation intentionnelle de l'expérience de l'autre" (cit. p. 90).

[91] Bonaventure, *I Sent.*, d. 10, a.2, q.1, concl. (I, 201a).

[92] Augustine, *De Trinitate*, op. cit. (B.A No. 15), Book V, c. XII, 13, p. 455: "we speak well of the Holy Spirit of the Father, but we do not speak in the opposite sense, i.e. of the Father of the Holy Spirit: one would in that case take the Holy Spirit for his Son. Likewise, we speak of the Holy Spirit of the Son, but not of the Son of the Holy Spirit: the Holy Spirit would in that case pass for his father." On the limits of this familial metaphor for expressing the Trinity, one could profitably consult B. de Margerie, *La Trinité*

theologically recognized by Bonaventure, bars an overly immediate transposition of the paradigm of human love onto divine love. It is from this, by way of a warning against this transposition, that the justification on the one hand (and in this case only) of the Augustinian distinction of *eros* (*amor/dilectio*) and *agapê* (*caritas*), and, on the other, the reluctance with respect to Richard's *condilectus*, understood here only as a "beloved friend" and not as an act of "loving the friend."[93] And although Richard guards himself against using this analogy of spouses by preferring instead the explanation by pure friendship (*amor purus*), Bonaventure nonetheless reproaches him, as I have emphasized, for deducing the Trinitarian community from a "mode of loving with respect to love" (*modum amandi circa amorem*)—namely from a fictitious perfection of human love—rather than first describing it *a priori* and in his *exemplar* starting from the "mode of emanating or proceeding from the origin" proper to the divine persons (*modum emanandi sive originis*).[94]

The imperative of the Trinitarian *a priori* and the descending approach particular to the *Breviloquium* remain always normative, or better *the* norm, and despite the fact that one might sometimes also use analogies, like the example of the spouses (*huius autem exemplum*), these pedagogical images are only too anthropomorphic in appearance. Indeed, no sooner does the Seraphic Doctor propose the spousal metaphor than he retracts it, yet without invalidating it, emphasizing that only "a certain form of emphasis" (*per emphaticum loquendi*) permits the affirmation of the fruit of the divine espousal as *Love* or the Holy Spirit (*amor*), even if a human child (*prolem*) always remains the *Beloved* of the parents (*amatus*) without ever identically meaning love itself.[95] The metaphor of the spouses must

---

chrétienne dans l'histoire, op. cit., Ch. VIII, 1, pp. 367-390: "Intersubjectivité et amitié familiales, première analogie révélée de la Trinité [Familial intersubjectivity and friendship: the first revealed analogy of the Trinity]."

[93] On the necessity of maintaining the distinction between *amor, dilectio,* and *caritas*—at least insofar as only the last one is specifically supernatural whereas the two others are natural (in the order of nature and of the will)—see Bonaventure, *III Sent.*, d.27, dub.I, sol. I (III, 616b): "to those who object that dilection and charity are the same thing (*quod idem est dilectio et caritas*), we must say that if they are the same thing in themselves (*si sint idem re*), there nonetheless exists some conceptual difference (*tamen aliqua differentia rationis est*): dilection in effect is broader than charity (*dilectio enim in plus est quam caritas*). We also usually say that love by nature (*quod amor est naturae*), dilection by the will (*dilectio est voluntatis deliberativae*), and charity by grace (*et caritas gratiae*)." This can be complemented by *I Sent.*, d. 10, dub.1 (I, 205a), which is cited, translated, and commented on above. The distinction between the *Beloved Friend* (Richard) and the *Act of Loving the Friend* (Bonaventure) is established above as well.

[94] Bonaventure, *I Sent.*, d.10, a.1, q.3, ad.4 (I, 199a).

[95] Bonaventure, *I Sent.*, d.10, a.2, q.1, concl. (I, 201a): "if this child had been produced by the concord of the will alone, it would be *Love* (*amor esset*); but in reality it is

thus be understood first in a symbolic sense in Bonaventure, and with this particularity: it extends the spousal theology that is "essentially limited to the *Ecclesia* in Augustine" to the whole of theology and especially, in my opinion, to the Trinity.[96] The nuptials of the husband and wife, so celebrated by Bernard of Clairvaux in the *Sermons on the Canticle of Canticles*—to speak of the Incarnation but without ever transferring the metaphor to or basing it in the Trinity itself[97]—is for Bonaventure, on the other hand, and with all the aforesaid precautions being taken, originally the celebration of the Trinity's *in-common*. In a medieval world where life in the familial state was hardly considered to approach the lofty spiritual summits of the consecrated life, except in the "Third Order" (a totally Franciscan creation!), the Seraphic Doctor shows in his writings on marriage that the sacrament, "without producing the love of man and woman" (*in hoc sacramento non fit desponsatio*), "nonetheless represents the marriage of God and the human soul" (*sed figuratur ipsa desponsatio quae est Dei ad animam*).[98] Bonaventure's innovation here, with respect to the Bernardian current, would scarcely appear clearly here (although the union of husband and wife expresses here in the proper sense, and not

---

the *Beloved* (*nunc vero est amatus*), unless one means a certain emphasis or connotation of Love (*nisi dicatur amor per emphaticum loquendi*)."

[96] Balthasar, *La Gloire et la croix*, op. cit., Styles I (monograph on Bonaventure), p. 239: "spousal theology in Augustine certainly had a foundation in the theology of the *Christus totus*, head and body, husband and wife, but it essentially remained limited to the *Ecclesia* in its whole…In Bonaventure, *spousal theology and spirituality are ubiquitous.* They take in everything, in a very natural way, and they are expressed with all the more force as the author approaches mystical heights" (my emphasis). Before the force of the object and the evident use of spousal theology in Bonaventure—reaching to the heart of the Trinity itself, as I shall show—one is surprised to read the following statement from the plume of Jacques-Guy Bougerol, *Introduction à saint Bonaventure*, op. cit. (Vrin, 1988), p. 91: "among the themes that the analysis has permitted us to group, there is one whose absence [in Bonaventure] *could be deplored*, one that is at the center of Bernard's mystical theology: that of *spousal love*" (my emphases).

[97] Bernard of Clairvaux, *Sermons sur les cantiques*, Paris, Cerf, Sources chrétiennes No. 431, 1998, t.2, sermo XXXI, I, 1, p. 427: "The Bridegroom-Word (*Verbum sponsus*) is often shown to souls of desire, but under diverse forms." On the meaning of such divine-human espousal (but once again, in my opinion, always applied to the Word or to God in general more than to the Trinity itself), one can profitably consult E. Gilson, *La théologie mystique de saint Bernard*, Paris, Vrin, 1931, Ch. III, p. 78-107: "schola caritatis." As for the relationship between Bonaventure and Bernard de Clairvaux—nevertheless without the distance between them being marked by the Trinitarian application of spousal theology—see (and despite a somewhat fastidious list of quotations) J.-G. Bougerol, "Saint Bonaventure et saint Bernard" in *Saint Bonaventure: Études sur les sources de sa pensée*, Northampton, Variorum Reprints, 1989, Ch. IV, pp. 1-79, esp. pp. 25-40 for the meaning of *dilectio*, albeit never re-interpreted in light of the Trinity.

[98] Bonaventure, *IV Sent.*, d.26, a.2, q.2, ad.3 (IV, 669a).

only in a figurative way, the union of the soul with God) if the soul were not always at the same time, as we have seen, a mirror (*fit speculum*) that monadologically reflects exactly what is in God.

For Bonaventure, since the nuptials of man and woman represent in themselves those of the soul and God, one must admit at the very heart of God, if only symbolically, certain nuptials between the Trinitarian persons capable of grounding in return, and in an exemplary and still more original way, those of the husband and wife with each other—and both with God. The social aspect of love shared between the Father and the Son (*amor socialis*) seals—within God—the contract of their shared life (*ad convivendum*). And this "intersubjective sphere of belonging" or this "community" (*Gemeinschaft*), to take up Husserlian terminology again, is indeed such that it cannot but "constitute, by its common intentionality, one and the same world": the Holy Spirit as fruit of their conjugal love (*amor coniugalis*).

Bonaventure does not consider the Holy Spirit as a child in the sense of being a begotten person, for this would risk falling, once again, into the confusions of paternity and filiality in God. He remains like a child, however, as a *link* between the Father and the Son (*nexus*), symbolically designating here not the act of their active unity, but the *passive result of their relationship*:

> to bind (*nectere*) means not that the Holy Spirit gives something to the Father and to the Son (*non significatur quod aliquid det Patri et Filio*), but rather that he receives (*sed quod magis recipiat*).[99]

For Bonaventure, the formula according to which "The Father and the Son love each other together by the Holy Spirit" ("*Pater et Filius diligunt se Spiritu Sancto*") does not indicate in this sense a third person who somehow actively unifies the first two—as, for Thomas, an action (e.g. the heating of fire) might also designate the effect produced (heat). The union by a third, which is both *notionally* and *essentially* true for the Angelic Doctor because for him a subsistent or essential third produces the reciprocal union of the first two, remains only *notionally* true but *essentially* false for the Seraphic Doctor, in the sense that the third hypostasis is received from the first, yet without ever actively producing their essential union.[100] Forbidding thus any deferment of the amorous

---

[99] Bonaventure, *I Sent.*, d.10, a.2, q.2, ad.4 (I, 203b).

[100] Compare, respectively, Bonaventure, *I Sent.*, d.32, a.1, q.1, concl. (I, 557b): "ista locutio (Pater et Filius diligunt se Spiritu sancto) falsa est, si tenetur essentialiter, vera autem, si tenetur notionaliter"; and Thomas Aquinas, *S. Th.*, Ia., q.37, a.2, resp.: "se-

reciprocity of the Father and of the Son toward a subsistent Love, their link (*nexus*) instead only signifies their common *donation* or *giving* (below, §10) to him who, at least from the intra-Trinitarian point of view, is but pure passivity and the reception of their communion of love: the Holy Spirit.[101]

Drawing the familial metaphor to a close, and to continue this phenomenological interpretation, let me propose, in one last hypothesis, that for Bonaventure the Holy Spirit shares something particular with a child (*prolem*): he expresses symbolically not only—and with certain reservations—an act of procreation, but also—and in a more obvious way—the characteristics of a birth, at least (and only?) as the place in which a passivity in itself is welcomed, always received from another and always returned to another: "one is born to self without ever being able to take one's birth upon oneself; it is I who am born, certainly, but even this very affirmation I can only declare to myself in the first person by the fact that others assumed it first and pronounced it in my name."[102] Like spouses giving their child his name in order to leave him to his own gift, and even more radically, as I will show (Ch. V), the *in-common* of the Father and the Son gives even to giving the gift itself (the Holy Spirit). In the height of their common abandon [*aban-don*][103], and there alone, our faith *will then sense* (*ut sentiat*) the extreme paradox of the *in-common* of God. This is where the Seraphic Doctor teaches us, like a good Franciscan, about the strangely proportional relationship between the poverty of being to the richness of giving. Because God gives in giving *himself* ("objective evidence") always more than what man can receive ("subjective evidence"), we ought to posit, at the heart of the Trinity itself, a radical (Franciscan?) "ontology of poverty" that retains "nothing for itself"—not even God himself (§10). Only thus will the Trinity, in the missions of its divine persons, be properly able to "manifest itself"

---

cundum quod essentialiter sumitur, sic Pater et Filius non diligunt se Spiritu sancto, sed essentia una" (the example of fire, heating, and heat [same reference]). For this whole question (although without a consideration of the opposition with Thomas), see W.-H. Principe, "Saint Bonaventure's Theology of the Holy Spirit with Reference to the Expression '*Pater et Filius diligunt se spiritu sancto*'," in *S. Bonaventura, 1274-1974*, op. cit. t. IV, pp. 243-269.

[101] W.H. Principe, ibid., p. 258: "the Holy Spirit's being bond of the Father and Son does not mean that the Holy Spirit exercises any active role with respect to them. When it is said that he joins together the Father and the Son, it means that he *proceeds* from each of them" (my emphasis).

[102] C. Romano. *Le possible et l'événement* (I), in *Philosophie*, No. 40, Dec. 1993, p. 92.

[103] Tr. n.: In French, *don* is "gift"; Falque here emphasizes the character of the gift at the heart of self-aban*don*ment for the sake of another.

to man—which is to say by "dwelling," "appearing," "descending," and "being sent" among us (§11).

PART THREE

THE MANIFESTATION AND NAMING OF GOD

At the beginning of this book, I started out by asking *how God has entered theology, and whether he is doing so again*. The question first demanded that we establish a framework or a method—theology itself (Part One)—by which descriptivity (Ch. I) as well as the twofold suspension of any statement in the form of a *quid* and of any proof for the existence of God (Ch. II) both prepare an entryway where the "arriving God" immediately reveals himself as a Trinitarian being. But it is at this beginning, prepared by man for the "arrival" of God in theology (subjective evidence), that the crucial step of his "appearance"—or better, his "influx" (objective evidence) takes place, at the very least in the sense in which the Trinitarian phenomenon always appears "by suddenly arising (it reaches me, it comes to me, and it overwhelms me)."[104] When God himself takes (the) control(s) "in the beginning" (Part Two), he demands two things: first, that he remain the unique *origin at work* in *the work* beyond any causal efficiency and in the unique fontality of a Father expressing himself by his Son (Ch. III); and second, that he constitute, this time with the Holy Spirit, a type of community, such that the *auto-affection of their divine experience*—even in man—might reveal, in their very union, the presence of a "common Friend" who has no other meaning than their unique desire for "Loving-in-common" (Ch. IV).

What has thus been prepared for welcoming God in a theological discourse (Part One) and what God reveals about himself in his exclusively Trinitarian form as Father, Son, and Holy Spirit (Part Two) now demand an encounter with the self, or better a self-fertilization (Part Three)—on the one hand so that what is perpetually contained in God from age to age might *be given* and *manifested* to man (Ch. V), and on the other hand so that man's quite Franciscan hyper-proximity to God might *be expressed*, here with the help of "metaphor." In this context, God's "quest for what is proper to him" nonetheless does not always allow him to remain specifically God (Ch. VI). Beyond any dialectic, then—since it is not a question here of contraries to be subsumed into some kind of higher unity, but only a coincidence of paths that makes Bonaventure's approach more an hodology (*itinerarium*) than an ontology[105]—the double aim

---

[104] Marion, *Étant donné, Essai d'une phénoménologie de la donation*, Paris, PUF, 1997, §14, pp. 185-197: *l'arrivage* (cit. p. 196).

[105] On the possible opposition, or at least the subordination, of ontology to hodology in mystical theology, see S. Breton. *Deux mystiques de l'excès: J.J. Surin et Maître Eckhart*, Paris, Cerf, 1985, p. 189.

of the "manifestation" and the "naming" of God (Part Three) has yet to be realized so that, in all logic and in keeping with Bonaventure's key principle, the "Trinity as Maker" (*Trinitas fabricatrix*) might be said to "shine forth" (*relucet*), and thus "be represented" (*repraesentatur*) and "be read" (*legitur*) by the believer in the immense book of Creation (cf. Conclusion).[106]

---

[106] Bonaventure, *Brev.* II, 12, No. 1 (V, 230a), Fr. tr. p. 123.

CHAPTER V

FROM THE ONTOLOGY OF POVERTY
(*Brev.* I, 3-4)
TO THE MANIFESTATION OF THE TRINITY
(*Brev.* I, 5)

It is the *gift* that *gives* love; it is not love that *is* or *makes* the gift, at least in a certain form of divine desire (*eros*). The impossibility of substantifying or reifying the gift now demands that we follow the movement of its own outpouring step by step. He who "gives," to take up here the beautiful words of Luke the Evangelist in his account of the widow's offering, "takes on his poverty (*ex eo quo deest illi*)" to put in his offering the "entirety of what [he] had to live on (*omne victum suum quem habuit*)" (Lk 21:4).[1] It may not suffice, then, for man at least (if not for God) only to give in order to be a "beggar" or to live "in poverty among the poor." It is also necessary to give *oneself*—or at the very least to give what constitutes the subsistence (*victus*) of what makes one's life. Bonaventure, recounting the life of St. Francis, writes:

> to the poor beggars, too (*pauperibus etiam mendicantibus*), not content to give what he *had* (*non solum sua*), he would have wanted *to give of his very self* (*verum etiam se ipsum cupiebat impendere*). And, when he had no more money in his hand, he gave them his clothes, sometimes tearing and dividing them in order to distribute them.[2]

---

[1] One can also find Bonaventure's commentary on the story of the widow's almsgiving in *Comm. in evang. S. Lucae* (VII, 511).

[2] Bonaventure, *Leg. maior*, cap.II, 6 (VIII, 507b), Fr. tr. *Vie de saint François d'Assise*, Paris, éd. franciscaines, 1968, pp. 28-29. On the originality of this type of beggarliness as the sole language of the flesh in its radical impoverishment, see my article "Saint François et saint Dominique: deux manières d'être chrétien au monde," in *Communio*, t. XIX, 3, No. 113, May-June 1994 (la spiritualité), pp. 59-76, esp. p. 64, "Saint François ou le langage de la chair."

"A purely *ontological* meaning is thus substituted for the *economic* meanings usually attached to poverty. Commonly defined as a dearth that does not affect the humanity of man, but rather leaves what he is absolutely intact, poverty instead appears to us here as *radical destitution*."[3] The exegesis proposed by Bonaventure, as a Franciscan master, forces us to examine, on the one hand, "the theological implications of his idea of poverty" (H. Schaluck) and, on the other hand, the significance of "the humility of God" that is bound to it (A. Gerken).[4] These concepts are so central to God's *condescension* (*condescensio*), but they ordinarily stop—or better begin (in a number of interpreters)—with the *Word's* kenosis: God only appears truly and fully himself, as himself, when, "humbly inclining himself" (*humiliter se inclinans*), he "assumes the *clay* of our nature into the unity of his person" (*limum nostrae naturae in suae asumpsit unitatem personae*).[5]

The idea of divine humility in the Incarnation, which comes directly from a Bonaventurian christocentrism, is powerful. Nonetheless, it must not be permitted to mask, in my opinion, the properly *Trinitarian* roots of this poverty.[6] For Bonaventure, God's condescension toward man cannot come without a certain condescension of God *in himself*, which is to say *independent* of the fact of the Incarnation and the Redemption. Wasn't it necessary, if we correctly interpret Bonaventure's account of the nativity in his mystical work on *The Tree of Life* (*Lignum vitae*), for God, as Trinity and from all eternity, to renounce somehow being merely "great and rich" (*cum magnus esset et dives*) so that he could then "choose to *come*, small and poor, for us" (*pro nobis effectus parvus et pauper elegit*)? God *comes* poor and small, lying in the manger at his epiphany, but he

---

[3] J.-Y. Lacoste, *Expérience et absolu, Questions disputées sur l'humanité de l'homme*, Paris, PUF, 1994, §63, pp. 205-207: "en deça de l'appropriation" (cit. p. 206, my emphasis). As for the necessity of abandoning *sub-sistence* and the *ousia*, see Marion, *Dieu sans l'être* (1982), Paris, PUF-Quadrige, 1991, pp. 140-146: interpretation of the parable of the prodigal son (Lk. 15:12-23).

[4] See H. Schaluck. "Les implications théologiques de l'idée de pauvreté chez saint Bonaventure," in *Actes du Colloque saint Bonaventure*, Études franciscaines, 1971, pp. 105-113 (a reprise of some of the themes in *Armut und Heil, eine Untersuchung über den Armutsdedanken in der Theologie Bonaventuras*, München-Paderborn, 1971); as well as A. Gerken, *La théologie du Verbe*, Paris, Éditions franciscaines, 1969, Ch. V, pp. 357-378: "l'humilité de Dieu."

[5] Bonaventure, *Nativitas domini*, sermo II, in *Sermones de tempore* (IX, 106b) and in *Sermones de Diversis*, new critical edition by J.-G. Bougerol, Paris, Éd. franciscaines, 1993, t. I, p. 93.

[6] On this non-foundation of the idea of poverty in the Trinity, see for example Schaluck, "Les implications théologiques de l'idée de pauvreté chez saint Bonaventure," op. cit., p. 106: "we have tried to demonstrate some anthropological, christological, and eschatological implications"—but no mention of Trinitarian ones.

does not become so; he has never really ceased to *be* as such nor to choose himself as such. The manger only makes fully visible what he already was from eternity to eternity—within the Trinity.[7] In this sense, the *Poverello* of Assisi is not content simply to follow the poor and naked Christ by wedding Lady Poverty (*sequela Christi*). Rather, in conforming himself to the Incarnate Word, he is somehow conformed to the Trinity itself (*conformatio Trinitatis*), making it fully visible in its kind of community. Thus, for example, the appearance of the "winged Seraph in the form of a cross" on Mount Alverne, far from representing merely the Stigmata of the Passion, also implies, by the symbolism of the six wings, the "six degrees of illumination" (*sex illuminationes scalares*)—from the contemplation of God in the traces he leaves in Creation through the blessed Trinity itself.[8] *Incipit speculatio pauperis in deserto*—"here begins the speculation of the poor one in the desert," as Bonaventure writes in opening the *Itinerarium*.[9]

§10. TOWARD AN ONTOLOGY OF POVERTY

"Blessed are the poor in spirit, for the kingdom of heaven is theirs" (Mt. 5:3): "this was the first word that Christ taught in the world," as Bonaventure says (*illud fuit primum verbum quod Dominus docuit in*

---

[7] Bonaventure, *Lignum vitae*, fructus I, No. 4 (VIII, 71b-72b): "qui, cum magnus esset et dives, pro nobis effectus parvus et pauper…elegit." John of God translates it: "bien que puissant et riche, il choisit par amour pour nous de *devenir* petit et pauvre" ["although powerful and rich, he chose to *become* small and poor because of his love for us"], in Œuvres spirituelles de saint Bonaventure, Paris, Libraire saint François, 1932, vol. III, *L'arbre de vie* p. 70. On the other hand, and more accurately, Valentin-Marie Breton translates it as: "bien que puissant et riche, il choisit par amour pour nous de *venir* petit et pauvre" ["although powerful and rich, he chose to *come* small and poor because of his love for us"], in *Saint Bonaventure*, Paris, Aubier, 1943, p. 243. The *effectus* used here does not imply a transformation in the very nature of God in the sense of a change or a "becoming," but only the visibility of the cause of which it itself is the effect: the poverty in God.

[8] Bonaventure, *It.* Prol. No. 3 (V, 295b), Fr. tr. (Duméry) p. 23: "the six wings of the seraph thus signify the six degrees of illumination (*sex illuminationes scalares*) that start from Creation and lead to God, before whom no one can manage to appear without passing through the Crucified One (*nisi per Crucifixum*)." The Crucified Jesus indeed seals here for Bonaventure the sole gate (*ostium*) for reaching God. But the "contuition of the Blessed Trinity," and it alone, remains the final goal of the path traveled (Ch. VI). As for the final repose (Ch. VII), it does not make one cross into some supplementary degree—these are limited to six—but only describes the state of grace of the one who has attained the last degree. Cf. RSPT, pp. 3-6: theological interpretation of the episode of the appearance of the "Seraph Winged in the Form of a Cross."

[9] Bonaventure, *It.* I, *incipit* (V, 296a), Fr. tr. (Duméry) p. 27.

mundo), and its meaning is not confined to the *spirit of Christ* in the sense of a lifestyle or a way of life—even though Bonaventure the Franciscan would have considered these fitting to adopt. The *spirit of poverty* indicates rather, in the Christian view, the *Spirit of Christ* himself—namely, the Holy Spirit, "given up" on the cross and "spread about" on Pentecost. Here, Bonaventurian poverty indicates, properly speaking, a theological and Trinitarian syntagma, on the one hand departing from any other strictly human form of poverty (that of John the Baptist, for example), and on the other hand surpassing the alleged naïveté of the Franciscan ideal of following the poor and naked Christ. This sort of poverty, be it *of the body* or *in spirit*, does not suffice to express what is specifically Christian about it. Following Bonaventure, only its eminently *Trinitarian* character truly makes sense of it. We can see it in two identifications: first, the identification of Christ himself as "first *Word*" (*primum verbum*) with the "first *word* taught" (*primum verbum docuit*) in the Beatitudes; and second, the identification of Christ's spirit of poverty with the Holy Spirit himself—who dispossesses himself, too, of the shared love of the Father and the Son, without ever growing tired of perpetuating the movement of the Trinity's circumincession.[10] The movement by which God somehow empties himself into another (*kenoein*), then, is not properly Trinitarian by the mere fact of the Incarnation of the Son: kenosis also somehow makes up the very nature of God, at least by extension from the communication of the idioms to the Trinity's appropriations: the Father can be recognized as originating principle of all donation (above, §7a), the Son as expressive and the aesthetic likeness of the Father (above, §7b), and the Holy Spirit at once as act of "Loving-in-common" (*condilectus*) and fruit that is yet always beyond the espousal of the Father and the Son (above, §9).

Thus, Bonaventure's famous *christological* insights, still relevant, must not mask the particularly *pneumatological* dimension of his teaching. Giving everything, even the gift itself—such will be the ultimate meaning, as we will show, of the Father's and the Son's gift of love in the Spirit, a

---

[10] Bonaventure, *Sermon for Epiphany*, Epiph. serm. I (IX, 147b), or the new edition in Bougerol, *Sermones de Diversis*, t. I, p. 188: "In evangelio Matthaei ubi dicit: *Beati pauperes spiritu quoniam ipsorum est regnum caelorum. Illud fuit primum verbum* quod Dominus docuit in monte." Bonaventure does not emphasize this formula, the possible identification of the *primum verbum* as the "first word" taught with the *primum Verbum* as the "Word Himself." The identity of the terms (*verbum*) nonetheless allows us to propose, in my opinion and leaning on that very formula, a Trinitarian interpretation of the first beatitude even if such was not Bonaventure's immediate goal in a sermon that was more directly didactic and less directly theological (on the meaning of this goal in Bonaventure's sermons, see J.-G. Bougerol, *Introduction à l'étude de saint Bonaventure*, op. cit., vol. II, pp. 200-201).

gift given without reserve. Perhaps one can in fact find in Bonaventure's pneumatology, as others have suggested, the outlines of a *theology of the Holy Spirit* to which certain contemporary religious practices bear particular witness, even if it does not supply them with their necessary conceptualization.[11] Neither a strictly social phenomenon nor an exclusively consecrated state, the theological idea of poverty as an act of being stripped of everything down to one's very self originally belongs, for Bonaventure, to the Trinity's movement of circumincession. In his view, the *ontology of poverty* does not mean some kind of "ontologism", as it has sometimes been wrongly accused of being. Instead, it should be understood here from the perspective of a *fundamental ontology* in the Heideggerian sense of the term: namely, as the "unveiling of a structure of being"—i.e., for us, in this context and with Bonaventure as our guide, as the auto-appearance of the Trinity to itself and to man in its complete givenness of self, a giving that takes it to the very most extreme point of its self-denuding.[12]

A) *THE GIFT, OR THE PASSAGE FROM SUFFICIENCY TO SUPERABUNDANCE*

The Father as *origin at work in the work* is defined, as we have seen, by the plenitude or fullness of his fontality, which gives him his absolute

---

[11] L. Mathieu, *La Trinité créatrice d'après saint Bonaventure*, op. cit., p. 297: "the recent rediscovery in the West of a theology of the Holy Spirit, and the attention paid to the Spirit in the groups of the 'Renewal' and in ecumenical encounters, can incite us to pay more attention to the Latin authors who had elaborated a very rich Trinitarian theology. It happens that precisely because of the nature of their approach, they are often qualified as 'mystics': Augustine, Richard of St. Victor, Bonaventure, Ruysbroek…to cite only the most famous. This qualification should be the recognition of the fact that their theology is not a pure adventure of the mind, a strictly intellectual approach, but rather the expression of a profound, interior experience; in short, their own spiritual life."

[12] For the fundamental impossibility of ascribing ontologism to Bonaventure, see the recent and definitive argument by D. Connel. "St. Bonaventure and the ontologist tradition," in *S. Bonaventura 1274-1974*, op. cit., vol. II, pp. 290-308. The other notes with precision that in spite of some apparent affinities of *Bonaventurian contuition* and *Malebranchist illumination*, the Seraphic Doctor keeps himself diametrically opposed to any direct illumination by virtue of the "mirror-like" structure of the human mind (*per speculum et in speculo*), which only reflects divine truth (see esp. pp. 305-308). And a capital point for our purposes is that it is precisely with a study on the meaning of Heideggerian ontology that he finishes his study, for, in a very Bonaventurian stroke here and like a mirror, Heideggerian ontology plays the game of the *hidden* and the *unveiled*: "Like Heidegger's Being, St. Bonaventure's God is always at the same time both manifest and hidden: manifest because he is the light apart from which nothing would appear to the understanding, hidden because what the light manifests directly is not the light itself but that in which the light is reflected."

primacy. But every expression of this fullness as source prevents him from being satisfied with his own sufficiency. In fact, there can only be knowledge of an ecstatic mode in God because it is "excess" (*excessus*) that first determines his mode of knowing.[13] Similarly, at the heart of the Trinity any possibility of sufficiency in this fullness (*plenitudo sufficentiae*) necessarily gives way to a superabundant fullness (*plenitudo superabundantiae*). The Father gives what he has—not first to strip himself of what he is (poverty in God, as in man, never implies a loss of identity), but instead only because that which he *is*, is totally—and nothing but— the givenness of what he *has*, i.e. himself and the overflowing of his own being in and from himself:

> the principle is only capable of proceeding (*ad influendum effi-cax*) if he has in himself original fontal fullness, a plenitude that is not only of *sufficiency* (*non tantum est plenitudo sufficentiae*), but also of *superabundance* (*sed etiam superabundantiae*).[14]

The *Father* thus neither gives nor gives *himself* according to the standard of sufficiency or satiety. Instead, he exceeds himself in his superabundance by pure liberality (*liberalitas*). And his outpouring is here such that the immediacy of his givenness (*velociter*) constitutes his very being.[15] As for the "eternally begotten" *Son* (*semper generat*), as we have seen, he makes manifest the very movement of the Father's complete donation, simultaneously as proclaimed Word (*Verbum prolatum*) and as expressive likeness (*similitudo expressiva*)—like a work of art, which bears in the opened character of its presence the very world that its author creates (*ibid.*). In view of the Father's expressivity, manifested in the Son by way of generation—"whoever has seen me has seen the Father (*qui videt me, videt et Patrem*)" (Jn. 14:9)—the *Holy Spirit*, spirated by the mode of the will, contains everything in a single name: "he is properly the Gift" (*cum proprium sit Spiritus sancti esse donum*). And although one might give him other names, too—"bind or charity (*nexum seu caritatem*)," and "*also* the

---

[13] Cf. RSPT, pp. 16-25: "l'*excessus* comme mode du connaître."

[14] Bonaventure, *Brev.* IV, 5, No. 5 (V, 346a), Fr. tr. p. 89.

[15] Bonaventure, *II Sent.*, d.23, a.1, q.1, fund.2 (II, 531b): "the excellence of divine liberality (*liberalitatis*) gives not only a superabundance of things (*non solum facit dare multa et magna*), but this also promptly (*sed etiam dare velociter*)." This is an implicit reference to Proverbs 3:28 (applied here to divine liberality): "Do not say to your friend: 'Go! You shall come back tomorrow and I will give to you then,' when you can already give to him now (*cum statis possis dare*)." On the different meanings of liberality, not only as a divine attribute but also as a moral virtue and as liberty, see Bonnefoy, *Le Saint-Esprit et ses dons selon saint Bonaventure*, op. cit., Ch. II, 1, art. 1, pp. 26-28: "diverses acceptions du mot 'liberalitas'."

Holy Spirit" (*esse etiam Spiritum sanctum*)—only the term Gift (*donum*)
defines him "characteristically" or "properly."[16] Revealing him in his very
self (*proprium*), however, the Gift is not only appropriated (*appropriari*) to
him—at least in the sense, which the *Breviloquium* emphasizes, that the
appropriated attributes "lead to the understanding and to the knowledge
of the properties (*ducunt ad intelligentiam et notitiam propriorum*)."[17]
In other words—and not forgetting the "sphere of ownness," which,
according to Husserl, is consitutive of every experience of the world—
the *ownness* of the Holy Spirit (*proprius*) cannot be reduced to any set of
properties (*propriorum*). And although this time he receives the attributes
of goodness, joy, finality, and benevolence (*Brev.* I, 6), he nonetheless
properly remains, and in a radically different sense, *gift* (*proprium...
donum*) (*Brev.* I, 3).[18]

Here, in Trinitarian theology as in phenomenology, "the experience
of ownness is the essence of experience." Indeed, the analysis of the flesh
in Husserl (*Leib*) and that of pneumatological givenness in Bonaventure
(*Donum*) have in common the fact that together they constitute—one
on the human level (the flesh) and the other relative to God (the Gift)—
on the one hand what is *most their own* as "the most originally mine,"
which distinguishes *me* from all the others (bodies or properties), and
on the other what is *closest to them* as absolutely inseparable from what
they really are.[19] Reducing every property to a more fundamental original
layer, ownness (*Eigen*) thus determines the *ego*—in man or God—as its
particular way of belonging to itself, beyond any reification in an "in
itself": for living man, not body (*Körper*) but flesh (*Leib*), for the third
divine hypostasis, not Spirit (*spiritus*) but gift (*Donum*). The insidious
substantification of the Holy Spirit wrongly suggested by the term of
spirit (*spiritus*) must thus for Bonaventure give way to or at least be
overshadowed by the term of gift (*donum*) as a synonym for the "relation
to a giver":

> we must say that 'gift' as well as 'spirit' (*tam donum quam spir-
> itus*) are names given relatively (*dicitur relative*). But the rela-

---

[16] Bonaventure, *Brev.* I, 3, No. 9 (V, 212a), Fr. tr. p. 75: "The Holy Spirit is properly
(*proprium*) the Gift; he is the bond or the charity of the two; he is also the Holy Spirit."

[17] Bonaventure, *Brev.* I, 6, No. 1 (V, 215a), Fr. tr. p. 93.

[18] Bonaventure, *Brev.* I, 3, No. 9 (V, 212a), Fr. tr. p. 75 and *Brev.* I, 6, No. 1 (V,
215a), Fr. tr. p. 93.

[19] For the phenomenological interpretation of the proper or the own (*Eigen*), consult
Husserl, *Méditations cartésiennes*, op. cit., §44: "Reduction of transcendental experience
to the sphere of belonging," as well as Didier Franck's commentary in *Chari et corps, sur la
phénoménologie de Husserl*, Paris, Minuit, 1981, pp. 92-93, esp. the formula "l'expérience
du propre est le propre de l'expérience."

tionship appears clearer in the name of *gift* than in the name of *spirit* (*sed tamen relatio magis apparet in hoc nomine donum quam in hoc nomine spiritus*) because the gift always connotes *the relationship to a giver* whereas the spirit does not (*quia donum semper dicit respectum ad dantem, spiritus autem non*). This name, in fact, can be taken absolutely.[20]

B) THE GIVABLE, OR THE ACT OF "GIVING THE GIFT"

But will it be enough for the Holy Spirit to *be given* (by the loving union of the Father and the Son) and to *give* (to creatures) in order for himself to be constituted—as Gift (*Donum*)? Again we must grant him the possibility of *giving himself*, supposing that the gift cannot truly give as long as he retains his ability to give to himself—otherwise, we run the risk of a conception in which he might retain even the act of donation to himself in the anticipation of a reciprocity in return. The whole power of the Holy Spirit's donation here, whether his passive power as a hypostasis or his active power as the regenerative breath of life, consists in the primacy of the *way* of giving (*quomodo*) over the gift itself (*quod*), a primacy that extends even over the giver himself (*quis*) and over the one to whom it is given (*ad quem*). We can apply here both Bonaventure's *donum* as much as Heidegger's *es gibt* (the German equivalent of "there is" or "there are", but literally meaning "it gives"—a sense that neither the English *there is* nor the French *il y a* connotes)—by which the act of "allowing" the entrance into presence always matters more than the presence of the very thing that enters: "*es gibt* means strictly: to allow the entering-into-presence (*Anwesenlassen*); it is no longer the presence of the being that summons the gaze, (*Anwesen*) but that on the basis of which it is detached in concealing it—to allow it itself (*lassen*), the givenness of the giving."[21] Paradoxically (unless the paradox is founded here on a theological structure implicit in the Heideggerian *Gegebenheit*) Bonaventure seeks in the affirmation of a pneumatological givenness precisely the conditions for "allowing" the entry into the mutual presence of the Father and the Son—and, for all creatures, into the presence of the whole Trinity—which, far from reducing the present to its mere presence, examines instead the gift of its presence or "the present that makes a

---

[20] Bonaventure, *I Sent.*, d.18, dub.I (333b-334a).

[21] Heidegger, *Séminaire du Thor* (1969), in *Questions IV*, Paris, Gallimard, 1976, p. 300.

present of itself."[22] In other words, and more trivially, whoever gives a present when he offers a present gives less the *presence of his present* (the beingness and the value of his gift) than the *modality of the presentation* of his present: this itself, as gift, says something of its manner of being by way of the giver). It is enough to read Bonaventure on the widow's alms in his *Commentary on the Gospel of Luke* (Lk 21:1-4):

> for indeed he gives abundantly who gives *more from his heart* (*copiosus namque donat qui ex majori* [sic] *corde donat*).[23]

This single formula shows how much the modal determination (*quomodo*) of pneumatological givenness, and thus also of poverty itself (see below, §10c), takes priority over its strictly substantial beingness. The defining characteristic of Christian giving, whether immanent or economic, does not measure the gift by the quantity of what is given nor by the prestige of the giver, but only by the *how* of the act of giving or of the givenness itself. Tell me how you give and I will tell you who you are, unless you are always already nothing but the very way of this giving: "more than matter, the given is registered as a manner of being—in fact, as the manner of Being."[24]

Among the numerous modes of the act of giving, "liberality" (*liberalitas*) characterizes precisely the particular *divine manner* of its donation. Jean-François Bonnefoy points out (yet without drawing out all the consequences of the observation) that Bonaventure poses a question at the beginning of his treatise on the Holy Spirit (*I Sent.* d. 10) that, in its very articulation, breaks with its classic formulation: "is there in God a procession *by means of liberality* (*per modum liberalitas*)? One would expect to read '*by means of the will*' (*per modum voluntatis*)."[25] The reason for this substitution of generous procession for voluntary procession, not at all "the result of negligence or distraction,"[26] is in my opinion to be found in the particular *mode* of the givenness that liberality exercises. "Because the Holy Spirit is properly the Gift," in the

---

[22] Marion, *L'idole et la distance*, op. cit. (Biblio/Essais), pp. 283-284: more essential to the present than its presence, seems to be the gift present, or better the present that makes present from itself."

[23] Bonaventure, *Commentarium in Evangelium Lucae*, c.XXI, No. 4 (VII, 521a). Cited and commented on, fairly, by Bonnefoy in *Le Saint-Esprit et ses dons selon saint Bonaventure*, op. cit., p. 30 (with an error in Bonaventure's pagination).

[24] Marion, *L'idole et la distance*, op. cit. (Biblio/Essais), p. 284.

[25] Bonnefoy, *Le Saint-Esprit et ses dons selon saint Bonaventure*, op. cit., p. 26. Leaning on Bonaventure, *I Sent.*, d.10, a.1, q.1 (I, 194-196): "utrum in divinis ponenda sit persona per modum liberalitatis."

[26] Bonnefoy, ibid. p. 26.

Breviloquium's words (*cum proprium sit Spiritus sancti esse donum*), all the determinations of the third hypostasis taken collectively (gift, charity, or link, and Holy Spirit) agree on a single common denominator: the "gift voluntarily given" (*datum voluntarium*) that properly designates (*nominat*) the gift.[27] An overly immediate interpretation of this voluntary given (*datum voluntarium*) would then consist either in making the will a possible mode of the donation (*giving with the will to give*), or in making the will the source or principle of every donation (*giving that begins with the will*). Divine liberality, on the other hand, does more—and in a different way—than giving voluntarily (*modus operari*) or giving by the will (*facultas*): instead, it gives the will itself. To be convinced, it should be enough for us to work with Bonaventure through the sharing that occurs between the two scopes of practice of divine liberality, depending on whether it means either the "reason for giving that is immanent" in God as the mode of the union of the wills of the Father and the Son in the Spirit (*ratio donandi*), or else the act of "actual economic donation," insofar as it just *is* the Holy Spirit, and is thus itself offered to creatures (*donatum*).[28] The chief point of distinction between these two modes of liberality is that the "actual given" (*donatum* or *datum*) in the Trinity's economic liberality is not to be identified with the "reason for giving" or the "principle of giving" (*ratio donandum*) in its immanent liberality. In other words, the Holy Spirit's actual, effective donation to man does not mean that this effectiveness should also have to be established in God as a rule or standard of all donation. If every gift, indeed, "indicates a relation between the one who gives and the one who receives" (*donum dicat respectum ad eum cui dicatur*), we should nonetheless further distinguish in God—and probably also in man—the "actual gift" having been given, or the actual given (*datus*); the "gift yet to be given," or the intentional

---

[27] Bonaventure, *Brev.* I, 3, No. 9 (V, 212a), Fr. tr. (modified; the *causal* relationship, or relationship of anteriority, of the Gift with respect to the Holy Spirit's other names is not perceived by the translator) p. 75: "because the Holy Spirit is properly the Gift (*cum proprium sit Spiritus sancti esse donum*), he is the bond or charity of the two (*esse nexum seu caritatem ambulorum*), and he is also the Holy Spirit (*esse etiam Spiritum sanctum*). *Gift* defines (*nominat*) him as being *voluntarily given* (*ut datum voluntarium*); and charity or bond as being *voluntarily given, as* principal, and Holy Spirit as *voluntarily given*, as principle and hypostasis."

[28] Bonaventure, *I Sent.* d.10, a.1, q.1, ad.1 (I, 195b): "we must say that emanation by the mode of liberality (*per modum liberalitatis*) is twofold: either as what is desired (*volitum*), or as reason for desire (*ratio volendi*); or again, either as what is given (*donatum*), or as reason for giving (*ratio donandi*). External creatures emanate by the first mode (*primo modo*), but the third person in the Trinity emanates (*emanat tertia in Trinitate persona*) by the second mode, because the reason for willing and the reason for giving are intrinsic and belongs to the perfection of the will (*quia ratio volendi et donandi est intrinseca perfectissimae voluntati*)."

donation (*dandus*); and the "givable" as pure reservoir or possibility of givenness (*donabilis*), independent of both its intentional fulfillment and its very intention:

> the gift (*donum*) indicates a relation between the one who gives and the one who receives in three possible ways: according to the act (*secundum actum*), because the gift *has been given* (*quia datur*); according to the intention (*secundum habitum*), because the gift is *going to be given* to someone (*quia donandum aliquando*); or according to possibility (*secundum aptitudinem*), because it *can be given*.[29]

We can certainly find in the *De Trinitate* of Augustine—of whom Bonaventure always remained an avowed disciple—some roots of the distinction between the gift (*donum*) and the given (*datum*).[30] But the great strength and originality of the Seraphic Doctor amounts to adding here the dimension of the pure "givable" or of the possibility of the giving as such (*donabilis*). In fact, it matters little, at the heart of the Trinity, whether the donation be actual or intentional; the only thing that really counts is its pure liberality—the sort that never causes the donation to be exhausted or fatigued in its act of giving. The purely givable (*donabilis*) here characterizes a Trinitarian framework in which "possibility is above actuality" (*höher als die Wirklichkeit steht die Möglichkeit*), in accordance with a rightful phenomenological inquiry and in opposition to an Aristotelian model that is once again full of *actuality* in theology ("actuality" in the sense of the unfolding of potentialities, an actuality that is seeing something of a revival in the discipline).[31] But it is not enough simply to reverse here the ancient primacy of actuality over potentiality and simply put its opposite into play: "a metaphysical concern still dominates the intention to surpass metaphysics."[32] The givable (*donabilis*) as pure possibility of givenness without reserve rather

---

[29] Bonaventure, *I Sent.*, d.18, a.un., q.2, concl. (I, 325b): "utrum Spiritus sanctus sit donum ab aeterno, an ex tempore." See the analysis of this pure, atemporal donation of the Holy Spirit in Bonnefoy, *Le Saint Esprit et ses dons*, op. cit. pp. 38-41, and Mathieu, *La Trinité créatrice d'après saint Bonaventure*, op. cit., pp. 261-265 (partial translation of this question).

[30] Augustine, *De Trinitate*, op. cit., (B.A No. 15), L.V, c.XV, 16, pp. 461-463: "the idea that we have of a *gift* (*donum*) is different from that of *what is given* (*donatum*). One may have a *gift* even before it is *given* (*donum potest esse et antequam detur*), but it is entirely impossible to speak of *something given* without it in fact being a gift (*donatum autem nisi datum fuerit nullo modo dici potest.*"

[31] Heidegger, Être et temps, op. cit. (tr. Martineau), §7, p. 38 (German pagination).

[32] Heidegger, *Temps et être*, in *Questions IV*, op. cit., p. 48.

abandons *at the same time* actuality and potentiality, metaphysics and the attempt to surpass it, to themselves.

Like a dazzling, unfading radiance, the possibility of giving in God is made paradoxically even more abundant for the fact that it gives without regard either for that which is given or for the one who gives or receives, and is instead attentive solely and exclusively to the act of donation itself. Not merely gift, the *givable gives the gift*—as if to keep the gift itself in the clutches of the giver, while actuality is again to be paid in exchange for the privilege of the donation. The "gift voluntarily given" (*datum voluntarium*), to return here to the *Breviloquium*'s formulation (*Brev.* I, 3), is thus only given (*datum*) because the will itself is given or is abandoned in the Gift (*donum*)—otherwise, the risk is that the gift seems to want to demand its due too much:

> the gift (*donum*) adds to the given (*dati*) the character of liberality, or of *non-returnability* (*conditionem liberalitatis sive irredibilitatis*).[33]

For Bonaventure, the Holy Spirit thus means the Gift—or better, the pure givable—because, in contrast to some kind of merchandise, "he cannot be sold" (*Spiritus sanctus dicitur donum quia non debet vendi*).[34] To restore the Holy Spirit as the pure givability (*donabilis*) of all reciprocity—such, for the Seraphic Doctor, in his *Commentary on the Gospel According to Saint John*, is thus the meaning of both Jesus' words to the Samaritan woman, "if you knew the gift of God" (Jn 4:10)— where "the gift means the Holy Spirit" (*si scires donum Dei: donum Dei est spiritus sanctus*)—and of the apostle Peter's sharp response to Simon, the recently converted disciple, who dared offer money for the gift of the Spirit and the power of the imposition of hands (Acts 8:20):

> may your wealth perish and you with it, because you have thought that you could have the free gift of God in exchange for money (*quoniam donum Dei existimasti pecunia possideri*).[35]

---

[33] Bonaventure, *I Sent.*, d.18, a.un., q.3, concl. (I, 327a). On the "non-returnability" (*irredibilitas*) in Bonaventure, see Bonnefoy, *Le Saint Esprit et ses dons*, op. cit., pp. 41-43. As for the distinction between *datum* and *donum* inherited from the apostle James (*James* 1:17), its theological roots can be found in John Scotus Eriugena, *De divisione naturae (Periphyseon)*, P.L. 72, Fr. tr. *De la division de la nature*, Paris, PUF, 1995, Book II, 565c, p. 339: "'any excellent thing given and any perfect gift (*donum*),' declares the apostle James, 'comes from on high and descends from the Father of Lights.'"

[34] Bonaventure, *Commentarium Evangelium in Ioanem*, c.IV, No. 18 (VI, 292a).

[35] Bonaventure, *Commentarium Evangelium in Ioanem*, c.IV, No. 18 (VI, 292a): "Jesus answered him and said, 'if you knew the gift of God' (*si scires donum Dei*) (Jn 4:10).

c) ABANDONMENT, OR "PERFECT POVERTY"

Consequently, the extreme wealth in God consists in his self-abandonment to the most extreme poverty: the very sort by which the widow "took on her poverty (*de penuria*) and gave all that she possessed, all that she had to live on" (Mk 12:44). The whole question of poverty, in God as in man, is not therefore knowing what I have, nor is it in measuring the value of what I have—as if taking it away from me would make me rediscover some kind of fictitious purity of what I am. Rather, it demands of me only that I make myself capable of transferring *what I have* into *what I no longer have* to make of the act of this donation the very thing that *I am*. *Having* and *Being*, like wealth and poverty, neither compete with nor oppose each other, since an *"allowing to be given"* in a donation without reserve (*donabilis*) takes priority over that which is *already given* (*datus*) and over that which is *yet to be given* (*dandus*). Instead, they convert each other, on the one hand in order to make of the *having* its very *being* (giving the *having* paradoxically remains the best means of "having"—as gift). "Retaining nothing for oneself" (*nihil prorsus retinet*): such, therefore, is the invaluable meaning of the reverse side of donation—poverty—in which Brother Francis receives the blessed share and to which Brother Bonaventure gives theological expression:

If you would be perfect, go, sell all you have (Mt. 19:21). This is *perfect poverty* (*ecce perfecta paupertas*), which retains nothing for itself (*quae nihil prorsus retinet*).[36]

The gift of God is the Holy Spirit (*donum Dei est Spiritus sanctus*) of whom it is said in *Acts* (2:38): 'convert, and let each one of you be baptized, and you shall receive the gift of the Holy Spirit' (*et accipietis donum sancti Spiritus*). The Holy Spirit is said to be the gift (*Spiritus sanctus dicitur donum*) because he cannot be sold (*quia non debet vendi*), as it says in *Acts* (8:20): may your silver perish and you with it, because you have judged that you could buy with silver the free gift of God (*quoniam donum Dei existimasti pecunia possideri*)." The reference is highlighted but not developed by Bonnefoy in *Le saint Esprit et ses dons*, op. cit., p. 41. The idea that "the formula *if you knew the gift of God* can here serve as a paradigm for all phenomenology of the gift" is drawn from Marion, *Esquisse d'un concept phénoménologique du don*, in *Archivio di Filosofia*, 1994, t.LXII, No. 1-3, Filosofia della rivelazione, pp. 75-94 (cit. p. 78). The hypothesis is taken up again, but in a less directly theological way, in the same author's Étant donné, Essai d'une phénoménologie de la donation, op. cit., §9-11, pp. 124-161: the triple *epoché* (of the giver, of the receiver, and of the gift itself).

[36] Bonaventure, *Brev.* V, 6, No. 5 (V, 259a), Fr. tr. p. 71 (the formula "ecce perfecta paupertas quae nihil sibi prorsus retinet" is unfortunately totally omitted from the fifth book of the *Breviloquium* by its translator, Jean-Pierre Rezette). This formulation of poverty as total dis-appropriation of self is explicitly inherited from St. Francis of Assisi: cf. *Lettre à tout l'ordre*, in Écrits, Paris, Cerf, *Sources chrétiennes* No. 285 (bilingual edition),

Three degrees of nakedness (*nuditas*) in the *Apology for the Poor* thus make the "poor one"—for which the Trinity, in my opinion, exemplifies the gift—the very one who "retains nothing for himself"—up to and including any concern for his own poverty.

(a) In a total movement of self-renunciation, the "extreme destitution of things" (*summa rerum penuria*) of whoever desires "to follow the naked Christ" (*nudum Christum nudus sequere*) first means that he renounces, in Bonaventure's opinion, "everything superfluous and any personal ownership (*omnis superfluitas et proprietariae possessionis*).[37]

(b) Next, on the second, higher level, extreme poverty consists in "renouncing all personal possessions (*consistit in abdicatione potestatis possidendi proprium*) and in abnegating one's own will (*et abnegatione propriae voluntatis*)."[38] When the true mendicant brother gives or gives himself in the vow of poverty, he in fact gives not only what he *has* but also his very power of having or of possessing (*potestatis possidendi*), not only what he *wants* but also his power to want (*propriae voluntatis*). This is not framed negatively, such that he should have to renounce all possession and desire to follow Christ, but strictly positively, such that the act of giving even the appropriation of the gift (having) and of himself (desiring) amounts precisely to conforming himself to Christ in his mode of giving: "no one takes my life; it is I who give it (*nemo tollit a me sed ego pono eam a meipso*)" (Jn. 10:18).[39] "Perfect poverty" (*perfecta paupertas*), for Bonaventure, does not merely turn the radicality of impoverishment into an ideal of life; instead, it establishes poverty itself as the very perfection of the mendicant brother. Perfect poverty—

1981, Admonition No. 29, p. 251: "retain nothing of yourselves (*nihil ergo retinet de vobis*) so that the one who gives himself to you entirely (*qui se vobis exhibet totum*) might receive you entirely (*ut totos vos respiciat*)."

[37] Bonaventure, *Apologia pauperum*, c.VII, No. 12 (VIII, 276a) for the formula of "supreme destitution" and No. 22 (VIII, 279b) for the first degree of evangelical poverty. The French translation – which Ephrem Longpré described as "the most perfect work of French literature" (*Dictionnaire d'histoire et de géographie écclésiastiques*, art. *Bonaventure*, t. IX, col. 774) – by Jean de Dieu, Œuvres spirituelles de saint Bonaventure, op. cit., vol. IV, pp. 21-218 (the cited passages are, respectively, from pp. 121 and 128). Let us finally point the reader to the valuable study by Jean Chatillon on this theme of evangelical poverty: "*Nudum Christum nudus sequere*, Notes sur les origines et la signification du thème de la nudité spirituelle dans les écrits de saint Bonaventure, in *S. Bonaventura 1274-1974*, op. cit., vol. IV, pp. 719-772 (analysis of Ch. VII of the *Apologia pauperum* on pp. 755-760).

[38] Bonaventure, *Apol. paup.*, Ch. VII, No. 22 (VIII, 279b), Fr. tr. (John of God), p. 128.

[39] Quoted and discussed by Bonaventure, *Commentarium Evangelium in Ioanem*, c. X, No. 23 (VI, 388a).

this, in reality, is what perfects the being who has voluntarily become poor. Only the *givenness of the gift* assures, at the heart of the Franciscan ideal, a complete givenness—which simultaneously suspends (*epochein*) the giver, the receiver, their reciprocity, and the gift itself.[40] Only then can the act of givenness appear in its pure nakedness—the only thing truly desired by the Franciscan in following the "naked Christ" (*Christum nudum*), which, after all, is the aim by which the receiver is "conformed," as much as possible, to the image of the giver (*conformatio*).

(c) The third and final degree of complete poverty (*summa penuria*)—of which the extreme act of donation in God really expresses the reverse side—amounts not only to an expectation of nothing for oneself, from the other, from reciprocity, and from the gift itself, but also to a final and paradoxical reduction or suspension that touches the very act of givenness:

> the third degree adds to the previous ones the renunciation of all transitory resources (*in abdicatione omnis transitoriae facultatis*) and accepts privation of and poverty in (*cum penuria et indigentia*) that which can assure a comfortable subsistence.[41]

Since even taking alms for oneself is rejected, nothing is left but the acceptance of total destitution (*penuria*)—better, nothing is left but the *gift of* destitution or the *gift for* desitution as such. The paradox reaches its height here and helps us understand the widow St. Paula, whom Bonaventure follows St. Jerome in praising: for her "desire to die as a beggar (*ut mendicans ipsa moretur*) aspires to this nakedness (*ad hanc nuditas aspirabat*)."[42] Death in fact attains the fullness of destitution not because it erases the gift of life, but precisely because it establishes the very *modality* by which life is lived. Paula's wish, to be clear, is not simply to die (which is another trivial form of possession of the gift of life, if only to destroy it), but to die *precisely* "as a beggar" (*ut mendicans*). The "end of control" or "the subject's experience of passivity" that every death implies (Lévinas) is here somehow anticipated in the experience of being a beggar. "Accepting that one is no longer able to do anything," even in one's own subsistence, as long as life lasts or at the dawn of death, since

---

[40] Marion, *Esquisse d'un concept phénoménologique du don*, op. cit., p. 79: "after reciprocity, the giver, and the receiver, givenness lastly implies—fourth argument—setting aside the gift itself."

[41] Bonaventure, *Apol. paup.*, Ch. VII, No. 22 (VIII, 280a), Fr. tr. (John of God), p. 128.

[42] Boanventure, *Apol. paup.*, Ch. VII, No. 23 (VIII, 280a), Fr. tr. (John of God), pp. 128-129.

it will soon cease to persist: this is the ultimate modality of the givenness of self as pure passivity—that which properly defines the Holy Spirit in his relation to the Father and to the Son (see above)—and which, far from losing me in darkest depths of destitution, instead brings me to the point of touching the extreme heights of its wealth.[43] The "nothingness" (*nihilitas*) proper to Bonaventure's corpus—well in advance of Meister Eckhart—thus does not let the creature do his renouncing in the mere nothingness of his vanity, even through the mere nothingness of his "detachment" (*abgescheidenheit* [sic]) from the world and himself.[44] The *annihilation* of Creation, to put it in contemporary terms, instead explicitly "re-attaches," according to Bonaventure, the creature not only to the magnanimity of its Creator but also, in a Trinitarian way, to the density of the creatures *monadologically* contained in him (cf. p. 98-99):

> the creature thus has of himself non-being (*de se habet non-esse*); he receives all his being from another (*totum autem esse habeat aliunde*). He was created so that thus, by his poverty (*pro sua defectibilitate*), he should always need his principle (*semper suo principio indigeret*) and so that the first principle, by his goodness (*pro sua benignitate*), should not cease to communicate himself to the creature (*influere non cessaret*).[45]

---

[43] On the properly theological sense of death as a *modality* of life and as a place of the subject's *passivity*, see my work *Le passeur de Gethsémani*, op. cit., Part 2. As for death as "the end of the subject's control," see Lévinas, *Le Temps et l'autre*, Paris, PUF, 1983, pp. 55-64 (esp. p. 62).

[44] Cf. Meister Eckhart, *Du détachement* (*abgescheidenheit*), Fr. tr. (G. Jarczyk and P.-J. Labarrière), Paris, Rivages/Poche, 1995, pp. 47-70 (and the introduction, pp. 11-23).

[45] Bonaventure, *Brev.* V, 2, No. 3 (V, 253b), Fr. tr. p. 37. Alain de Libera (cf. *Albert le Grand et la philosophie*, Paris, Vrin, 1990, p. 84, and *Penser au Moyen Age*, Paris, Seuil, 1991, pp. 219-320) have been able to show, and to reveal, the particularly Bonaventurian source of Eckhartian *humilitas*, in the Franciscan's adoption not only of a humility of distrust [of self] (connected to sin), but also a properly speaking ontological sort (inherent in reduction to nothingness of man and of Creation before the grandeur of God). See Bonaventure, *Quaestio disputata de humilitate*, in *Quaestiones disputatae de perfectione evangelica*, q.1, concl. (V, 120a): "consequently, since all created things emanate from a single principle (*ab uno principio manant*) and are produced from nothing (*et de nihilo sunt producta*), he is truly wise who recognizes his *nothingness* and that of others (*qui veraciter recognoscit suam et aliorum nihilitatem*) and the sublimity of the first principle." The distance between Bonaventure and Meister Eckhart, especially on the status of humility (*humilitas*), as a syntagma of the "theological" in the former and a "properly philosophical virtue" in the latter (cf. A. de Libera, *Albert le Grand et la philosophie*, ibid., p. 281, and *Penser au Moyen Age*, p. 321), remains to be examined in a later work (especially in the context of a commentary on the *Breviloquium*'s treatises on Creation (*Brev.* II) and on grace (*Brev.* V).

The ontology of poverty, which we have shown does not in any way diminish the criticism of ontologism, thus gives rise to a world, or better, another mode of being for our own world: that of every existing being that, in its very nudity (*nuditas*), does not depend or no longer depends on itself alone to subsist—otherwise running the risk of sinking in the most extreme vanity (*vanitas*). *Dependence* in poverty against the *autonomy* in wealth: such is, finally, the specifically Christian meaning of poverty—which is to say it is Trinitarian. The Trinity itself in fact never parts from this law of a proportional relationship between poverty and dependence; on the contrary, it exemplifies it, since the need for an impossible autonomy in the subsistence (dependence) of the Persons responds *de facto* to the reciprocal gift of the Persons in what they are (poverty). The mutual gift of the Father to the Son, and together to a third (the Holy Spirit), makes up their very being in their radical Trinitarian interdependence.

Furthermore, the Gift—to take a New Testament perspective on the Holy Spirit—implies or denotes the very *medium* or the "milieu" of all givenness. As the first Gift (*primum donum*) or the exemplary principle of all givenness, the Holy Spirit is in fact such for Bonaventure neither simply because he gives, nor because he accepts being given, nor even because "every gift amounts to a gift" (*omne donum reducitur ad donum*), but essentially because "he is the gift *in which* all the other gifts are given" (*Spiritus sanctus est donum in quo alia dona donantur*).[46] His apparent recapitulation of Augustine thus must not obscure the distance between the two thinkers: givenness gives *in* the Gift (*in quo*) for the Seraphic Doctor, and not *from* or *by* the Gift (*a quo / per donum*), as it does for the Doctor of Hippo when he comments on the Pauline formulation of how the "Spirit brings forth all these gifts and distributes them to each as it pleases him" (I Cor 12:12).[47] The Gift, in an original way in Bonaventure,

---

[46] Bonaventure, *I Sent.*, d.18, a.un., q.1, fund. 3 (the first gift) and concl. (the gift in which all the other gifts are given).

[47] Augustine, *De Trinitate*, op. cit., (B.A., No. 16), L.XV, c. XIX, 24, p. 34: "each person does not have all the gifts: some have these, and others have those; but all have the Gift itself (*ipsum donum*) *from which* (*a quo*) the gifts that are proper to each flow, or in other words the Holy Spirit" ["chacun ne possède pas tous les dons: les uns ont ceux-ci, les autres ceux-là, bien que tous possèdent le Don (*ipsum donum*) *duquel* (*a quo*) découlent les dons qui sont propres à chacun, autrement dit l'Esprit Saint."] The [French] translator, P. Agaësse, here renders *a quo* by "*from which the gifts flow.*" Without definitively solving the question here of the meaning of this use of the ablative, either indicating the origin (from which) or the means (by which), the presentation of the Holy Spirit as an active agent of an external donation who does not contain this donation in himself can be discerned in the formula "*per donum quod est spiritus Sanctus*" (by the gift which is the Holy Spirit) is not taken into account in the translation. On the shift from the *per*

is not "the one who gives" (*per*)—be it in the union of the Father and the Son in God or by sanctifying grace in man—but that "in which" (*in quo*) everything is given: in the mode of generosity or the givenness of the gift. In other words, and to take up here a current expression, the Gift gives all the more as it seeks all the less to give than to show "what it gives" of the giving (*quomodo*). The Holy Spirit "is because he gives" (*ideo est quia donum*) and does not first give because he is, as Bonaventure emphasizes in a remarkable formulation:

> if one should object that the Spirit is related more to being than to the gift (*quod magis spiritus dicit habitudinem repicientem esse quam donum*), we must say that it is true in those who receive being as gift (*quod verum est in his quibus accidit esse donum*), but that the Holy Spirit himself *is because he gives* (*sed in Spiritu sancto, qui ideo est quia donum*).[48]

Gift without being—or better *Gift before being* (avoiding here the pitfall of some hasty readings reducing a work to the mere misunderstanding of its title): precisely this, for Bonaventure, is the ultimate meaning of the Holy Spirit, for whom the "gift crosses Being / being" In the *donabilis* as pure "givable," or the possibility of giving, "the gift (here) encounters Being/being, cancels it by a sign, and finally opens it, as opening a window, onto a moment that remains unspeakable according to the language of Being."[49] Adopting *this new language of the gift*, or entering into *the Word of pure givenness*, has thus demanded first that "what we ought to think (*quid sentiendum*) and how we ought to speak (*qualiter loquendum*) about the sovereign Trinity be sufficiently clarified" (*satis claret*), to take up the *Breviloquium*'s own words (*Brev.* I., 4).[50] In order to *think* of the Trinity (*ad sentiendum*)—or better to feel it, since for Bonaventure the one cannot be without the other[51]—

---

to the *in* from Augustine to Bonaventure, see Mathieu, *La Trinité créatrice d'après saint Bonaventure*, op. cit., pp. 179-186.

[48] Bonaventure, *I Sent.*, d. 18, dub.I (I, 334a).

[49] Marion, *Dieu sans l'être* (1982), Paris, PUF/Quadrige, 1991, p. 147 (la croisée de l'Être).

[50] Bonaventure, *Brev.* I, 4, No. 6, (V, 213b), Fr. tr. p. 85: "his intellectis, satis claret, et *quid sentiendum* et *qualiter loquendum* sit de summa trinitate divinarum personarum."

[51] I have shown above that for Bonaventure there can be no pure thought *about* the Trinity without there also being a sensing or a feeling on the part of the believer *according to* the Trinity (*sentire de Deo*). The *quid sentiendum* formulated here (*Brev.* I, 4), before any false division of mysticism and theology, thus simultaneously designates for Bonaventure "what must be thought" *and* "what must be sensed or felt." The amphibology of this *sentire* (perceiving by the senses or experiencing in oneself *and* perceiving by the intellect

we have tried to sense *with God*, i.e. to experience how he experiences *himself* in his own self-affection or his Trinitarian in-common (§8). And in order to speak of it (*ad loquendum*)—to translate it or talk about it—I have attempted here (§10), following the Seraphic Doctor, to give all its rights to the act of pure givenness by which divine generosity demands of itself *and* of man a total self-giving to the most extreme point of poverty, indeed of destitution, in the ideal of mendicancy. Of the many discourses on pure givenness (even on ontic and purely rational non-predication), nothing remains except *prayer* or the "discourse of praise," meaning by this, as the *Breviloquium* puts it, the modality proper to man's welcoming of a wealth that simultaneously comes from an Other and is dug into us by the openness of our own poverty:

> prayer (*oratio*) inclines us to receive the divine charisms. God wants us to pray to him (*Deus orari vult ad hoc*) that he might share his gifts (*ut munera largiatur*).[52]

To the one who places his "faith" in the Trinity (*fides Trinitatis*) and thus prays to it (*oratio*), the Trinity gives, precisely in its extreme liberality, the gift of welcoming its complete and radical manifestation without ambiguity (*Brev.* I, 5).

§11. THE TRINITARIAN MANIFESTATION

Now that we have admitted (a) the possibility of a descriptive theology as a place to receive the Trinitarian *a priori* (Ch. I); (b) the necessity of suspending any statement in the form of *quid* or *quis* in speaking of God's entry into theology (Ch. II); (c) the unfolding of the origin as alone being capable of effecting a departure from metaphysics (Ch. III); and finally (d) the amorous perichoresis of the three persons of the Trinity, diffusing from the self already at the very heart of their divine community (Ch. IV), I must, in this unique movement of divine disappropriation, lay the groundwork for the presence of the Trinitarian being in the world

---

or thinking), from which the *sententia* itself is drawn, is incidentally attested in common Latin usage (cf. Gaffiot, F. *Dictionnaire Latin-Français*, op. cit., art. *sententia* and *sentio*). As for the sense of *sentire* as "experiencing in oneself."

[52] Bonaventure, *Brev.* V, 10, No. 2 (V, 263b), Fr. tr., p. 103. On the meaning and the modalities of prayer as a "discourse of praise," especially in an analysis of Dionysius, see Marion, *L'idole et la distance*, op. cit., (Biblio/Essais), §16, pp. 219-243: "le discours de louange."

that simultaneously delivers—almost phenomenologically—the *how* of its appearing. Paul Claudel, very close to Bonaventure here, writes:

> the world without God is not only incomplete, but also reduced to chaos, to nonsense, and to nothingness. I would gladly change the saying so that instead of *a visibilibus ad invisibilium amorem rapiamur* (let us be carried from the visible to the love of the invisible), I would say: *ab invisibilibus ad visibilium amorem et cognitionem rapiamur* (let us be carried from the invisible to the love and knowledge of the visible). For there are various revelations: that of a plain and simple truth, but also that of the water that reveals the seed planted in the ground by making it grow.[53]

Despite the sometimes warranted accusation of a "flight into mysticism" in Bonaventure,[54] the downward movement of the *Breviloquium*—diametrically opposed to that of the *Itinerarium* (which rises degree by degree from the sensible to the intelligible)—leads or leads back "from the invisible to the visible" (*ab invisibilibus ad visibilium amorem*), as Paul Claudel writes, and not the opposite. Better, leading or leading back the invisible Trinity toward "the love and knowledge of the visible" begins with the discussion of the Trinity (*Brev.* I, 5)—and paradoxically even before any treatment of Creation (*Brev.* II):

> alongside the *ascendant analogia entis* that scarcely comes into consideration, there is a much stronger, *descendent* one: the Eternal Word of Expression knows better and expresses what each thing means better than each thing itself can.[55]

The reason is that for Bonaventure—and in this, for example, showing his originality with respect to John Scotus Eriugena—the Father needs nothing of the world, neither from its nature nor even from its existence, to make himself manifest. Instead, his paternal origin only requires his

---

[53] Claudel, P. *Lettre inédite à H. Lemaître* (1 August 1937), cited in Lagarde & Michard, *Le XXe siècle*, Paris, Bordas, 1962, p. 182: introduction and presentation of Paul Claudel. The letter was unfortunately not reprinted in Claudel, P. *Correspondances 1911-1954*, Paris, Gallimard, 1995.

[54] Balthasar, *La gloire et la croix*, t.I (Apparition), op. cit., p. 316: "the spiritual senses in Albert the Great and Bonaventure disappear in the inaccessible heights of mystical contemplation, and thus lose interest in theology" (cited and discussed in RSPT, pp. 44-47: "de la chair du monde comme conquête de nouvelles terres à la réitération d'une fuite"

[55] Balthasar, *La gloire et la croix*, t.II (Styles I), op. cit., pp. 265-266 (my emphasis).

own Son to express himself, but this fully, because the Father's givenness is sufficiently abundant *in the Son alone*.[56]

A) The expression of the Trinity: the beauty and grandeur of God

Bonaventure's schema of the *expressio* is unique and original in that it is centered, in the person of the Word alone, on the entire act of the Trinity's manifestation: on the one hand, insofar as the Father "conceives" the Son not only as an act of some anticipatory intellection but first as a place of a life-giving self-begetting (the double sense of the *verbum conceptum*); and, on the other hand, insofar as this "conceived" Son is such not only in view of some self-contemplation of God in himself, but more in the intent of a "proclamation" or a "presentation" of the Father's paternity, which he expresses (*verbum prolatum*), both toward man and toward the whole of Creation (cf. p. 96). Since this expressive schema of the Trinity, as we have seen, protects Bonaventure from the accusation of not having "taken expressionism all the way to the immanence that it implies,"[57] to continue following the order of the *Breviloquium*'s prescriptions we must now think of it according to an eminently "aesthetic" mode—the only one fully appropriate for it:

> that which is supremely beautiful (*pulchrum*) and splendid (*speciosum*) possesses the cause of expression (*exprimendi*) and exemplarity (*exemplandi*); this is why it is fitting that exemplarity should be appropriated to the Son (*appropriandi exemplaritatem Filio*).[58]

---

[56] John Scotus Eriugena, *De divisione naturae (Periphyseon)*, p. L, No. 62, Fr. tr. *De la division de la nature*, Paris, PUF, 1995, Book III, 678c, p. 167: "we must thus understand that God and the creature do not constitute two distinct realities, but rather one and the same reality. For it is by a mutual cooperation that the creature subsists in God and that God *is created* in an extraordinary and inexpressible way in the creature, *by manifesting* himself." The idea of a self-creation, indeed of a self-manifestation, of God first in his creatures remains here diametrically opposed to Bonaventure, at the very least in the sense that God would have to require creatures to express himself. God in fact has no need for the world in order either to be or to manifest, according to Bonaventure, since the Father *is* and is already and always manifested, fully so, in his one Son in whom all creatures are also contained. Creation thus only lets appear what has already been contained from all eternity in the Word.

[57] G. Deleuze. *Spinoza et le problème de l'expression*, op. cit., pp. 163-164. For criticism of this criticism.

[58] Bonaventure, *Brev.* I, 6, No. 4 (V, 215b), Fr. tr. (modified) p. 97. The unjustified omission of any transcription of the term *speciosum* in this translation is to be regretted.

The origin at work *in* the work *makes* its work, I have said; and for that reason it opens a world—or better makes its (divine?) world into an opened world. The Son is then almost *aesthetically* the Father's work of art, "supremely beautiful and splendid (*summe pulchrum et speciosum*)" through the glory of the Father: as "cause of expression" (*ratio exprimendi*), he manifests, like any work, the depths of his origin or of his author; and as "cause of exemplarity" (*ratio exemplandi*), he is addressed to man to make man see, by way of a prototype this time, the brilliant, sense-giving intuition whose manifestation he, for his part, offers. The two of them—Father and Son—are thus "one in the beautiful," and they present themselves to the believer to be seen as such.[59]

But for Bonaventure, the grandeur of God, even more than his beauty, does not consist merely in being great (*magnus*), greater (*maior*), or even the greatest (*maximus*) in an infinite transcendence or a semi-invisibility with respect to creatures, as it does for Anselm. It consists instead in the fact that God finds, *in himself,* someone (*aliquis*) "as great" as him (*sicut*)—and is thus able to be given to man, who is obviously always less great:

> this diffusion reaches so far (*haec diffusio est ultimata*) that the one who produces (*ut det producens*) gives all that he can (*quidquid potest*). But the creature cannot receive all that God can give (*creatura recipere non potest quidquid Deus dare potest*) ... It is thus necessary that this diffusion, because of all of its power, be in someone (*in aliquo*) than whom nothing greater can be thought (*quo maius cogitari non potest*). Now, it is possible to think of something greater (*maius*) than any creature, and the creature itself can conceive of something greater than itself. But in the Son, production is *as* in the Father (*sed in Filio est productio sicut in Patre*). Consequently, if nothing can be thought that is greater than the Father (*si ergo Patre nihil maius cogitari potest*), the same is true of the Son (*ergo nec Filio*).[60]

---

[59] Balthasar, *La gloire et la croix*, t. I (Apparition), ibid., p. 518 ("l'attestation de la figure"): "The Father is the foundation, the Son is the manifestation; the Father is the content, the Son is the form in the unique way that it appears in revelation. But here as elsewhere there can be no base without manifestation, no content without form. The two are *one in the beautiful*; they repose in each other; and he who would perceive the beautiful must understand this reciprocity: 'Learn and understand that the Father is in me and I am in the Father (John 10:38)."

[60] Bonaventure, *Hex.* XI, 11 (V, 382a), Fr. tr. (modified), *Les six jours de la création*, op. cit., pp. 282-283.

Bonaventure's achievement becomes clear here: because nothing can be thought greater than the Father, and because the Son alone is (at least) *equal* to the Father (*in Filio est productio sicut in Patre*), only the Son is revealed as being capable of receiving the fullness (*ultimata*) of the Father's donation. The excess (*excessus*) of this donation is such in God that the Father gives himself first totally, and in a Trinitarian way, into his Son. It is not that he unfairly refuses to give himself to man in this way, but no creature, always as limited as imperfect, could receive this kind of divine indwelling.[61] In other words, where in the greatest *distance* from man to God Anselm sees at least a way of arriving at his existence, if not a full proof of it (*the ontological argument*), Bonaventure sees an indication of man's *hyper-proximity* to God, a proximity contained in the complete equality of the Father and the Son (the Trinitarian *a priori*).[62]

The insertion of the ontological argument at the heart of the Trinity's perichoresis thus raises the Anselmian formula (*id quo maius nihil cogitari potest*) to its true—or at the very least to another (?)—place: no longer deployed to prove God by the idea of his hyper-transcendence, it is instead to let him express himself, as himself, starting only with the presentation of his paternal givenness to his own Son. If God is thus not proven for Bonaventure (§5a), it is first because he makes himself fully known by himself (§5b); and he does this best by the expressed likeness in his Son (§7b), the only one capable, we now see, of manifesting at once the beauty (the aesthetic model) and the grandeur (the borrowed and converted Anselmian argument) of Trinitarian theophany. Only in the character of the Son manifesting the depths of the Father and uniting in the divine love of a third, the Holy Spirit (§11), can the Trinity rightly be said to "dwell, appear, descend, be sent, and send" (*Brev.* I, 5).

---

[61] Cf. RSPT, pp. 20-25: "le dépassement de la métaphysique: l'excès de la donation du Père."

[62] For the formulation of the "so-called" ontological argument, see Anselm of Canterbury, *Proslogion*, op. cit. (Cerf), t.I, Ch. XV, p. 267: "for God is greater than can be thought (*quod [Deus] maior quam cogitari possit*)." As for Kant's reduction of this argument to an "ontological" form that yet does not belong to him, see, respectively, Kant, *Critique de la raison pure*, Paris, PUF, 1980, trans. Tremasaygues-Pacaud, p. 425-431 (the ideal of pure reason): "on the impossibility of an ontological proof of the existence of God"; and Marion, "L'argument relève-t-il de l'ontologie?" in *Question cartèsiennes* (1), Paris, PUF, 1991, pp. 221-258. It will be noted, however, that no Trinitarian interpretation of the argument is proposed here (unless very indirectly by the development of the idea of the Good), precisely because such is not Anselm's intent – by contrast to Bonaventure – in the development of his argumentation.

B) The Divine Indwelling: Mission and Inhabitation, Acts of Appearing, Manifestation

Far from being reduced to the mere experience that we have of it, the *Trinity's appearing* is in fact no less given to man under the modalities of its acts of appearing, whose intentional aim justifies, as I have said, if not a comprehensive grasp of it (*cognitio comprehensionis*), at least an apprehensive approach (*cognitio per apprehensionem*). Neither empirical nor solely experiential, the theologian's "vision" of this "essence" (*Wesens-Schauung*), to express it in phenomenological terms, paradoxically, in my opinion, supposes more the aspect (*eidos*) than the pure Idea (*Idee*). The divine Trinitarian being is in fact given phenomenologically to every believer only by a multiplicity of adumbrations (*Abschattungen*) that, very precisely, constitute at once the unity and the diversity of its appearance. The "return to the things themselves," since it here concerns the Trinitarian God, consists first in "interrogating (*him*) inasmuch as he gives himself" and not only *me* inasmuch as I have the empirical experience of him giving himself—although this experience may often be or seem to me, in many ways, normative. Returning progressively from Husserl to Bonaventure,[63] to make the appearing of "the (divine) object in its how" (*das Objekt im wie*) appear no longer unilaterally in its *quid* (*sein Was*)—i.e. "in the how of his modes of givens" more than in that very thing that is given—such is probably, in my opinion, the final tension of the whole of Part I of the *Breviloquium*. The statement in its fifth chapter, treating precisely of "the unity of the divine nature in its multiple acts of appearing (*apparitionum*)," demonstrates this by the insertion of a concession—"nonetheless" (*nihilominus*)—that marks the complete passage to another order: from the metaphysics of the *quid* of the divine essence to the mysticism of the *quomodo* of his act of appearing to man:[64]

---

[63] This quick detour through Husserlian phenomenology in fact has as its sole aim, at least in this work, to renew the interpretation of Bonaventure by posing him new questions and in leaving the concern to treat with precision the repercussions for Husserl himself of this theological application of his phenomenology for later—or to others. On the points here emphasized, see especially E. Husserl, *Ideen I* (1913), op. cit., (Tel/Gallimard), intr. p. 9 (distinction *Idee/eidos*); §3, pp. 19-24 (the vision of the essence, the departure from the *quid*, the multiplicity of adumbrations, and the original donating intuition); §19, pp. 63-67 (the return to the things themselves as an interrogation of the givenness of the object, the cardinal flaw of its confusion with empiricism, and vision not as sensory, empirical vision but as original donating consciousness); §132, pp. 444-445 (the object in the *how* of its modes of givens).

[64] I refer here to my hypothesis of "a logic of mysticism as a logic of transcending metaphysics," which I develop elsewhere (RSPT, esp. pp. 15-16). The hypothesis is for-

according to divine teaching, we must hold that God (*Deus*) is without limit, invisible, and unchangeable. *Nonetheless (nihilominus)*, he dwells in a special way (*habitat specialiter*) in sanctified human beings; he has appeared (*apparuit*) to the patriarchs and to the Prophets; he has descended (*descendit*) from heaven; and he has sent (*misit*) his Son and his Holy Spirit for the salvation of the human race.[65]

Without going deeper here into a full clarification of the Trinity's appearing at the heart of the soul as well as at the center of the world, let us note that from the beginning this already orients the whole of Bonaventure's theology toward an "ontology of the sensible": indwelling in sanctified mankind, appearing to the patriarchs and prophets, descending from heaven, and the sending of the Son and the Holy Spirit for the salvation of the human race. It is not that man's experience of the Trinity is reduced to its merely sensible effects; rather, the Trinity's appearing *even in and to* the sensible guides the whole development of the *Breviloquium*, and that from its very first lines.[66] The hypothesis of possible *Trinitarian appearances* in Part I's Chapter 5, which an initial and overly hasty reading (*Brev.* I) might take as a kind of *hapax legomenon* in the middle of a more metaphysical set (unity of the essence, Trinity of persons, appropriations, etc.), instead marks, in my opinion, the summit, indeed the fundamental orientation, of the *Brief Discourse* in general, for it opens, this time explicitly, onto the properly *Biblical* affirmation of the Trinity as offered to man: indwelling, appearing, descending, being sent, and sending.

Situated between the affirmation of persons (Ch. 2-4) and the explanation of the appropriations (Ch. 6-9) of the three Persons of the Trinity, the whole chapter (Ch. 5) is ordered around a single question: the multiplicity of the divine nature's *acts of appearing* and their agreement with its unity (*De unitate divinae naturae in multiformitate apparitionum*).[67] That God appears or gives himself to man to be seen —even if it is only his back (Ex. 33:23)—seems very well to be the fundamental fact of Judaism and of the whole theology of Scripture

---

mulated but not developed by O. Boulnois in his preface to the translation of the *Hexaemeron* (Ozilou), op. cit., p. 10.

[65] Bonaventure, *Brev.* I, 5 (V, 213b), Fr. tr. p. 85.

[66] This hypothesis belongs to a work to follow this one which would discuss the rest of the *Breviloquium*, as has already been noted, and which would have as its title: *St. Bonaventure and the Ontology of the Sensible: The* Breviloquium *as a* Summa Theologica (Brev. *II-VII*).

[67] Bonaventure, *Brev.* I, 5 (213b), Fr. tr., p. 84 (chapter title).

taken up and developed by Christianity: it is "so that they might believe" (*ut credant*) that the Lord God "appeared" (*apparuit*) to Moses and that his staff was miraculously changed into a serpent (Ex. 4:5).[68] But the questions of the *visibility* and of the divine acts of appearing can yet still be obscured by those of its *invisibility* and its *non*-appearance, at least in the general framework of Latin Trinitarian theology. In Augustine, as in fact in Thomas Aquinas, the visible mission of the Son or the Spirit is always doubled in an invisible mission that overshadows and grounds it: not only the invisible Father, for example, but also "the invisible Father, at the same time as his Son, who is invisible with him, (*cum Filio secum invisibili*), has sent the Son in making the Son visible" (Augustine).[69] Every historical perspective set aside, Irenaeus, for example, would counter this primacy of invisibility—sundered from the Son's and the Spirit's visibility—with the necessity of taking into account a "knowledge of the Father who is identically the manifestation of the Son (*agnitio enim Patris est Filii manifestatio*)": namely, at last, and in a new way, taking Jesus' words to Phillip seriously—"whoever has seen *me has seen* the Father (*qui videt me, videt et Patrem*)" (Jn. 14:9)—and which one scarcely finds in the subsequent tradition of Trinitarian theology in the Latin world.[70] Even if it is impossible to show that Irenaeus had any direct and explicit influence on Bonaventure,[71] some echoes can nonetheless be heard, at least from the conceptual point of view—as some commentators have already noted on the subject of sin.[72]

---

[68] Vulgate, *Biblia Sacra*, Paris, 1938, Ex. 4:4-5: "Dixitque Dominus: extende manum tuam, et apprehende caudam ejus. Extendit, et tenuit, verasque est in virgam. Ut credant, inquit, quod apparuerit tibi Dominus Deus patrum suorum, Deus Abraham, Deus Isaac, et Deus Jacob."

[69] Augustine, *De Trinitate*, op. cit., L.II, 5, 9, p. 204: the invisibility of the Son; and (from the same author) ibid., II, 5, 10, p. 207: the invisibility of the Holy Spirit. The same primacy and the division of visibility and invisibility of the Son and the Spirit is found in Thomas Aquinas, *Super Boethium De Trinitate*, XXIII, 3. For the hypothesis of this refuge in invisibility, see Corbin, M. *Essai sur le mystère trinitaire*, op. cit., especially pp. 35-38 and pp. 51-53.

[70] Irenaeus, *Adversus Haereses*, IV, 6, 3, Fr. tr., *Contre les hérésies*, Paris, Cerf, 1984, pp. 419-420: « The Father, totally invisible and unlimited as he is in comparison to us, is known by his own Word and, as inexpressible as he is, is expressed by him…thus the Son reveals the knowledge of the Father by his own *manifestation*: the knowledge of the Father is this manifestation of the Son, for all things are manifested by the mediation of the Word." On the meaning and the necessity of this visibility in God, consult my article "Hans Urs von Balthasar lecteur d'Irénée ou la 'chair retrouvée,'" in *Nouvelle revue théologique*, t.115, No. 5, Sept.-Oct. 1993, pp. 683-698.

[71] Bougerol, *Introduction à l'étude de saint Bonaventure*, Paris, Desclée, 1961, p. 60.

[72] J. Plagnieux. *Aux sources de la doctrine bonaventurienne sur l'état originel de l'homme: influence de saint Augustin ou de saint Irénée*, in *S. Bonaventura, 1274-1974*, op.

The resolution in the *Commentary on the Sentences* of what a visible mission is —*quid sit missio visibilis (I Sent.* d. 16 q. 1)—in this sense suggests to Bonaventure a distinction in the movement that goes from God toward man between mission (*missio*) and indwelling (*inhabitatio*), appearance (*apparitio*), and manifestation (*manifestatio*).

(a) *Mission (missio)*, according to the Seraphic Doctor, results from the sending of the divine persons starting from the Father. What characterizes a Trinitarian mission is thus in the first place the mode of emanation (*modum emanationis*)—generation and procession or spiration—and precisely in this consists "the rather great difference" (*differentia est maior*) between the Trinitarian persons.[73] These Trinitarian "missions" (*missiones*), however, when they are given to the believer in the act of their diffusion (*diffusio*), really determine, for Bonaventure, a sort of "divine dwelling" (*habitare*)—close in this sense to Heidegger's "residing" or "staying" (*bauen*)—at least when it is accompanied by an "acceptance" on the part of the faithful (*cum acceptatione*):

> to dwell (*habitare*) implies a spiritual effect (*dicit effectum spiritualem*) to which corresponds an acceptance (*cum acceptatione*).[74]

To say of "the whole Trinity" (*tota Trinitatis*) that it "dwells within us" (*inhabitare in nobis*) is first to recognize in our conscience "the effect of sanctifying grace (*effectus gratiae gratum facientis*) that ... makes God have us (*et Deum facit nos habere*) and be had by us (*et haberi a nobis*)."[75] The *indwelling* of the Trinity in the soul of the righteous remains no less real for the fact that it does not "appear" (*apparere*) to the senses. And nothing would force us here—as if in a trivial empiricism—to keep expecting "something to happen or appear to the senses" in order for this indwelling of God in man to take place. Nonetheless, for Bonaventure the Trinitarian missions never leave the effect brought about in the believing subject, even though it is at the heart of his Trinitarian auto-affection

---

cit., t. III, pp. 311-328.

[73] Bonaventure, *Brev.* I, 4, No. 6 (V, 213b), Fr. tr. p. 83: "for this reason there are in God only three ways of differentiation: according to the modes of being or emanating (*secundum modos essendi sive emanandi*)..., according to the modes of being in relation (*secundum modos se habendi*)..., and finally according to the modes of [our] understanding (*secundum modos etiam intelligendi*)...The first difference is the greatest (*prima differentia est maior*) that can be found in God; it is this that is between the *supposita* to the point that one cannot be called the other."

[74] Bonaventure, *Brev.* I, 5, No. 2 (V, 214a), Fr. tr. p. 87. As for the reference of "dwelling" as "remaining" and "staying," see Heidegger, "Bâtir, habiter, penser" (1951) in *Essais et conférences*, Paris, Gallimard, 1954, pp. 172-173.

[75] Bonaventure, *Brev.* I, 5, No. 2 (V, 214a), Fr. tr. pp. 87-89.

(cf. p. 110 sq). In fact, and to force the line of thought somewhat here, the first "mission" of the Trinity when it gives itself *to man* is perhaps nothing other than God's attempt to dwell in him (*habitare*) or to "make his dwelling" in him (Jn. 15:4), once he consents to receive it (*cum acceptatione*): for example, we have seen signs of his effective presence in the burning bush of Horeb (Ex. 3:2), in the staff of Moses (Ex. 4:5), or in the cloud on Mount Sinai (Ex. 19:9).

(b) This mission as (in-)dwelling of the Trinity in man next becomes *appearance* (*apparitio*) once it is also made manifest to the senses:

> *appearing* (*apparere*) designates a sensory effect (*effectum sensi-bilem*) with an express meaning (*cum expressa significatione*), as the Holy Spirit who appeared (*apparuit*) under the form of a dove.[76]

In this sensory appearance we can see the particularly New Testament character of Trinitarian givenness, exemplified, of course, by the divine incarnation. As the *Breviloquium* emphasizes:

> when one says that the Holy Spirit has appeared under the form of tongues of fire and a dove (*in linguis igneis et in columba ap-paruisse*), it is not because of a new connection (*hoc non est prop-ter novum vinculum*) or a special effect (*vel effectum specialem*); but because of the union (*sed propter unionem*) that exists be-tween the one who is signified and the sign (*quae est inter signa-tum et signum*) assigned to him in conformity with the original mode (*sibi specialiter et modo et origine deputatem*).[77]

In other words, and to tie this to more contemporary perspectives, for Bonaventure the *appearing* of the Trinity (*apparere*) originally binds a *symbolic* structure of signification of the "sensory effect" (*effectum sensibilium*)—the dove—to the "express meaning" (*cum expressa significatione*)—the Holy Spirit—in that the "union" (*unio*) established here between the sign (*signum*) and the signified (*signatum*) is such that the one cannot be said without the expression of the other. The *symbol* of the dove as "operator between one signifier and other signifiers," to take up here the famous analysis of Edmond Ortigues, thus defines the very being of the Holy Spirit—contrary to the burning bush on Horeb or the staff of Moses—since it says *in itself* something of what he *is* himself

---

[76] Bonaventure, *Brev.* I, 5, No. 3 (V, 214a), Fr. tr. (modified), p. 89.

[77] Bonaventure, *Brev.* I, 5, No. 3 (V, 214a), Fr. tr. (modified), p. 89.

(the Spirit of God who "hovers" over the waters in the Book of Genesis as prelude to a new creation in the baptism of Jesus).[78] When the *Trinity appears* (*apparere*), for the Seraphic Doctor, there is thus no simple, purely arbitrary line from the invisible to the visible; on the contrary, it shows this time how much the visible can be devoted to being, in a New Testament regime, the eminent and worthy bearer of the invisible.

(c) Finally, the Trinity's *manifestation* (*manifestatio*)—a term that does not appear as such in the *Breviloquium* (*Brev.* I, 5), but does in the *Commentary on the Sentences* (*I Sent.* d. 16, q. 1)—designates a kind of intermediate state, at the heart of which (*in quo*) something appears when it itself, as such, does not appear:

> the affirmation that a mission is a manifestation (*missio est manifestatio*) does not mean an act (*non intelligitur actu*) but a disposition (*sed habitu*), because *something is made or is shown* (*quia aliquid fit vel ostenditur*) in which (*in quo*) the emanation from a person can be manifested (*manifestari*), which the act of appearance (*apparitio*) implies of itself (*de se*).[79]

More than a simple "indwelling" (*inhabitatio*) or an "act of appearing" (*apparitio*) of the Trinity, the "manifestation" (*manifestatio*) of the divine missions designates here less *the one* in whom it is shown (the indwelling) or *what* is shown (appearance) than *"in what"* or *"how"* (*in quo*) precisely that which is shown shows itself.[80] Put differently, or speaking phenomenologically, in order for something to show itself, it is not enough that *the thing* be shown (*quid,* a dove), nor even that there be *someone from whom* that might be shown (*quis,* the Father sending the Spirit), nor again *someone for whom* it might be shown (*ad quem,* the Son or man); once again the *showing oneself* must instead manage to show itself in its own *way* of showing itself (*quomodo,* divine liberality).[81] If, in fact, to take up Bonaventure (*above*), "by the affirmation that a mission is a manifestation (*missio est manifestatio*), we understand not an act (*non intelligitur actu*) but a disposition (*sed habitu*)," it is because in

---

[78] E. Ortigues, *Le discours et le symbole*, Paris, Aubier, 1962¹, 1977², p. 65. As for the symbolism of the dove, see *La Bible de Jérusalem*, reviewed and expanded edition, Paris, Cerf, 1998, Note f on Matthew 3:16.

[79] Bonaventure, *I Sent.* d. 16, a.un., q.1, f.4 (I, 279b-280a): "quid sit missio visibilis" (statement of the question).

[80] Bonaventure, *ibid.* "missio visibilis est apparitio, *in qua* manifestatur divinae personae emanatio et inhabitatio" (statement of the conclusion).

[81] On the phenomenological meaning of this showing (of the phenomenon), see Heidegger, *Être et temps*, op. cit. (trans. Martineau), § 7, pp. 29-31 (German pagination): "le concept de phénomène."

reality the three persons of the Trinity "manifest" (*manifestant*), together
this time, the *habitus* in which is shown *everything* that is shown about
God: the mode of "liberality" or of the "givenness of the gift" (cf. p. 142
sq.). What is given in this manner here—in being abandoned—is not
seen (the appearance) nor even reduced to its produced effects in the
soul of the believer (the indwelling). It is instead a sign, and only this,
toward that "in which" or the "how" (*in quo*) by which is given all that
is given: a "disposition" of God himself (*habitus*) that, like the definition
of the phenomenon in Heidegger, "first of all and most frequently does
not show itself"; it is a disposition that falls to the theologian, as the
phenomenon does to the phenomenologist in a different order, to "let
come to light."[82]

Only the *manner* in which all this is shown (liberality or generosity)
can thus take us, finally, to the crux of the meaning of the divine missions.
All told, and together, they rest in a *manifestation* ("the givenness of the
gift") that, not appearing as such, nevertheless allows all that appears to
appear at all. Hence precisely, to return to the statement in the chapter
of the Breviloquium under consideration here (*Brev.* I, 5), "the unity
of the divine nature in its multiple appearances" (*de unitate naturae in
multiformitate apparitionum*): *multiple appearances* by their modes of
emanation, indwelling, and appearances; but *unified* in their common
mode of manifestation: divine liberality or "perfect poverty" (cf. p. 145
sq.) Far from being limited to their mere "effects" in the soul of the believer
(*inhabitatio*) or to their "sensory apparitions" (*apparitio*), the Trinitarian
missions (*missiones*) thus find instead in their common liberality *the*
mode and *the* support for their own "manifestation" (*manifestatio*)—
even in and to the sensible. In this sense, and in this sense only, their
appearing at once as three and one (understood here in the broad sense
of the manifestation as "givenness of the gift" or as "perfect poverty") *is*
their very *being*.

c) *The Trinitarian theophany: "so much appearance so much being"*

In this context we ought to go back to Augustine to recover a
systematically Trinitarian, and thus Christian, interpretation of the
theophanies of the Old Testament (*De Trinitate*, II, 2): among them, of
course, the three angels who appeared to Abraham at the oak of Mamre

---

[82] Heidegger, ibid., p. 35. On the theological implications of this phenomenological
method, see my article "The Phenomenological Act of *Perscrutatio* in the Proemium of St.
Bonaventure's Commentary on the Sentences," in the English-language journal *Medieval
Philosophy and Theology*, vol. 9, No. 2, Autumn 2000.

(Gen. 18), but also the angel of the Lord who appeared to Moses in the fire of the burning bush (Ex. 3), and again in the vision of the cloud on Mount Sinai (Ex. 19), as well as of the Son of Man seated on his throne, where he is beheld by the prophet Daniel (Dan. 7).[83] Besides the question of *which* of the three persons of the Trinity (or the three at the same time) appeared in these various theophanies—which, after all, solely fixes the questioning on the *quid* of the unity of the substance or the *quis* of the plurality of persons (cf. p. 55 *sq.*)—the Bishop of Hippo paradoxically invokes the divine apparitions less to reveal their modes of appearing, as in the *Breviloquium*, than to end instead, in the struggle against Arianism, at the very invisibility of the being of the divine. God appears, in Augustine, in fact, less visible as *himself* the more he appears *through* a creature. His appearance under a form that is not directly his own (an angel, a cloud, a bush, etc.) remains somehow the surest gauge of his very non-appearing and the constitutive element of his being that is most properly his own.[84]

Bonaventure, on the other hand, as a good Franciscan master and in a way free of the danger of a devaluation of the divine to the level of the creaturely (Arianism), attempts to rediscover the authentic meaning of a visibility of the Trinity itself at the heart of these theophanies. Of course nobody could give to Abraham the immoderate and unbiblical claim of a face-to-face vision of the Father, the Son, or the Holy Spirit. But in paradoxically interpreting the angelic mediation less as an impenetrable veil than as the *revealing negative* of an appearance, the Seraphic Doctor makes possible an *appearance of the Trinity* properly speaking that is *not* at the same time its *disappearance* under the numerous layers of the sensory,

---

[83] Augustine, *De Trinitate*, op. cit., L.II, respectively 9, 19-12, 22, pp. 231-239 (Abraham's vision of the three angels); 13, 23-14, 24, pp. 239-245 (Moses's vision of the burning bush); 15, 25-17, 32, pp. 245-263 (Moses's vision of the cloud on Mt. Sinai), 18, 33-18, 35, pp. 263-269 (Daniel's vision of the Son of Man on his throne). On all these Old Testament theophanies and their Trinitarian interpretation, one would do well to consult Lebreton, J. *Histoire du Dogme de la Trinité*, t.II, Note G, pp. 663-677 (as well as the note from Augustine's *De Trinitate* that gives all the references to the divine theophanies, op. cit., [B.A vol. 15], Note 7, p. 570).

[84] Augustine, *De Trinitate*, op. cit., L. II, 18, 35, p. 269: "of the passages of Holy Scripture that we have been able to examine, insofar as it seemed useful, this alone seems to come out of a humble and prudent study of the divine mystery: one cannot rashly judge which Person of the Trinity it was who appeared to the patriarchs and prophets in a thing or a sensible image, unless the tone of the text contains some probable indication. As for the nature, or the substance if you will, or the essence, or any other name that is given to that which constitutes or is God, whatever this might be, *one cannot see it sensibly* (*corporaliter videri non potest*). On the other hand, we must acknowledge that the Son and the Spirit, without doubt, but also the Father have revealed themselves to human senses in the form of a sensible image through a creature subject to God (*per subjectam creaturam*)."

as impassible as they are inscrutable. Where Augustine only invokes the Trinity's appearance to conclude ultimately that it is impossible that is should appear in itself, Bonaventure finds a way to liberate precisely this kind of sensible and visible appearance of the Trinity itself (*in se*)— necessarily through a sensory mediation that, far from acting as its veil, instead manifests a certain mode of its being:

> indeed, the witness (*testimonium*) of the Trinity is given in the Old Testament in figures (*in figuris*) as in words (*quam in verbis*). Among the figures, the most true (*maxime authentica*) is the one that was revealed to Abraham, the father of our faith. It is said in effect in Chapter 28 of the Book of Genesis that three men appeared to him (*tribus viris sibi apparentibus*). He certainly *saw* (*quidem vidit*) the three, but he adored a single one of them; he speaks of the three as of a single one. In this the mystery of the Trinity becomes comprehensible *in itself* (*in se*) and implies other mysteries (*insinuans aliis*).[85]

The *in itself* of the Trinity, comprehensible in itself (*in se*), is thus again given *to us* (here Abraham)—but this time under the modality of certain sensible appearances: so much so, according to the Prologue of the *Itinerarium*, that the Trinitarian vision of the cruciform winged Seraph will even "show through in the flesh," e.g. by the stigmata of Francis (*in carne patuit*).[86] There again—allowing ourselves once more a rapprochement with Heidegger, but here moving from the Trinitarian missions to the theophanies of the Old Testament—the "showing itself" (*phainesthai*) of the Trinity in its theophanies very well designates with Bonaventure "what is shown in itself," the manifest (*das Offenbare*), and not simply the appearance (*der Schein*) of "that which is shown as that which it in itself is not"[87]: the three men or the three angels who appeared to Abraham are really a sign pointing more toward "the showing itself of the Trinity's mystery in itself (*in se*)" (the manifest), in conformity with the God's Franciscan appearance in the sensible, than toward "the showing itself as if not showing itself" of the justified reaction of the bishop of Hippo against Arianism (the false seeming, or the appearance).

---

[85] Bonaventure, *De myst. tr.*, q.1, a.2, concl. (V, 55a-b).

[86] Bonaventure, *Itinerarium*, Prol. 3 (V, 295b), op. cit., (Vrin), Fr. tr. p. 23. Cf. RSPT, pp. 4-6 and pp. 34-44: "la chair ou l'en-deça de la métaphysique."

[87] See Heidegger, *Être et temps*, op. cit., trans. Martineau, §7, p. 28-31 (German pagination): distinction between the manifest (*Offenbare*), the appearance (*Schein*), and the act of appearing (*Erscheinung*).

Whether in Trinitarian missions or in divine theophanies, the phenomenological identification of being and appearing—"so much semblance so much being" (*wieviel Schein jedoch soviel Sein*)[88]—finds also, ahead of its time, and setting aside any anachronism, an exemplary model in Bonaventure's conception of the Trinity's appearance. As he admirably notes in the *Breviloquium* (*Brev.* I, 6):

> the true (*verum*) is knowable (*cognoscibile*) in that it is *not suscep-tible to being separated from its own appearance* (*habet per indivi-sionem sui a propria specie*).[89]

In other words (to touch here what is probably the foundation of Bonaventure's theology), the truth of a thing is paradoxically less the *adaequatio intellectus et rei*—even if this metaphysical definition plays a role there as well—than the bringing to light of the impossibility of separating (*indivisio*) the particular being of a thing (*sui*) from its mode of appearing (*a propria specie*)—which, properly speaking, defines the very specific framework of the *expressio* carried by the Word:

> this resemblance or this Word *is* the truth (*est veritas*). What is the truth according to the definition? Adequation of the intellect and the thing perceived by the intellect (*adaequatio intellectus et rei intellectae*)...But (*vero*) because a thing is only imperfectly adequate (*perfecte non adaequatur*) to the idea that expresses or represents it (*rationi quae exprimit eam vel repraesentat*), every creature is an untruth, according to Augustine. Besides, the ade-quate thing is not its adequation (*res autem adaequata non est sua adaequatio*): consequently, the Word or resemblance or reason is necessarily the truth. It is here that resides the truth of the crea-ture (*ibi est veritas creaturae*).[90]

---

[88] Heidegger, ibid., p. 36.

[89] Bonaventure, *Brev.* I, 6, No. 2 (V, 215a), Fr. tr. p. 95 (modified; *species* here des-ignates in my opinion less "species," in an anti-Bonaventurian logicism, than the image or the form where the phenomenon itself shines through). On the aesthetic meaning of *species* and its relationship with *splendor*, see von Balthasar, *La gloire et la croix*, op. cit., t.I (Apparition) p. 17 (definition of a theological aesthetic starting from the *species/splendor* pair). As for the three senses of *species* as form ("expressive image"), expression ("mediating image"), and beauty in Bonaventure, see *La gloire et la croix*, op. cit., t. II, 1 (Styles), p. 269.

[90] Bonaventure, *Hex.* III, 8 (V, 344b), Fr. tr. *Les six jours de la création*, op. cit., p. 154.

To hear Bonaventure affirm so frankly here—in a solidly phenomenological vein, although obviously this was unknown at his time—that "the adequated thing is not its adequation" (*res adaequata non est sua adaequatio*), on the one hand totally disproves any overly hasty exegesis that would count him among the number of onto-theological metaphysicians, and on the other hand allows us to recognize that the "saturation" of the phenomenon over the knowing subject takes priority here over the traditional dominance, in the history of philosophy, of the knowing over the known by the *adaequatio intellectus et rei*.[91] What is true, for Bonaventure, is thus not primarily the adequation of the intellect and the thing, but *that which is expressed* (*expressiva*) in an appearing— in a paradigmatic way in precisely the One who "*is* the Truth (*ego sum veritas*)" (Jn. 14:16).[92] Against the impossibility of complete adequation of phenomena with our mode of knowing, and as if to come to terms with the uncertainty of their fluctuation for man ("possibility," "vanity," or "non-being"), true being (*verum esse*) implies the center or the seat of expression starting from which any rejection of manifestation must also be interpreted as a complete non-truth.[93]

The essence of truth for Bonaventure, to turn at last to Heidegger's famous analysis (*Vom Wesen der Wahrheit*), and following a parallel that has recently been advanced (by Désiré F. Scheltens), means the act by which the theologian in his *ek-stasis* is opened to the being of the existing being—here the divine Trinity—in order to "reveal" it (*alêthein*) and to "let it be" as such.[94] In this opening or openness, and in it alone, God

---

[91] Cf. RSPT, pp. 16-25: "l'*excessus* comme mode du connaître." Hence the comment by M. Ozilou: "in Bonaventure's exemplarist conception, *adequation is always second*, since it is essentially insofar as they are *expressed by the Word* that things are manifested. Consequently, the critique of the Western tradition that Martin Heidegger develops, for example in *Being and Time* (§44), *does not apply in this sense to Bonaventure*, nor to the Franciscan tradition generally" (my emphasis); cf. Ozilou, *Les sept dons du Saint-Esprit (Bonaventure)*, Paris, Cerf, coll. Sagesses chrétiennes, 1997, Note 8, pp. 93-94.

[92] Bonaventure, *Commentarium Evangelium in Ioanem*, c. XIV, No. 7 (VI, 437a).

[93] Bonaventure, *I Sent.*, d.8, p. I, a.1, q.1, concl. (I, 151b): "Magister et Augustinus et Hieronymus vocant enim verum esse, quod nihil habet de possibilitate, nihil habet de vanitate, nihil de non entitate."

[94] Heidegger, *De l'essence de la vérité*, in *Questions I*, Paris, Gallimard, 1968, pp. 161-194 (esp. pp. 175-176); and Scheltens, Désiré F. "L'absolu et le relatif dans la doctrine bonaventurienne, le dernier horizon de la pensée," in *Eros and Eris, Contributions to a Hermeneutical Phenomenology*, Kluwer Academic Publishers, Dordrecht/Boston/London, No. 127, 1992, pp. 79-91: "in Bonaventure's teaching one can find ideas that approach Heidegger's…: the relation between the essential opening of the mind and the access to the divine world" (cit. p. 79). On this whole question of the status of the truth in Bonaventure and the impossibility of reducing it to a "subsistent universal itself" (p. 163), one should consult J.-M. Bissen. *L'exemplarisme divin selon saint Bonaventure*, Par-

manages to conduct all the way to us (*nobis*), in a hyper-knowledge (cf. p. 71 *sq.*), that which he is now in his very being: a Trinity given "to be seen" or "to appear." Once again then—again, like the phenomenological *logos* whose "function consists purely and simply in the "*making visible*" of something[95]—we must find or delimit this time a type of *discourse* capable of "gathering" (*legein*) without destroying the purity of the phenomenon of the Trinity in its appearance:

> if one understands this, then what must be thought [or felt] (*quid sentiendum*) and how one must speak (*qualiter loquendum*) of the supreme Trinity of the divine persons appears clear.[96]

---

is, Vrin, 1929, p.II, Ch. 1, pp. 162-174: general conditions of truth in God and in the creature.

[95] Heidegger, *Être et temps*, op. cit. (trans. Martineau), §7, p. 34 (German pagination): the concept of *logos*. As for the definition of *legein* not first as speaking or an act of discourse but as a "way of gathering" or of "holding in a sheaf," see (from the same author) *Qu'appelle-t-on penser* (1959), Paris, PUF, 1983, pp. 165-226 (esp. pp. 184-192): interpretation of Parmenides's formula "it is necessary to say and to think that the being is."

[96] Bonaventure, *Brev.* I, 4, No. 6 (V, 213b), Fr. tr., p. 85.

CHAPTER VI

EXPRESSING GOD
(Brev. I, 4 and *Brev.* I, 6-9)

In passing from the "sense of God" (§8) and his "Trinitarian manifestation" (§11) to an attempt to "speak about and express God," or to "translate" him into human words, it will no longer be enough simply to accept "that which must be held (*quid tenendum*)" about the Holy Trinity (*Brev.* I, 2) or that which must be comprehended according to a "sound understanding" (*intelligentia sana*) (*Brev.* I, 3). Instead, we must now also discover a "mode" (*modus*), or better a type of "expression" (*expressio*) that is here called "catholic"—or, in other terms, adequate—for translating this Trinitarian faith (*De istius fidei expressione catholica* [*Brev.* I, 4]).[1] Now, a one-sided reference to the "writings of the holy doctors" (*secundum santorum Doctorum documenta*), found at the beginning of the chapter in which Bonaventure begins to discuss this (*Brev.* I, 4) might lead us to believe that he introduces nothing original here.[2] Moreover, the division of modes (*modi*) on the subject of the divine persons—modes of predication, supposition, designation, speaking, and differentiation— could not be more commonplace in medieval philosophy in general, at least with regard to the agenda imposed by the *Book of Sentences* (Peter Lombard).[3] Thus, without going back over a set of distinctions that, to tell the truth, are as technical as they are complex, we can nevertheless examine a comment of Bonaventure's that properly manifests, in my

---

[1] Bonaventure, *Brev.* I, 4, No. 1 (V, 212b), Fr. tr. p. 75: "the catholic expression of this faith" (chapter title).

[2] Bonaventure, *Brev.* I, 4, No. 1 (V, 212b), Fr. tr. p. 75: "here, according to the writings of the holy doctors, we have the catholic expression of this faith when we speak of the divine persons." As for the absence of any originality particular to Bonaventure in this chapter, it is this that Luc Mathieu might suggest, at least in counter-relief here, when he says that the Seraphic Doctor only expresses "common notions of Scholastic philosophy" despite a "remarkable effort of precision and economy of language" (ibid., Note 24, p. 126).

[3] P. Lombard, *Liber Sententiarum, I Sent.,* d.22 (modes of predication), *I Sent.,* d. 23 (modes of signification), *I Sent.,* d.25 (modes of supposition), *I Sent.* d. 26 (modes of differentiation).

opinion, his Franciscan turn, in that it argues once more in favor of man's *hyper-proximity* to God (§5b and §11b). In effect, once again, just as with the Trinity's appearances in Chapter 5 of the *Breviloquium* (cf. p. 154), the concession—or rather here the supposition—seems to have to be established as a rule:

> the first principle is perfect and at the same time very simple. Anything that implies a perfection must be affirmed of it properly and truly (*proprie et vere*). But one cannot affirm on this subject whatever carries some imperfection, *unless* (*aut si*) this affirmation concerns the human nature assumed by the Word (*secundum assumptionem humanae naturae dicuntur*), or unless one is speaking metaphorically (*vel translative*).[4]

Since this is concerned not only with accepting (*Brev.* I, 2), sensing (*Brev.* I, 3), and seeing something of the Holy Trinity being manifested (*Brev.* I, 3), but also with attempting to "express" it with "catholic" or adequate words (*Brev.* I, 4), Bonaventure holds that we can no longer content ourselves with simply differentiating the persons of the Trinity— even when this is done in the best possible way, i.e. by their modes of emanation (§7). We must instead go one step further and determine a "mode of predication" (*modus predicandi*) for speaking of them that befits each of them in particular—and this precisely so that we can speak of them well.[5] Classically limited to the double connection between the predicates and the substance or the relation—like the statement of the thesis (*per modum substantiae et relationis*)—this "predicative mode" finds the paradigmatic (or at the very least, its specifically Bonaventurian) reason for its being in the narrow but effective distinction between what can be "properly and truly affirmed on the subject of the first principle" (*de ipso dicuntur proprie et vere*), and what "carries some imperfection" (*quae autem imperfectionis sunt*)—this then being uniquely predicated either with respect to "the assumption of human nature" by the Word (*secundum assumptionem naturae dicuntur*), or "metaphorically" (*translative*). Determining what is "properly and truly" predicated of the divine persons is thus in fact the finale of Bonaventure's treatise on the Trinity (Ch. 6-9), and it has, as we shall see (§13), no other end than to center the *quest for what is proper to itself* of this Trinitarian figure around the Word—albeit an uncreated and not yet incarnate one.

---

[4] Bonaventure, *Brev.* I, 4, No. 2 (V, 212b), Fr. tr. p. 77.
[5] Bonaventure, *Brev.* I, 4, No. 1 (V, 212b), Fr. tr. p. 77.

But beyond his famous doctrine of "appropriations"—already amply developed elsewhere (L. Mathieu—and I shall come back to this point)[6]—the very approach that Bonaventure employs in attributing human qualifiers and imperfections to God in one of two ways, i.e. either "by the divine assumption of our humanity" or "by metaphor," is nonetheless exemplary of this attempt for making the Trinity—the unceasing gift of the Father in his Son, and in him to humankind—always "closer" and "better known" by the one who contemplates him. If the concession, or rather the supposition, is to be turned into a rule—*aut si*—we must establish with the Seraphic Doctor a certain *use of metaphor*, one possible and even necessary in theology, since we are here concerned with speaking of how the divine approaches the human and somehow adopts human modes of being that are always "imperfect" (*quae autem imperfectionis*) in order to give itself to man (*below*, §12). Only then will we be able to determine and justify, always following Bonaventure and according to a duly arranged classification, the inevitable *quest for what is proper to itself* of each divine person (*below*, §13).

§12. THE USE OF METAPHOR

A) CATEGORIES AND THE CORPOREAL WORKS OF GOD

"Imperfect" attributes, or in other words those attributes proper to human finitude, can be predicated of God by virtue of the "human nature assumed by the Word" (*secundum assumptionem naturae dicuntur*). From the treatise on the Trinity onward (*Brev.* I), and even before any consideration of restoration or redemption (*Brev.* IV), the incarnation of the Uncreated Word seems at least envisaged, if not prefigured. The reason is that of Aristotle's ten categories, in the words of Boethius (*De unitate Trinitatis*), only the first five are appropriate for speaking of God: substance, quantity, relation, quality, and action (cited in the same way in the *Breviloquium*).[7] As for the last five, Bonaventure emphasizes, following Boethius—passion or undergoing, place, time, position, and having—they are not truly worthy of God, for "they properly concern things that are corporeal and subject to change" (*quinque ultima proprie*

---

[6] Mathieu, *La Trinité créatrice d'après Saint Bonaventure*, ibid., Ch. II-V, pp. 59-194: the appropriations.

[7] Boethius, *De unitate Trinitatis*, *Patrologia Latina* t. 64, Migne, 1847, Ch. IV, col. 1252-1243, Fr. tr. *La Trinité* in *Courts traités de théologie, Opuscula sacra*, Paris, Cerf, col. Sagesses chrétiennes, 1991, Ch. IV, pp. 135-139. These five categories attributed properly to God are taken up by Bonaventure, *Brev.* I, 4, No. 2 (V, 212b), Fr. tr. p. 77.

spectant ad corporalia seu mutabilia).[8] What makes the predication of certain categories impossible for appropriation to God is either their *corporeity* (passion or having, for example)—which is opposed to divine immateriality—or their *mutability* (especially place, time, and position)—which is opposed to divine immutability. But it goes without saying that the Incarnation itself demanded that the Incarnate Word assume both of these properly human paradigms: corporeality and mutability. To this, for example, the *Breviloquium* bears witness, but this time in the treatise on the Incarnation (*Brev.* IV), because it is precisely there that the suffering and the passion of Christ are explained (*De passione Christi quantum ad statum patientis*):

> the pains ... that are the evidence of a true humanity (*testificati-vae humanitatis verae*), not a false one (*non simulatae*), are above all those that concern [human] nature in general, like hunger and thirst in the absence of food, sadness and fear in the presence of a prejudice: consequently, Christ had to assume them (*debuit assumere*), and he did assume them (*et assumpsit*).[9]

What is said here in a corporeal or temporal mode on the subject of man holds also, and first of all, for the Word himself, at least inasmuch as he "assumes human nature" (*secundum assumptionem naturae dicuntur*). In this sense, and in this sense only, God takes on corporeal categories since here they apply to the Incarnate Word "according to the thing" itself (*secundum rem*), and not only according to our modes of comprehension or denomination (*secundum impositionem*)[10]: he experiences needs (hunger and thirst), feels passions (sadness and fear), lives in a particular place (Israel) for a limited time (33 years), etc.

But all this becomes much more complex when we consider attributing not just to the Son but to the whole Trinity a certain number of these so-called "imperfect" categories—or better "corporeal acts" or kinestheses (*actus corporales*) that first belong properly to man. One cannot "attribute corporeal or material acts (*actus corporales sive materiales non attribuntur*) like sleeping and walking (*ut dormire et ambulare*)" to "God Almighty" (*De omnipotentia Dei*), for example—and thus including the Father here and according to the doctrine on appropriations, to which we will have to return (below, §13)—as Bonaventure underscores in the *Breviloquium*,

---

[8] Bonaventure, *Brev.* I, 4, NO. 2 (V, 212b0, Fr. tr. p. 77.

[9] Bonaventure, *Brev.* IV, 8 ("the suffering of Christ"), No. 4 (V, 249a), Fr. tr. (modified), p. 111.

[10] Bonaventure, *I Sent.*, d.22, a.1, q.3, concl. (I, 395b): "utrum omnia nomina dicantur translative."

"except by metaphor (*nisi forte transsumptive*)."[11] Metaphor thus comes into play not to justify any form of application of the corporeal categories to God—since "according to the thing" (*secundum rem*) they are "properly" (*proprius*) attributed to the Incarnate Word (*above*)—but only to define a type of process capable of moving or "transferring" (*translatio*), at least from the point of view of human language, attributes assigned in the Bible to God and which nonetheless do not seem, theologically at least, to befit him. Thus, for example, God—namely the Father and Creator in a Christian re-reading of the Old Testament—is in fact said in the Book of Genesis to "sleep" and rest (*dormire*) on the seventh day of Creation (Gen. 2:2), even though he could never suffer fatigue since he is subject neither to temporality nor toil; or again he is said to "walk" and go about (*ambulare*) in the Garden of Eden (Gen. 3:8), though nothing could justify any such movement on his part, since he has in himself, quite unlike any ordinary person out for a stroll, ubiquity.[12]

As I have shown, in light of the *Breviloquium*'s Prologue, a mode of theological *expositio* (the metaphor) corresponds to the scriptural *descriptio*'s manner of proceeding (God "sleeping" on the seventh day of Creation, or "walking" in Eden, or looking for Adam), such that, for Bonaventure, the two might constitute a unity or "chiasmus" of scriptural descriptivity and theological discourse. Precisely at this point the metaphor comes into play—"except by metaphor" (*nisi forte transsumptive*)[13]—for it alone is capable of ensuring, this time theologically, the well-founded application of attitudes or manners of being that are specifically human (sleeping, walking, etc.) to God—thus drawing us somehow ever closer to him.[14]

---

[11] Bonaventure, *Brev.* I, 7, No. 1 (V, 215b), Fr. tr. p. 99.

[12] This paradox of a possible attribution of corporeal categories to the Father himself comes into Christian theology on the strong foundation of a Trinitarian reading of the Old Testament, and in particular through the discernment of the figure of the Father in that of Yahweh creating man and seeking him in the Garden of Eden. For this interpretation and the question (at least raised here) of the attribution of corporeal categories to the Father, see Augustine, *De Trinitate (The Trinity)*, Paris, DDB, B.A No. 15, 1955, Book II, X, 17, p. 225: "quel était le promeneur divin dans le paradis (*quae Persona in Paradisio deambulat*)?"

[13] Bonaventure, *Brev.* I, 7, No. 1 (V, 215b), Fr. tr. p. 99.

[14] Cf. E. Jüngel. *Dieu mystère du monde* (1977), Paris, Cerf, Cogitatio fidei, No. 116-117, 1983, t.II, p. 103: "the difference between God and man, which constitutes the essence of the Christian faith, is thus *not that of some dissemblance that is always growing*, but on the contrary the difference of a *resemblance that is always growing* between God and man at the heart of such a great dissemblance [*pas celle d'une dissemblance toujours encore plus grande*, mais tout au contraire la différence d'une *ressemblance toujours encore plus grande* entre Dieu et l'homme au sein d'une si grand dissemblance]" (my emphasis). The

B) THE METAPHORICAL TRANSPOSITION (*DÉPLACEMENT*)

Though Bonaventure holds, following Boethius, that the last five categories (passion, place, time, position, and having) are not befitting of God as such, they *can* be worthy of him, he adds in the *Breviloquium*, not only in that the Word takes them on (see above), but also "figuratively and by transposition" (*ideo non attribuntur Deo nisi transsumptivo modo et figurativo*).[15] More than Augustine or Boethius, who only transform the mode of being of these categories in order to justify the legitimacy of their emphasis on the divine substance—by designating them as relative terms (Augustine) or by classifying them as accidental attributes (Boethius)[16]— Bonaventure instead confers on them a specific and exemplary linguistic status, precisely in the usage of the "metaphor." Ever since Aristotle (*Poetics*), it has been almost universally known—though perhaps here not by Bonaventure[17]—that the metaphor is at least rhetorically defined as the process of "applying an improper name by transposition (*metaphora*) from genus to species, from species to genus, from species to species, or by an analogical relation."[18] Metaphor thus effects a "transfer"—hence its Latin name, "*translatio*"—of a term properly attributed to one substance (e.g. man) toward a meaning that is not proper to the thing described but is nonetheless correct, i.e. toward another substance unable to receive it adequately (e.g. God). It is thus "properly" (*proprius*), or according to what is his own, that a man may be said to "sleep" (*dormire*) or "take a walk" (*ambulare*), whereas it is improperly, or better by a transposition of the proper onto the improper, or by metaphor (*translative*), that such corporeal acts or kinestheses may also be applied to the Father. The *Commentary on the Sentences* (*I Sent*. d. 22), however, implies that it is not

---

thesis is developed on pp. 118-119 and is applied to the *symbolic* relationship between the "sign" (*signum*) and the "thing signified" (*res significata*), p. 113.

[15] Bonaventure, *Brev*. I, 4, No. 2 (V, 212b), Fr. tr. p. 77.

[16] Boethius, *De unitate Trinitatis*, op. cit. (Cerf), Ch. IV, p. 135: "accidental attribution"; and Augustine, *De Trinitate*, op. cit., (B.A No. 15), Book 5, IV, 5-V, 6, pp. 431-435: "accident and relation."

[17] Cf. A. de Libera, *La philosophie médiévale*, op. cit., p. 361: the first Latin translation of Aristotle's *Poetics* was done late—namely by William of Moerbeke in 1278 and thus four years after Bonaventure's 1274 death. Rather than a simple and fortuitous conceptual coincidence between the authors (Bonaventure and Aristotle), it is probably also because the theory of metaphor in Bonaventure does *not* come from Aristotle that it has real originality. Indeed, far from being a simply rhetorical or discursive device, it is in fact constructed only to be properly befitting of the first principle when it seeks to express itself to man. Hence the eminently *theological*, rather than philosophical, character of the metaphor for Bonaventure.

[18] Aristotle, *La Poétique*, Paris, Seuil, 1980, 57b6, Ch 21, p. 107.

enough to let the metaphor designate only a *deficient,* or better *derived* mode of the analogy, as Thomas Aquinas would later say (but from a very different perspective; see *Summa theologiae* Ia. q. 13).[19]

Without returning here to the Thomistic "construction" of an analogy of being (*analogia entis*) by the double movement of the transposition of the analogy of proportionality onto the attribution, and then of its "focalization" on being in general,[20] let us only note for our purposes here that Aquinas invokes "metaphorical" attribution (*metaphorice*) simply in order to guard against the possibility of the failure of the proper or "analogical" (*analogice*) attribution that actually agrees better with any predication of the divine. It is only when the kind of attribution that in itself befits God—i.e. what is said of him "by priority" (*per prius*), such as goodness, wisdom, justice, etc.—no longer exactly suffices to speak of him from a Scriptural perspective that it then becomes fitting—"for us" this time (*pro nobis*) and almost in a provisional way—to envision him differently, and thus *metaphorically*, starting from our own knowledge of creatures (possessing the "strength of a lion," "sleeping, "walking about," etc.). Put differently, and along the lines of an hypothesis that has yet to be explored in depth, the Thomistic preference (*per prius*) for the terms properly attributed to God and then analogically attributed to creatures (goodness, justice, perfection, etc.), is surreptitiously moved in priority, in my opinion, from the analogy itself onto the metaphor—since the *in itself* of the thing known is substituted for and takes priority over the *for us* of the knowledge.[21]

---

[19] Thomas Aquinas, *Summa Theologica,* Ia, qu.13, a.6, resp. Fr. tr. (Cerf), p. 243. The affirmation of the primacy of analogy over metaphor is explicit – the mode of attribution being "primarily" (*per prius*) fitting for God and only "secondarily" (*per posterius*) for creatures, according to a mode of hierarchical participation (*secundum ordinem*): "it is necessary that all the names that are attributed by analogy (*analogice dicuntur*) be attributed with respect to a single one (*dicantur per respectudm ad unum*)...; and it is necessary that this name be attributed primarily (*per prius*) to the one term of the analogy which figures into the definition of the others, and secondarily (*per posterius de aliis*), following the order (*secundum ordinem*) according to which they more or less approach the first."

[20] The famous operation of Thomas Aquinas on Aristotle is studied in detail by P. Aubenque. "Ambiguïté ou analogie de l'être?" in *Le Langage, Actes du XIIIᵉ congrès des sociétés philosophiques de langue française,* Neuchâtel, La Baconnière, 1966, pp. 2-14; as well as (from the same author): "Les origines de la doctrine de l'analogie de l'être, sur l'histoire d'un contre-sens," in *Les Études philosophiques,* Jan.-Mar. 1978, No. 1, pp. 3-12. On this point, I refer you to my philosophy master's thesis (unpublished), *De l'impossible analogie de l'être chez Aristote et de sa réalisation chez Thomas d'Aquin,* Université Paris X-Nanterre, June 1986 (under the direction of J. Brunschwig and A. de Libera).

[21] Thomas Aquinas, *Summa Theologica,* I, qu. 13, a.6, resp., Fr. tr. ibid. p. 243: "from this we must conclude that if we consider the thing signified by the name, each name

Despite a certain "meaning effect of the metaphorical in analogy" (at least from the predicative point of view), we should take stock the distance between our two doctors, which is probably unbridgeable if, in Paul Ricœur's words, "the explicit purpose of the Thomistic doctrine of the analogy is to establish theological discourse on the level of a science and thus to *shield it entirely from poetic frames of religious discourse*, even though it should come at the cost of a *rupture* between the science of God and the Biblical hermeneutic"—precisely what Bonaventure, as we have seen, was unable to accept or adopt.[22]

While he does not neglect the grounds for the distinction between the analogical and the metaphorical—by the twofold sharing of that which is "proper" to oneself and "improper" to oneself, on the one hand, and the "in itself" and the "for us," on the other—the Seraphic Doctor nonetheless maintains, at once biblically and theologically, the metaphorical in its (rightful?) place—namely as the most privileged and exemplary axis of the theological. To respond, for example, to Dionysius, in whose words "*every* divine attribution is metaphorical" (*omnis nominatio Dei translativa est*)[23], Bonaventure is not content in his *Commentary on the Sentences*, like Thomas later in the *Summa Theologica*, but once again from a completely different perspective (*utrum sacra doctrina sit scientia*), to invoke here a simple "difference in reasoning" (*non est eadem ratio*)—namely a completely speculative rupture—between the metaphorical (strictly Scriptural) and the other forms (theological) of attribution, among them analogy.[24] Remaining instead at the very heart

---

is said by priority (*per prius*) of God, not of the creature: for it is from God that these perfections are derived in creatures."

[22] Ricœur, *La métaphore vive*, Paris, Seuil, 1975, 8ᵉ étude (metaphor and philosophical discourse), p. 344. As for the "meaning effect of the metaphorical in analogy" but with a purely speculative aim because of this radical "rupture" with Aquinas between "biblical (or poetic) discourse" and "theological discourse," see respectively (ibid.) p. 356 and p. 354.

[23] Free interpretation of Dionysius by Bonaventure, *I Sent.*, d.22, a.un., q.3, ad op.3 (I, 394b).

[24] Thomas Aquinas, *Summa Theologica*. I, qu.13, a.6, ad.2, Fr. tr., ibid., p. 244: "one cannot reason in the same way (*non est eadem ratio*) about the names attributed to God by metaphor (*de nominibus quae metaphorice de Deo dicuntur*) and about the others (*et de aliis*)." The *question* treating of the status of the metaphor with respect to analogy ("*utrum sacra Scriptura debeat uti metaphoris*" [q.1, a.9]) remains in fact taken, in my opinion, in the general direction of the first question of the *Summa Theologica* as it is set down in Article 2: "*utrum sacra doctrina sit scientia*" (q.1, a.2). The movement from the expression "*sacra doctrina*" (Art. 2) to "*sacra Scriptura*" (Art. 9), not conveyed in the French translation (Cerf), in my opinion indicates how great a division is already established in Aquinas between theology in itself on the one hand and Sacred Scripture on the other – precisely what distinguishes the (theological) approach of analogy and the (exclusively Scriptural)

of the Dionysian ambition, but without failing to nuance it, the Seraphic Doctor on the one hand explicitly recognizes the "excellence" of the metaphor as mode of divine attribution ("*quamvis mystica nominet Deum translative quantum ad proprietates excellentiae*") and on the other refuses nonetheless to establish it as a norm for all theology ("*tamen non solum sic nominat, sed etiam per abnegationem; et ideo non solum translative*").[25]

In other words, in a new and perpetual compenetration of the symbolic and the speculative,[26] *granting nothing* to metaphor, according to Bonaventure, would mean losing theology in an abstraction far from the experience of the divine, while *attributing too much to it* would mean forgetting that God himself, though he expresses himself to man so brilliantly in the adoption of man's own *kinestheses* (sleeping, walking, etc.), can nonetheless not be reduced to such figurative language.

"Symbolic theology" (*theologica symbolica*) somehow uses corporeal categories and metaphorical transpositions to speak of God, since it teaches us, according to the *Itinerarium*, what "in the sensible world is useful" for returning to him (*recte utamur sensibilibus*). Thus, symbolic theology only ever means, very precisely, a single one of the "three modes" (*triplicem modum*) or of the "triple view" (*triplicem aspectum*) by which the theologian looks at both God and the world.[27] It may be thanks to Dionysius that we can distinguish the three aims of theology (symbolic, speculative, and mystical), yet for Bonaventure we can neither expel metaphor as a mode proper to theology itself—even if only symbolically (Thomas)—nor extend it to all of theology, at the inverse risk of losing the meaning of all properly speculative discourse (Dionysius). Hence Bonaventure's attempt to restore metaphorical transposition to its true and rightful place:

---

use of metaphor. Bonaventure, for his part, more faithful in this regard to the Augustinian tradition, tries less to establish theology as speculative discourse than to translate according to speculation – like a mirror of the world or *speculatio* (*fit speculum*, §5c) – the very movement of Scripture. Far from opposing one to the other, let us only affirm here that our two protagonists each pursue two *divergent* perspectives as a function of their different intents (*speculatio* as a mode of Christian *sapientia* or of the theologian's *scientia*).

[25] Bonaventure, *I Sent.*, d.22, a. un., q.3, ad.3 (I, 396b).

[26] See my article, "The Phenomenological Act of *Perscrutatio* in the Proemium of St. Bonaventure's Commentary on the Sentences," in the English-language journal *Medieval Philosophy and Theology*, vol. 9, No. 2, Autumn 2000.

[27] Bonaventure, *It.* I, 7 (V, 298a), Fr. tr. p. 35: "The incarnate Word has taught us the knowledge of the truth according to the three modes of symbolic, speculative, and mystical theology: the symbolic (*per symbolicam*) teaches us the right use of the sensible; the speculative (*per propriam*) teaches us the right use of the intelligible; the mystical (*per mysticam*) takes us to the joys and the movements of the spirit."

we must affirm that in God some names are metaphorical (*aliqua nomina translativa*), but not all (*non omnia*).[28]

So, whereas Aquinas, chronologically after Bonaventure, places a rupture between the speculative and the mystical in order to establish theology as a science (*scientia*)—which comes at the cost of privileging analogy over metaphor (*above*)—Bonaventure instead distinguishes them at the heart of theology in maintaining that, to reach God, it is possible and even first necessary to pass through symbols or metaphorical terms (symbolic theology) in order, perhaps, to go beyond them afterwards (speculative and mystical theology). In Bonaventure's theology there is no more a primacy of the analogical over the metaphorical than there is a superiority of the speculative over the mystical or of the ontological over the hodological.[29] The "journey" (*Itinerarium*)—like the path and the transposition of meaning that the metaphor effects (attributing, for example, the strength of a lion to God)—is not only the title of one of Bonaventure's works; it is also, and above all, the very mode of his theology. It belongs to theology in its mode of exposition (*expositio*), and not only to Scripture in the latter's mode of description (*descriptio*), to use metaphors—or better, to make the meanings of such transferred metaphors explicit by extracting them from their symbolic casing. As the Seraphic Doctor tells us in a reflection on the paradisiacal origins of man:

> it is by mysterious and symbolic forms (*aenigmaticis ac mysticis figuris*) that the eye of the rational intellect (*intelligentiae rationalis oculus*) is led to grasp the truth of divine wisdom…These sacred veils (*sacra velamina*) are the symbolic descriptions of Holy Scripture (*sunt mysticae in sacro Eloquio descriptiones*), by which the divine ray is veiled and obscured in order to be adapted to our view (*ut nostris contemperetur aspectibus*).[30]

Far from effecting a simple transposition (*translatio*) only to make sense of some transferals of meaning in passing from the creatures to God in Scripture (sleeping, walking, being strong as a lion, meek as a lamb, etc.), metaphor again becomes, beyond the simple rhetorical process, "truth-revealing" (*poïêsis*): on the one hand, to follow Bonaventure's text (*above*), in that it "is addressed to our intelligence" (*intelligentiae rationalis oculus*), and on the other, in that it "is adapted to our view"

---

[28] Bonaventure, *I Sent.*, d.22, a. un., q.3, concl. (I, 396b).

[29] On the relation between the ontological and the hodological and the subordination of the former to the latter. S. Breton. *Deux mystiques de l'excès*.

[30] Bonaventure, *Tract. de plantatione paradisi*, NO. 1 (V, 575a). Quoted and translated by Bougerol, *Introduction à l'étude de saint Boanventure*, op. cit., pp. 120-121.

(*ut nostris contemperetur aspectibus*). In this twofold function, at once cognitive and heuristic, then, the metaphor's own virtue is defined and made "living," this time since it tries to say something of God at the heart of an "experience of reality in which inventing and discovering coincide."[31]

c) *THE METAPHORICAL TRUTH*

According to Paul Ricœur, metaphor not only involves the transfer of one term to another by resemblance (rhetoric), or even of one attribution to another (semantics), but also the very specific power to describe in a new and different way any reality that is always immediately grasped in a certain type of discourse (hermeneutic). The *poem* of the metaphor, in the Greek sense of the *poïêsis* as the "pro-duction" of an external work (as opposed to the *praxis*),[32] is not content simply to let some previously unseen meaning or another on the subject of the divine emerge (for example, a God who sleeps on the seventh day or walks in Eden); instead the poem creates a "new frame of reference" for its author, at the very least in the sense that the metaphorical meaning that it produces allows a "textual world" (*poïêsis*) to arise at the same time that it transforms the one who strives after it (*praxis*):[33]

> we can risk speaking of *metaphorical truth* in order to designate *the realistic intention* that is attached to the re-descriptive power of poetic language.[34]

With respect to this effort to bring forth meaning, for Bonaventure it is all as if what was at first posed only "for us" in the order of knowing (*pro nobis*), the metaphor, stealthily turned into the best means of understanding God "in himself" (*in rem*). Even though the Seraphic

---

[31] Ricœur, *La métaphore vive*, op. cit., p. 310: "as the junction between fiction and redescription suggests, the poetic sentiment also develops an experience of reality in which inventing and discovering cease to be opposed and where creating and revealing coincide."

[32] Aristotle, *Nicomachean Ethics*, IV, 5, 1140b, Paris, Vrin, 1983, pp. 285-286: "whereas production (*poïêsis*), in fact, has another end than itself, it is not so for action (*praxis*), right praxis being itself its own end."

[33] Ricœur, *Herméneutique philosophique et herméneutique biblique*, in *Du texte à l'action, Essai d'herméneutique II*, Paris, Seuil, 1986, p. 126: "our general hermeneutic invites us to say that the necessary step between structural explication and self-comprehension is the unfolding of the world of the text; it is this that finally forms and transforms the self-being of the reader according to the intention."

[34] Ricœur, *La métaphore vive*, op. cit., p. 311.

Doctor would also take immense care, as Thomas Aquinas would later, to distinguish on the one hand what is expressed of God "in himself" (*in rem*) from, on the other hand, what we attribute to him strictly "metaphorically" (*translative*) (*I. Sent.* d. 22, q. 3),[35] he nonetheless favors metaphorical or "improper" predication as a type of paradoxically appropriate attribution—if not for expressing God himself, at least for addressing him; this he does in an original way here and with another distinction on the Trinitarian appropriations (*I Sent.* Distinction 34 a. un., q. 4).[36] Since the divine has no other aim but to reveal itself "to us" (*nobis*) in a hyper-knowledge (cf. p. 71 *sq.*) and to manifest itself "for us" (*pro nobis*) in its Trinitarian persons (cf. p. 150 *sq.*), the modes of metaphor that are symptomatic of his extreme proximity to the created world's ways of being ("strength of a lion," "meekness of a lamb," "cleverness of a serpent," etc.) somehow take primacy here, at least from the point of view of our understanding, over those of his attributions in himself (God as righteous, good, perfect, etc.).

As for the grounds for the usage of metaphor to express God—*utrum in divinis ponenda sit translatio*—two consummately "poetic" functions of the *translatio*, i.e. functions that elucidate meaning and which could just as well serve as the model of any discourse, are then attributed to it: (a) "praise" on the one hand (*laus Dei*) and (b) the "conduct of our intellect" on the other (*manuductio intellectus nostri*).[37]

(a) If, for Bonaventure, being a good Franciscan here, God is "most worthy of praise" (*Deus multum est laudibilis*),[38] the very act of praising him appears even more, this time in the *Hexaëmeron*, the fourth and final fruit of wisdom—precisely that by which the theologian, too, and in his own language, is made to sing of creation.[39] The reason is that "the signs and the forms," or in other words the metaphors that apprehend God

---

[35] Bonaventure, *I Sent.*, d.22, a. un., q. 3, concl. (I, 395a): "non omnia nomina de Deo dicuntur translative: quando enim significant rem, cuius veritas est in Deo et oppositum in creatura, nullo modo transferuntur."

[36] Bonaventure, *I Sent.*, d.34, a.un., q.4 (I, 593-594): "utrum in divinis ponenda sit translatio."

[37] Bonaventure, *I Sent.* d.34, a.un., q.4, concl. (I, 594a): "dicendum quod ratio vel finis translationis duplex est: una, inquam, est laus Dei, alia manuductio intellectus nostri."

[38] Bonaventure, *ibid.*

[39] Bonaventure, *Hex.* XVIII, 21-25 (V, 417b-418a), Fr. tr, *Les six jours de la création*, *ibid.*, p. 403: "the fruit of wisdom comes from the four last antitheses, and includes four actes, for wisdom comforts (*confortans*), contends (*collutans*), contemplates (*contemplans*), and praises (*collaudens*)...These four fruits come in order (*per ordinem oriuntur*)...From the fourth fruit of wisdom, namely from a distance (*e longiquo*) is born in us – with respect to the signs and forms – the praise of God in all things (*nobis in nascitur collaudatio Dei in omnibus*)."

"from afar" (*e longiquo*)—i.e. starting from created beings—serve also for the theologian, as for the psalmist in Scripture, as a final recourse for expressing God while, at least liturgically, any purely speculative language about his divinity keeps silent:

> in view of the praise of God, one must have recourse to meta-phor (*propter laudem Dei necessaria est translatio*). Since in fact God is most worthy of praise (*Deus multum laudabilis*), and in order that the praise never cease for want of words (*ne propter inopiam vocabulorum contingeret cessare a laude*), Holy Scripture has taught us (*sacra Scriptura docuit*) to transpose the names of creatures onto God (*nomina creaturarum ad Deum transferri*).[40]

There is almost nothing more banal than recognizing the frequent use of metaphors in Scripture. Dionysius, whom Bonaventure explicitly draws on and cites on this point, unquestionably praises the fact that Scripture brims with it. Hence, for example, the numerous biblical formulas that the Pseudo-Areopagite cites as model metaphors: "I, Jesus ... I am the *brilliant morning star*" (Rev. 22:16); "the Lord your God is a *consuming fire*; he is a jealous God" (Deut. 4:24); "I will be for Israel *like the dew*; she will flourish *like the lily*" (Hos. 14:6); "I am the *vine*; you are the *branches*" (Jn. 15:5), etc.[41] Bonaventure, however, differs from Dionysius on this point—once again, without failing to express the thrust of his work explicitly and to justify it deliberately—in that he is less keen on praising theologians who, in an apophatic perspective, are made *capable* of "praising the Universal Cause *for* having no name and yet possessing every name" (Dionysius), than he is on calling them *constantly* to find names for God, even if they can only do so thanks to metaphors, "so that praise should never cease for want of words" (*ne propter inopiam vocabulorum contingeret cessare a laude*)."[42] Put otherwise, where Dionysius makes the absence of words—or better the fact of being beyond all words (apophaticism or negative theology)—the very summit of all theology, Bonaventure instead seeks some ultimate succour in words themselves—those of praise—precisely so that the theologian who expounds what the psalmist describes might not "run out of words" for speaking of man's proximity to God (cataphaticism or affirmative theology)..Better, by using transpositions of meaning drawn from creatures—like "the strength of a lion" (*ut leo fortitudinem*), "the

---

[40] Bonaventure, *I Sent.*, d.34, a.un., q.4, concl. (I, 594a).
[41] Dionysius the Areopagite, *Noms Divins*, I, 6, 596a, in Œuvres complètes, Fr. tr. M. de Gandillac, op. cit., pp. 74-75.
[42] Bonaventure, *I Sent.*, d.34, a.un., q.4, concl. (I, 594a).

meekness of a lamb" (*agnus mansuetudinem*), "the solidity of a rock" (*petra soliditatem*), and "the cleverness of a serpent" (*serpens prudentiam*)[43]— neither the theologian nor the psalmist falls for the dual risks, according to Bonaventure, of either dumbness or ineffability, since Creation itself always appears inexhaustible in its diversity, in its foundation as in its manifestations. The *Commentary on the Sentences* adds:

> an unlimited number (*et hoc in numero indefinito*) [of metaphors must be used] so that, just as all creatures praise God (*sicut omnis creatura laudat Deum*), God might also be praised through the names of all his creatures (*ex omni nomine creaturae*).[44]

The "unlimited number" of transpositions or metaphors (*et hoc in numero indefinito*) for speaking about God thus establishes the inexhaustible character of the literary device, since the sum of "all creatures' names" (*ex omni nomine creaturae*) must enjoy a diversity at least as great in magnitude as the multiplicity of creatures themselves praising God, and these names are such that God himself can also be praised by them. Even though some creatures' names obviously are not worthy of the magnificence of God—"like the devil, the toad, or the fox (*ut diabulus, bufo, vulpes*)"[45]—nevertheless both the psalmist in his *descriptio* and the theologian in his *expositio* will still have access to a plurality and diversity of words, or of meanings, since creatures in general diversely express the modes of being of the divine. Beyond the transpositions of terms, then (the rhetorical function), or indeed of meaning (semantic function), the metaphor thus appears in an exemplary way as an inventive and creative mode of discourse itself (hermeneutic function). Indeed, in attributing to God traits or attitudes proper to created beings (strength of a lion, meekness of a lamb, solidity of a rock, etc.), the psalmist describes anew, but in different terms, the reality that theology, too, strives after.

The theologian, then, finding himself in a veritable "chiasm" or "back and forth" with the psalmist, but far from poetically producing new metaphors in his turn, tries only to extract their meanings inasmuch

---

[43] Bonaventure, *I Sent.*, d.34, a.un., q.4, concl. (I, 594b).

[44] Bonaventure, *I Sent.*, d.34, a.un., q.4, concl. (I, 594a). The relationship between Bonaventure and Brother Francis's *Canticle of Creation* seems to be exemplary here. The poor man of Assisi is not content to celebrate the formal beauty of creatures. Instead, he requires them—in the movement from the first to the second strophe—as an original way of relaying the impossibility of naming God and yet doing so through his creatures: "All praise is yours, all glory and honor, O Most High, and no man is worthy *to name you*. / Be praised, my Lord, through all creatures…" (Francis of Assisi, *Canticle of the Sun* or *Creation*, in *Saint François d'Assise*, Documents, éd. franciscaines, 1968, p. 169).

[45] Bonaventure, *I Sent.*, d.34, a.un., q.4, concl. (I, 594b).

as they furnish him with an original a type of discourse adequate for telling the (metaphorical) truth about God—the truth about a divine being who, drawing near to man, makes himself our neighbor and "dwells among us" (Jn. 1:14). It is not only "*man* [who] abides as a poet" through Biblical metaphors, to draw on Hölderlin's words here, but even more so *God* himself: by making himself so close to us, he makes us see, according to a mode (psalmody) that is now proper to him, that "it is poetry that, in the first place, makes a dwelling a dwelling" (Heidegger).[46] For in the *Breviloquium* (*Brev.* I, 5), as we have seen, God is not satisfied with "appearing" to the patriarchs, or with "descending from heaven," or with "sending" or "being sent" (depending on the divine person in question): for he "also *dwells*, in a special way, in holy men (*tamen habitat specialiter in sanctis viris*)."[47] Is not the possibility of God's inhabiting *in* man, by the use of metaphors that make him somehow so close to our own (human) way of being in the world, the consequence of God's dwelling *among* men—according to the mode of the Word in the Old Covenant and according to the flesh in the New Covenant? "Inhabiting means a spiritual effect accompanied by an acceptance," as Bonaventure has already emphasized in the *Breviloquium* (*habitare namque dicit effectum spiritualem cum acceptatione*).[48]

Since God "dwells in us" (*inhabitare in nobis*), or better, since "it is the whole Trinity (*immo simul tota Trinitas*) that dwells in us,"[49] we ought to receive him there, within ourselves. But how can we welcome or "accept him" (*cum acceptatione*) if our very discourse is not converted into a place of welcome—or a vessel or receptacle (*legein*)[50]—for the divine presence in us? The usage of the metaphor in Biblical description (*descriptio*), as well as the revelation of its meaning in theological exposition (*expositio*), thus very broadly exceeds the bounds of the simply rhetorical or semantic form of the transfer. It no longer suffices to attribute to God some of the created world's modes of being out of a merely aesthetic concern (rhetoric) or through literary ingenuity (semantics). To speak *metaphorically* of God is rather to weave a mode of discourse (hermeneutics) through which the desire for his indwelling in man in fact is fulfilled.

[46] Respectively, F. Hölderlin. *En bleu adorable*, in Œuvres, Paris, Gallimard, coll. "Pléiade," 1967, p. 939; and Heidegger, *L'homme habite en poète*, in *Essais et Conférences*, Paris, Gallimard, 1958, pp. 224-245 (quote pp. 226-227).

[47] Bonaventure, *Brev.* I, 5, No. 1 (V, 213b), Fr. tr. p. 85.

[48] Bonaventure, *Brev.* I, 5, No. 2 (V, 214a), Fr. tr. p. 87.

[49] Bonaventure, *ibid.* Fr. tr. p. 89.

[50] Heidegger, *Être et temps*, op. cit., §7, p. 34 and *Qu'appelle-t-on penser ?* op. cit., p. 184-192: interpretation of the *logos* as "place of welcome" or "receptacle" of the appearing phenomenon.

The hermeneutic aim of the metaphor is thus very clear here, inasmuch as it itself produces the truth of which it speaks (*poïêsis*): it is not that the Biblical metaphor should have to 'invent' God—far from it. Rather, it brings forth the truth of which it speaks in the sense that God himself never ceases to use metaphors to reveal himself to mankind—to put himself, somehow, within man's reach. The metaphor then comes "alive" here in that it translates the very *life* of God through the most ordinary mundaneness and temporality in our own life:[51] the twinkling of a star, the burning of a consuming fire, the morning dewfall, the vine and the branches, the strength of a lion, the meekness of a lamb, the solidity of a rock, etc. Instead of seeking another world, then, Bonaventure's theological reflections on the Biblical usage of metaphor instead indicate just how much God "dwells" (*inhabitare*) in our own world: in his Incarnation he weds himself to everything—except for sin—of our own way of being in the world.

Moreover, Christ himself is made or becomes *metaphor*—in a translation or transposition (*translatio*) or passage (*transit*)—at the very least in the sense in which, dwelling in our world, it is precisely he who, as the ultimate *Passeur* ("ferryman" or "people smuggler"), lets this world pass over (*transire*) to the Father:

> we can take the sensible world as a mirror through which we pass over (*transeamus*) to God, the supreme artisan. We will then be true Hebrews, crossing over (*transeuntes*) with Christ from this world to the Father.[52]

Constantly drawing the divine and the human ever closer together, like the prophets and Christ himself, the "metaphorical truth" assumes for Bonaventure this "*realistic intention* that is attached to the descriptive power of poetic language"—perhaps even more for Bonaventure than for Thomas Aquinas (the only one of the two, however, whom Paul Ricœur cites).[53] The reciprocity of the theologian and the psalmist again

---

[51] Ricœur, *La métaphore vive*, op. cit., p. 314: "it is in a philosophy of life that the pact between image, time, and contemplation is sealed."

[52] Bonaventure, *It.* I, 9 (V, 298a), Fr. tr. *Itinéraire de l'âme vers Dieu*, op. cit., p. 35 (modified). The hypothesis of Christ as one who *passes* [*passeur*], although with etymological allusion to "passage" rather than "passion" and therefore in a sense different from Bonaventure's, is at the heart of my work *Le passeur de Gethsémani*, op. cit., esp. pp. 123-124: "pâtir du monde." As for the particularly Bonaventurian sense of the passage (*transitus*), see Ménard, A. *Spiritualité du transitus*, in *Bonaventuriana IV, 1274-1974*, pp. 607-635 (citation from *It.* I, 9, p. 631).

[53] Ricœur, *La métaphore vive*, op. cit., p. 311. One will be surprised to see that Bonaventure is never cited at the heart of this book, whereas the author struggles—that

comes into play for Bonaventure here since somehow the theologian must always be changed into a cantor for God—and indeed, from the opposite perspective, the psalmist must be transformed into a Schoolman. Bonaventure, as theologian, ponders the point in the *Hexaëmeron*:

> indeed, all creatures confess God (*omnes enim creaturae effantur Deum*). And I, what shall I do (*quid ego faciam*)? I shall sing with them (*cantabo cum omnibus*)…The signs and figures in Scripture (*figurarum signa in Scriptura*) are in fact taken from all creatures and turned to the praise of God (*ad laudandum Deum*), as we read in the Psalm: "praise the Lord from the heights of the heavens" (Ps. 148:1).[54]

(b) These "signs in the form of figures" (*figurarum signa*), when they are read poetically in Scripture as metaphors or transpositions of meaning (a star's twinkling, morning dewfall, the vine and the branches, etc.), are inadequate for speaking about God in his fullness if their meanings are not also, and first of all, discerned by the theologian himself (in order to speak here, for example, of "the name of Jesus" [Rev. 22:16], the "grace of God" given to Israel [Hos. 14:6], or the "bond of dependence" from Christ to his disciples [Jn. 15:5]). Bonaventure warns in the *Hexaëmeron*:

---

goes without saying—to find some originality in the metaphorical discourse coming from St. Thomas Aquinas (pp. 344-356). The difference in perspectives between the two Doctors is in my opinion exactly what probably makes it impossible for the interpreter here to take the reflection to its end, at least starting from the Thomistic corpus alone. Hence Paul Ricœur's own perplexity in claiming on the one hand that the notion of analogy in Aquinas "widens the gap between speculative and rhetorical discourse" (p. 346) and on the other hand that one can nonetheless speak of a "metaphorical sense of the analogy" (p. 356).

[54] Bonaventure, *Hex.* XVIII, 25 (V, 418a-b), Fr. tr. *Les six jours de la création*, op. cit., p. 403. The spiritual implications of a theological reflection on the Biblical use of metaphor really are immense, especially when one recognizes with Bonaventure that one of its ends is in praise ("*una ratio vel finis translationis est laus Dei*" [*I Sent.*, d. 34, ibid., V, 594a]). See for example Loew, J. *Dans la nuit j'ai cherché*, Paris, Bayard, éd. Centurion, 1988, pp. 13-16: "how does God go about making himself known *to us*? Our Bible is full of puzzling *descriptions*: God *is compared to humans* in their most human actions: he speaks, he listens, he sees, he senses, he laughs, he whistles: he has eyes, ears, feet – and he puts these on a footstool…Sometimes he walks in the cool of the evening, inspecting his property like a landowner; sometimes, like a grape harvester, he works the winepress; he himself closes the door of Noah's ark, and often he does not disdain resembling a valiant warrior. He goes further: even *the actions of animals* serve him as a comparison to show an aspect of his strength (the lion, the bear, the panther, the eagle…)…He experiences our feelings: joy, disgust, repentence. And all that to put in our heads the fact that he is *Someone*, a person, not an idea or a theory. He is a living being" (my emphasis).

the signs are worth nothing (*signa nihil valent*) if the things are not understood.[55]

The hypothesis of some kind of mysticism in Bonaventure distanced from all true speculation, then, is once again just as far from the reality of the Franciscan master as the hypothetical appraisal of the *Itinerarium* as vastly superior to all the rest of his corpus (seen over the course of history) is from the real value of his other works—especially the *Breviloquium*.[56] Even though one might well find that "the spiritual doctrine of St. Bonaventure, rife with *unctuousness*, with *poetry*, constitutes a singular moment in mystical literature" (E. Longpré), in my opinion it would nevertheless be wrong to omit the fact—by fallaciously overemphasizing the mystical over the theological—that precisely in this "poetry" a conceptual doctrine, too, is constructed, one that regulates and justifies the right use of the metaphor.[57] The theologian cannot and must not abstract himself from Biblical metaphors if he is to forge a *theology* that can "welcome" or "receive" (*legein*) God *as* God expresses himself in Scriptures, any more than the psalmist can be content with simple metaphors if either he or another does not open their meanings.

Descriptio and *expositio*—Scriptural metaphor and theological analysis—are thus once again subjected to each other in an irreducible chiasm. And their mutual fruitfulness is again here such that the theologian will not *find* his subject matter without the psalmist's praise and the psalmist will not *know* the meaning of his song without the theologian's interpretation. The "living metaphor," in its twofold "heuristic" and "cognitive" function (Ricœur), thus finds in Bonaventure probably one of its most exact representatives. Not only the "praise of God" (*laus Dei*) in man's heuristic search for God, the linguistic transpositions worked by

---

[55] Bonaventure, *Hex.* XIII, 3 (V, 388a), Fr. tr. *Les six jours de la création*, op. cit., p. 302.

[56] Although it is the most popular (and sometimes the only) work by which Bonaventure is accessed today, the *Itinerarium*'s mystical journey can only be understood in light of the theological route it is tracing at the same time. Thus, if one is to understand this, one must have access to Bonaventure's more properly speaking theological texts, especially the *Breviloquium*.

[57] E. Longpré. "Saint Bonaventure." *Dictionnaire de Spiritualité*, Paris, Beauchesne, 1936, t. 1, col. 1842. The reduction of Bonaventure's corpus to a classification as simply mystical—though Emile Longpré does not otherwise fall completely into this trap (even if he is writing here for a dictionary said to be of "spirituality")—probably remains one of the most serious dangers caused by an overly hasty interpretation of our doctor. Praising his mysticism frequently serves as a means of distancing him even further from any real claim of theological originality—and especially with respect to his relationship with Thomas Aquinas. Working against this exclusion of the theological in the name of an alleged over-concentration on the mystical is thus one of the goals set for the present work.

Biblical metaphors (*translationes*) also lead our intellect cognitively, as if "by the hand" (*manuductio*), toward God: "*alia ratio vel finis translationis est manuductio intellectus nostri.*"[58]

The metaphors have in common the fact that they lead all things toward God by a particular type of sensory—or better sensitive—experience that they describe: the twinkling of a star, the dewfall in the morning, the burning of a fire, the strength of a lion, the meekness of a lamb, etc. Once again, to know God as a theologian is for Bonaventure not first to make abstractions or theories about him, but to be born with him[59]—in the knowing of co-birth or the "feeling" of him.[60] If we must thus let ourselves "be led by the hand" (*manuductio*) by Biblical metaphors (*translationes*), it is in that of which the diffusion is made possible, according to the *Commentary on the Sentences,* not only by the unlimited number of creatures (*above*), but also the plurality of their very names:

> because we arrive at the knowledge of the Creature by creatures (*per creaturas ad cognoscendum Creatorem venimus*), we must also transfer onto God various creatures' names (*ideo oportuit plura nomina transferri ad Deum*).[61]

The secondary status of the "metaphorical" in the book of Scripture with respect to the "symbolic" in the book of the world, appears here with force. No one could understand what it means, for example, when in the Book of Revelation Jesus receives the name "*brilliant morning star*" (Rev. 22:16) if he has not also had this experience of seeing a star rise when a new dawn has already broken—an experience all the more exceptional for the fact that it can be had in the ordinary course of daily existence.

Yet the human soul, in its post-lapsarian state, can no longer *directly* discern the Trinity in Creation, but only "*through* its mirror" (*ut per speculum*) or "*in* its mirror" (*et ut in speculo*).[62] "Being fallen" and "having

---

[58] Bonaventure, *I Sent.*, d.34, a.un., q.4, concl. (I, 594a). As for the double function of the "living metaphor" in its hermeneutical dimension, see (in addition to Paul Ricœur's text) Jean Greisch's presentation of it in *L'univers philosophique*, PUF, 1990, t.2, p. 3673.

[59] [Tr. n.: In modern French, the distinct Latin origins of the verbs for "to be born" and "to know" intimately converge to allow for some wordplay: *naître* ('to be born') and *con-naître* ('to know', or as the wordplay would have it, 'to be born with').]

[60] Formulation of "knowledge" ("*connaissance*") as "co-birth" ("*co-naissance*") (Claudel): above, note 73, p. 83.

[61] Bonaventure, *I Sent.*, d.34, a.un., q.4, concl. (I, 594a-b).

[62] Bonaventure, *It.* I., 5 (V, 297b), Fr. tr., *Itinéraire de l'esprit vers Dieu*, op. cit., Vrin, p. 31. To address a common error, the "mirror" (*speculum*) for Bonaventure is not Creation, but the soul or mind (*mens*) of the man who seeks to discover the presence

lost knowledge," to take up a famous passage of the *Hexaemeron* (*Hex.* XIII, 12), man requires alongside other creatures "another book" (*alius liber*) besides the *book of the world*, which "has become dead and obscured ... in order to *interpret* the metaphors of things (*ut acciperet metaphoras rerum*)."[63] This other book—the *book of Scripture* here—then supplies the key, or serves as a "pre-text," for a new (re-)reading "of the metaphors of the things written in the book of the world" (*metaphoras rerum in libro mundi scriptarum*), even as far as reordering the whole world to the "knowledge" and the "praise" of God (*ad Deum cognoscednum [et] laudandum*)—i.e. precisely the aim hoped for by the usage of the metaphor in Bonaventure (cf. p. 173):

> but when man had fallen and lost his knowledge (*cadente autem homine cum ammisset cognitionem*), there was no one to lead Creation back to [the praise of] God (*non erat qui reduceret eas in Deum*). This book (*unde iste liber*), i.e. the world (*scilicet mundus*), then became as if dead and obscured (*quasi emortuus et deletus erat*). For this reason another book was necessary (*necessarius autem fui alius liber*), by which man was enlightened and shown how to interpret the metaphors of things (*per quem iste illuminatur ut acciperet metaphoras rerum*). This book is that of Scripture (*hic autem liber est Scripturae*), which explains the resemblances, the properties, and the metaphors of things written in the book of the world (*qui ponit similitudines, proprietates et metaphoras rerum in libro mundi scriptarum*), and which reorders the whole world to the knowledge, praise, and love of God (*liber ergo Scripturae reparativus est totius mundi ad Deum cognoscendum, laudandum, amandum*).[64]

---

of God there: "fit speculum" (above, §5c). Although Creation as a "vestige" (*vestigium*) might in this way lead the human mind *toward* the contemplation of the Holy Trinity (*It.* I-II), this very mind is nonetheless no longer capable of seeing it there *immediately* in its post-lapsarian state. It is not that the Trinity is not there—far from it—but simply that man is no longer able to discover it *directly* there (without the help of the "book of Scripture," as I shall show). Cf. RSPT, pp. 10-11: "l'enjeu d'un regard: le passage du *per* au *in*."

[63] The translation of *accipere* by "interpret" is justified by Blaise, A. *Dictionnaire latin-français des auteurs chrétiens*, op. cit., Art. "*accipio*," p. 42, col.b, sense 4 (cf. Augustine, *De baptismo*, VII, 53, 102). Translation followed by Ozilou, M. *Les six jours de la création* (Bonaventure), op. cit., p. 308.

[64] Bonaventure, *Hex.* XIII, 12 (V, 390a), Fr. tr. *Les six jours de la création*, op. cit., pp. 307-308. I give all of the Latin of this fundamental text here, following word for word Ozilou's translation.

Here the grounds for the metaphor and the necessity of the Biblical text are presented and justified—translating the whole set of now-illegible, or at least unbefitting, symbols in the created world as so many Scriptural transpositions to aid man in his return to God. The Biblical metaphors inscribed in the "book of Scripture" (*liber Scripturae*) thus serve as a link to the symbols of Creation in the "book of the world" (*liber mundi*), and make Biblical hermeneutics—at least in the words of Paul Ricœur (who, though without citing Bonaventure, is nonetheless more concerned with the opacity of Creation)—the source point of any philosophical or theological hermeneutic.[65] In other words, and in a more common way this time, even though man might no longer see God iconically in the act of contemplating "the brilliant morning star" or in the admiration felt before "the strength of a lion," he will at least manage to rediscover him through Scripture, which tries to call him back, in a radical experience of conversion, to this original experience. Only in this condition—i.e. at the heart of this reference from the Biblical metaphors to the symbols of the created—will he easily enter into the fraternity of the created world and see, rightly this time, and following Brother Francis, a "brother" in Master Sun or a "sister" in the shining of the moon."[66]

Letting ourselves be led "by the hand" (*manu-ductio*), or better led back "in our intellects" (*intellectus nostri*) toward the knowledge of God by Biblical metaphors, amounts first to recognizing that human intelligence is not in itself, and in itself alone, its own guide. Far from inventing God, it *finds* him instead, or rather discovers him, all along its "journey"— i.e. in the "double frame of reference" that the metaphor produces: namely, in the link of the "symbol" of the creature experienced at the heart of Creation (first frame of reference) to the Biblical "metaphor" rediscovered and discerned this time in its "name," which is written in Scripture (second frame of reference).[67] The theologian will not be content to interpret metaphors for guiding the psalmist along the path of meaning if he doesn't also celebrate poetry (praise), just as the cantor who sings of Creation will not be satisfied in sensing God in the immediacy of naked or sheer faith if he does not also cling to the demands imposed by

---

[65] Ricœur, in an article that is a historical milestone in philosophy as much as in theology: "Herméneutique philosophique et herméneutique biblique," in *Du texte à l'action, Essais d'herméneutique II*, Paris, Seuil, 1986, pp. 119-133, esp. p. 129: "the Biblical hermeneutic is simultaneously a particular case of the general hermeneutic described above, and a unique case."

[66] Cf. RSPT, pp. 31-34: "l'*epoché* sur le sensible: de l'emprise technique à la déprise mystique."

[67] Ricœur, *La métaphore vive*, op. cit., p. 311: "the new application concerns the reference itself and the claim of the metaphorical statement to attain reality in some way."

the necessity of *interpreting* Scripture (hermeneutics). Both of them, and each of them *like* the other, share the same faith: "all those who do not have this faith (*omnes qui non habent hanc fidem*)," Bonaventure bitterly observes in the *Hexaemeron*, "have their hand cut off."[68] Eyes, or the mode of comprehension—to draw the comparison anew here—are not sufficient for the theologian to decode the meaning of metaphors. Once more, and above all, he must "have hands"—or in other words faith— to grasp its meaning. To open the "manual" of Creation, which sin has made almost illegible, indeed invisible, Bonaventure demands that the brother-theologian also use his hands—in other words his faith—to discern the meaning anew. Precisely in this way he will be led "by the hand" (*manu-ductio*) in his reading and his understanding of the text, unlike "the illiterate lay brother who holds a book but doesn't know what to do with it (*sicut laicus nesciens litteras et tenens librum non curat de eo*)."[69] Because he is trying to discern the meaning of the metaphors, the true reader (*lector*) recognizes his twofold dependence at once on Creation itself (since he must discover symbolic meaning there) and on that of which the psalmist sings in following Scripture but without necessarily understanding it (precisely since it falls to him to produce or bring forth its meaning). In this sense, and in this sense alone—i.e. *without* the "illiterate lay brother" from the point of view of theology, but *with* him in the same conviction in faith for the metaphorical praise of God—the theologian's intellect becomes capable of letting itself be guided, as "by the hand" (*manuductio*), by the transpositions of meaning supplied in Scripture.

Before Bonaventure, incidentally, Hugh of St. Victor and John Scotus Eriugena were not mistaken when they understood "*manuductio*" as the very mode of the intellect progressing toward God by signs.[70] But

---

[68] Bonaventure, *Hex.* III, 9 (V, 345a), Fr. tr., *Les six jours de la création*, op. cit., p. 155.

[69] Bonaventure, *Hex.* II, 20 (V, 340a), Fr. tr. p. 136. The figure of the illiterate man, here applied to the "lay brother" by Bonaventure, is drawn from Hugh of St. Victor, *Eruditionis didascaliae libri VII*, *Patrologia Latina* 176, 1854, cap. I (*De tribus invisibilibus Dei*), col. 814b: "the totality of the sensible world (*universus mundus iste sensibilis*) is like a book written by the finger of God (*quasi quidam liber est scriptus digito Dei*)…but if an illiterate person sees an open book (*quaemadmodum autem si illiteratus qui apertum librum videat*), he sees shapes (*figuras aspicit*) but does not recognize the letters (*litteras non cognoscit*)."

[70] See Hugh of St. Victor, *Commentaria in Hierarchiam caelestem S. Dionysii Areopagitae*, *Patrologia Latina* 175, Migne, 1854, Ch. I, 1, col. 923a-928b ("de differentia mundanae theologiae atque divinae et de demonstrationibus earumdem") as well as John Scotus Eriugena, *Expositiones super Ierarchiam caelestem S. Dionysii*, *Patrologia Latina* 122 1853, Ch. II, 1, col. 143-146. On the twofold origin and the importanc of the *manuduc-*

is it not enough, for the Seraphic Doctor, for us to let ourselves be "led by the symbols" in the midst of Creation (*manuductio materialis*); once more we must recognize that sin makes reading the book of Creation not only "difficult," but in fact "impossible."[71] All the metaphors in the Bible are first written "for us" (*pro nobis*)—supposing that God himself has no need, as far as he is concerned, to be compared to a star, a lion, or a lamb—but inasmuch as this "for us" of the apprehension of God primarily designates the best that can be discerned of his "in himself" while we try to reach him here below in our post-lapsarian state. As Eriugena emphasizes:

> indeed, the human mind was not made for Holy Scripture (*propter divinam Scripturam factum est*), for which it would have no need had man not sinned. Rather it is Holy Scripture, composed of diverse symbols and teachings (*in diversis symbolis atque doctrinis contexta*), that was made for the human mind (*sed propter humanum animum sancta Scriptura*). And this is so in order that, by its introduction (*ut per ipsius introductionem*), our rational nature (*rationabilis nostra natura*), which by transgression is fallen from pure contemplation of the truth, might be led back again (*reduceretur*) into the primitive height of pure contemplation.[72]

Put differently, to paraphrase here the famous Gospel saying on the Sabbath (Mk. 2:27): Scripture is made for man, and not man for Scripture. The metaphors are thus indeed "for us" (*pro nobis*), as Thomas emphasizes, too, but this time not in the sense of an "in itself" that prevails over them (the analogy). Scripture's "for us" (*pro nobis*) or "for the human mind" (*propter humanum animum*) is "for us" first in the sense that the Biblical text itself, at the root of all theology, is composed and inspired "for us" precisely since we have sinned and no longer know how to read, or decipher, the book of Creation. According to Bonaventure, we must therefore recognize in Scripture itself the places where metaphors

tio as the "foundation of Bonaventurian Biblical theology," I refer you to Marc Ozilou's brief but suggestive comment: *Les six jours de la création* (Bonaventure), op. cit., Note 66, p. 324.

[71] The distance between Hugh of St. Victor and Bonaventure with respect to the status of the book of the world (which, in Hugh's opinion, is not necessarily replaced by a second book, contrary to Bonaventure and Eriugena before him [*below*]) is in particular emphasized by M. Ozilou in *Un Deutero-Bonaventure, La symbolica theologica de Richard Rufus de Cornouailles* (unpublished), EPHE thesis, 1990, op. cit., p. XXXVIII.

[72] John Scotus Eriugena, *Hier. cael.*, op. cit. (*Patrologia Latina* 122), Ch. II, 1, 146c. The passage is translated in a note by Ozilou in *Les six jours de la création* (Bonaventure), op. cit., Note 49, p. 308.

are woven since they speak to *us* in the best way of God, provided that we know how to decode them when they assume, or translate in a different way, the symbols of Creation. Thus it is "in the metaphorical mode" (*sub metaphora*), for example, that a sermon on the nativity discovers "the truth of the new nativity of Christ explained by the flesh" (*nativitatis Christi novae per carnem veritas explicatur*) in the image of "the glorious rainbow held by the hands of the Most High" (Eccl. 43:12); or again "metaphorically" that a sermon after Pentecost sees a "good man" (*bonus homo*) beneath the image of the "good tree" (*bona arbor*) that bears good fruits (Mt. 13:24); or finally "under the most fitting metaphor" (*sub convenientissima metaphora*) that a sermon after Epiphany recognizes the homology between "the man who has sewn good seed in his field" (*homo qui seminavit bonum semen in agro suo*) and "our Lord Jesus Christ" (*dominus noster Jesus Christus*) announcing the Kingdom of Heaven (Mt. 13:24).[73] Bonaventure's *Sermons*—the metaphorical process of which has already been, if not explained, at least identified elsewhere[74]—thus employ this *theology of the right use of the metaphor*, which I have tried, for my part, to develop here: on the one hand in that the metaphorical mode permits us to address God liturgically in praise (*laus Dei*), and on the other in that it also demands an interpretation, this time theologically, by guiding our intellect (*manuductio*). Far from being merely a rhetorical approach or a simple appendix to theological discourse, then, the use of metaphor grounded in reason proves instead, and again if need be, the perfect harmony of the theologian and the mystic in the person of Bonaventure. As theologian, the Franciscan Doctor is never satisfied with a naïve or rationally groundless spirituality; and as a mystic he also takes on his role as minister of the order and addresses his brothers in his *Sermons* by a type of (metaphorical) discourse accessible to all—from the "lay brothers" holding the book without understanding it to the future teachers of theology for whom the *Breviloquium* was composed.

As a repercussion and starting from the use of the metaphor defined here, we ought to contrast the Seraphic Doctor's own so-called "proportional" method against the famous analogical method attributed

---

[73] See, respectively, Bonaventure, *Sermones de tempore, sermones in nativitate domini*, sermo IV (IX, 113a): image of the rainbow; *Sermones de dominica septima post pentecosten*, sermo III (IX, 385b): image of the good tree; *sermones de dominica quinta post epiphaniam*, sermo I (IX, 192b).

[74] M. Shumacher. "Mysticism in Metaphor," in *Bonaventuriana II, 1274-1974*, op. cit., (1974), pp. 361-386 (with the references cited above, pp. 372-373): "what is undeniably certain, however, is that a study of word-choice and image in the *Sermones* of Bonaventure reflects these expressions as being in direct contact with his mystical experience" (cit. p. 386).

to Aquinas.[75] In other words, according to Bonaventure, and once again at the expense of Thomas Aquinas, the non-conversion of the Aristotelian analogy of proportion (*ana-logia*) into an analogy of attribution (with the "*pros hen*" structure) and its non-focalization on being together preserve the original meaning of analogy: a real and possible proportion or "identity of relationship between the different terms" (*ana-logia*) of man and God—even if it is never conceived precisely as such, obviously, in any divine-human relationship of the Aristotelian sort. Even if Étienne Gilson did not perceive how only the use of the metaphor allows us to speak *theologically* of God in the same terms—and with the support—of the most ordinary human experience (the twinkling of a star, the strength of a lion, the meekness of a lamb, etc.), we should nonetheless give Gilson his due for his claim that there is a "universal analogy" in the Seraphic Doctor, at least in the sense in which some *proportion* always remains (in my opinion, by metaphor) from the Creator to the creature—even though the creature, who by sin loses the original proportion written in the symbols of the book of Creation, nonetheless finds it again in the "transfers of meaning" (*translationes*) wrought by the book of Scripture:

> above all concerned with closing any path that could lead to pantheism and therefore with forbidding any substantial communication of being between God and his creatures, St. Thomas always insists much more readily on the distinguishing meaning of an analogy than on its unitive meaning ... But the fundamental tendency in Bonaventure is exactly the *opposite* of that of St. Thomas. The philosophers he constantly targets are not those who exalt the creature and confuse it with the divine being, but those who do wrong to the immensity of the divine being by attributing a certain independence to him and an excessive self-sufficiency to the creature. Where St. Thomas proves himself to be above all preoccupied with establishing the creature *in its own being* in order to prevent it from making claims on the essence of the divine, St. Bonaventure shows himself to be above all preoccupied with revealing the *bonds of kinship* and *dependence* that bind the creature to the Creator so as to prevent a complete self-sufficiency from being attributed to nature and to prevent nature from being posited as an end in itself.[76]

---

[75] Bougerol, *Introduction à l'étude de saint Bonaventure*, op. cit., pp. 120-122: "the method of proportion."

[76] Gilson, *La philosophie de saint Bonaventure*, op. cit., p. 190 (my emphasis). Although here the famous interpreter does not connect the *universal analogy* to the use of the *metaphor*, which alone (in my opinion) grounds it (in Scripture and in theology), the

At the heart of these "bonds of kinship and dependence" between man and God, then, the Biblical metaphor—sung by the psalmist (*laus Dei*) and interpreted by the theologian (*manuductio intellectus nostri*)—unceasingly weaves one and the other into a shared web, having no other end than to make *manifest* in the Son—but here according to an adequate or "catholic" mode of discourse (*Brev.* I, 4)—the presence of the Trinity in each man (§11). Espousing, then, creaturely ways of being by the images conferred on him (the lion's strength, the lamb's meekness, etc.), the Creator approaches his creature all the more closely by deliberately letting himself be circumscribed—in the figure of his Incarnate Son—in the very narrow limits of the properly human experience of the world: feeling hunger and thirst, being affected by sadness and fear, etc. (§12). But the danger of their confusion, by pantheism or anthropomorphism, would nonetheless ruin the homogeneity of the doctrine if Bonaventure himself had not also conceived the copy, distinguishing this time with exactitude and in an implacable coherence, *what is proper to* each divine person in God—precisely that by which the transcendence of the Creator neither dissolves into the mere immanence of creation nor yet refuses to speak through it (§13).[77]

§ 13. THE SEARCH FOR WHAT IS PROPER TO GOD

"God is beyond any genus": *Deus est extra omne genus.* This expression from the *Breviloquium*, drawn from the twofold argument of the infinity and the simplicity of the divine being, serves as a rampart against any overly hasty reduction of the transcendence of God to the immanence of the world.[78] God deliberately expresses himself, in fact, to men by the

---

whole chapter (Ch. VII, pp. 164-191) can be read profitably; it probably constitutes the center of the work, at least with respect to the relationship between Bonaventure and Thomas Aquinas.

[77] Hence the necessary limits of metaphor in its theological use that should now be excavated—not in order to suppress metaphor, but rather to reintegrate it into the divine archetype. See for example Siewerth, G. *Philosophie der Sprache*, Einsiedeln, Johannes Verlag, 1962, p. 35: "no comparison, no reflection is capable of explaining the mystery of the Lamb by *transposed* images like those of meekness and patience. All this remains dull and secondary before the power of the image itself…It is the *archetype* of love emptying itself that has inspired the figure of the Lamb as such, and it evokes the symbols and images that come from human hearts in order to guide us all the way to the depths of its mystery" (cited by H. Urs von Balthasar, *La Théologique II*, op. cit., Note 110, p. 303).

[78] Bonaventure, *Brev.* I, 8, No. 8 (V, 217b) Fr. tr. p. 113. The formula is expressed in the *Commentary on the Sentences*, I *Sent.*, d.8, p. II q.4, concl. (I, 173b): *Deus nec est in*

mode of metaphor—thus adopting, somehow, man's own ways of being in the world—yet he will not relinquish being God and not man. One will thus not find in the Seraphic Doctor, at least at first, any similarity between the "wisdom of God" (1 Cor. 2:7) and the wisdom of man, since "God's wisdom (*sapientia Dei*) knows all things clearly (*omnia*)...both those which are incomprehensible to us and those which are infinite (*ac per hoc incomprehensibilia nobis et infinita*)":

> if one seeks something similar in the creature (*si autem huius simile in creatura requiratur*), it must be said that this, wisdom, is really *proper* to the divine exemplar (*hoc est illius exemplaris proprium*).[79]

Contrary to what we might have expected, then, precisely in order to leave the initiative for divine-human proximity to God alone, we can now discern in Bonaventure an explicit desire to ground Creation, and every act of naming in general, *starting with God* (*a parte Dei*) "properly as the exemplar" of everything (*hoc est exemplaris proprium*)—rather than starting with man or with Creation in general (*a parte creaturae*). The question of naming the divine depends very directly on the relationship from the Creator to his creatures, yet again without "the creaturely world of God" (*Brev.* II) ever leaving the "Trinitarian perichoresis" (*Brev.* I). Metaphor, as we have seen, designates God first *a parte creaturae* since it confers on him a certain number of ways of being that are proper to Creation (strength of the lion, meekness of the lamb, etc.), so how can God stay God and avoid the indirect and undesired consequence of being totally locked within such linguistic transpositions?

A) WAYS OF EXPRESSING GOD

Two ways present themselves explicitly to the thirteenth-century Schoolman for thinking about the relationship between the Creator and his creature: either, as Thomas Aquinas emphasizes in his *Commentary on the Sentences* (1253-1256), written just after Bonaventure's (1250-1253), Creation unfolds *a parte Dei* when all creatures "emanate from the first principle" (*a primo principio exierunt*) and "return to God as to their final end" (*et in finem ultimum ordinantur qui Deus est*), and the task of contemplating him falls to the *theologian* (*sed theologus considerat*);

---

aliquo determinato genere, nec in pluribus.

[79] Bonaventure, respectively *Brev.* I, 8, No. 1 (V, 216a-b), Fr. tr. p. 103; and *Brev.* I, 8, No. 8 (V, 217b), Fr. tr. (modified) p. 111.

or, on the other hand, the status of Creation is first defined starting from creatures (*a parte creaturae*) such that they are only considered "in themselves and in their own nature" (*in propria natura consistunt*), and it belongs exclusively to the *philosopher* to define their condition (*philosophi enim creaturas considerant*).[80] The choice between these two ways (*a parte Dei / a parte creaturae*) simultaneously distinguishes two types of approaches (theology and philosophy) and very broadly spills beyond the mere question of the status of the created. The words we use to express God are always our own (nobody knows any language other than a human one, even if one inspired by God), and at the same time the attributes proper to the divine also designate attitudes that we esteem, although somewhat less familiar to us (omnipotence, perfect wisdom, pure goodness, etc.); and so the question of the grounds of a discourse that is specifically *a parte Dei* arises here—and that all the more compellingly for the fact that the reduction of all discourse to the sole way *a parte creaturae* would immediately invalidate the very equilibrium of Bonaventure's whole doctrine: the metaphorical naming of God *a parte creaturae* (§12)—which Bonaventure never, incidentally, considers philosophical as such, since it remains, as we have seen, thoroughly Biblical and theological)—would indeed fall into a trivial anthropomorphism if the *quest for what is proper* for God were not justified in itself and by itself (*a parte Dei*).[81] Even though we ought to recognize as necessary, at least in part, the way "*a parte creaturae*"—since it alone exhibits the right (Biblical and theological) usage of metaphor—this way nonetheless remains, according to Bonaventure, quite insufficient (a) as much from the perspective of the recourse to philosophy (b) as from that of the restriction of all discourse to its purely metaphorical meaning.

(a) The creaturely return to God (*a parte creaturae*) in itself is not at first enough, and is indeed useless and vain, if one unilaterally considers the creatures' ascent toward the Creator as a simple ascent from cause to cause, i.e. toward a foundational and universal cause. The originally Aristotelian hypothesis of a terminus for the infinite regression of causes

---

[80] Thomas Aquinas, *Commentum in secundum librum Sententiarum*, in *Opera omnia*, Paris, Vivès, 1873, t.8, prologus, p. 1: "*creaturarum consideratio pertinet ad theologos et ad philosophos, sed diversimode. Philosophi enim creaturas considerant secundum quod in propria natura consistunt: unde proprias causas et passiones rerum inquirunt; sed theologus considerat creaturas, secundum quod a primo exierunt, et in finem ultimum ordinantur qui Deus est.*" On the meaning of these two ways (though here their relation to the status of the metaphor is not pointed out) and the divergence between Bonaventure, Albert the Great, and Thomas Aquinas, see Losa, D.R. *Un trait original du tempérament intellectuel de saint Thomas*, in *Revue Thomiste*, No. 50, 1950, pp. 157-171 (and especially pp. 159-162).

[81] See Tr. Mouiren, *Introduction au Breviloquium II*, op. cit. (éd. franciscaines), pp. 20-23: "le refus de partir de la création."

by the *causa prima* in fact leaves, according to Bonaventure, the eternal and crucial question of the "how" (*quomodo*) of the creaturely dependence on his Creator totally unanswered: its extent, its nature, the prospective coexistence of other principles, etc.[82] In other words, a philosophical return to God proceeding only from creatures irredeemably incurs the risk of remaining forever nothing but a properly human path—finding at the end of its journey only what it had already posed in its beginnings: a philosophical or metaphysical God, in the sense of a fundamental principle (§6a). Only the descent *from* the divine exemplar—in which everything is already contained (§5c) and duly named as Father, Son, and Holy Spirit (§7 and §9)—can fully assure us, according to the Seraphic Doctor, that we are speaking about not just any god but the God of the Christians (but of him in his fullness), and that we are rising to the level of "true metaphysicians" or true theologians.[83] The *Itinerarium*, incidentally—when it is read scrupulously and without tying it too hastily to the Bernardian theology of the ladder of ascent—does not deceive anyone who, like the *Breviloquium* (Prol. 1), starts out by invoking "the First (Trinitarian) Principle from which every illumination *descends* (*a quo cunctae illuminationes descendunt*)*," and only then evokes the episode of the apparition of the winged seraph in the form of a cross (Prol. 2) to set in motion the ascent to God: vestiges (Ch. 1-2), images (Ch. 3-4), divine names (Ch.5-6), and finally the "contuition" of the Blessed Trinity (Ch. 7).[84]

(b) Moreover, the way *a parte creaturae* is insufficient, since the metaphor (§12)—and no longer simply the ambitious *philosophical* attempt to attain God by starting from man—is one of its modes. Actually, by using the law of turning the concession into a rule (*aut si / tamen / nihilominus*)—either to speak of the Trinity's acts of appearing (§11b), or to attribute to the Word certain bodily pains (hunger, thirst, sadness, fear, etc.) (§12a), or finally to transfer to the Father various

---

[82] Bonaventure, *II Sent.*, d.1, p. I, a.1, q.1 (II, 14a): "*ideo hoc supposito, scilicet quod res habeant principium causale aliquo modo, est quaestio, utrum res sint productae omnino, hoc est secundum principium materiale et formale, an tantum secundum alterum principium.*"

[83] Bonaventure, *Hex.* I, 13 (V, 331b), Fr. tr., p. 108: "the metaphysician (*metaphysicus*) may well rise to this Being insofar as he has the notions of principle, means, and final end, but he cannot by the Father, Son, and Holy Spirit...When he considers this being under the notion of the exemplar of all things, he does not share it with anyone and he is a true metaphysician (*et verus est metaphysicus*)." On the meanings of and distinction between "metaphysician" (*metaphysicus*) and "true metaphysician" (*verus metaphysicus*) in Bonaventure, see RSPT, pp. 20-25: "le dépassement de la métaphysique: l'excès de donation du Père" (exégèse détaillée de ce texte).

[84] Bonaventure, *It.* Prol. No. 1 (V, 295a), Fr. tr. p. 27

human *kinestheses* (sleeping, walking, etc.) (§12b)—Bonaventure notes that we are dealing precisely with a concession here, indeed an exception, and that the rule, for its part, must always remain that of an expression of what is "properly" divine:

> the first principle is perfect and at the same time entirely simple. All that perfection implies must be affirmed of it properly and truly (*proprie et vere*). But one cannot affirm on this subject anything that contains some imperfection, unless (*aut si*) this affirmation concerns human nature [assumed by the Word], or (*vel*) if one takes care to speak in a metaphorical sense (*translative*).[85]

Metaphor may in fact tell us how extreme man's proximity to God really is, but it cannot express the entirety of his divinity. Yahweh may be "strong" as a lion, "meek" as a lamb, "solid" as a rock, and "jealous" as a consuming fire (cf. p. 174), but he nonetheless remains in himself—in a different and exemplary way this time—strong, meek, solid, and jealous. Without denying here the absolute primacy of the metaphor in our mode of accessing God nor even subordinating it analogically to an "in himself" from which it would be derived only by a mode of participation, Bonaventure holds that this is only a question of recognizing that in calling what is proper to the divine being "Trinitarian," God refuses to be simply reduced to merely human modes of being—since he consents to enter, as *himself*, into theology (*Brev.* I, 6-9). In place of the *participatory* virtue of the analogy that does not permit a mode of relation between the divine *esse* and the creaturely *ens* (Thomas), Bonaventure thus substitutes, ahead of his time, in my opinion, the *identifying* power of the Trinitarian appropriation, according to which on the one hand the divine is not reduced to the human, and, on the other—but now in an exemplary way—God takes on a face for man—for "one of the characteristics of St. Bonaventure's Trinitarian theology … is that he never considers the divine essence abstractly, but rather always contemplates it in the three persons who possess it."[86]

If some distance must therefore be affirmed between the Creator and his creation, so that the former might not be reduced to the latter, creation nonetheless somehow moves, in a fair reading of St. Bonaventure, *to the very heart of God*. Far from separating God from all other beings by the mere consideration of the human *ens* relative to the divine *esse*, the search for a distance capable of counterbalancing a possible metaphorical fusion

---

[85] Bonaventure, *Brev.* I, 4, No. 2 (V, 212b), Fr. tr. p. 77.
[86] Mathieu, *Introduction au Breviloquium I, La Trinité de Dieu*, ibid. p. 40.

introduces instead, *in God himself,* a mode of appropriation of which the Trinitarian characteristics—and only these—identify him simultaneously as *not being* man and yet, because he is Trinitarian, capable of offering a determinate face *to* man. Contrary, then, to any *causa sui* as distant as it is metaphysical, "praying," "falling to your knees," "making sacrifice," "playing," "singing," and "dancing" (Heidegger) thus retain their significance before this God who is at once three and one.[87]

Thus, in place of Bonaventure's well-known—and already broadly discussed (Gilson)— rejection of a "separated philosophy" based exclusively on the way *a parte creaturae* (even if the very originality of the metaphorical approach is rarely taken into account),[88] we must substitute, in my opinion, the other question—much more "difficult" because it is closer to the very act of naming God—of the divine appropriations (*lectio difficilior*). More than a "ladder" (*scala*) for ascending to God (*a parte creaturae*), we ought to speak here of a "sphere" (*sphera*), since everything proceeds from God (*a parte Dei*) and returns to him (*a parte creaturae*) only and precisely insofar as nothing, ever, can truly escape him—except through sin:

> God is an intelligible sphere (*Deus est sphera intelligibilis*) whose center is everywhere and whose circumference is nowhere (*cuius centrum est ubique et circumferentia nusquam*).[89]

If both the worshiper and the theologian nonetheless tramp up and down a ladder in a two-pronged approach that is at once ascending

[87] Heidegger, *Identité et différence*, in *Qu. I*, op. cit., p. 306: "*Causa sui*. Such is the name that befits God in philosophy. To this God man can neither pray nor offer sacrifice. Before the *Causa sui* he cannot fall to his knees full of fear, nor play instruments, nor sing nor dance." Quoted and discussed in RSPT, p. 6.

[88] Bonaventure, *Hex.* XIX (V, 422a), Fr. tr. p. 415: "the worst of the dangers is to descend to philosophy (*descendere autem ad philosophiam est maximum periculum*)...This is why teachers must guard against overestimating or commending too highly what the philosophers have said (*ne nimis commendent et appretientur dicta philosophorum*), for fear that at this the people will turn back to Egypt, or follow their example and abandon the waters of Siloam, where the highest perfection is found, to drink the water of the philosophers (*et vadas ad aquas philosophorum*) where eternal deception is found." For an exegesis of Bonaventure's criticism of a separated philosophy, see Gilson, *La philosophie de saint Bonaventure*, ibid., Ch. II, pp. 76-100: "La critique de la philosophie naturelle" (and especially p. 99: "With that, Bonaventure turns his back on the separated philosophy of modern times.")

[89] Bonaventure, *It.* V, 8 (V, 310a), Fr. tr. pp. 89-91. Drawn from Alain de Lille, *Theologiae regulae*, regul. 7. For the meaning of this expression and its distance from the interpretation that Pascal would later give it, see *above*, pp. 00-00: on the monadological hypothesis.

(*Itinerarium*) and descending (*Breviloquium*), the reason is merely that every ascent and every descent, for the Seraphic Doctor, necessarily take place at the very heart of God, and of the created world in him. For Bonaventure, there is thus no rung that can somehow permit us to "build a wall," or, in a Platonic mode, to escape either the world or God. In this sense, in my opinion, the accusation of a "flight from the sensible" at the end of Bonaventure's spiritual approach (H. Urs von Balthasar) too quickly forgets how much the sensible, always contained in God, is never suppressed nor surpassed. Without ever separating them or privileging one over the other, Bonaventure, Franciscan through and through, always keeps together the two poles of his theology: the Trinitarian God *and* the intimate dependence of the creature on its origin.[90]

For the Seraphic Doctor, seeking "what is proper to the divine exemplar" (*hoc est illius exemplaris*) thus does not consist, as if by a ricochet or a final paroxysm, in trying to dissociate the creature from his Creator—either by a claim of creation's self-subsistence or by a hypothetical respect for an absolute transcendence separate from man. The essential thing is not, and perhaps never has been, in guaranteeing an autonomy or some kind of independence either to one or the other, to man or God. It is that the image of one (man, who has issued forth from the hands of the Creator) is answered by the image of the other, forever illuminating him (the radiance of the Creator himself before his own creature). The Trinitarian God thus comes before the gaze of the man seeking the essence of God, in a way revealing his own face to him—Father, Son, and Holy Spirit.

---

[90] The accusation of a "flight from the sensible" is often repeated, in many exegetes, but this is contrary to Bonaventure's thought. Hans Urs von Balthasar himself does not escape it; he concludes his chapter on the spiritual senses in the first volume of *La gloire et la croix* by regretting that "the spiritual senses in Albert the Great and Bonaventure disappear in the inaccessible heights of mystical contemplation and thus lose theological interest" (*La gloire et la croix*, t.I [Apparition], ibid., p. 316). After deploring this "repetition of a flight" myself, following Urs von Balthasar, at the end of the Bonaventurian journey (RSPT, pp. 44-47), I nonetheless believe today that the enveloping character of the divine nature is such in the Seraphic Doctor as actually to prohibit this kind of transcendence. The world, always remaining "held in God," could not serve solely as a point of support—in a completely exterior way—from which to spring toward God. There can be no flight toward God since no advance can ever go beyond the divine horizon, which is always already there, except in the case of "sinful evasion" (*Brev*. III). What is perhaps true of Albert the Great ("the flight from the sensible") it not necessarily the case for Bonaventure.

B) DIVINE APPROPRIATION

In this search for a representation and a particularity, or "singularization," of the divine, "what is proper to the exemplar" can be understood by (a) the divine essence with respect to creation in general (*Deus in proprio*), (b) the appropriation of each of the persons of the Trinity as the way they relate to their common essence (*persona in propria*), or finally (c) the delimitation of each person in what "properly" belongs to him—which is to say what belongs to him in a manner distinct from that of the other persons (*persona et proprietae earum*).[91]

(a) The definition of an appropriated attribute (*Deus in proprio*)—wisdom, for example—does not first mean that this property should belong *properly*, i.e. *exclusively*, to one of the divine persons, namely to the Son in this case. What is "proper to this exemplar (*illius exemplaris proprium*)"[92] indicates first of all, and just for the time being, that a distance must be affirmed between man and God (creature-Creator relation), yet nevertheless without rendering, through a "return shock" every type of metaphorical discourse obsolete. For evidence, although the *Breviloquium* refers explicitly enough to the Father, to the Son, and to the Holy Spirit in the introductory chapter on the appropriations (*Brev.* I, 6), it remains the case that none of the subsequent examinations of the appropriated attributes—omnipotence (*Brev.* I, 7), wisdom (*Brev.* I, 8), and will (*Brev.* I, 9)—refer to the Father, the Son, or to the Holy Spirit (at least not explicitly). Instead, at least with respect to their titles and in order to indicate the complete sharing of this type of attribute (power, wisdom, goodness), each relates to the *entirety* of the divine nature—God:

> the omnipotence *of God* (*De omnipotentia Dei*), the wisdom *of God* (*De Dei sapientia*), and the will *of God* (*De voluntate Dei*).[93]

Far from respectively pointing to the Father, the Son, and the Holy Spirit, this globalizing formula ("God") only means, in my opinion, that the distinction of what, according to Bonaventure, is proper to each person (power for the Father, wisdom for the Son, and will for the Spirit) effects at the same time, and in God himself (*see above*), the distinction of

---

[91] I reconstruct this classification starting with Bonaventure, *I Sent.*, d.26, a.1, q.2 (I, 621-622): "utrum res sint in Deo ratione essentiae, vel personae"; and from *I Sent.*, d.12, a. un. (I, 220-227): "de processione Spiritus sancti in comparatione ad Patrem et Filium."

[92] Bonaventure, *Brev.* I, 8, No. 8 (V, 217b), Fr. tr., p. 111.

[93] Bonaventure, *Brev.* I, 6-9 (V, 214-219), Fr. tr. pp. 99-119 (respective titles of the chapters *Brev.* I, 7; *Brev.* I, 8; *Brev.* I, 9).

the Creator from the whole of Creation. In other words, and taking up an argument that I have already developed elsewhere,[94] naming the Trinity 'Good' necessarily takes priority over the name of 'Being' as essence, since for Bonaventure the consideration of the Trinity always first means God's own "taking himself into view" (*aspectus*) starting from himself ("contemplation of the Blessed Trinity *in* its name [*in eius nomine*]), whereas focusing on Being always keeps us tied to the merely human "view" (*oculus*) of the divine ("contemplation of divine unity *by* his primary name [*per eius nomen primarium*]").[95] In this sense, for example, to say that wisdom is "proper to the exemplar" first means distinguishing the wisdom of God from the wisdom of man—not in excluding one from the other to the point of prohibiting any metaphorical proximity (*above*, §12), but only in recognizing that the limitation of man's wisdom is yet always counterbalanced by the affirmation that it is always contained *within* God's wisdom. This act of appropriation thus determines the essence of God with respect to Creation in general, establishing a distance here that elevates neither pure fusion nor simple separation, and at the same time does not condemn the use of the metaphor, either.

(b) We must distinguish "what is proper" to God (*Deus in proprio*) relative to creatures in the sense emphasized in the *Commentary on the Sentences* (*I Sent*. d. 36) from—yet without entirely abandoning—what is proper to each person of the Trinity in a doctrine of the appropriations (*persona in propria*): in the first case (*above*) it means the "relation to things" (*relationem ad res*) and conceives of "things in God as contained in the cause" (*res in Deo ut in causa*), whereas in the second (*below*) it considers the shared and absolute essence in God (*in divinis est considerare essentiam quae est communis et absoluta*) and this time describes the appropriated properties as "essential attributes considered in the persons" (*sic ratione appropriatorum quae sunt essentialia considerata in personis*).[96] In other words, and as an example, whereas in the creature-Creator relationship God's wisdom is distinguished from man's because the former totally exceeds the latter and entirely contains it, in the second way, in the doctrine of the appropriations wisdom is properly appropriated to the Son not because it belongs to him exclusively—since it also belongs to the Father and to the Spirit—but only because it determines him in a *mode* or in an original way of intentionally relating to the common essence:,

[94] RSPT, pp. 11-15: "les régions de l'Être et du Bien."
[95] Bonaventure, respectively *It.* VI (the name of the Good) and *It.* V (the name of Being), (V, 308-312), Fr. tr. pp. 83-89. See RSPT, pp. 11-15.
[96] Bonaventure, *I Sent.*, d. 36, a.1, q.2, concl. (I, 622b).

although (*licet*) all the essential properties are equally and indif-
ferently befitting of each of the three persons, unity is *nonetheless*
(*tamen*) proper to the Father, truth to the Son, and goodness to
the Holy Spirit.[97]

(c) Finally, *what is proper* to each person also defines him in his
"properties" (*personae et proprietates earum*), in that these determine
the type of relation of one person to another person (*relationem ad
personam*) to the exclusion of any other. A property, as another passage
from the *Commentary on the Sentences* emphasizes, is strictly speaking
"incommunicable" (*non habere ab alio*) in that it denotes each person
in his "ipseity" (*proprietatem sive solitudinem*).[98] The *Breviloquium* states
very precisely:

> each person possesses a *property* (*quaelibet personarum unam ha-
> bet proprietatem*) by which he is *principally* known (*per quam
> principaliter innotescit*)[99]—

—or better, in my opinion, *princepally* known, to bring out the sense
of being the *principal*..

Thus, for example, as we have seen in analyzing the different modes
of emanation (*Brev.* I, 3), it is exclusively the Father who is innascible and
unbegotten (§7a), only the Son who is the Word as expressed likeness
(§7b), and the Holy Spirit alone who is given as a "bond of charity
between the two (§9c).[100] What one has does not belong to the other,
and what is proper to each—or better what is the "property" of each
(*proprietas*)—here designates, to restate it in phenomenological terms
(Husserl), a kind of "sphere of belonging that is constitutive of every
ego"—though in this case it is divine and not unilaterally human.[101]

---

[97] Bonaventure, *Brev.* I, 6, No. 1 (V, 214b), Fr. tr. p. 93.

[98] Bonaventure, *I Sent.*, d.12, dub. III (I, 227a-b). Far from designating the solitude
or independence of the persons, the *solitudo* of each person as his exclusive property
(*proprietas*) must on the contrary be understood, in my opinion, as the *solus ipse* that
constitutes his specificity and yet never locks him into any kind of solipsism.

[99] Bonaventure, *Brev.* I, 3, No. 6 (V, 212b), Fr. tr., p. 73.

[100] Bonaventure, *Brev.* I, 3, No. 6 (V, 212b), Fr. tr., p. 73: "what is proper to the
Father (*proprium sit Patris*) is to be innascible and unbegotten"; No. 8 (V, 212b), Fr. tr.
p. 75: "likewise (*similiter*), the Son is Image, Word, Son"; No. 9 (V, 212b), Fr. tr. p. 75:
"the Holy Spirit is properly (*proprium*) the Gift, the bond or the charity between the two."

[101] Husserl, *Méditations cartésiennes*, Paris, Vrin, 1980, §44, pp. 77-82: "reduction
of transcendental experience to the sphere of belonging." This rapprochement between
the Trinitarian *ego* and the transcendental subject has of course, for the moment, only
a suggestive value. Husserl, for his part, would certainly and radically reject … in the

At the end of this study, *the search for what is proper* to the divine being (§13), distinguished from *the use of the metaphor* (§12), is thus defined as relative (a) first to creatures (God-man), (b) next to what is "in itself" Trinitarian (power, wisdom, goodness, etc.), and (c) finally to the specificity of each person in his incommunicable and individual property (Father, Son, Holy Spirit). In my opinion, the originality of Bonventure's Trinitarian thought consists precisely in the equivocity of the *proprium*. The fact that the property of "omnipotence" belongs to one (*Brev.* I, 7), "wisdom" to another (*Brev.* I, 8), and finally "will" to a third (*Brev.* I, 9), is not only a prior determination of what is proper to each of the persons of the Trinity (Father, Son, and Holy Spirit); it is also, and above all for the human soul, a subsequent recognition of a *Someone* (*quis*) in the one who is revealed to the soul through his *way* (*modus*) of *indwelling* within it and taking up residence there. In this affirmation Bonaventure is drawing from John Scotus Eriugena, and he goes on to explain that

> the [word] God not only means the divine essence (*non enim essentia divina Deus solumnodo dicitur*), but also the *mode* (*sed etiam modus ille*) by which God reveals himself to intellectual and rational creatures, according to the capacity of each one of them (*prout est capacitas uniuscuiusque*).[102]

In other words, and in a more ordinary way, it makes little difference to man whether power be attributed to the Father, wisdom to the Son, and goodness to the Spirit *if* these *modes of being* of God do not also identify him as so many *ways* that properly constitute him in the *way* that he gives himself to man. Without taking up the entirety of the doctrine of

---

name of the necessity of "excluding God's transcendence" in the quest for the "pure me" or a reduced ego (cf. *Idées directrices pour une phénoménologie, Ideen I*, Paris, Gallimard, 1950, §58, pp. 191-192). Nonetheless the path toward a *theological* and indeed also *phenomenological* reinterpretation of the problem of the act of appropriation by way of the Trinitarian doctrine of the appropriations remains open, in my opinion. Without falling into an "indecent theologization," let us at the very least note that a "rapprochement" remains possible and that it has been evoked by others (cf. Marion, *L'idole et la distance*, ibid., Biblio/Essais, repectivegly pp. 293 and 296).

[102] John Scotus Eriugena, *De divisione naturae (Periphyseon), Patrologia Latina*, 1853, t. 122, Book I, col. 446d, Fr. tr. (modified) *De la division de la nature*, op. cit. (PUF), p. 73. This is a link between Bonaventure and Eriugena that would be worth exploring further, while nonetheless noting that the Irishman, contrary to the Seraphic Doctor, never directly imposes a Trinitarian reading of divine theophany, and this despite the urgent necessity, shared between the two of them, of not staying at the level of the mere essence designated by the word *God*.

appropriations, which has already been broadly developed elsewhere,[103] and without entering into the technicalities of a debate in which one would probably be wrong to reproach Bonaventure for his "classifying mania,"[104] we should nonetheless show here, staying faithful to our phenomenological perspective, how each mode of attribution can be thought of as an original way by which each divine person intentionally relates to the common essence.

Among the various sets of appropriations—of which the *Breviloquium* explicitly counts four[105]—only the *first* (unity, truth, goodness) seems to Bonaventure to act as the principal appropriation, or better the *princepal* appropriation, "from which" (*et iuxta hanc*) proceeds, properly speaking, a sort of intentionality specific to the Trinitarian God that has as its object his own essence. Bonaventure emphasizes:

> *from there* (*et iuxta hanc*) [i.e. from the first series of attribution]
> is drawn a second set of appropriations (*sumitur secunda appro-*
> *priatio*) ... and *from there*, a third (*iuxta hanc sumitur tertia*) ...
> and *from there*, a fourth (*et iuxta hanc sumitur quarta*).[106]

In other words, all of the appropriations (eternity, beauty, delight; principle, exemplar, end; power, wisdom, benevolence) seem to be determined solely and exclusively by the first set: unity, truth, goodness. A *hierarchy* would thus seem to be established, in the purest sense of a philosophical trichotomy, starting from Platonic transcendentals (one, true, good) and descending to every other type of transcendental or appropriation. But the finale of this same chapter (*Brev.* I, 6)—confirming the idea of the reciprocal fruitfulness of the Scriptural and the theological

[103] Mathieu, *La Trinité créatrice d'après saint Bonaventure*, op.c it., Ch. II-V, pp. 59-194 (completely devoted to the doctrine of the appropriations); as well as (by the same author) *Introduction au Breviloquium I, La Trinité de Dieu*, Éditions franciscaines, ibid., pp. 39-48.

[104] H. de Lubac, *Exégèse médiévale, Les quatre sens de l'Écriture*, Paris, Aubier, 1964, t. 4 (II, 2), p. 270: "let us admit that, by their artificial character, by the accumulation of tripartite divisions and subdivisions, [Bonaventure's] exposés are often tiresome." For a criticism of this point of view that proves, in my opinion, a certain misunderstanding of the "dynamic sense" of classification in Bonaventure, see my article, "The Phenomenological Act of *Perscrutatio* in the Proemium of St. Bonaventure's Commentary on the Sentences," in the English-language journal *Medieval Philosophy and Theology*, vol. 9, No. 2, Autumn 2000.

[105] Bonaventure, *Brev.* I, 6, No. 1 (V, 214b-215a), Fr. tr. p. 93: unity/truth/goodness; eternity/beauty/joy; principle/exemplar/end; power/wisdom/benevolence (see the table of appropriations that Mathieu sets up in *Introduction au Breviloquium I*, ibid., p. 43.

[106] Bonaventure, *Brev.* I, 6, No. 1 (V, 214b-215a), Fr. tr. p. 93.

and the creature's act of praising the Creator—shows us that this is not so. Indeed, after considering each of these attributions in this order, the Seraphic Doctor indicates in passing (but his audacity is always hidden within such passages) that only the *last* (power, wisdom, benevolence), and not the *first* (unity, truth, goodness), deserves to be studied:

> the last attributes, power, wisdom, and will, are above all (*potissime*) those by which Holy Scripture (*ex quiubus in Scripturis*) praises the sovereign Trinity (*laudatur Trinitas summa*). Therefore we must now speak of them (*et ideo de his aliquid dicendum*) briefly and summarily.[107]

In the choice of these "last attributes" (power, wisdom, will)—"we must now speak of them" (*et ideo de his aliquid dicendum*)—there is hidden, once again, one of those *tours de force* to which the Seraphic Doctor keeps the secret to himself. Instead of a simple recitation of the Hellenistic transcendentals (unity, truth, goodness), Bonaventure in fact explicitly stands up for the other option (power, wisdom, and will), because simultaneously, he says, it is "inspired by the Scriptures" (*ex quibus in Scripturis*) and expresses "the praise addressed to the Supreme Trinity" (*laudatur Trinitas summa*). The appropriation that seemed at first to have no other end but to enlighten our intellects by speculation— and there is nothing more abstract and repulsive, at least at first glance, than the technicality of this doctrine—is thus somehow grounded here on that which constitutes what is proper to metaphorical language: rootedness in Scripture and invitation to praise (*above*, §12c). Once again, but with the enigma now revealed to anyone who knows how to read it, the most abstract element of Bonaventure's thought (the doctrine of appropriations) is conveyed primarily by what is most concrete in Christian practice (Scripture and praise).

The doctrine of appropriations thus will only constitute an "event" for the believer (*Ereignis*)—to put it in phenomenological terms and to return toward the sense of divine intentionality—inasmuch as what is proper (*proprium*) to the face of God arrives [*ad-vient*] by the same doctrine: or, in other words, as it "makes its ownness come to itself" (Heidegger).[108] In fact, ownness somehow appropriates God, no longer

---

[107] Bonaventure, *Brev.* I, 6, NO. 5 (V, 215b), Fr. tr. (modified), pp. 97-99.
[108] Heidegger, *Temps et Être*, in *Questions IV*, Paris, Gallimard, 1976, p. 43. One will find this rapprochement of the *Ereignis* and Trinitarian appropriation at least suggested, if not developed, in Marion, *L'idole et la distance*, op. cit. (Biblio/essai), p. 296: "posé que l'*Ereignis* et Dieu sont d'autant moins à confondre que d'abord ils ne sont ni l'un ni l'autre à la manière des étants, on ne peut esquiver le rapprochement."

in the sense that it exclusively determines each person in the "sphere of belonging," but merely in that the community accepts itself as so many *intentional objects* of a common essence:

> the properties are essential attributes (*essentialia*) considered in the persons (*considerata in personis*).[109]

Divine appropriation does not mean that each person keeps one or the other attribution to himself (power, wisdom, will, etc.)—as if each were assuming office, or worse, grabbing for possessions. Instead it amounts to the recognition, at the very heart of the Trinity's circumincession (where the love of the first for the second is never jealously denied to a third), that each person deploys his own particular intentional aim on what they all are together. Each somehow receives from the two others the aim that properly constitutes it and is thus itself recognized through a property—not one that it gives to itself, but one it receives from another. The person of the Son, for example, does not appropriate wisdom to himself as *his* exclusive attribute any more than the person of the Father appropriates power or the Holy Spirit goodness, as their exclusive possession. Rather, all of them share the same attributes, but nonetheless consent to being "properly" named by one attribute rather than another. They supply at the same time the access code to their *properties* (*proprietates*), i.e. their determination as Father, Son, and Holy Spirit—according to the original relations that are neither interchangeable nor communicable:

> these attributes (unity, truth, goodness, etc.) are said to be appropriated (*haec autem dicuntur appropriari*) not because they *become proper* (*non quia fiant propria*) [to one or the other] while remaining *common* (*cum semper sunt communia*), but because they lead to the understanding and the knowledge of the *properties* (*sed quia ducunt ad intelligentiam et notitiam propriorum*), i.e. of the three persons (*videlicet tria personarum*).[110]

Like Bonaventure's teaching on metaphor (§12), but now in another mode (§13), the doctrine of the Trinity's appropriations has no other purpose than to give us a way to access the understanding and knowledge of the divine persons. But it nonetheless has the peculiar characteristic that the *appropriated attributes* (unity, truth, goodness, etc.) adopt the creaturely mode of being no longer *only* for the Trinity to reveal itself

---

[109] Bonaventure, *I Sent.*, d.26, a.1, q.2, concl. (I, 622b).
[110] Bonaventure, *Brev.* I, 6, No. 1 (V, 215a), Fr. tr. p. 93.

to man (strength of a lion, meekness of a lamb, solidity of a rock, etc.), as with the metaphors; rather, they also indicate the very intentional object that God sets for himself, at least in the words of the Scriptures (recall Bonaventure's deliberate choice of the appropriations *in Scripturis*: power, wisdom, goodness). Thus, they let us see an authentic (divine) image of the Trinitarian God and are meant to make us definitively reject any idolatry of a neutral God: "the prayer of believers is addressed to the divine persons and not to an anonymous divinity."[111] The operation of the *reductio*, in which the specificity of Bonaventure's theological movement is laid out (§5), is thus no longer uniquely applied to God in his wholeness (in his relation to Creation), but also to each of the persons of the Trinity respectively (simultaneously in the community and in the specificity of the relations that they maintain amongst themselves).

c) The reductio, appropriated

The *Breviloquium*, at least, seems to have made its choices pretty definitively: first, and obviously (*et ideo*), (a) "omnipotence" must be appropriated to the Father (*Brev.* I, 7), (b) "wisdom" to the Son (*Brev.* I, 8), and (c) "will" to the Holy Spirit (*Brev.* I, 9). To analyze its content now, this triple attribution reveals the true face of God in that it is as much in conformity with Scripture (*ex quibus in Scripturis*) as with the act of glorification of the sovereign Trinity (*laudatur Trinitas summa*).[112]

(a) When "omnipotence" (*omnipotentia*), for example, is attributed to the Father (*Brev.* I, 7), this appropriation indicates neither that the attribute be absent from the Son and the Spirit (*above*), nor that it should have no other end but to annihilate, in some kind of Promethean force symptomatic of a profound inability to understand medieval philosophy, all creatures.[113] On the contrary, the "all" (*omni-*) of the "power" (*potentia*),

---

[111] Mathieu, *La Trinité créatrice d'après saint Bonaventure*, op. cit., p. 64.

[112] Bonaventure, *Brev.* I, 6, No. 5 (V, 215b), Fr. tr. pp. 97-99. ""

[113] H. Jonas. *Le concept de Dieu après Auschwitz, une voix juive*, Paris, Rivages Poche, 1994, pp. 27-28: "we affirm in effect, for our image of God as well as for our whole relation to the Divine, that we cannot maintain the traditional (*medieval*) doctrine of an absolute, limitless power…It follow from the simple concept of potency that omnipotence is a notion that is in itself contradictory, one destined to abolish itself and one that is indeed meaningless" (my emphasis). Without getting into a debate that would be worth a more developed argument, it seems at the very least clear here that Hans Jonas can only substitute the idea of an "impotence of God" (pp. 27-40) for that of the "omnipotent God" through a certain failure to understand the meaning of the medieval *potentia*. The whole project of the Middle Ages consisted precisely, and on the contrary, in showing that God himself is not only defined as the "absolute power" to do anything (*potentia*

the *Breviloquium* notes, has only a "distributive" sense (*et ideo distributio addita ei distribuit*), such that the power *of the* whole (the whole set of possibilities) can never and must never be confused with the power *of* the all (the unconditioned realization of all these possibilities):

> from this point (*ex his*) it appears finally that the *impossibili-ty* of doing certain things (*quod aliquorum impossibilitas*) does not contradict *true* omnipotence (*simul stet cum vera omnipo-tentia*).[114]

When the Father is thus said to possess omnipotence (*omnipotentia*) "as his own," he deprives neither the Son nor the Spirit of it; instead he exemplifies it, in that from his own power as a property (*proprietas*) or "the sphere of belonging of his own ipseity (*above*)" (i.e. the power of begetting) comes also the "shared power" of the three persons of the Trinity, as power to create with him (the power of the Word) and to guide the world providentially (the power of the Spirit). In appropriating to one person in particular (the Father) one of the Trinity's attributes (power)— and thus proceeding along an exclusively downward path this time (*a parte Dei*)—the creative totality of the divine as such is distinguished, by the same stroke, from the created world in general: the Father, for example, on the one hand is thus himself revealed, and him alone, to

---

absoluta), but also as "ordered power" by the laws that he himself has established (*potentia ordinata*). For a reaction to Hans Jonas's misunderstanding of this point, but which in my opinion does not negate the validity of his interrogation, I refer you to Solère, J.-L. "Le concept de Dieu avant Hans Jonas: histoire, création et toute-puissance," in *Mélanges de science religieuse*, Lille, t. 53, No. 1, Jan.-Mar. 1996, pp. 7-38 (especially pp. 34-35 for the meaning of the distinction between *potentia absoluta* and *potentia ordinata*): and for another, my work *Le Passeur de Gethsémani*, op. cit., pp. 87-95: "indétermination et puissance impuissante de Dieu."

[114] Bonaventure, respectively, *Brev.* I, 7, No. 2 (V, 216a), Fr. tr. pp. 99-101 (distrib-utive sense of totality) and *Brev.* I, 7, No. 3 (V, 216a), Fr. tr. p. 103 (the impossibility of making certain things non-contradictory with true omnipotence). This is an original position of Bonaventure's, especially with respect to Abelard, and it consists in simultane-ously maintaining the absoluteness of God's omnipotence in the order of possible things as "potential"—thought not actualized—and God's self-limitation through possibilities that he himself *has* actualized in his works. Cf. *I Sent.*, d.43 q.4 (I, 775a). On this point see also Ozilou, *La puissance et son ombre, De Pierre Lombard à Luther*, Paris, Aubier, 1994, p. 193, in Boulnois' translation of and commentary on Bonaventure, *I Sent.*, d.43, q.4 (I, 775a): "utrum ratio divinae potentiae se extendat ad infinita." As for the position of Abelard which, on all points according to Bonaventure, limits the omnipotence of God in reducing it to his mere works or to his acting (*facere*), see Abelard, *Theologia Christiana*, *Patrologia Latina*, 178, Book V, col. 1324a-1330c: "quaerendum arbitror utrum plura facere possit Deus vel meliora quam faciat, aut ab his etiam quae facit ullo modo cessare posset, ne ea unquam videlicet faceret" (cit. 1324a).

be an inexhaustible reservoir of possibilities, and on the other hand nonetheless consents to binding himself to the laws of the Creation that he himself has instituted. By the appropriation of power to the Father, the first person of the Trinity even assumes a face for us—nevertheless without being reduced to the false images fueled by an unconditional usage of metaphors (the absoluteness of unconditional power given to the lion, for example), and without forbidding a certain validity to this linguistic transposition (since God himself, somehow, also limited his own power at least in the effectiveness of his operations).

(b) When "wisdom" (*sapientia*) is attributed to the Son (*Brev.* I, 8), the very heart of the doctrine of the appropriations—or better, the center of the Trinitarian God—is revealed: "these three (eternity, wisdom, and beatitude) are reduced to a single one (*haec tria reducuntur ad unum*), wisdom (*scilicet ad sapientiam*)."[115] In my opinion, however, the originality of this appropriation consists not only in making the Word the one by whom the Father is expressed and declared—which I have already shown.[116] It also reveals a divine mode of knowing from which, paradigmatically this time, all other modes of knowing must be derived, even the specifically human ones. The *Breviloquium* emphasizes the point:

> in itself and by itself (*in se et per se*), wisdom knows all things that are other than itself (*omnia alia a se*).[117]

In other words, and to express it in the phenomenological terms of intentionality (*above*), for God knowing is not first apprehending something exterior to himself—in the double fiction of a purely idealist (Plato) or empiricist (Aristotle) objectivism—but rather carrying "in himself" (*in se*) something "other than himself" (*omnia alia a se*), just as phenomenologically speaking "every state of consciousness in general is, in itself, consciousness *of* something."[118] Because God already contains

---

[115] Bonaventure, *Brev.* I, 2, No. 5 (V, 211b), Fr. tr. p. 69. Taken from St. Augustine, *De Trinitate*, ibid. (B.A No. 17), L.XV, V, 7-VIII, 9, pp. 435-443 (but the attribution of wisdom to the Son is peculiar to Bonaventure here – hence his original and not immediately Augustinian christocentrism."

[116] See on this point the major work of Gerken, A. *La théologie du Verbe*, Paris, éd. franciscaines, 1970, especially pp. 49-83 on the double word of the Father.

[117] Bonaventure, *Brev.* I, 8, No. 5 (V, 217a), Fr. tr. p. 109.

[118] Husserl, *Méditations cartésiennes*, Paris, Vrin, 1980, §14, p. 28: "the word intentionality signifies nothing but the fundamental and general particularity that the consciousness has of being conscious of something, of carrying the *cogitatum* in itself by virtue of its *cogito*." For the medieval roots of this phenomenological definition of

all things in his Word, like a monad but open to the other persons of the
Trinity, the Father and the Spirit somehow together *grasp* the known in
the Son to whom wisdom is properly ascribed: for the act of knowing
nonetheless always begins by an act of "re-cognition"—or better by the
admission of a presence—of "the other in itself": "*perfectio sapientiae
... omnia alia a se cognoscit in se et per se.*"[119] When the appropriated
attributes are thus defined as "essential attributes considered in the
persons (*essentialia considerata in personis*),"[120] we not only make the
divine being vary in three distinct though not separate persons (avoiding
the double danger of modalism or tritheism), but rather first *recognize*
their common essence precisely in that each of the three, while sharing
his perspective with the others in the concurrence of their encounter
(circumincession), maintains his own particular intentional aim on this
same essentiality. Like the omnipotence of the Father, which does *not*
imply the annihilation of man and of creation in general, the wisdom
of the Son somehow teaches *us*, revealing his true face to us and in us,
how much he belongs to God himself, not only by being omniscient—
although this consideration is one of the most important and most
developed points in Bonaventure—but also by showing us everything
with him in his Word, like a true "mirror" (*speculum*).[121]

(c) The appropriation of the "will" (*voluntas*)—or better of
benevolence (*benevolentia*)—to the Holy Spirit (*Brev.* I, 9) will then have
no other end than to make us, too, participate, as creatures, in the same
love that reciprocally unites the Father and the Son in a third. In other
words, and in a more common way, the very thing that is produced *in
God* in the order of his own will is also accomplished *in us* in his divine
providence:

> nothing arrives visibly and sensibly in this vast and immense
> republic of Creation (*in ista totius creaturae amplissima quadam
> immensaque republica*) that is not either ordained or permitted

---

intentionality, see the judicious and well-documented article by J.-L. Solère "La notion
d'intentionnalité chez saint Thomas," in *Philosophie*, No. 24, Autumn 1989, pp. 13-36.

[119] Bonaventure, *Brev.* I, 8, No. 5 (V, 217a), Fr. tr., p. 109. This quote, which one
can compare to the citation from Saint Augustine that concludes Husserl's *Cartesian Meditations*, in an emblematic way serves to emphasize, once again, the generally implicit
convergence of the philosophical and the theological: "do not flee from yourself; but
rather go within yourself, for the truth is within man" (*noli foras ire, in te redi, in interiore
homine habitat veritas*).

[120] Bonaventure, *I Sent.*, d.26, a.1, q.2, concl. (I, 622b).

[121] Bonaventure, *Brev.* I, 8, No. 2 (V, 216b), Fr. tr. p. 105: "as divine wisdom is
the reason by which things seen and accepted are known, it is called a mirror (*dicitur
speculum*)."

by the interior, invisible, and intelligible court of the Supreme Emperor (*quod non de interiore invisibili atque intelligibili aula summi Imperatoris*).[122]

If God extends his dominion over the created world by his good will or his Providence, it is not, here again, so as to reduce all his creatures to enslavement to him or merely to his allegedly despotic fancies. The *Breviloquium* clearly emphasizes this point:

> the divine will *cooperates* with the things that it has created (*cooperetur rebus quas creavit*) by letting them act by their own movements (*ut eas agere proprios motus sinat*).[123]

In Trinitarian theology, what is proper to the Holy Spirit as "cooperation" (*cooperetur*) with the created world in a single "act" or "work"—primarily in the aesthetic sense here—is thus substituted for the false images of divine arbitrariness in his action on the world, in order to lead man to take responsibility for, with God, the inescapable weight of the laws of the world that has been subjected to sin.[124]

Against the naïve temptation on the one hand (and already underscored many times) of a radical opposition of Bonaventure and Thomas Aquinas, and in order to guard on the other hand against any attempt to suggest that metaphor might be an abandonment of the human in the name of the hyperproximity of the divine, the Seraphic Doctor ultimately indicates, as the Second Vatican Council later would, that "created things and societies themselves have their own laws and values" (since they "act by their own movement"), yet without the possibility that one could ever claim that the "autonomy of the temporal" should be understood as meaning that "created things do not depend on God and man can dispose of them without reference to the Creator" (precisely

---

[122] Bonaventure, *Brev.* I, 9, No. 2 (V, 218a), Fr. tr. p. 115. From St. Augustine, *De Trinitate*, L.III, c.4, No. 9, B.A No. 15, ibid., p. 289.

[123] Bonaventure, *Brev.* I, 9, No. 6 (V, 218b), Fr. tr. (modified) p. 117. Drawn again from St. Augustine (*City of God*, L. VII, c. 30), but explicitly adding to it here the schema of "cooperation" (*cooperetur*) that is originally absent from it.

[124] If, in conformity with the whole Latin medieval tradition, Bonaventure derives the insupportable burden of existence (anguish, suffering, death…) directly from sin, for my part I have tried to show elsewhere and from a more contemporary perspective that a "non-sinful finitude" is also thinkable in both theology and philosophy—one according to which sin consists precisely in locking oneself in on oneself. Cf. Falque, *Le Passeur de Gethsémani*, op. cit., Part One, pp. 17-58: "le vis-à-vis de la finitude."

since, quite to the contrary, "the divine will cooperates with things").[125] By letting "things act through their own movement," but nonetheless "cooperating" with them, the appropriation of "benevolence" to the Holy Spirit thus teaches the believer that he never remains alone in his own actions, and yet they never cease to be his own—and only his own. In making us participate in the divine nature, the Spirit reveals to us that we, too, participate and cooperate in his work of creation. The virtue of this appropriated attribute thus makes manifest, once again, that what is proper to God with respect to the created world (the divine will) is first properly revealed in a person of the Trinity (the Holy Spirit)—yet without suppressing either the meaning of the metaphor or the deliberate proximity of the divine and the human.

Simultaneously (a) as *Father* who does not take the power of all but yet concentrates in himself the all of power (in the reserve of possibilities), (b) as *Son* who is not only omniscient but is also the very paradigm of all knowledge and who "re-cognizes" first of all the presence of the other in himself (intentionality), and (c) as *Holy Spirit* who is not the arbitrary will of the divine imposed on the human but who is rather the cooperator in the work of creation, God in fact assumes a face for man through the doctrine of the appropriations. As Father (§7a), Son (§7a), and Holy Spirit (§9), he adopts "ways of being" that—far from reducing him by metaphors to merely human modes (§12)—are properly his own: (a) possessing omnipotence and yet limiting it deliberately, (b) sufficient in himself and yet welcoming the other in himself, and (c) ruling the world and yet giving to man, too, the power to cooperate in the act of creation. Neither staying in the pure incommunicability of whatever *Styxes* or *Phoenixes one imagines,* nor being conflated with the human until he has lost himself, the Trinitarian God instead makes the choice to take with him, and in him, man himself in this movement of appropriation of the self—or of the act of appropriating. In other words, God only comes *to what is proper to him* in assuming and in fact in inviting into himself, in a final return (*rediens supra se*), what is *not proper* to him—man:

> the first and supreme unity, returning to itself by a perfect and complete return (*rediens supra se ipsam reditione completa et per-*

[125] Vatican II, *Gaudium et spes, L'Église dans le monde de ce temps* (1965), in *Vatican II, Les seize document conciliaires,* édition de poche Fides, 1967, §36, No. 2-3, p. 206: "right autonomy of terrestrial realities." On the Bonaventurian inspiration of Vatican II, and the more Thomistic inspiration of Vatican I, see Mouiren, Tr. *Introduction au Breviloquium II*, op. cit. (Éditions franciscaines), pp. 41-43: "Saint Bonaventure et Vatican II." See also on this point my article, "Dieu nous éprouve-t-il ou faut-il sauver la providence" in *La vie spirituelle*, No. 734, March 2000, pp. 71-91.

fecta), is omnipotent; likewise truth, returning to itself, is omniscient; and goodness, returning to itself, is the highest benevolence.[126]

At the heart of Bonaventure's treatise on the Trinity's appropriations, then, the return to the self or the act of the *reductio* in the *Liber de causis* passes from the mere consideration of the essence of God (in Proclus or its unknown author) to its *princepally* Trinitarian intentional object.[127] It is thus not enough, or no longer enough, for God in his wholeness and unity to bring about an act of return toward himself. Rather, each person of the Trinity must respectively accomplish it in himself and for himself—such that (a) the Father, in coming back to himself (*rediens supra se*) and encompassing everything in him, appropriates his own power as Father (i.e. the power dependent on the Son and on the created world in him); (b) the Son, in returning to himself, makes himself able to reveal the presence of the other in him; and (c) the Holy Spirit, moving back to himself, finally harmonizes the will of man with the will of God. The simple *reductio of the essence of God* (§5) now (§13) gives way to the terms of a *reductio that is appropriated* to each of the divine persons.

Before the profundity of the mystery of the Trinity—at once "singularly admirable" (*singulariter admirabile*) and "admirably singular (*mirabiliter singulare*),"[128]—one cannot, and must not, silence every discourse that has something to say. In an ultimate cry raised at the end of this first treatise (*Brev.* I)—principial more than principal (*in principio*)[129]—Bonaventure deliberately makes himself deaf to the "why" (*quare*) and the "who" (*quis*) of the many interrogative inquiries on the subject of God—and *"at last"* imposes "silence on human loquacity" (*hic oportet silentium imponere humanae loquacitati*):

if someone asks himself why (*quare*) grace is given more abundantly to one sinner than to another, we must impose silence on human locquacity (*hic oportet silencium imponere humanae loquacitati*) and exclaim with the Apostle: O the depths of the

---

[126] Bonaventure, *Brev.* I, 6, No. 5 (V, 215b), Fr. tr. p. 97.

[127] Proclus, *Liber de causis*, op. cit., Prop. 15: "all knowledge that knows its essence goes back to its essence in a complete return." For the difficulty of definitively attributing this treatise to Proclus.

[128] Bonaventure, *De myst. Trin.*, q.2, a.2, concl. (V, 65b): "since the plurality of persons does not divide their unity and since their unity does not absorb their plurality, the divine being appears singularly admirable (*mirabiliter singulare*)."

[129] Bonaventure, *Brev.* I, 1, No. 1 (V, 210a), Fr. tr. (modified) p. 59: "in the beginning (*in principio*), it must be understood that sacred doctrine, which is to say theology, which speaks princepally of the first principle...."

richess, wisdom, and knowledge of God! How immeasurable are his decrees, how incomprehensible his ways! Who indeed has ever known the mind of the Lord? Who has ever dared counsel him? Or again who has given a gift to him so as to be paid in return? For all things are from him (*ex ipso*), through him (*per ipsum*), and to him (*in ipso*). To him be glory forever. Amen.[130]

---

[130] Bonaventure, *Brev.* I, 9, No. 7 (V, 218b), Fr. tr. p. 119 (finale of *Brev.* I).

CONCLUSION

FROM THE "BRIEF SUMMARY" TO THE POEM
ON CREATION

It was somehow fitting to "fall silent about God by surpassing language,"[1] at the end of a path that forces at least the theologian to bow before God's *Trinitarian* entrance into theology. And yet this silence is not the equivalent of dumbness or mutism—if it were, it would risk converting the absence of words into a negation of his presence. And Bonaventure knows this; he opens Part II of his *Breviloquium* precisely with the necessity to "express" (*dicenda*) once more the Trinity's appearance, or better to let it express itself, this time through the "creaturely world of God" (*De creatura mundi*):

> after this summary review (*summatim*) of the Trinity of God (*de Trinitate Dei*), something must be said (*dicenda sunt aliqua*) of the creaturely world of God (*de creatura mundi*).[2]

Far from considering brevity to be the sole norm of all discourse, the "summary" (*summatim*) word on the subject of the Trinity means here not only a statement in the form of a "summary"—even if it is a brief one. The *summary* of the *Brief Discourse* in its entirety, as a succession of subjects, now consists entirely and *theologically* in its first part alone: the "summary of the Trinity of God" (*summatim de Trinite Dei* [*Brev.* I]), summarizing at its heart the totality of a world that remains contained in it and is laid out by it (*Brev.* II-VIII). Since, in spite of the silence imposed on human talkativeness (conclusion of *Brev.* I), "something must also be said of the creaturely world of God" (*above, Brev.* II), I hope that I might both find the luxury and the grace to *continue to take* this word, and, like Bonaventure, do nothing but *receive*: "if one finds anything correct in this treatise (*si quid vero rectum*), may God alone be given honor and

---

[1] E. Jüngel. *Dieu mystère du monde*, op. cit. t. II, p. 52-61: "taire Dieu pour surren-chère de langage."

[2] Bonaventure, *Brev.* II, 1, No. 1 (V, 219a), Fr. tr. p. 55.

glory (*soli Deo honor et gloria referatur*)."³ Again, something *had to be said*—and perhaps everything when it is a question *of the all*—"of the Trinity of God" (*Brev.* I) and of the type of "theology" that supports it (*Brev.* Prol.) as a *way* of letting "God enter theology."

I have answered the question of "how God entered theology, and whether he is doing so again," with Bonaventure, by saying that only theology itself (Part One)—in its pure descriptivity on the one hand (Ch. I) and the suspension of any statement in the form of *quid*, as well as, on the other hand, any proof for the existence of God (Ch. II)—prepares an entry for him that does not force him to stay there other than as he *is* and as he wishes to present himself: as Trinity. But when God himself "begins" (Part Two), the Father then demands on the one hand that he remain the sole "origin at work *in* the work" by expressing himself almost aesthetically through his Son, and beyond any causal efficiency (Ch. III); and he demands on the other hand that the two of them constitute, together with the Holy Spirit, a type of community such that the auto-affection of their divine sense is totally laid out in their unique desire to tend toward a "Common Friend"—or better, their desire to "Love-in-Common" (Ch. IV). At the intersection of this theological space prepared by man for the divine indwelling (subjective evidence) and of the eminently Trinitarian expression of the One who reveals himself to have been there in the beginning (objective evidence), God "manifests himself" and "expresses himself" to the believer (Part Three) first by "abandoning himself" in a Trinitarian way in the most perfect poverty, even to the point of "appearing" in his very "being" (Ch. V), and next by using "metaphors" that somehow adopt his specifically human ways of being or dwelling in the world, yet without ever letting himself be reduced to or renouncing "what is proper to him" (Ch. VI).

Over the course of the *Breviloquium*, the baton is handed from the theologian who "speaks about" or "expresses" the Trinity of God (*de Trinitate Dei*) as soon as it "manifests itself" and bows, with God, too, to the norms of an adequate theological discourse—i.e. "descriptive" (Ch. I)—to another way of speaking about or expressing God: this time in the magnificence of his "entry into the world"—*De creatura mundi* (*Brev.* II). "Every creature is a word of God (or divine word)"—*Verbum divinum est omnis creatura*—in the words of Bonaventure himself:⁴ for "they all have a relationship of dependence on their Creator (*omnes creaturae respectum habeant et dependentiam ad suum Creatorem*)."⁵ The attempt to speak

---

³ Bonaventure, *Brev.* Prol. 6, No. 6 (V, 208b), Fr. tr. p. 123 (cited in the Foreword, above).

⁴ Bonaventure, *Com. in Eccl.*, c.I (VI, 16b): "verbum divinum est omnis creatura, quia Deum loquitur; hoc verbum percipit oculus."

⁵ Bonaventure, *Brev.* II, 12, No. 2 (V, 230a), Fr. tr. p. 125.

of God is thus not limited, or no longer limited, to merely expressing him in himself—whether by metaphor or in the search for what is proper to him (Ch. VI). Better, God is only expressed—in a Franciscan mode—through that which can be seen or touched (the Creation, and the experience of the stigmata, for example), rather than his speaking of himself: "the science of interpretation, hermeneutics, has its limits," as Bernard Bro writes; "it will always be the maid that prepares the bed, but lying in it is not her task."[6] The Franciscan way of being in the world as "word of the body" or as "language of the flesh" conveys first, to express it again in phenomenological terms, "the pure and, so to speak, still mute experience that is to be brought to the expression of its own meaning."[7] God somehow presents himself as an "open book" in Creation, according to the *Breviloquium* (*Brev.* II), not only in the sense that he lets himself be circumscribed in a book—a dead letter, vellum or book—but only in that he is only seen "at work in the act" "through" (*per*) and "in" (*in*) the "works" of his creatures:[8]

> the created world (*creatura mundi*) is like a book (*est quasi quid-am liber*) in which the Creative Trinity, or the Trinity as Maker (*Trinitas fabricatrix*), shines forth (*relucet*), is represented (*repraesentatur*), and is read (*legitur*).[9]

Reading (*legere*) the book of the Creation and the radiance (*relucere*) by which the Trinity is *phenomenalized* in it matters more here than the book itself—with the legions of words, structures, and literary devices that accompany it. The *quomodo* (§4) of the Trinity's act of appearing (§11) and of its interpretive keys is replaced by the *quomodo* of its manifestation or its revelation through *its creatures' diverse modes of being*—and of their apprehension by man:

---

[6] B. Bro. *La beauté sauvera le monde*, Paris, Cerf, 1990, p. 66. On the limits of hermeneutics and the impossibility of its total reconciliation with phenomenology, see Janicaud, D. "Articulations / désarticulations" (Ch. IV), in *La phénoménologie éclatée*, Éd. de l'éclat, Paris, 1998, pp. 70-93. For the double Franciscan reference to the *Canticle of Creation* and to *the experience of stigmata*, see respectively RSPT, pp. 31-34 ("de l'emprise technique à la déprise mystique.") and RSPT, pp. 42-43 ("de la croix à cœur ouvert aux stigmates de frères François").

[7] Husserl, *Méditations cartésiennes*, Paris, Vrin, 1980, §16, p. 33. On the meaning and the necessity of this mute (phenomenological and descriptive) experience—in theology, too—see my work *Le Passeur de Gethsémani*, op. cit., pp. 138-139: "vers une expérience muette."

[8] See RSPT, pp. 10-11: "l'enjeu d'un regard: le passage du *per* au *in*."

[9] Bonaventure, *Brev.* II, 12, No. 1 (V, 230a), Fr. tr. p. 123. The ranslation, contrary to the current usage, of *Trinitas fabricatrix* by "fabricative Trinity" or "Trinity as Maker" rather than as "creative Trinity" is justified (above, pp. 89-90).

the *way* or the *mode* (*quomodo*) by which God conceals himself (*lateat*) within all the objects of sensation or knowledge is obvious (*in omni re, quae sentitur sive quae cognoscitur*).[10]

"To be a vestige is not an accident for any creature, something that the piety of viewing it can add to it; it is the very being of the thing: its *way of being* is to be bound and dependent, to reflect."[11] The hypothesis of an "ontology of the sensible" in Bonaventure—if not developed, at least evoked in this work[12]—will consist first in recognizing, and in proving, that only a truly Franciscan vision of the world finally manages to counterbalance, at least in theology, the inflexible legacy of the "Platonic postulate according to which the divine world is purely spiritual, and thus can express itself in sensible images only inadequately and, for us men, deceptively."[13] The delay that, for a time at least, is imposed upon me in anticipation of realizing "the work"—in another (and different) thread of this vast project[14]—will thus steer me, without ever leaving the present "beginning" (*Brev.* I), toward the complete development of this "Bonaventurian *Summa Theologica*," in which the aesthetic consonance of its harmonics (creation, sin, incarnation, grace, sacraments, and final ends) resonates again with its principal tonality (Trinity):

by itself, the large string of the zither does not sound good (*grossa chorda in cithara per se non bene sonat*), but with the others it is harmonious (*sed cum aliis est consonantia*).[15]

"No one can see the beauty of a poem (*nullus potest videre pulchritudinem carminis*)," the *Breviloquium*'s Prologue warns, "if he does not cast his gaze over the whole of it (*nisi aspectus eius feratur super totum*

---

[10] Bonaventure, *De reductione artium ad theologiam*, No. 26 (V, 325b), Fr. tr. (modified) *Les six lumières de la connaissance humaine*, Paris, Éditions franciscaines, 1971, p. 85.

[11] Mouiren, *Introduction au Breviloquium II*, op. cit., (Éd. franciscaines), p. 26 (my emphasis).

[12] *Above*, Note 4, p. 88; Note 2, p. 99; and Note 3, p. 154.

[13] Balthasar, *La gloire et la croix*, t. I (Apparition), op. cit., p. 352 (passage taken up as an introductory problematic in my article "*Vision, excès, et chair…*", RSPT, p. 3). To return to this postulate: such seems to us to be a great breakthrough of Hans Urs von Balthasar in theology, and not among his least. Again we should articulate its philosophical—or rather phenomenological—translation, and give both theology and phenomenology the chance to cross-fertilize. My own research is very explicitly dedicated to the realization of this task.

[14] This work would be entitled: "St. Bonaventure and the Ontology of the Sensible: the theological summary of the *Breviloquium* (*Brev.* II-VIII).

[15] Bonaventure, *Hex.* XVIII, 25 (V, 418a), Fr. tr., *Les six jours de la création*, op. cit., p. 403.

versum)."[16] In this sense, though no one of them is superimposed over any other, the seven ages that constitute the history of the world—as well as the seven parts of the *Breviloquium*—chant various verses of a song that are linked by a single refrain: the Trinity itself (*Brev.* I). Once more I will have to imagine, sometime in the near future, and as briefly and densely as the *Breviloquium*, a way to unfold its course or chant its hymn (*Brev.* II-VII). In that case only Madame Gervaise's declaration at the beginning of another "poem"—*The Portal of the Mystery of Hope* (Péguy)—will translate in the same way (but now for the twentieth and twenty-first centuries) an eminently Bonaventurian, and thus original, perspective on the cosmic fraternity between man and the world—initiated by the Trinity itself and received by the believer from the paternity of God for each of his creatures, inexorably borne in his Son:

The faith I love best, says God, is hope.
That is not surprising.
I shine so brightly in my creation.
In the sun and in the moon and in the stars.
In all my creatures.
In the lights of the firmament and the fish of the sea.
In the universe of my creatures.
On the face of the earth and on the face of the waters.
In the movements of the stars that are in the sky.
In the wind that blows over the sea and the wind that blows in the valley.
In the calm valley.
In the quiet valley.
In the plants and in the beasts and in the beasts of the forests.
And in man.
My creature.[17]

---

[16] Bonaventure, *Brev.* Prol. 2, No. 4 (V, 204b), Fr. tr. (modified), p. 101. For an interpretation of the beauty of the poem (*pulcherrimum carmen*), inherited from Augustine (*De vera religione* XXII, 42) but applied here by Bonaventure to salvation history, see H. Urs von Balthasar, *La gloire et la croix*, t. II, 1 (Styles), pp. 282-283.

[17] Péguy, *Le porche du mystère de la deuxième vertu*, Paris, Pléiade, Œuvres poétiques complètes, 1957, p. 529. Péguy's monologue is not, of course, without reminiscences of Brother Francis's *Canticle of Creation*. The affinitiy between the two authors (with the Seraphic Doctor as exegete of Franciscan intuition) remains, however, to be deepened—and especially with respect to the Trinitarian perspective of Péguy's theology. Like Bonaventure in the 13th century, Charles Péguy can probably be considered "the best representative of a theological aesthetic at the beginning of the 20th century" (see H. Urs von Balthasar, *La gloire et la croix*, Paris, Aubier, 1972, (Styles II), monograph on Péguy, p. 277).

AFTERWORD: ST. THOMAS AQUINAS AND THE ENTRANCE OF GOD INTO PHILOSOPHY

THEOLOGICAL LIMIT AND PHENOMENOLOGICAL FINITUDE[1]

One will probably be surprised to find an afterword on St. Thomas Aquinas as a conclusion to a work on St. Bonaventure. The book that you just read through shows this over and over. A real gap is visible between the one and the other: hypercognizibility and analogy, search for the "how" and quest for "why," monadology and exit into the created, paternity and principiality, givenness and substance, poverty and perfection, manifestation and existence, trinity and concept, identity and connaturality, etc. And yet I have said, and we should reaffirm it, the Seraphic Doctor and the Angelic Doctor celebrate the same "poem to creation," whether by the canticle of creation (St. Francis, St. Bonaventure), or by the ways of arriving at it (St. Dominic, St. Thomas). Their difference lies not, therefore, in content first, but rather in approach. The opening to the present work has fully shown this ["Confrontation with Étienne Gilson"]. I *myself* have *also* followed the path that goes from Bonaventure to Thomas Aquinas. And yet it is in no way a question of leaving the one (the Seraphic Doctor) to turn towards the other (the Angelic Doctor). Rather, we should hold onto them both, be it non-simultaneously and according to differentiated modes.[2]

I have said this from the preface to the present work onward. There is, or we have read here, a *St. Bonaventure and the Entrance of God into Theology*. Far from being confined only to the debate with metaphysics (Gilson), or from wanting to exit from it (Heidegger), *my* St. Bonaventure attempted to "describe" rather than to "explain," to

---

[1] This text initially appeared in the *Revue des Sciences Philosophiques et Théologiques*, Colloque du Centenaire, July-Sept. 2008, vol. 92 n° 3, pp. 527-556 under the complete title "Limite théologique et finitude phénoménologique chez saint Thomas d'Aquin" (text translated and reworked for the occasion).

[2] See *Crossing the Rubicon*, trans. Reuben Shank, New York, Fordham University Press, 2016, ch. 5, pp. 121-136: "Tiling and Conversion" [Duns Scotus, Thomas Aquinas, Bonaventure].

show *how* the mystical is said in the phenomenological, or also to what extent this God, hyper-known to us (manifestation), is also said through metaphors made to express him rather than in order to conceptualize him (interpretation). But perhaps there is now also what it is fitting to call a *St. Thomas Aquinas and the Entrance of God into Philosophy* (and no longer only into theology). I have, moreover, emphasized this, but in a debate with and concerning St. Augustine this time: "God comes 'into philosophy' only when he enters *also and at the same time* 'into theology.' Here the hypothesis of onto-theo-logy collapses of itself: not only in the sense that it is historically inaccessible (except in Thomas of Erfurt, the pseudo-Duns Scotus on whom the young Martin Heidegger worked), but because it remains in principle impossible within the insoluble *tension of metaphysics and theology*."[3] We will therefore maintain here the hypothesis of a double entrance, or rather of a single double-wing door: *the entrance of God into theology* on the one hand (St. Bonaventure) and *the entrance of God into philosophy* on the other (St. Thomas Aquinas). But in both cases, as in all cases, it is still a question of the "same God" who enters, whether it is a question of his coming to us by concepts (natural theology) or by revelation alone (revealed theology).

We will certainly hold onto *theo*-logy, but without failing at the same time to aim at its counterpoint in theo-*logy*. There is no reason why God would have given us "reason," which is what is proper to man, according to Thomas Aquinas, if he were not to say with that very (natural) reason that which at least in part concerns himself. Everything would then occur as if the creative act amounted to denying himself, preferring to turn away from the most precious thing he had given and refusing it all access to him, as if he wanted, as it were, to get rid of it, or at the very least to mistrust it. Suspicion with regard to so-called "natural" reason has perhaps had its day, including within the framework of phenomenology. Not that we should this time boldly return to metaphysics against phenomenology, according to a backlash that would be quite inappropriate – but only because *his* nature gives itself to *my* nature and because "there also" he comes to manifest himself fully.

The "phenomenology of the limit" developed here (my perspective, inherited both from Bonaventure [the incarnate] and Thomas Aquinas [the limited]) is, then, certainly distinct from the "phenomenology of the saturated phenomenon" (Jean-Luc Marion's perspective, inherited from Denys the Areopagite). Let us be careful, however, and I have insisted on this from the *incipit* of the present work onward. It is not a question of opposition but rather of making visible the possibility of a differentiated,

---

[3] *GFO*, p. 26.

other path: a "phenomenology from below and of carnal ordinariness" on the one hand and a "phenomenology from above or of the saturation of phenomena" on the other.[4] One never wins by speaking "against," for one always remains "entirely against." Moreover, recognizing one's debt is not committing parricide but rather acting such that the child grows and that, once an adult also, he will be able to emancipate himself. I will therefore here follow my own way, sure that on this route, and precisely, I must now come across Thomas Aquinas, after having followed Bonaventure along such a good path.[5]

In the manner of Étienne Gilson in his time, (cf. Opening), the effigy of the Angelic Doctor indeed rises up as a tutelary figure for every medievalist who is committed not only to the plural tradition of a differentiated Middle Ages (a current largely asserted in France precisely against Étienne Gilson) but who dares to stand facing the greatest ones, against whom he cannot avoid measuring himself. In this debate, or, better, this "loving struggle," I will not interrogate, or will no longer interrogate here, the question of the aforementioned ontotheology, of the status of beingness (étantité), or of the sense of alterity, having, moreover, already treated of it[6] – but rather that of "finitude" or of the "limit" that is assigned to it. There is indeed an originality of Thomas Aquinas in relation to Martin Heidegger, which brings them closer just as much as it separates them: the "limit" (or finitude) is not only stated in a Christian system, it is, in a sense, wanted and desired by God. Paradoxically, the distinction of the created and the uncreated does not come, for Aquinas, to make the believer leave his humanity in order to insert him into divinity, but on the contrary it teaches him to stand within and even to sink ever further into the human, for it is there that the divine first stands. God "wants" the limit and "wants us" in the limit. This is the great teaching of Thomas Aquinas, not against Bonaventure (the limit in corporeality) but otherwise than him (the limit in the created). In them both, one takes "ways" (*viae*), but in two divergent senses: a steep climb or verticality on the one hand (Bonaventure) and a winding path or horizontality on the other (Thomas Aquinas). Whereas for the former

---

[4] See *The Metamorphosis of Finitude: An Essay on Birth and Resurrection*, trans. George Hughes, New York, Fordham University Press, 2012, § 5, pp. 19-20: "Christian Specificity and the Ordinariness of the Flesh".

[5] Concerning the whole of this journey, see my work that is quasi-autobiographical, or that at the very least retraces an intellectual intinerary in debate: *Parcours d'embûches: S'expliquer*, Paris, Editions franciscaines, 2016 (response to the collection *L'analytique du passage: Dialogue et confrontations avec Emmanuel Falque* (dir. Cl. Brunier-Coulin), Paris, Ed. franciscaines, 2016 (730p.).

[6] See *GFO*, ch. 1 (Augustine), ch. 2 (Scotus Erigena), ch. 8 (Thomas Aquinas) respectively.

it is a question of raising oneself by degrees up to the *apex affectus* by which we unite ourselves to God (*Itinerarium*), one needs, for the second, to walk along another path, only pulling oneself up to God in order to access the possibility of recognizing oneself as a created human, and therefore of needing the uncreated divine to differentiate oneself (*S. th.* Ia, q. 2).[7]

That man *is not* God: such is the aim, and the principal originality, of Thomas Aquinas – not because the human would regret not being the divine, as if he had fallen from an identification that never existed, but because he does not have to be the divine since he is created. In this sense, the contemporary avowal of finitude as the blocked horizon of existence (phenomenology) could not be indifferent to its rootedness in the created as the Being-there[8] of man, called first to be and to remain human, albeit "in" the Son of Man, through whom God became man (medieval philosophy). Moreover, and to differentiate the traditions without, however, opposing them, the aim in Thomas Aquinas is not only humanization (Latin vision) but also divinization (Greek vision). Or more precisely, it is here divinization (Greek vision) in that it first passes through its pure and simple humanization (Latin vision). It is Thomas Aquinas's domain, and perhaps what is proper to him, to have known how to unite Latin and Greek in his concept of analogy (proportionality and eminence). The contemporary phenomenologist cannot, then, ignore this and must draw the lesson from it, provided that he endeavors no longer only to dictate to the theologian what he must do, for lack of knowing how to practice it, but that he needs on the contrary to learn and to receive from him a possibility for thinking that he had not envisioned until now: namely, a "conversion" or a "metamorphosis" of concepts that he had first developed, the horizon of "finitude" in particular.[9]

---

[7] This perspective of the limit of the created and the uncreated, which founds the act of the Eucharist understood as a "passage from animality to humanity" (in descent) and not only as a way going from "humanity to divinity," is largely developed in *The Wedding Feast of the Lamb: Eros, the Body, and the Eucharist*, trans. George Hughes, Fordham University Press, 2016, chapter 7, pp. 177-198: "The Passover of Animality" (a limit also envisioned in *Eros*, chapter 6, pp. 133-172: "Embrace and Differentiation").

[8] [In accordance with standard convention, whenever être or étant appear as nouns, "Being" translates the former and "being" the latter, except within quotations from Thomas Aquinas, in which the noun "being" always translates être. (Étant does not appear as a noun in any of the quotations from Aquinas employed here.) To avoid confusion, whenever the standard English translation of Aquinas reads "being" but neither être nor étant appears in the French, I modified the translation to eliminate the word "being" and follow the French more closely. – Trans.]

[9] This is precisely the entire sense of the work *The Metamorphosis of Finitude: An Essay on Birth and Resurrection*, trans. Hughes, New York, Fordham University Press, 2012.

Introduction: Limit and finitude

A. *Thomas Aquinas and phenomenology*

The multiple interpretations and confrontations of Thomistic thought with phenomenology certainly do not date from today – a proof, if there is one, that the relevance of Thomism has never ceased to haunt phenomenologists. The examples are multiple and even genealogical, such that a veritable tradition, even a lineage, can be established from the rise of phenomenology to Thomas Aquinas. Husserl first, who via Brentano inherited the concept of "*intentio*," of which recent studies, in analytic philosophy as in phenomenology, have shown the direct link with the *Summa Theologica*.[10] Edith Stein next, who, on the occasion of Husserl's 70th birthday (1929), offered an "essay of confrontation between the phenomenology of Husserl and the philosophy of St. Thomas Aquinas" (sic.), even brutally opposing phenomenological "egocentrism" to Thomistic "theocentrism."[11] Or also, and of course, Martin Heidegger taking up the "Thomistic philosophy of the *ens creatum*," wrongly accusing it, moreover, of a reduction of the concept of "creation" to that of "production," and this even as the concept of *actum essendi* in Aquinas could have cast much light on the famous forgetting of Being in the eyes of the philosopher from Freiburg.[12] To which one will finally add, at least in order to remember them, on the one hand the Thomistic debate led by E. Gilson concerning a sense of "Christian philosophy" for today and the Heideggerian accusation that it is a "square circle";[13] and on the other

[10] See, as pioneers, Elizabeth Margaret Anscombe for analytic philosophy [*Intention*, Oxford, Blackwell, 1957] and A. de Muralt for phenomenology [*La métaphysique du phénomène: Les origines médiévales et l'élaboration de la pensée phénoménologique*, Paris, Vrin (Reprise), 1985 (articles from 1958 to 1963)]. And for today, D. Perler (ed.) [*Ancient and Medieval Theories of Intentionality*, Boston, Brill, 2001], and J. Benoist [*Les limites de l'intentionnalité*, Paris, Vrin, 2005].

[11] E. Stein, "Husserl and Aquinas: A Comparison" (1929), in *Knowledge and Faith*, ed. Walter Redmond, Washington, D.C., Institute of Carmelite Studies, 2000, p. 32.

[12] On the error of identifying "creation" with "production," see M. Heidegger, "The Origin of the Work of Art," in *Poetry, Language, Thought*, trans. Albert Hofstadter, New York, Harper & Row, 1971, p. 29: "The inclination to treat the matter-form structure as *the* constitution of every being receives a yet additional impulse from the fact that on the basis of a religious faith, namely, the biblical faith, the totality of all beings is represented in advance as something *created*, which here means *made*." As for the Heideggerian forgetting of the Thomistic *actum essendi* as a counter to the forgetting of Being, I will refer to J.-B. Lotz, *Martin Heidegger et Thomas d'Aquin* (1975), Paris, PUF, 1988, 2nd treatise, pp. 29-48: "l'être selon Heidegger et Thomas d'Aquin."

[13] See É. Gilson, *The Spirit of Medieval Philosophy* (1932), trans. A. H. C. Downes, New York, Charles Scribner's Sons, 1936, pp. 49-51 [Metaphysics of Exodus and Chris-

hand Jean-Luc Marion's "joyful retraction" (sic.) to make visible a "God without Being" who would not, however, be "without act of Being," be it simply to save Aquinas from the great shipwreck of the supposed "ontotheologians" of the history of philosophy.[14]

It is not, however, or it is no longer, the moment to know who among the ancient or medieval philosophers must be counted among the holders of ontotheology – such a posture in reality only designating a certain Avicenian figure of Duns Scotus [Thomas of Erfurt], falsely erected in 1915 by Martin Heidegger as a paradigm of all metaphysical thought.[15] We will be no more satisfied next, and this in the manner of numerous commentators, simply to juxtapose on the one hand what concerns the *actum essendi* in Aquinas and on the other what concerns "*Sein*" in the philosopher from Freiburg. The reunion with the former (Being in Thomas) cannot, indeed, so cheaply console us for the denunciation of its forgetting in the latter (Being in Heidegger).[16] We will not, finally, be content to focus Thomas Aquinas's relation to modernity solely on the epistemological field of logic [analytic philosophy], as the examination of the structures of consciousness and of language in the 13th century certainly has its philosophical importance but does not bring out, in my view, what concerns the type of experience and the relation to the world that is involved with it [phenomenology].[17] As a phenomenologist,

---

tian philosophy]; and M. Heidegger, *Introduction to Metaphysics,* trans. Gregory Fried and Richard Pold, rev. ed., New Haven, Yale University Press, 2014, p. 8 [the accusation that Christian philosophy is a "square circle"].

[14] J.-L. Marion, "Saint Thomas d'Aquin et l'ontothéologie," in *Revue thomiste,* Jan.-March 1995, note 2, p. 65: "Such was my position, following many others, notably in *God Without Being* [the calling into question of the primacy of Being and the contestation of Thomas Aquinas's fundamental position]. It is clear that I must, and with joy besides, today present a *retractatio* on this point." [My translation. – Trans.]

[15] See A. de Libera, *La philosophie médiévale,* Paris, PUF, "Que sais-je?," n° 1044, 1992 (2nd ed. revised), pp. 72-73: "For a medievalist, this (onto-theo-logical) characterization of the essence of Aristotelian metaphysics in fact applies principally to *one of the Latin interpretations of Avicenna* that was imposed in the School." [My translation. – Trans.] This interpretation was in reality based on Martin Heidegger's *Habilitationsschrift* on a pseudo-Duns Scotus [Thomas of Erfurt], *Duns Scotus' Theory of the Categories and of Meaning* (1915), trans. Harold Robbins, Chicago, DePaul University, 1978.

[16] Such was the attempt, praiseworthy in its time, of numerous commentators: the accusation of forgetting Being did not resist the affirmation of the *actum essendi* in Thomas Aquinas (cf., and according to different aims: E. Stein, J-B. Lotz, J. Caputo, W. Richardson, B. Rioux, M. Lindblad, etc.). We will not, however, confine ourselves to this, precisely because the debate about Being opens onto the debate about the limit and finitude, which is at least as fundamental and demanding as the former.

[17] As for the renewal of Thomistic studies by way of his analytic reading, I refer the French reader to R. Pouivet, *Après Wittgenstein, saint Thomas,* Paris, PUF, 1997, p. 5: "Even though Wittgenstein is assuredly not a commentator on Thomas Aquinas, he, bet-

therefore, and as a medievalist according to a path that today has largely been established, I will attempt, for my part, to say only, but radically, that which is, in my view, "the thing itself" of the whole Thomistic attempt in view of our modernity: namely, a veritable thought of the "limit," understood here as philosophical finitude, also reread in light of theology.[18]

B. *Homo viator*

We must affirm this from the start: the couple, or better yet, the marriage, of the "theological limit" *and* "phenomenological finitude" does not go without saying. Edith Stein, however, had already, in her era (1929) and some two years after the publication of *Being and Time* (1927), pronounced its sentence, commenting precisely on Aquinas's thought in light of Husserl's phenomenology: "At our goal, both what we know *in via* [on our earthly journey] and what we take on faith *in via*, we know in another way. The possible extent of our knowledge *during our pilgrimage on earth* is fixed; we cannot *shift its limits*."[19] We will, therefore, have to resign ourselves to this: "God is not," according to Thomas Aquinas, and this from the *prima pars* of the *Summa Theologica* onward (q. 88), "*for us* the first object known" – *Deus non est primum quod a nobis cognoscitur.*[20] That which God is "in himself" (*in se*) is a thing, and we can certainly demand to know him even as he remains unknown to us – on which, moreover, Thomas here bases the "natural desire" to know God.[21] But that which God is "for us" (*pro nobis*), or "starting from us" (*a nobis*), is, however, truer "in our home (*chez nous*)"

---

ter than any other, could assure an access to Aquinas's philosophy by calling into question a modern conception of spirit and thought that appeared with Descartes." [with such diverse Anglo-Saxon authors as Anthony Kenny, Elizabeth Anscombe, Peter Geach, John Haldane, Fergus Kerr, etc.]. A "declared anti-Cartesianism" ["l'anti-Descartes" (pp. 31-47)] probably marks the distance from the phenomenological interpretation of Thomas Aquinas (supported by Husserl's *Cartesian Meditations*).

[18] Cf. [for the justification of the method] my work *God, the Flesh, and the Other*, Evanston, Illinois, Northwestern University Press, 2015, Introduction, pp. 12-19: "The Sealed Source."

[19] E. Stein, "Husserl and Aquinas: A Comparison" (1929), op. cit. [*Knowledge and Faith*], p. 13 (emphasis added). [Translation modified to follow more closely the wording of Falque's quotation from the French. – Trans.]

[20] Thomas Aquinas, S. th. Ia, q. 88, a. 3, resp.: "Whether God is the first object known by the human mind?" trans. The Fathers of the English Dominican Province, Christian Classics Ethereal Library. [Translation modified to follow more closely the wording of Falque's quotation from the French. – Trans.]

[21] S. th., Ia q. 12 a. 1: " Whether any created intellect can see the essence of God?"

(*apud*) because that is the place where *we* live and where, indubitably, *we* stand: "In our universe – or rather 'in our home' (*apud*) –," as Aquinas emphasizes concerning the simplicity of God (q. 3), "composite things are better than simple things."[22]

This crucial Thomistic distinction between man "*in via*" and man "*in patria*" must also be counted among those major epistemological ruptures in the history of thought, of which it is unsure that we have taken the full measure, at least in relation to its pertinence for contemporary philosophy. Aquinas is certainly a theologian of transcendence. But he first deploys a "philosophy of immanence," endeavoring thereby to rejoin the question of "the human per se" – not independently of God (in which he here differs from contemporary philosophy), but because it is on the contrary the task of God's creative project itself to inscribe man in a finitude that both *respects the human condition as a creature* and maintains it in its *incompressible distance from the Creator.* "For everything that is finite by its nature is *limited* according to the nature of some limited genus (*omne quod secundum suam naturam finitum est, ad generis alicuius rationem determinatur*)," as the *Summa Contra Gentiles* insists, by way of a leitmotif. This is why "it is therefore evident that the consideration of creatures has its part to play in building the Christian faith."[23]

The hypothesis, also maintained [*The Metamorphosis of Finitude*], of the human "per se" as the point of departure of a metaphysics first rooted in finitude, be it to then be metamorphosed into God, thus finds its most radical confirmation in the Thomist consideration of the "mere human being" (*ab homine puro*), taken and rooted "here below" in its properly "mortal" life. Neither against God nor absent from him, the human "per se" will indeed serve in St. Thomas, as in contemporary philosophy, as a point of departure to a theological metaphysics rooted in finitude, even though the Trinity in St. Bonaventure would also call for an "upheaval" of this humanity in God (Trinitarian monadology): "God cannot be seen in his essence by a *mere* human being," as Aquinas remarkably emphasizes from the first beginnings of the *Summa Theologica* [Ia q. 12] onward, "*except he be separated from this mortal life (nisi ab hac vita mortali separetur).* [...] But our soul, *as long as we live in this life (quandiu in hac vita vivimus),* has its being in corporeal matter, hence naturally it knows only what has a form in matter, or what can be known

---

[22] S. th. Ia, q. 3 a. 7, ad. 2: "Whether God is altogether simple?" [Translation modified to follow more closely the wording of Falque's quotation from the French. – Trans.]
[23] CG (*Contra Gentiles*), I, 43 n° 4 ["That God is infinite"], trans. Anton C. Pegis, and II, 2 n°6 ["That the consideration of creatures is useful for the instruction of the faith"], trans. James F. Anderson, respectively. [Translation of the first quotation modified to follow more closely the wording of Falque's quotation from the French. – Trans.]

by such a form. [...] Hence it is impossible for the soul of man *in this life* (*secundum hanc vitam viventis*) to see the essence of God. [...] It is not possible, therefore, that the soul *in this mortal life* (*quandiu hac mortali vita vivitur*) should be raised up to the supreme of intelligible objects, i.e. to the divine essence."[24]

Man is therefore first pilgrim man (*homo viator*) in Thomas Aquinas as "mortal man" or in his "state of mortality" (*homo mortalis*), though always and of course oriented towards beatitude. If death is neither the condition nor the domain of finitude, as with its later deployment in Martin Heidegger, it nonetheless marks, and as if in counter-relief[25] in Thomas Aquinas, the point on the basis of which the consideration of "this life" (*hac vita*) becomes meaningful "for us" (*pro nobis*), and in particular in our relation to God. Far from denying all relation to the divine – since we know of its existence [Ia q. 2] while nonetheless being ignorant of its essence [Ia q. 3] – the Thomistic *double vision* "of this earth" and "of the fatherland" therefore orders the entirety of his thought and likewise also his relation to a certain mode or form of finitude. Far from aiming at God only within the framework of the beatific vision, and even though that vision will forever remain the goal, the human will take up here below the means to consider his humanity "per se" in order to see in it the God who, for his part, made the choice to dwell in it (kenosis): "[This] should be understood as referring to the vision had in this life (*de visione viae*)," as Thomas clarifies in *De veritate*, "in which a person sees God through some form or other. [...] Hence [*in via*] we do not know what God is (*quid est*), but only what he is not (*sed quid non est*)."[26]

C. THEOLOGICAL LIMIT AND PHENOMENOLOGICAL FINITUDE

In what does the "theological limit of man," such as it is positively wanted by God even and including in his creative project, rejoin, then, the "phenomenological finitude of *Dasein*," as it is noted at the horizon of our world in its pure immanence? – such is the object of the present

---

[24] S. th. Ia, q. 12, a. 11: "Whether anyone in this life can see the essence of God?" (emphasis added).

[25] [The locution *en creux* has the figurative meaning of "implicitly" and could be translated thus, but especially as it later stands in opposition to *en plein* ("in full"), I have chosen to render it as "in counter-relief" to preserve the image it offers. Note also that the word later translated as "hollow" is *creux*. – Trans.]

[26] *De veritate*, q. 8 a. 1 ad. 8, trans. Robert W. Mulligan. See also the accurate commentary of J.-P. Torell, *Saint Thomas Aquinas, Vol. 2: Spiritual Master*, trans. Robert Royal, Washington, D.C., The Catholic University of America Press, 2003, p. 30.

study, with all the risks that a contemporary rereading of the thought of Thomas Aquinas presents, but that it also necessitates: "One will perhaps say," Karl Rahner says, simultaneously accusing and justifying himself, from the first pages of *The Spirit in the World* (*Geist in Welt*), "'But you are giving an interpretation of St. Thomas drawn from modern philosophy?' Far from considering such an assessment as a criticism, the author accepts it as praise. For ultimately, I ask you, can St. Thomas interest me other than in accordance with the questions that disturb my spirit and that philosophy debates today?"[27] It is necessary, then, to call phenomenologically for the *roots of finitude* in the limit in theology (1st part), in order to then discover, as if *in counter-relief*, its emergence at the beginning of the *Summa Theologica* (2nd part), in order to finally demand philosophically, as well as theologically, a veritable *consistency of the ens finitum* that phenomenology itself would be wrong to forget (3rd part). The "limit in theology" illuminates "finitude in phenomenology," not only because the former furnishes the latter with its roots but also because it imposes on the world a "consistency" that is yet more radical, once it is wanted by God rather than simply noted by man.

I. THE ROOTS OF FINITUDE

1. THE STATUS VIAE OR THE HORIZON OF FINITUDE

None, frankly, could doubt that finitude, that is (to put it briefly), the "consciousness of the blocked horizon of existence," marks "the figure of modern man" (M. Foucault). One will certainly be able to object, and this with the support of Thomas Aquinas, that this very finitude could not be thought in theology "in an interminable reference to itself." It remains, however, no less for all that the base, or at the very least the foundation, starting from which our modernity can and must be thought.[28] As I have said, everything is therefore a matter of the "point of departure." What we discover "first" (*primo*) is neither man *in patria* nor the angel, and still less is it God himself, but man *in via*. The "way" (*via*)

[27] K. Rahner, *Spirit in the World* (1957), trans. William Dyck, London, Bloomsbury Academic, 1994 (cited and translated by J. Doré in *K. Rahner, Aimer Jésus*, Paris, Desclée, Coll. Jésus et Jésus-Christ n° 24, Postface, p. 97). [To follow more closely the wording of Falque's quotation from the French, this is my translation. – Trans.]

[28] M. Foucault, *The Order of Things*, translator not listed, New York, Vintage Books, 1994, p. 312-318: "[O]ur culture crossed the threshold beyond which we recognize our modernity when finitude was conceived in an interminable cross-reference with itself. [...] [M]odern man [...] is possible only as a figuration of finitude" (p. 318).

is from the beginning a "state" in Thomas Aquinas (*status viae*) – that
of pilgrim man held within the horizon of his created Being, although
oriented and inhabited by beatitude – whereas it principally appears as a
"path" in St. Bonaventure (*Itinerarium*). The *status viae* takes precedence,
at least with regard to the departure, over the *Itineriarum*, in that the
"way" says *the Being of man here below* or "the state of the present life"
(*status praesentis vitae*), rather than the too-immediate desire to be rid
of it or to leave it: "Since the human intellect in the present state of life
(*secundum statum praesentis vitae*) cannot understand even immaterial
created substances," clarifies the *Summa,* in search of a point of departure
for knowledge that is in conformity with our nature, "much less can it
understand the essence of the uncreated substance."[29]

We must, therefore, accept the detour, or rather never omit to make
the return. The path is always "longer" (*longior*) for the spiritual and
corporeal creature first called to remain in his creaturely state (man)
than for the purely spiritual creature directly contemplating God in an
immediacy that, here below, is not accessible to us and does not even
deserve to be missed (the angel): "Man according to his nature (*secundum
suam naturam*) is not like the angel," as Aquinas clarifies in his treatise on
the angels, but in reality in order to define man. "Man was not intended
to secure his ultimate perfection *at once* (*statim*), like the angel. Hence
a longer way was assigned to man *than to the angel* (*longior via data est
quam angelo*) for securing beatitude."[30] Negative theology, to which I will
return, comes not from the excess of the known over the knower in the
unlimited (Denys), but conversely from the limitation of the known to
the knower by a pure and simple respect for the limit (Thomas Aquinas).

2. THE KANTIAN LEGACY OF THOMISM

The consideration of the "fatherland" or of "finitude" as a necessary
"point of departure" for the long way [that of man] and contrary to the
short way [that of the angel], certainly makes one think of the Jesuit
Joseph Maréchal's "*Point de départ de la métaphysique*" [*Point of Departure*

---

[29] S. th. Ia q. 88 a. 3, resp.: "Whether God is the first object known by the human
mind?"

[30] S. th. Ia q. 62 a. 5 ad. 1 (trans. modified [relative to the ed. du Cerf]): "Whether
the angel obtained beatitude immediately after one act of merit?" [Translation modified
to follow more closely the wording of Falque's quotation from the French. – Trans.]
Thomas Aquinas always avoided the false direction of angelism, the trail of which one
will find in my work *God, the Flesh, and the Other,* op. cit. ch. 8, pp. 231-253: "Angelic
Alterity (Thomas Aquinas)."

of Metaphysics] that established, in his era and with all the acerbic criticisms
of which he was the object, the renewal of post-Kantian Thomism.
The father, in a sense, of Karl Rahner in his own relation to Thomas
Aquinas, Maréchal probably allowed him to discover in Thomas the sense
of a "metaphysics of finite knowledge" (the subtitle of *The Spirit in the
World*).[31] Let us not err here, however. If finitude as the possible horizon
of Thomist thought cannot stray from its relation to Kant, a point on
which I agree with Maréchal or Rahner, it is not at all a question here of
reducing it to a simple epistemological or gnoseological consideration.

More linked to space and time as "a priori forms of intuition"
(Heidegger) than to the imagination in its schematism (Rahner) or
to the categories of the understanding (Maréchal), the *philosophical*
interpretation of Thomas Aquinas will here find its renewal not in the
negation of earlier positions but in their radicalization up to the position
of man's Being-there. The "state of being on the way" (état de voie) in the
Angelic Doctor (*status viae*) does not fix merely the bounds of natural
knowledge of God [neo-Kantian perspective] but indicates the positive
limits of our "Being-there" per se, up to the affirmation of the positivity
of the limit itself [Heideggerian perspective]. Moreover, it would be a
blunder, this time from the *theological* point of view, not to relate the
"limit" (in theology) to "finitude" (in phenomenology). For, if there is a
gap from the one to the other – from "theology" to "phenomenology" – it
is not because the former (theology) does not treat of the same objects
as the latter (phenomenology) but because what is simply noted by the
former (the horizon of finitude in phenomenology) becomes strangely
desired and wanted by the latter (creation within the limit in theology).
That one cannot and should not remain confined to Martin Heidegger's
existential analytic – which *The Metamorphosis of Finitude* sought to
demonstrate – does not therefore, exempt us from passing through it, at
the risk, on the contrary, of entirely missing our modernity and, firstly,
the necessity of recognizing ourselves as limited Beings.

---

[31] See, respectively, J. Maréchal, *Le point de départ de la métaphysique*, Paris, Fe-
lix Alcan, 1926 [in particular the 5th notebook: "une ontologie de la connaissance"]; K.
Rahner, *Spirit in the World* (1957), Bloomsbury Academic, 1994 [in particular pt. 2, § 1,
pp. 57-64: "The Point of Departure: The Metaphysical Question"]. ([The subtitle of *Spirit
in the World* does not appear in the English translation. – Trans.]) As for the relation of
the one to the other, one may profitably read L. Roberts, *The Achievement of Karl Rahner*,
New York, Herder and Herder, 1967, pp. 13-15. As for the history of the lineage from
J. Maréchal to Thomas Aquinas, see the accurate clarification of B. Pottier, "Maréchal
et Thomas d'Aquin," in P. Gilbert, *Au point de départ, Joseph Maréchal entre la critique
kantienne et l'ontologie thomiste*, Bruxelles, Lessius, 2000, p. 27-47.

3. *The theological legacy of finitude*

Paradoxically, Martin Heidegger himself, in a text recently brought
to light (the course of 1938-1939 [GA vol. 60]), insists on the necessity
of this link between "phenomenological finitude" and "theological limit,"
emphasizing in particular the rooting of the former in the latter: "The
expression '*finitude*' (*Endlichkeit*) is chosen within the framework of an
inevitable *historical comprehension* and of a revocation of the questions that
have been posed up to the present. This word is susceptible to numerous
misinterpretations [...]. One can relate it to the *Christian representation*
of the created character of every being, and one can even become the
victim of the trap of dialectic, according to which it is necessary to think
that with the position of the '*finite*' an '*infinite*' would also always be
thought. Everywhere here the '*finite*' (*Endliche*) is taken in the sense
of a *limited* (*Beschränkten*) and, in truth, of a *limitation* of the being
(*Beschränkung von Seiendem*); '*finitude*' is thought in a metaphysical
fashion. The finitude of Being signifies, however, something entirely
different: the abyssal character (*Abgrunlichkeit*) of the interval to which
belongs not a negativity understood as a lack or a limit but as a distinctive
mark (*Auszeichung*)."[32]

From this crucial text of the philosopher from Freiburg, we will
retain at least three points for my remarks, which the journey through
Thomistic philosophy will have as its task, if not to carry out, then at
least to evaluate. (a) The concept of finitude (*Endlichkeit*), according to
Heidegger himself, finds its roots in "the Christian representation of the
created character of every being." Said otherwise – and this will be a
crucial point in my aim – only the position of a transcendence is at least
historically able to bring forth a horizon of immanence, albeit in order
to break with it thereafter. *Qua* created or produced, the world will break
with the transcendence that engendered it better than if it were simply
posited as unable to be derived from some transcendentality (the distance
between creation as production *ex nihilo* in Thomas and simple change
in Aristotle). Christianity indeed constitutes in this sense, and probably
in an exemplary fashion in Thomas Aquinas, the "point of departure"
for contemporary thought concerning finitude. (b) "Finitude" cannot be
identified right from the start with the "finite." That is, in Heidegger's
view as also in my own, one of the most frequent errors in the entire
modern theological corpus, which takes up for itself the concept of
finitude: "In order to uncover the finitude of man, it is not enough to

[32] M. Heidegger, *Besinnung*, in *G.A.* vol. 66 [course of 1938-1939], Frankfurt-on-
Main, Klostermann, 1990, p. 87-88. Cited and translated by A. Gravil, *Philosophie et finitude*, Paris, Cerf, coll. "La nuit surveillée," 2007, pp. 411-412. [My translation. – Trans.]

adduce at random any one of his many imperfections," the philosopher from Freiburg precisely indicates in *Kant and the Problem of Metaphysics* (1929): "In this way we state at best only that man is a finite being."[33] Finitude or "the fallen Being of Dasein," to say it this time in the terms of *Being and Time*, (1927), "must not be taken as a 'fall' from a purer and higher state. Not only do we lack any experience of this ontically, but, ontologically, we lack any possibilities or clues for interpreting it."[34] In short, one who says finitude (*Endlichkeit*) does not necessarily say "finite" (*Ende*) either at the beginning [when leaving the finite] or at the end [when deriving the finite from the infinite]. We will interrogate in this sense numerous contemporary phenomenologists. A sort of "Cartesian preemption of the infinite over the finite" indeed marks, in my view, French phenomenology, be it a question of the "face" (Levinas), of the word (*parole*) (Chrétien), of auto-affection (Henry), or of the "saturation of phenomena" (Marion). Thomas anticipates the danger of ontologism, to which I will return, and could well teach phenomenologists themselves not to leave too quickly the "plane of immanence" to which, however, phenomenology itself was initially linked.[35] (c) Without any contrary therefore, finitude is therefore in Heidegger's view a "distinctive mark" (*Auszeichnung*) of the being as such. Probably it is necessary, here again, to retain henceforth the lesson that the creature's finitude in Thomas Aquinas is not the degradation or the limitation of an infinite or of an unlimited that should belong to it. From the beginning to the end, that is, from its birth to its glorification, and this by passing via death, the creature remains in its creaturely state, that is, within the limit that

---

[33] M. Heidegger, *Kant and the Problem of Metaphysics*, trans. James S. Churchill, Bloomington, Indiana University Press, 1962, § 39, p. 226: "The Problem of a Possible Determination of the Finitude in Man." [Translation modified to follow more closely the wording of Falque's quotation from the French. – Trans.]

[34] M. Heidegger, *Being and Time* (1927), trans. John Macquarrie and Edward Robinson, New York, Harper & Row, 1962, § 38, p. 220. [Translation modified to follow more closely the wording of Falque's quotation from the French. – Trans.]

[35] Cf. my remarks addressed to J.-L. Marion dans *Le combat amoureux: Disputes phénoménologiques et théologiques*, Paris, Hermann, 2014, ch. 4 ["Phénoménologie de l'extraordinaire"], pp. 178-183: "théologie naturelle et retour de l'ontologisme" [pp. 50-53]: "The ontologism of revelation, which Thomas Aquinas [justly] blamed, in opposition to Anselm […], has perhaps not finished producing certain of its transformations. The essential question today, in phenomenology as in theology, is not uniquely that of the "phenomenon of revelation" or of "God" (with or without Being) but rather that of man or of the receiving subject in his capacity to say, or not, the phenomenon or God: either on the basis of the phenomenon itself or of God in his act of self-revelation [the descending ontological way], or on the basis of man and of his conditions of existence (*in via*) that render impossible any direct access to some beyond (*in patria*) [ascending cosmological way(s)]" (cit. pp. 181-182).

is consubstantial with its very Being and never thought as negative. Beatification, and even resurrection, to which I will return, is not for Aquinas the rupture of limits but their assumption for a transformation. Including in the beatific vision, the limit remains because the creature never leaves its creaturely state, even though it becomes capable of welcoming the unlimited in itself. Rather than accusing Christianity of having diverted finitude from its vocation of immanence as soon as Christianity gave birth to it, we will show, contrary to this presumption of Heidegger, and with the support of Thomas Aquinas, that immanence itself is never scorned in a Christian system, even though it relies on transcendence as its principle.

It remains, then, to think otherwise, or anew, Thomas Aquinas himself, and this beginning with the opening and the procedure of the *Summa Theologica*, that is, in light of the horizon of this duly sought-for finitude. Certainly nothing appears more daring than to claim to read, or to reread differently, the beginning of the *Summa* [q. 1-3]. Everything, or almost everything, seems to have been said about a text of which it is often predicted that it will say nothing more, at least about what we know of it in the bulk of its interpretations. It remains that this would be to doubt the force of this Thomistic thought that is still capable of engendering us. An indefatigable fidelity to the letter of Aquinas, to which I will return, sometimes obscures his spirit. Returning to his intention and ridding ourselves of our preconceptions will therefore show, on the contrary, that the respect for the "limit of man" in Aquinas's theological aim joins with, and reinforces to the highest degree, the "sense of finitude" in the phenomenological aim of Martin Heidegger and of many others after him. The quest for the *full* (the beatific vision *in patria*) always lets appear the sense of the *hollow* (the distance between man and his necessary limit *in via*). Far from falling in a void, the hollow here marks a "horizon" – precisely that of finitude: first in the relation of philosophy to theology (q. 1), then by the status of the ways to access God (q. 2), and finally in the simplicity accorded to God alone and not to the creature (q. 3). The "deficiency of man" understood as limit rather than as sin (q. 1), the redefinition of the "ways for God" as so many "ways for man" (q. 2), and the imperative of the simplicity of God making visible "our own composition" (q. 3) thus constitute so many theses to be (re)discovered in the hollow/counter-relief of the human that also constitutes, for us today, its fullness.

II. Finitude in Counter-Relief

1. Philosophy and Theology

I will neither redo nor retrace here the long history of the Thomistic relation of philosophy to theology. Such is neither my aim, nor my proposal, nor my ambition. Within the framework of an attempt at the determination of finitude in Thomas Aquinas himself, I will, nonetheless, want to show – and this will be my first point – that the limit of the finite Being, certainly conceived on the basis of the unlimitedness of an infinite Being, does not necessarily need to relate itself to the unlimited to discover itself in the state of pilgrim man. As I have said, what distinguishes the *itinerarium* in Bonaventure from the *homo viator* in Thomas Aquinas lies in a difference of perspectives rather than in an opposition of ways. Whereas for the former, the pilgrim knows that he is going somewhere, along an ascending pathway (the itinerary that goes from sensible apprehension to the *apex affectus*), for the latter he sees himself on the contrary as on the path (*sur le chemin*) (in the limit of the *pro nobis* or the *in via*). The "way" (*via*) or the "itinerary" (*itinerarium*) in Bonaventure is rather a "state" (*status*) in Thomas Aquinas, for which reason a determination of finitude in the latter [Thomas] rather than in the former [Bonaventure] will legitimately be sought.

The time of finitude or of the limit as such thus properly marks the time of *philosophy* for Thomas Aquinas, even though it always remains embedded in theology: "In the teaching of philosophy (*in doctrina philosophiae*)," clarifies the *Summa contra Gentiles*, "which considers creatures in themselves (*secundum se*) and leads us from them (*ex eis*) to the knowledge of God, the first consideration is [therefore] about creatures (*prima est consideratio creaturis*); the last, of God (*et ultima de Deo*). But in the teaching of faith (*in doctrina vero fidei*), which considers creatures only in their relation to God (*non nisi in ordine ad Deum*), the consideration of God [therefore] comes first (*primo est consideratio Dei*), that of creatures afterwards (*et postmodum creaturarum*)."[36] Everything is thus a matter of the point of departure, and of a difference of views, and not of a distinction of objects: creatures come "first" and God "last" in philosophy, and God comes "first" and creatures "last" in theology. Moreover, it is the very relation to the divine that is envisioned here, with theology always referring directly to its model, whereas philosophy restricts itself to the simple consistency of things as such: "the teaching of the Christian faith deals with creatures so far as they reflect a certain

---

[36] CG, II, 4, n° 5.

likeness of God (*quaedam Dei similitudo*) [...]," clarifies the *Summa contra Gentiles*. "[H]uman philosophy considers them as they are [...]." [37]

Without falsely opposing an ascending philosophy to descending theology, since the theologian also discovers the effects of grace, as the philosopher discovers the effects of creatures, it is therefore the proper task of the "human approach to philosophy" (*philosophia humana*) to be able to consider creatures "in themselves" (*secundum se*) or "according to their proper mode" (*secundum quod huiusmodi*), and to not envision them "uniquely in relation to God" (*non nisi in ordine Deum*), which, moreover, does not exclude them from being positively thus related. Such a "consideration of the creatures" (*consideratio creaturarum*) henceforth appears as crucial for the entire history of philosophy, in that it turns the Bernardine *consideratio* away from only contemplating God [*Treatise on Consideration*] towards the world itself and the proper density that it requires [*Summa Theologica*]. Discovering himself in the state of a man "on" the path (*"sur" le chemin*) rather than "en" route (*"en" chemin*), and considering creatures as a philosopher (*consideratio creaturarum*), "the mere human being" thus first takes note of his Being-there [*Dasein*] to discover himself next as already open to God. The famous adage of the *Summa Theologica* – "*cum gratia naturam non tollat sed perficiat*" ("grace does not destroy nature but perfects it")[38] – here founds a metaphysics of finitude that we will take at least as a point of departure, waiting also this time for God to indicate the point of arrival.

We will wonder, then: is such a departure by philosophy really necessary? Should we not confine ourselves only to the Bonaventurian perspective in which God enters into philosophy only by not entering into it, entering precisely, and only, into theology? *St. Bonaventure and the Entrance of God into Theology* (the work) here paradoxically finds its counterpoint in what I now call a *St. Thomas Aquinas and the Entrance of God into Philosophy* (the afterword). It is not that the ways are entirely opposed, as I have said, but that they are complementary, differentiated, and above all committed otherwise.[39] For if phenomenology appears, in a sense, to be of Bonaventurian inspiration in the consideration of the absolute rather than of the limit (the face, the word (*parole*), autoaffection, flesh, the saturation of phenomena), it also waits to find again its Thomistic perspective that originally marked its birth certificate (the horizon, the limit, the world, the thickness of the flesh, etc.). In short, if there is a "theological turn in French phenomenology" (D.

---

[37] CG, II, 4, n°1.
[38] S. th. Ia q. 1 a. 8, ad. 2.
[39] See *Crossing the Rubicon*, § 17, pp. 128-131: "On 'Tiling' or Overlaying," [Duns Scotus, Thomas Aquinas, Bonaventure].

Janicaud), this amounts less to accusing phenomenologists of some infidelity to phenomenological orthodoxy than to interrogating the unthought decision for a primacy of the absolute (more Bonaventurian) over necessarily maintaining the point of departure in finitude (more Thomistic).[40] In order no longer arbitrarily to oppose "Christianity of revelation" on the one hand and "atheism of finitude" on the other, we will therefore maintain that "revelation" and "finitude" together belong to the perspective of Christian theology, depending on whether one gives oneself for point of departure either the "unlimitedness of the Trinity *in patria*" (Bonaventure) or the "limit of our state *in via*" (Thomas). A *positivity of the limit,* impossible to derive from sin and therefore impossible to reduce to a mere *limitation* is also seen in Thomas Aquinas from the opening of the *Summa Theologica* onward: "Whether sacred doctrine is nobler than other sciences?" (Ia q. 1 a. 5).

2. DEFICIENCY AS LIMIT

Whether it is indeed a question of "doubt for us" (*dubitatio pro nobis*) in what concerns articles of faith or sacred doctrine's need to use the philosophical sciences "as of the lesser, and as handmaidens" (*tanquam inferioribus et ancillis*), the Angelic Doctor offers one and the same reason: the "weakness of our intelligence" (*propter debilitatem intellectus nostri)*" [ad. 1] or the "weakness of our spirit (*propter defectum intellectus nostri)*"[41] (repeated twice [ad. 1 et ad. 2]). One will here notice the prudence of the translators, who take care to not transcribe *debilitas* as a form of "debility" issued from an understanding corrupted by sin, or *defectio* as a sort of "deficiency," or even a sort of "defeat," of a soul that supposedly did not succeed at maintaining itself in its state of perfection. By translating it as "weakness," the contemporary editors of the *Summa Theologica* here preserve a neutrality that it is precisely the interpreter's task to question.[42]

---

[40] See *The Metamorphosis of Finitude,* § 5, pp. 16-19: "The Preemption of the Infinite."

[41] [Translation modified to follow more closely the wording of Falque's quotation from the French. – Trans.]

[42] One will note here the gap between the translation of the edition of the "Revue des jeunes" ["debility"] and that of the Éditions du Cerf ["weakness"]. The latter precisely grants more liberty to the commentator in that it draws, at least in a manner one can envision, the nature of the human spirit to the side of the "limit" (weakness) rather than that of "limitation" or even "corruption" (deficiency or debility). Probably all the originality of Thomas Aquinas lies in that he envisioned it thus, making of the state of man *in via* the state of a man limited by his nature (as a corporeal and spiritual being),

If the "doubt" (*dubitatio*) that can arise regarding the articles of faith "is not [indeed] due to an uncertainty in the things themselves (*incertitudinem rei*), but to the weakness (*debilitatem*) of our intelligence"[43] it is not therefore, in my view, because the thing is "doubtful" in itself or because we can simply "err" with regard to it. Taking up Aristotle word for word, and therefore here outside any framework of sin, it is the dazzling character of the truth that first makes the articles of faith difficult for us to understand – "like the owl's eye faced with the sun's light" [*Metaphysics,* Alpha 1.2 [993b9]]: "Nothing prevents (*nihil prohibet*)," as Aquinas emphasizes, here citing the Stagirite, "what is in itself the more certain (*certius secundum naturam*) from seeming to us the less certain (*esse quoad nos minus certum*)" [ad. 1].[44] Although failure as "insufficiency" or "error" in the act of knowing certainly appears in the *respondeo* simply to mark the degree of certainty of purely human knowledge [the "certitude from the natural light of human reason [...] can err (*postest errare*) [...]", "error" or rather the "weakness of our intellect" (*debilitas intellectus nostri*) is not, therefore, of the same nature in the *ad primum* of the same article [q. 1 a. 5], for one who knows how to read or how to perceive it. On the one hand, there is man who can err with respect to the infallible truth of sacred science [*respondeo*], and on the other hand, there is the limit of our intelligence that cannot affirm that it knows certainly, as pilgrim man, the articles of faith [*ad primum*]. Finitude indeed stands there, *in counter-relief,* in our state *in via* (doubt about the articles of faith [a. 5, ad. 1 et ad. 2: limitation of our sight]), while the superiority of sacred doctrine over the other sciences seeks to be said, *in full,* in the aim of man *in patria* ([a. 5 resp.], here supported by the "science of God and the blessed" [a. 2, resp.: dazzle of the light]).

This reading *in counter-relief* of the *Summa Theologica,* which from the inaccessibility of the light recognizes first and positively our own obscurity, in my view accounts precisely for the famous subalternation of philosophy to theology. The gnoseological aim (the debate about natural theology) indeed could not be understood independently of its existential and ontological foundation (the limited condition of our human Being-there). Certainly "our spirit is weak," understood here as "limited" (*defectus intellectus nostri*), and therefore the absolute superiority of sacred doctrine over the philosophical sciences is imposed. But this

---

rather than the state of an inveterate sinner from another condition that he would have to envy (the temptation of angelism or of the creature that is purely spiritual and is stripped of the carnal or of the limit).

[43] [Translation modified. – Trans.]

[44] [Translation modified to follow more closely the wording of Falque's quotation from the French. – Trans.]

weakness, or, better, this "limit," is also what constitutes its force – to the point that the unlimited precisely needs the limit to be said to man: "Besides (*et hoc*)," as Aquinas insists in a concession always turned into a rule, "that sacred doctrine thus uses the other sciences is not due to its own defect or insufficiency, but to the weakness of our spirit, which is more easily led (*facilius manudicitur*) by what is known through natural reason (from which proceed the other sciences) [...]" (a. 5 ad. 2).[45] One could not, therefore, be clearer. The unlimitedness of revelation does not regret the limit, certainly of reason, but also of the body or of sensation. On the contrary, it wants it and requires it because the limit is more in conformity with our status *in via* and even with our state as creatures in general. Whereas the limit yet results only from the *excess* of the unlimited (the dazzle of the sun's light for the owl's eye in the Thomistic reprise of Aristotle and then of Denys [ad. 1]), it this time positively becomes its *auxiliary* to *make visible* what it itself teaches, but by another way – certainly more limited (natural reason), but also more accessible (in direct conformity with our status *in via*): "[Sacred doctrine] can in a sense depend upon the philosophical sciences, not as though it stood in need of them, but only in order to make its teachings more manifest (*ad maiorem manifestationem*)" (ad. 2).[46]

The ambition here is clearly displayed. The "limit" or "finitude" is the way that suits our state of being on the way (*status viae*), in that it takes our nature in its "Being-there" and does not dispose of it before having definitively established a foothold in our "here below." A double "quasi-phenomenological" relation of philosophy to theology thus forms here under the pen of Aquinas, provided that we still dare to spin the metaphor: relation of "finitude" first, in the limit of the reason that does not necessarily, or at least consciously, call for unlimitedness ("the *weakness of our spirit* [...] is more easily led by what is known through natural reason"), and relation of "manifestation" or of phenomenality next, in the role of epiphanic auxiliary that revelation precisely confers on reason ("to make its teachings *more manifest*"). Although everything is given by the unlimitedness of Revelation in the framework of a *Summa Theologica*, "nothing prevents," therefore, the limit of the body or of the reason from being able in part to say it in its departure (finitude) and even from manifesting it (phenomenalization). The *concession*, I have said– "nothing prevents (*nihil prohibet*)" [ad. 1] or "besides" (*et hoc*) [ad. 2] – in each case becomes a *rule*, once no obstacle is any longer posed

---

[45] [Translation modified to follow more closely the wording of Falque's quotation from the French. – Trans.]

[46] [Translation modified to follow more closely the wording of Falque's quotation from the French. – Trans.]

to the possibility of saying God and of first saying oneself within the framework of the limit of our creaturely state. Thus the cosmological ways to God (q. 2) are less "positively" modes of access for going to the divine (a. 3) than "negatively" the only possibility or possibilities that remain (the works) once no direct or immediate way appears practicable any longer (a. 1).[47]

3. THE WAYS TO GOD AS WAYS TO MAN

I will not retrace here the multiplicity of ways, so well-known that one does not know what more to say about them. The wedding of "theological limit" and "phenomenological finitude" compels us, however, to celebrate the undying marriage in which they find themselves bound. We know that Thomas's originality lies less in the ways or in their multiplicity (q. 2 a. 3: "Whether God exists?") than in the manner of introducing them (q. 2 a. 1: "Whether the existence of God is self-evident?"). As a proof of this, when the Angelic Doctor sets out the ways, in the *Contra Gentiles* for example, he speaks less of "his ways" than of "arguments by which both *philosophers* and *Catholic teachers* have proved that God exists" (CG I, 13, emphasis added); and when he calls for a multiplicity of ways, this list appears neither exhaustive nor even absolutely necessary, at least in that the *Compendium Theologiae*, written at the same time as the *prima pars*, only produces, for its part, a single one of the ways.[48] The originality, once again, comes from the limit (our state *in via*) and not from exceeding it (the rush towards the *patria*) or from its goal to be reached (the object, God himself). The first necessity for the human is not to rejoin the divine immediately, at the risk of losing in the supposed identification with the Creator that which is the distance from the creature. It amounts rather and on the contrary to accepting the "detour," for what will reveal itself, *in fine*, as a "return": passing *first* via man to go to God, be it on the basis of works that he arranged *for us* in order for us to ascend to him.

---

[47] This law of the concession being turned into a rule here serves as a principle for a reading in counter-relief of finitude in Thomas Aquinas. Constantly repeated – *nihil prohibet* (q. 1 a. 5 ad. 1; q. 2 a. 2 ad. 1), *et hoc* (q. 1 a. 5 ad. 2), *nihilominus* (q. 7 a. 3 ad. 3)… –, a detailed study of this, put to the test of the text, would probably authorize a renewed reading of Thomas Aquinas in his distance from Denys rather than in his coincidence: a negative theology by the test of the "limit" of man *in via* (proper to Thomas Aquinas) rather than by the excess and dazzle of the "givenness" of God *in patria* (Denys and his current revival in the framework of phenomenology).

[48] Consult on this point the judicious remarks of L. Renault, *Dieu et les créatures selon Thomas d'Aquin*, Paris, PUF, 1995, pp. 32-38.

The adversary aimed at from the opening of Question 2 onward is in reality known – and so famous even in the eyes of Aquinas that it becomes useless to name him. I have, of course, here invoked the *Proslogion* of Anselm of Canterbury and his famous so-called ontological argument, as it is explained by Thomas Aquinas: "But as soon as the signification of the word "God" is understood, it is at once seen that God exists. For by this word is signified that being than which nothing greater can be conceived (*id quo maius significari non potest*)" (q. 2 a. 1 obj. 2).[49] Despite the transformation of the formula (*significari* and no longer *cogitari* [obj. 2]), its statement in a logical form (identification of the subject and the predicate [resp.]), and the opposition of thought and of reality as existing in itself [ad. 2], the Angelic Doctor's exposition clearly shows that the argument is understood, and even often taught, but repeating it is not first his aim. The intention is different: not the validity of the argument, but its impossible practicability for us: "Therefore I say that this proposition "God exists," *of itself* (*in se*) is self-evident, for the predicate is the same as the subject [...]. Now because *we* do not know the essence of God (*sed quia nos non scimus de Deo quid est*), the proposition is not self-evident *for us* (*non est nobis per se nota*); but needs to be demonstrated by things that are more known *by us* (*quoad nos*), though less known in their nature – namely, by effects (*scilicet per effectus*)" (a. 1, resp.).[50]

We must resign ourselves, and this in spite of the multiple and false interpretations of the Angelic Doctor that would seek to turn us away from this, and make us believe that he would still be seeking a proof if he took here the concept of God as his principal object. *We* are the real object of the proof, or, better, of the way, more than God himself. Or rather, *proving ourselves* constitutes the exact "argument," rather than God as such. It matters little, indeed, whether we ascend to God by movement, by efficient causes, by contingency, by degrees of being, or by ends. The multiplication of the ways only shows that the ways matter little. "Do we have the means to prove, and by what means can we prove?" – such is the quasi-transcendental, and surprisingly modern, question that Thomas Aquinas poses here, and this against all the reductions to a pure objectivism that do not belong to him. To this interrogation, which therefore determines our belonging to finitude, the response sounds clearly and distinctly for the one who knows how to hear it: immediate access to God, of the type of the Anselmian argument (identification of essence and existence), belongs to the angels rather

---

[49] [Translation modified to follow more closely the wording of Falque's quotation from the French. – Trans.]

[50] [Translation modified to follow more closely the wording of Falque's quotation from the French. – Trans.]

than to men. Not having the means *in via* to know a proposition that is evident "in itself" (*in se*) concerning God's existence, we must "for us" (*nobis*) pass through what is better known "by us" or "starting from us" (*quoad nos*). If the "invisible perfections of God are made visible to the intellect by means of his works,"[51] to take up the famous adage, cited by Thomas, from the epistle to the Romans (Rom. 1:20 [a. 2 sed contra]), this exegesis of the world comes in reality less from the cosmos itself than from the necessity, *in what concerns us,* of finding a means adapted to the limited Being that we are in order to ascend to God: "Demonstration can be made in two ways: one is through the cause (*per causam*), and is called 'a priori,' and this is to argue from what is prior absolutely. The other is through the effect (*par effectum*), and is called demonstration 'a posteriori'; this is to argue from what is only first *in the order of our knowledge* (*per ea quae sunt priora quoad nos*). When an effect is better known *to us* than its cause (*nobis est manifestior quam sua causa*), from the effect we proceed to knowledge of the cause" (Ia q. 2 a. 2, resp., emphasis added).[52] In short, and the thing itself manifests itself once one knows how to read (it): the knowing subject takes precedence over the known object in the clearing of the ways in Thomas Aquinas, and nothing is more to be feared than the presumption of a direct access to God or the danger of ontologism (knowledge of the Absolute in its very Being). The first affirmation of "existing" in Thomas (*an sit*) is not a declaration of objectivity, as is sometimes wrongly believed: "the *first thing* we must know of any being is whether it exists" (*primum enim quod oportet intelligi de aliquo est an sit*) [a. 2 sed contra, emphasis added].[53] The declaration concerns what is "first to be known" rather than the "existence" of what is known. It does not address the object itself but on the contrary marks the subjective avowal of a finite being that must first pass through its proper limits and those of the world (cosmological ways) in its impossibility of directly accessing God (ontological way). The cosmological ways – the last resort of an angelism that is not only inaccessible but is as perilous as it is undesirable here below – here serve as a bridge for an ontological argument that is certainly *valid* in the beatific vision (knowledge of essence) but *impracticable* in the state of wayfaring

---

[51] [Translation modified to follow more closely the wording of Falque's quotation from the French. – Trans.]

[52] [Translation modified to follow more closely the wording of Falque's quotation from the French. – Trans.]

[53] [Translation modified to follow more closely the wording of Falque's quotation from the French. – Trans.]

man (passage by existence).[54] Whereas numerous interpreters bet on a *positive excess of essence* relative to the negative narrowness of existence, we will, on the contrary, have to recognize for ourselves (*pro nobis*) a *positive limit of existence* relative to an essence that is forever inaccessible here below. The "owl" that knows (Thomas), rather than the dazzling sun (Denys), accords with man's limit in Thomas Aquinas, and this well before Duns Scotus, who, on this point, gives only the reprise: "it is not the sun but the owl's eye that explains why it does not see the sun."[55]

III. HOLDING ONESELF TO THE LIMIT

Recognizing that the "ways for God" are "ways for man" thus demands of man that he *hold himself first to his limits,* even though God himself has given him by his works, which are also limited, the means to ascend to his unlimited Being. This is a holding of oneself to the self that, in my view, founds, with the necessary respect for a *de facto* if not *de jure* finitude (q. 2), [1] first the argument of the famous *preambula fidei* (a. 2), [2] next the organicity of the ways in general (a. 3), [3] and finally the possible treatment and resolution of a phenomenology of the inapparent. Three stages, or three steps, that lead us, at least in a first movement, from the *preambula fidei* to the horizon of finitude as such – without ever leaving the horizon of "this" world by which we are first constituted.

1. FROM THE PREAMBULA FIDEI TO THE HORIZON OF FINITUDE

[1] Against any "anthropological reduction" and its false accusation (Balthasar / Rahner),[56] the "preliminary truths" in reality matter less in

---

[54] The somewhat caricatural opposition of "Being" and "gift" should in this sense be nuanced according to the context of its enunciation. St. Thomas imposes the primacy of existing over engendering not of itself [a necessary retraction regarding my *St. Bonaventure and the Entrance of God into Theology* but only in virtue of the not immediately accessible character of the gift or of essence for man here below. The danger of "ontologism" should in this sense be pointed out not only with regard to medieval philosophy (Anselm or Bonaventure facing Thomas) but also with regard to contemporary philosophy and phenomenology in particular. Cf. "Phénoménologie de l'extraordinaire (à propos de J.-L. Marion)," in *Le combat amoureux*, op. cit., ch. V, pp. 198-183: "Théologie naturelle et retour de l'ontologisme" (*supra*, note 33).

[55] See Gilson, in a commentary on Duns Scotus, but which applies already here to Thomas Aquinas, *Jean Duns Scot, Introduction à ses positions fondamentales*, Paris, Vrin, 1952, p. 466. On this point, see GFO, ch. 9: "The Singular Other (John Duns Scotus)" (in particular pp. 260-262: "The Limitation of Nature to My Nature").

[56] See Balthasar, *Love Alone is Credible*, trans. D. C. Schindler, San Francisco, Ignatius Press, 2004, ch. 2, pp. 31-50: "The Anthropological Reduction."

their constraining prism of a divine truth that is ceaselessly limited by human prerogatives than in the "path to be traveled" (*ad articulos*) that they demarcate by a simple respect for our *status viae* that compels us to pass through the world to go to God (cosmological ways): "The existence of God and other like truths about God, which can be known by natural reason, as the Apostle says (Rom. 1:19), are not articles of faith (*non sunt articuli fidei*), but *preliminary truths that lead us to the articles* (*sed preambula fidei ad articulos*)" (a. 2 ad. 1, emphasis added).[57] By separating too much the *preambula fidei* from their process of finitude in which they remain always caught, the critics have progressively erected as an in-itself what in reality is true only of our state *in via*. The path towards what is to be demonstrated (*ad articulos*) indeed imposes the preliminary truths of the faith (*preambula fidei*) and not the preliminary truths of the path to be traveled. The existence of God becomes precisely "demonstrable" in Aquinas (*demonstrabile* [a. 2]) not on the basis of the Dionysian radiance of the truth to be demonstrated (Anselmian ontological argument), but by the strangely modern virtue of our own capacities for demonstration supported by the world that is given to us (Thomistic cosmological ways). Finitude lies precisely in the fact that it is necessary to pass via man and via his own limits to go to God. In this lies the fundamental sense of demonstration: less in the objective act of "demonstrating" (*demonstrare*) than in the subjective capacity to demonstrate or to render the thing "demonstrable": *utrum Deum esse sit demonstrabile?*[58]

For the same reason and in the same article [q. 2 a. 2], in a relation of philosophy to theology that it here remains to question again, "faith presupposes natural knowledge (*fides praesupponit cognitionem naturalem*), even as grace presupposes nature, and perfection supposes something that can be perfected (*sicut gratia naturam, et perfectio perfectibile*)" ([ibid.] a. 2 ad. 1). The famous adage could not here be understood outside of its context, precisely that of finitude, or at the very least of the limitation of "nature" to "my" nature. The *presupposition of natural knowledge by faith,* or of *nature by grace,* does not mark, as is sometimes repeated at will, an objective in-itself of the world that would precede us or the hypothesis of a possible Being of God that would only follow the Being-there of man. On the contrary, it establishes *for us,* as also *for God* in his act of creation and of redemption, this world as the true world because we here gain a foothold by way of a point of departure of our knowledge, once we are rooted in it. The limitation of "nature" to "my" nature is not folded into itself in a critical subjectivism, of which one is often wrongly accused,

---

[57] [Translation modified to follow more closely the wording of Falque's quotation from the French. – Trans.]

[58] Ia, q. 2, a. 2 [title].

but on the contrary is an openness to the world on the basis of an I, my own, that respects its creaturely state and its distance from the Creator as it is also wanted and desired by God himself. Once again, the *limit* is not here a *limitation* in the sense of an apophatism that crushes us in the dazzle of its light as it is nostalgic from being unable to aspire to more. The consideration of the "limit" marks, on the contrary, respect by God himself for my creaturely state *in via* and his ultimate desire that "nature" be also "mine," in a sharing of properties that makes it so that nothing that is mine in my "here" remains foreign to what is his in his "over there": "[Demonstration] through the effect (*demonstratio per effectum*)," as the *respondeo* insists in an originality that should be emphasized, [a posteriori demonstration], "is *first* in the order of *our* knowledge (*per ea quae sunt priora quoad nos*)" (a. 2 resp.).

[2] Whence the true stake of the ways, in their organicity in general: not only, in my view, at their end (J.-L. Marion), but at their beginning (my own hypothesis). If the first of the ways – by movement – appears, according to Thomas, as "the most manifest" (*manifestior*), it is because "it is certain, and evident to our senses, that in the world some things are in motion" (Ia q. 2 a. 3, resp.). What matters here is not the end: the "*quod omnes dicunt Deum*" (and this we call God), concerning which one could wonder, rightly or wrongly, if it is not necessary to read in it an indication of ontotheology and of the identification of God's icon with the idol of his concept.[59] It is found rather in its beginning: the most manifest (*manifestior*) is the most evident "for us" (*nobis*) because it is first a question "of us" (*quoad nos*). Reading the ways upside down, or rather right side up (from their beginning), restores their true right: that of anchoring us in the finitude of our own limit rather than making us bend beneath the excess of a glory that always exceeds its concept. There are in reality "ways" to God, precisely because we are "on the way," that is, *in our own existence*. It is known that the "path of the world" or the cosmological ways are not proofs. But that the ways themselves are only a "path for our state of being on the path," (état de chemin) – such is what is found in the necessary rereading for today of the "theological limit" as "phenomenological finitude" in Thomas Aquinas. There are no *viae* in Aquinas (a. 3: the five ways) independent of the *status viae* that precisely constitutes our state here below (a. 2: critique of the ontological

---

[59] J-L. Marion, *The Idol and Distance: Five Studies* (1977), trans. Thomas A. Carlson, New York, Fordham University Press, 2001, p. 10: "In short, the question of the existence of God is posed *less before the proof than at its end*, when it is no longer a question simply of establishing that some concept can be called *God*, nor even that a certain being (étant) puts that name into operation, but more radically that that concept or that being (étant) *coincides* with God himself ['that which we call God']" (emphasis added).

argument). Whence the diversity of ways, which indicates less, in my view, a plurality of itineraries than the importance of remaining in what constitutes the Being-there of man as "Being on the way." Rather than the goal (God himself), the method or the manner of reaching it matters more here (the ways of our world). And in this "method," precisely, resides man's Being-there: *meta ê odos* – on the way.

[3] Hence the paradoxically retrospective resolution, precisely for the reading of Thomas Aquinas, of the conflict that invigorates all phenomenology and the hypothetical "phenomenology of the inapparent." I have said, and even written, that French phenomenology suffers today, like Anselm, from an excess of ontologism that could make us wrongly believe in a direct access to the absolute in the overflow of the event over the everyday (the face, the word (*parole*), autoaffection, saturation of phenomena, etc.). Dominique Janicaud, in his famous *turn*, had, however, foreseen, "Is there a trait that distinguishes [French phenomenology] decisively from the time of the first reception of Husserl and Heidegger? And is this trait *the rupture with immanent phenomenality?*"[60] Thomas's ways show us, in this sense, the way, and now for today. If phenomenological finitude (the point of departure, even the anchoring in immanence) is at the same time a desire for the theological limit (the project of creation wanted by God himself), we must first pass through our "humanity per se" or through the "mere human being (*ab homine puro*)," to go to God. In the "simplicity" *in full* of God's existence and of the equivalence of his essence and his existence lies in reality *in counter-relief* the thickness of our own "composition" and of the inadequation, in principle, of our Being to its definition. Nothing is "simple," therefore, and especially not man. Simplicity is fulfilled by God alone [q. 3: "Of the simplicity of God"], who, *in excess* in his simplicity, makes visible, *in the narrow space* of our composition, the richness of our Being-there: "in our universe" – or, better, "*in our home*" (*quaod apud*) – as I have noted precisely regarding God's simplicity (q. 3) – "composite things are better than simple things (*nos composita sunt meliora simplicibus*)" (Ia q. 3, a. 7, ad. 2).

2. NOTHING IS SIMPLE, EXCEPT GOD

Paradoxically, therefore, and I have announced this, the more one advances in the *Summa Theologica* as a determination of God, the more in reality one sinks into the thickness and the limit of man. Certainly,

---

[60] D. Janicaud, "The Theological Turn of French Phenomenology" (1991), trans. Bernard G. Prusak, in *Phenomenology and the "Theological Turn": The French Debate*, New York, Fordham University Press, 2000, p. 17 (emphasis added).

and we must say this from the beginning, negative theology remains that which, first, works at the heart of the treatise on the names of God: "how God is not" (*quomodo non sit* [q. 3-11]), "how he is known by us" (*quomodo a nobis cognoscatur* [q. 12]), and "how he is named" (*quomodo nominetur* [q. 13]). But, still according to the same procedure, the Angelic Doctor, indicating *in full* what God "is not" – body, composite of matter and form, of substratum and essence, of essence and existence, of genus and difference – says in reality *in counter-relief* what "we are." The method of elimination in reality more makes *us* visible as "composites" than it designates God as "simple" – remaining, moreover, always unknown to us in his essence (q. 3). What is essential in "the simplicity of God" is therefore neither God nor simplicity, any more than what is primordial in the ways lies in the ways, but in the possibility *for us* of having access to them. The appeal to "simplicity" (*simplicitas*) therefore does not aim only at the nature of God, even though it is opposed to the composite. It seeks first and implicitly to formulate what we are, even though it treats more explicitly of what he is. Rather than determining the essence of God, "simple" (*simpliciter*) here marks rather "the radical distinction between the created and the uncreated," that is, "the fundamental ontological hiatus that Thomas places at the source of all differences."[61]

The "distance" imposed by God relative to his creature indeed states neither his indifference, nor his remoteness, nor even his splendor – quite the contrary. It marks, inversely, the density of the human and the positivity of its limit in its disproportion to the divine: *Deus non est mensura proportionata alicui* – "God is not a measure proportionate to anything," as Question 3 insists, as if nothing mattered more in God's "simplicity" than remaining *for our part* more within "composition." By letting God be God, man always becomes more a man. Such is the paradox of "proportionality in difference" that always aims at the aforementioned analogy of Being, and this independently of all the duly justified technical considerations that distinguish "attribution" from "proportionality." Nothing, frankly, should be more coveted than remaining in our creaturely state, and therefore in "difference," for thereby we paradoxically fulfill our Creator's "desire for the limit." Far from any "angelism," we are first caught in our "humanism" – not as some current to be overcome or as an era to address, but because our "pure and simple" humanity (*ab homine puro*) is primarily that in which our creatureliness consists. God's desire is therefore first, and paradoxically, that we "remain men" and thereby faithful also to his project of creation.

---

[61] See L. Renault, *Dieu et les créatures selon Thomas d'Aquin*, op. cit., p. 38.

The divine never goes against the human (in a proposition that is certainly not reciprocal), and the *limit* is not bad in itself and only becomes so in its accusation and its transvaluation into a *limitation*. We are "composites" because God is "simple," and such a simplicity is for us neither desirable nor enviable because it belongs only to God and does not demand to define us. "Our" composition makes our humanity, even though "his" simplicity makes his divinity. Such is the ground of our finitude, in which God also takes on a body, at least in his sharing of our pure and simple humanity.

3. A QUESTION OF BEING

But there is more, and better, in my view, in the Thomistic determination of God's simplicity as an affirmation *in counter-relief* of man's finitude. The Heideggerian exegesis of the Thomistic questions has greatly (as I have said), and even too much, centered the debate only on the question of "Being." The famous "forgetting" of Being would not in reality be a forgetting in light of Thomas Aquinas, and the distinction between "Being" (*esse*) and the "act of Being" (*actum essendi*) would permit us to bring out a positive and dynamic concept of Being that Heidegger himself had not seen: "Being is said in two ways," as Question 3 [The Simplicity of God] emphasizes. "It may mean the act of essence (*actum essendi*), or it may mean the composition of a proposition (*compositionem propositionis*) [...]" (Ia, q. 3, a. 4, ad. 2).[62] Certainly the examination is just and deserves to be developed.[63] But the question today is another one. It is not that the question of Being had one day to be overcome (God "with" or "without" Being), but that behind or at the heart of ontology lies, frankly, the question, also crucial, of the possibility for man of maintaining himself within his own Being, following very precisely in this God's design according to Thomas Aquinas. Saying indeed of man that his "existence is caused by another (*habeat esse causatum ab alio*)," and that in him "existence differs

---

[62] [Translation modified to follow more closely the wording of Falque's quotation from the French. – Trans.]

[63] In particular J.-B. Lotz, *Martin Heidegger et Thomas d'Aquin*, op. cit., p. 43: "Compared to the Being of Heidegger, I will retain Being as Thomas conceives of it, as follows: human thought, and in general all human accomplishments, are carried out within the horizon of Being that has always already manifested itself [...]. Aquinas reaches a Being that simultaneously exceeds finite essence and the corresponding act of Being because it is their common foundation: the Being that signifies absolute plenitude [...]. Thomas Aquinas penetrates these ultimate depths that Heidegger does not wrest from *forgetting* and that alone give access to God." [My translation. – Trans.]

from [his] essence (*esse est aliud ab essentia sua*)" (Ia q. 3, a. 4, resp.) is not only establishing the "dependence" or the "participation" of man in God, in the profound intimation of the act of Being to all beings at the heart of a creation newly defined as "relation" (Ia q. 45 a. 3 resp.). This avowal of reception opens also and first to the way of contingency: "that which is not its own being (*non est suum esse*)," as this time the *Contra Gentiles* asserts, "is not through itself necessary (*non est per se necesse est*)" (GC I, 22).[64] The formula certainly does not indicate that everything is contingent or that everything could just as well "be or not be," (être ou ne pas être)[65] God alone excepted. But it emphasizes at the very least that all necessity, probably like all contingence, can itself only be received from God. I have said this repeatedly, and we must now insist on it. Finitude is wanted in Thomas Aquinas because the created Being is never subsistent by itself (*ipsum esse*); finitude is on the contrary endured or noted in Aristotle because no creation indicates an intention that would be capable of creation (*ex nihilo*): "Creation *is not change* (*creatio non est mutatio*), except according to our mode of understanding," as Aquinas indicates, here in an abandonment (*déprise*) rather than a reprise (*reprise*) of the Stagirite. "Creation places something in the created being (*ponit aliquid in creato*) according to relation only (*secundum relationem tantum*) [...]."[66] Respecting the creation that is "his own," God also respects what constitutes its genus and does not destroy what he originally initiated. Created within the limit, man therefore remains limited, even though the unlimitedness of resurrection will come to metamorphose him, without, nevertheless, ceasing to assume the limit: "For everything that is finite by its nature is *limited* according to the nature of some genus *that is itself limited*," as we have already noted and as the *Summa Contra Gentiles* states definitively [CG I, 43].

To Étienne Gilson's famous pages about the difference between the God of Aristotle and the God of Thomas as far as creation is concerned, we must now add at least this note: the God of St. Thomas is not only "a God Who loves," nor that of Aristotle "a god who lets himself be loved" (in an opposition that, besides, leaves something to be desired), but the God of St. Thomas is a God of "the transcendence that opens onto a possible immanence," whereas the God of Aristotle is a "God of such

---

[64] [Translation modified to follow more closely the wording of Falque's quotation from the French. – Trans.]

[65] [Note that this French phrase is the French translation of Hamlet's famous question, "To be or not to be." – Trans.]

[66] S. th., Ia q. 45, a. 2 ad. 2, et a. 3 resp., respectively. [Translation modified to follow more closely the wording of Falque's quotation from the French. – Trans.]

a great distance" that he cannot *want* anything, not even immanence.[67]
The horizon of finitude is indeed historically liberated on the basis of the
"Christian representation of the created character of every being," as I
have indicated following Martin Heidegger [*supra*], and this Thomistic
historicity is still incumbent upon us today in that it sounds the charge of
a God who will never only take refuge in the hindmost worlds of his own
privacy. The limit as a simple resultant of divine excess in Denys, and
therefore as a mode of limitation, therefore here becomes, paradoxically,
the proper place of the Being-there of man *in via* in Thomas Aquinas.
The obscurity of God does not, or no longer, results from his dazzling
character in the cloud but from our having been made as limited Beings:
"We must say that God is incomprehensible to every intellect and
impossible *for us* (*nobis*) to contemplate in his essence […]," emphasizes
Thomas, commenting on and, in my view, modifying Denys's *On the
Divine Names*, "and this is true of our *terrestrial life* – or, better, of our
'state of being on the way' (*hoc est statu viae*)."[68] Ignorance, though it
be already erudite here, does not therefore come from the *excess* of the
source of light (Denys or J.-L. Marion), but on the contrary from the
natural *narrowness* of its receiver (Thomas or my own interpretation):
"It is not the *excess* that constitutes the difficulty," emphasizes Thierry-
Dominique Humbrecht, articulating together *Théologie négative et noms
divins chez Thomas d'Aquin*, [*Negative Theology and Divine Names in
Thomas Aquinas*] "but the failure to reach it," or even, I dare add, the
limit *for us* of what remains forever unreachable here below.[69] The *hollow*
of finitude therefore here perfectly reaches its *fullness*, as is clearly evident.
When man is paradoxically summoned by God to the point farthest from
him ("to see the essence of God is possible to the created intellect by
grace, and not by nature" [Ia q. 12, a. 4, *sed contra*]), he paradoxically
discovers himself at the point closest to what he himself is in his creaturely
state and therefore also to God in his creative and redemptive project.
Against all expectations, the disproportion of man to God demands not a
disproportion or a rupture of the human to make himself like the divine

---

[67] See Gilson, *The Spirit of Medieval Philosophy* (1932), trans. A. H. C. Downes,
New York, Charles Scribner's Sons, 1936, p. 75. [Translation modified. – Trans.]

[68] Thomas Aquinas, *In librum beati Dionysii de Divinis nominibus*, Cap. 1, lect. 1.
[My translation of the French quotation. – Trans.]

[69] See Th-Dom. Humbrecht, *Théologie négative et noms divins chez Thomas d'Aquin*,
Paris, Vrin, 2005, p. 405, commenting on another formula of Thomas Aquinas's *Commentary* on Denys's *On the Divine Names*: "after all the knowledge that we have of God *in
the present life*, what God is remains hidden from us" (*De Divinis nominibus…*, expositio
n° 68, cité p. 404). [My translation. – Trans.] This formula marks, in my view, a distance
with relation to Denys [position of the "limit"] rather than a simple reprise [repetition
of "excess"].

(the Greek perspective of divinization), but a proportion of God who, by choice, bends and gives himself to man's portion (the more Latin aim of the humanization of God): "Now, God is the most perfect agent," emphasizes the *Summa contra Gentiles* with regard to creation. "It was his prerogative, therefore, to induce his likeness into created things most perfectly, *to a degree suited to created nature (quantum naturae creatae convenit)*" (CG, II, 45, n°2, emphasis added).[70]

IV. THE CONSISTENCY OF THE ENS FINITUM

Phenomenological finitude, primarily drawn out as a philosophical horizon, therefore now appears, ultimately, as a "theological limit" wanted and desired by God. Brought back to the divine will and to his project of creation as "relation," man is first called to remain in his humanity, by which precisely and paradoxically he bears a greater resemblance to the divinity who came to become incarnate. But we could not be content, as I have said, to derive the limit from the unlimited. Having discovered the *primacy of the limit* ["deficiency as limit" (q. 1) and "the ways for God as ways for man" (q. 2)] by *relating it to the unlimited* as its creative and intentional principle ["nothing is simple, except God" (q. 3)], it now remains to make of this finitude itself a veritable *"distinctive mark"* of man [*Auszeichung* (Heidegger)], to follow here the program initially set out (*supra*). A "law of proportion" thus dictates its measure, which first accounts for our knowledge of God here below, then clips the wings of our pretention to angelism, and finally establishes *us* as a "limited phenomenon" rather than a "saturated" one.

1. THE ADAGE OF THE LIMITED PROPORTION

We have only just emphasized this: God imprints his likeness in created things only "to a degree suited to created nature (*quantum naturae creatae convenit*)" (CG II, 45 n°2). Very early, and this from his first writings onward (*Commentary on the Sentences*), Thomas Aquinas thus shares the intimate conviction of a necessary "measure" of the participant to the participated – in which, moreover, in my own view, he was not first the disciple of Denys, but on the contrary his most secret attacker, seeing in the Dionysian ineffable all the limits that it has, precisely in its

---

[70] [Translation modified to follow more closely the wording of Falque's quotation from the French. – Trans.]

unlimited character. The opening of the *Commentary on the Sentences* testifies to this in a formula of "proportionate participation" that one could well erect as a principle: "anything that participates in something is in it *in the mode of what participates* (*in eo per modum participantis*) because nothing can receive *beyond its own measure* (*quia nihil potest recipere ultra mensuram suam*). Since, therefore, the finite mode of every created thing is finite, every created thing receives a finite being" (*Sup. libros Sententiarum* L. I, d. 8 q. 1, a. 2 s. c. 2).[71] The adage is exemplary here; that is the least one can say. The *Summa Contra Gentiles* even makes it its spearhead, of which some will say that the formulation characterizes Aquinas's thought definitively and in its specificity: "*quidquid recipitur ad modum recipientis recipitur*" – "everything that is received is received in the manner of the one who receives" (CG II, 79, n° 7).[72]

Man certainly receives and participates in the subsistent Being that he himself is not, thus receiving his limit from the very Being of God, who always and forever wants that limit thus: *omnis creatura habet esse finitum* –"every creature has a finite being," as the *Commentary on the Sentences* emphasizes from the beginning.[73] But the limit is not, or no longer only is, a "state that gives itself" insofar, then, as we are created. It is and becomes also an "aim that is intended," by man and for this man this time, if indeed not every vocation could so easily free itself from its condition. The "manner of the one who receives" (*modum recipientis recipitur*) therefore also accounts for "that" which is received (*quidquid recipitur*). Said otherwise, and to recall anew here the "decisive test" of the anthropological reduction [*Cordula*], the taking into account of the receiver also moves as a condition of the givenness of the giver. No one, be it God himself in his supposed "objective evidence" (H. Urs von Balthasar [*La gloire et la croix*]), gives at just any time, or just anywhere, or to just anyone. The question of the "type of receiver that Christianity presupposes" (K. Rahner [*Foundations of Christian Faith*]) also matters, provided that this act of restriction or contraction of the unlimited to the limit articulates less philosophically "a measure of God taken (*prise*) and understood (*comprise*) by man" than it kenotically exposes a "measure of

---

[71] Thomas Aquinas, *Super libros Sententiarum,*. lib. I, d. 8, q. 1, a 2, s. c. 2. Cité et traduit par G. Gravil, *Philosophie et finitude*, op. cit. (Cerf), p. 109. [My translation of the French quotation. – Trans.]

[72] [My translation of the French quotation. – Trans.] See J.-P. Torell, who raises this formula to the rank of the no less famous "*cum gratia naturam non tollat sed perficiat*" ("grace does not destroy nature but perfects it" [S. th. Ia q. 1 a. 8, ad. 2]). *Saint Thomas Aquinas, Vol. 2: Spiritual Master*, op. cit., p. 252.

[73] Thomas Aquinas, *Super libros Sententiarum,*. lib. I, d. 8, q. 5, a 1, s. c. 2. Cité et traduit par G. Gravil, *Philosophie et finitude*, op. cit. (Cerf), p. 108. [My translation of the French quotation. – Trans.]

oneself by God offered to man."[74] The participated (God) dictates his law to the participant (man) only insofar as the participated himself (God in his unlimitedness) has made the theological choice of the participant (man in his limit). The Incarnation and redemption paradoxically sign this *decision to restrict,* which alone is capable of offsetting the *excess of givenness.* Through them, a new mode of dwelling at the heart of the limit itself is established.

This law of restriction or of concentration even becomes such, or so central in the eyes of Aquinas, that God himself comes to the point of submitting himself to it, independently of any mode of reception of man. Able to not create such and such a being in his "absolute power" (*potentia absoluta*), the Christian God kenotically makes the choice to bow to it in his "conditioned power" (*potentia ordinata*). The miracle "outside of nature" (*extra naturam*) is never "against nature" (*contra naturam*), insists Aquinas, precisely and paradoxically because the "limit imprinted on the laws of creation" is also that within which God paradoxically makes the choice to confine himself: "the existence of a non-round coin is possible," emphasizes Thomas, duly commented on by J.-P. Torell, "whereas it is impossible [including for God] for a circle not to be round (*circulum autem non esse rotundonum est impossibile*)," at least once his laws have been enacted.[75] Announcing here, and as in advance, the later debate with Descartes on the creation of the eternal truths, it is not submitting God "to the Styx and the Phoenix" to say that he himself bends under the weight of his own laws, provided that the choice to embrace man's limit is first theological (creation and incarnation) and not simply philosophical (crushing God under an intellectual evidence unworthy of his power). Man's challenge is to be caught between animality and angelism, and Aquinas seems, for his part, to have decided. So be it, bestiality lies in wait for us, and everyone will be able to avoid it. But there is something worse, or more devious, than man's mere "becoming animal": namely, his pretention to identify himself with a sort of angelism that does not belong to him. A "body without conscience," certainly man will fall into sin (limit hypothesis of animality). But a "conscience without body," he will not for all that be exempt from sin (limit hypothesis of angelity). Remaining a body from beginning to end, from his birth to the final resurrection, man's corporeality is not only, for Aquinas, an addition to a

---

[74] See V. Holzer, *Le Dieu Trinité dans l'histoire, Le différend théologique Balthasar – Rahner,* Paris, Cerf, Cogitatio fidei n°190, 1995, p. 333: "If Rahner stated a measure of God for man, he did *not* think it *as a measure of God taken and understood by man,* but as a *measure of himself by God offered to man.*" [My translation. – Trans.]

[75] CG II, 55, n° 3. Taken up and commented on by J.-P. Torell, *Saint Thomas Aquinas, Vol. 2: Spiritual Master,* op. cit., p. 239.

psyché that only struggles to manifest itself. On the contrary, it marks the constituent that is most proper to him, which certainly distinguishes him from angelity, but which also constitutes his proximity to the incarnate Word. In the vis-à-vis with the angel, man remains in his limit: that of his carnal Being-there by which finitude this time takes on the figure of his corporeality.

2. THE TEMPTATION OF THE ANGEL

Paradox of paradoxes, there has existed not only the angel who sometimes was tempted to defy God, but also man who frequently wants to rival the angel. We often wrongly suppose that Aquinas merely restricts matter to the reception of a form, such that the body would only be the inadequate receptacle of an (angelic) soul capable of overflowing it: "Now the contraction of the form comes from the matter (*coarctatio autem formae est per materiam*)" as we read concerning "God's knowledge" (Ia q. 14 a. 1, resp.). But it remains, however, for us to understand which, matter or form, makes the choice for such a restriction or coercion. Said otherwise, does man possess by nature an unlimited intellect of which his body negatively marks the limit (finitude as "limitation"), or is his intellect already so limited that it in reality seeks only in its body the wherewithal to be realized (finitude as a "distinctive sign")? Aquinas's response comes bluntly. To the question "Whether the intellectual soul is properly united to such a body?" Thomas responds straight away that "since the form is not for the matter (*formam non sit propter materiam*), but rather the matter for the form (*sed potius materia propter formam*), we must gather from the form (*ex forma*) the reason why the matter is such as it is (*sit talis*); and not conversely (*et non e converso*)" (Ia q. 76 a. 5, resp.). A veritable reversal, and even a quasi-Copernican revolution, must therefore occur here. Our body does not limit an unlimited spirit, in the view of the Angelic Doctor, but our spirit, which is limited because it was created thus, also seeks the limit in order to unfold. The limit (of the spirit) tends toward the limit (of the body) and does not seek to transgress itself into the unlimited. "Remaining in the limit" – is the ground, in Aquinas's view, of the unwavering union in man of the soul and the body: "But nature never fails in what is necessary," the same article continues. "[T]herefore the intellectual soul had to be endowed not only with the power of understanding (*non solum haberet virtutem intelligendi*), but also with the power of feeling (*sed etiam virtutem sentiendi*)" (Ia q. 76 a. 5, resp.). A limited spirit therefore seeks and finds for itself a limited body, rather than a limited body restricting and enclosing an unlimited spirit. The desire of a body for the soul is not simply a lack but is properly "creative or productive of an object" (Deleuze): we are a body because the spirit requires it, desires it, and wants it, and not the reverse.[76]

Everything is, in this sense, a matter of "connaturality" or affinity, to say it this time in the terms of finitude. For the angelic intellect, it is "connatural (*connaturale*) to know natures that are not in matter," since the angel is not a body, nor does it seek a body for itself, save exceptionally in order to manifest itself to man [the angel of Tobias, for example]. But such knowledge remains "the natural power of the intellect in our soul in the state of its present life (*secundum statis praesentis vitae*)," as the same article clarifies, "united as it is to a body (*quo corpori unitur*)" (Ia q. 12 a. 4, resp.).[77] Far from creating an obstacle, the body here serves as a vehicle or *medium* for our intellectuality, to speak here with Paul Claudel.[78] Should one want to leave it, one would forget that in which our humanity consists: "The weakness of human knowledge in relation to angelic knowledge does not lead Thomas Aquinas to regret that man must, in order to know, start with sensation," as A. Gravil justly emphasizes. *"It would be absurd to wish to have a knowledge that was not appropriate for our nature."*[79]

Whence the ultimate consequence, this time from the eschatological and not only protological point of view. The beatific vision itself and the resurrection remain also, in Aquinas's view, within finitude or the limit, certainly in order to inhabit it otherwise or to metamorphose it, but without ever, paradoxically, wanting to transgress it: "the created light of glory received into any created intellect cannot be infinite (*non possit esse infinitum*) [...]" foresees Question 12 concerning beatification (Ia q. 12, a. 7, resp.); and the soul, separated from the body in death, waits for the resurrection of the body to complete what it lacks in order to shine fully and anew as a "composite," certainly limited but also inhabited –

---

[76] See G. Deleuze et F. Guattari, *Anti-Oedipus: Capitalism and Schizophrenia* (1973), trans. Robert Hurley, Mark Seem, and Helen R. Lane, Minneapolis, University of Minnesota Press, 1983 p. 25-26: "To a certain extent, the logic of desire misses its object [...]. From the moment that we place desire on the side of *acquisition* [...] which determines it primarily as a *lack*: a lack of object, a lack of the real object. [...] If desire is *productive*, it can be productive only in the real world and can only produce reality. [...] The real flows from it [...]. Desire does not lack anything; it does not lack its object" (emphasis added). [Translation modified to follow more closely the wording of the French. – Trans.]

[77] [Translation modified to follow more closely the wording of the French. – Trans.]

[78] P. Claudel, "Sensation du divin," in *Présence et prophétie*, Fribourg, Egloff, p. 55: "It is not the spirit alone that speaks to the spirit; it is the flesh that speaks to the flesh." [My translation. – Trans.]

[79] A. Gravil, *Philosophie et finitude*, op. cit. (Cerf), p. 129. [My translation. – Trans.]

by God's glory, that is: "Perpetually, then, the soul will not be without a body," as the final part of the *Summa Contra Gentiles* explains and promises (CG IV, c. 79 n°10, trans. Charles J. O'Neill). The evangelical imperative to "become *like* angels" (Luke 20:36) does not make angels of us – far from it – but rather sends us back to our specific vis-à-vis as a humanity facing the divinity. By reading Thomas Aquinas today, one therefore learns of what we are really made – and what constitutes the "thing itself" of our humanity *in via*: the "limit" as the phenomenon that is most proper to us, wanted by God (theological limit) as well as noted by man (phenomenological finitude).

3. The limited phenomenon

In view of the first questions of the *Summa Theologica* revisited in light of finitude, the "human phenomenon" therefore does not appear to us first as "saturated," even though a glory could always precede it, even at the risk sometimes of crushing it. Man is, and remains, first "(the) limited phenomenon," at least in that God himself embraces and desires the limit within which he created him. From "saturation" (J.-L. Marion), we will therefore distinguish "limitation," or rather the "limit" (my own perspective), less to deny the glory of the divine than to recognize the thickness of the human.[80] Denys, certainly able to serve as a spearhead for the distance of the ineffable, could not so easily play that game in Aquinas. Positively *limited* in its "distinctive mark" (*Auszeichung*), rather than nourished by regretting a "(negative) *limitation* of the being" (*Beschränkung von Seiendem*) [*supra*], the creature therefore expects of the Creator less that he suppress and exceed our own limits than, rather, that he inhabit them to transform them from the inside, but without ever, nevertheless, claiming to rupture them. That we remain "humans": such is, as I have said, the dearest wish of the "divine," not against the angel (that we are not) but for the man (that we are always called to become to a greater extent).

By passing also through the Thomistic prism of the (theological) limit, the (phenomenological) finitude of man therefore corresponds, in a sense, to a *vocation*. Whereas the "limit" was previously nothing but

---

[80] See [for the saturated phenomenon], see its first formulation in J-L. Marion, "The Saturated Phenomenon," trans. Thomas A. Carlson, in *Phenomenology and the Theological Turn: The French Debate*, New York, Fordham University Press, 2001, pp. 176-216; and its development in *Being Given: Toward a Phenomenology of Givenness*, (1997), trans. Jeffrey L. Kosky, Stanford, Stanford University Press, 2002, § 21-22, pp. 199-221: "Sketch of the Saturated Phenomenon."

mistrust (Gnostic tendency) and would later become a mere convenience (phenomenological neutrality), it responds, this time and specifically for Aquinas, to a *double call*: the call for man to hold himself to it and the call for God to come into it. The "diversity of creatures" does not mean, in this sense (only), the effort of the limited creature to raise itself towards the unlimited Creator [q. 2: ways to go to God]. It announces and requires, rather, the kenotic condescension of a God searching for creatures as "limits" in which evermore to give himself [q. 47: Treatise on the Creation]. Rather than transgressing the limits and thereby denying the finitude of the world, the God of Christianity therefore multiplies, on the contrary, the "created" or "limited Beings," as so many receptacles of the divine that are always impossible to exceed, and precisely thereby ensuring that he remains fully within them rather than exceeding them: "God brought things into being in order that his goodness might be communicated to creatures, and be represented by them (*et per eas repraesentadam*)," as we read, magistrally, at the heart of the *Summa Theologica.* "[A]nd because his goodness could not be adequately represented by one creature alone, he produced many and diverse creatures (*produxit multas creaturas et diversas*), that what was wanting to one in the representation of the divine goodness might be supplied by another (*ut quod deest uni ad repraesentandam divinam bonitatem, suppleatur ex alia*)" (Ia q. 47, a. 1, resp.).

CONCLUSION: THE QUEST FOR AN IN-COMMON: REASON OR FINITUDE?

Theological limit *and* phenomenological finitude, the conclusion is simple: we are men forever and always, and we will remain so rather than being angels. Finitude is shared among all men today more than yesterday ("modern man who only exists as a figure of finitude" [M. Foucault (*supra*)]) and marks in this sense, and in the final analysis, the limits of an "in-common" or of a "common trunk" of all men amongst themselves, rather than a specificity as such. Whereas Aquinas yesterday sought in "natural reason (*ratio naturalis*)" that "for lack of anything better" that was, however, suited to all men, and in particular to those who share in neither the Old (the Jews) or the New Testament (the heretics) [*Contra Gentiles*, I, 2], we will therefore, in my view, today call for "finitude" or the sense of the "limit" as the veritable community of humanity, itself also waiting to be metamorphosed.[81]

---

[81] Today I attribute this crucial place to Thomas Aquinas in the relation between philosophy and theology [moment of tiling]. See *Crossing the Rubicon*, § 5, Tiling and

Suited to all, to the "good" as to the "bad," the simple recognition of the "limit" constitutes our existence as well as our common presence. Christianity is still waiting for its *common and purely human base* on which it will this time deserve to be built. Yesterday natural and limited reason (Thomas), and today finitude as mortality (Heidegger). The approach remains the same, but the terms are different. Grace certainly is given to all, but it is, however, welcomed only by a few. Nature, on the contrary, albeit in its "worst-case scenario," constitutes "our all" and immediately concerns every one of us: "As the knowledge of God's essence (*per essentiam*) is by grace, it *belongs only to the good* (*non competit nisi bonis*)," proclaims the Angelic Doctor, in the best of cases. "[B]ut the knowledge of him *by natural reason* (*per rationem naturalem*)," admits Aquinas, this time in all cases, "can belong to both good and bad (*potest competere bonis et malis*)" [Ia q. 12 a. 12, ad. 3]. The *fullness* (knowledge by grace) reveals once again the blessing of the *hollow* (knowledge by nature). Our state of living "here below" (*status viae*) first demands that we content ourselves "in common" with the "little that we have" (finitude, nature, or reason?) in order then for "everyone in his own right" to live on "all that we are" (grace, perfection, illumination). That there is not necessarily a "drama of atheist humanism" as *The Metamorphosis of Finitude* sought to show, is not a concession to the contemporary world, and still less a deduction from Thomas Aquinas, but it precisely fulfills this quest for a "community for today" (finitude rather than reason) that, by the act of the incarnation and of the resurrection, can in Christ be both assumed and transformed (metamorphosis).[82]

(Translated by Sarah Horton)

Conversion, p. 130 ["The Natural and the Supernatural"]: "The model advanced by Bonaventure or Pascal of the relay of philosophy by theology [...] no longer suffices without running the risk of leaving no place for the God-man to assume the human dimension. At least at this stage of the meeting of the human and the divine, Aquinas's model of overlaying is preferable after it is somewhat transformed." Duns Scotus (finitude) – Thomas Aquinas (tiling) – and Bonaventure (conversion) mark, in my view, the three "medieval" movements of a renewal of the relation between philosophy and theology today.

[82] *The Metamorphosis of Finitude*, chapter 3, pp. 30-40: "Is There a Drama of Atheist Humanism?"

INDEX

A

Abelard, Peter liv, 205
Abraham, Patriarch 154, 158, 159, 160
Albert the Great 5, 114, 148, 192, 196
Alexander of Hales 5, 29, 31, 37, 38, 39, 40, 41, 42, 68, 69, 73
Anselm of Canterbury, St. xxxiv, 22, 30, 44, 45, 46, 47, 50, 51, 52, 81, 82, 95,
    96, 103, 105, 106, 107, 108, 109, 112, 150, 151, 232, 240, 242, 245
Aquinas, St. Thomas vii, ix, xv, xx, xxi, xxii, xxv, xxvi, xxviii, xxx, xxxi, xxxiii,
    xxxv, xxxix, xl, xli, xlvii, xlviii, li, lii, liii, lv, lxi, 5, 6, 11, 18, 30, 31, 32,
    33, 34, 35, 38, 41, 42, 44, 48, 49, 50, 51, 52, 65, 66, 67, 74, 78, 80, 86,
    87, 88, 89, 95, 105, 106, 108, 109, 114, 122, 154, 171, 172, 174, 175,
    180, 181, 182, 189, 190, 191, 192, 208, 219, 220, 221, 222, 223, 224,
    225, 226, 227, 228, 229, 230, 231, 232, 233, 234, 235, 236, 237, 238,
    239, 240, 241, 242, 243, 244, 245, 247, 248, 249, 250, 251, 252, 253,
    254, 255, 256, 257
Areopagite, (Pseudo-)Denys xxi, xxxiii, 52, 66, 88, 116, 177, 220
Aristotle liv, 32, 49, 65, 66, 70, 74, 78, 88, 167, 170, 171, 175, 206, 231, 237,
    238, 248
Arius 39, 65
Aubenque, Pierre liv, 171
Augustine, St. xx, xxviii, xxxvii, xxxviii, xl, liii, 12, 17, 22, 29, 30, 31, 32, 33,
    38, 40, 42, 55, 56, 57, 58, 69, 73, 80, 81, 82, 98, 103, 119, 121, 133, 139,
    145, 146, 154, 158, 159, 160, 161, 169, 170, 184, 206, 207, 208, 217,
    220, 221
Austin, J. L. 24

B

Bacon, Francis liv, lxi, 4
Balthasar, Hans Urs von 6, 14, 31, 59, 63, 71, 72, 81, 83, 84, 101, 113, 121,
    148, 150, 154, 161, 190, 196, 216, 217, 242, 251, 252
Bernard of Chartres xxvi
Bernard of Clairvaux, St. xxviii, xl, 73, 96, 121
Boethius liv, 167, 170
Bougerol, Jacques-Guy xxxvi, xlix, lxi, 2, 3, 4, 13, 14, 19, 21, 37, 46, 66, 68,
    72, 74, 94, 96, 97, 98, 101, 102, 115, 121, 130, 132, 154, 174, 189